Religion in the Age of Romanticism

Religion in the Age of Romanticism

Studies in Early Nineteenth Century Thought

BERNARD M. G. REARDON

Formerly Head of the Department of
Religious Studies in the University of
Newcastle-upon-Tyne

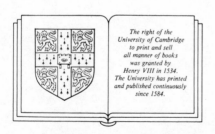

The right of the
University of Cambridge
to print and sell
all manner of books
was granted by
Henry VIII in 1534.
The University has printed
and published continuously
since 1584.

CAMBRIDGE UNIVERSITY PRESS

Cambridge
London New York New Rochelle
Melbourne Sydney

Published by the Press Syndicate of the University of Cambridge
The Pitt Building, Trumpington Street, Cambridge CB2 1RP
32 East 57th Street, New York, NY 10022, USA
10 Stamford Road, Oakleigh, Melbourne 3166, Australia

First published 1985

Printed in Great Britain at the University Press, Cambridge

Library of Congress catalogue card number: 84-23174

British Library Cataloguing in Publication Data
Reardon, Bernard M.G.
Religion in the Age of Romanticism: Studies
in Early Nineteenth Century Thought.
1. Religion – History – 19th century
2. Romanticism – History – 20th century
I. Title
200'.1   BL65.R6
ISBN 0 521 30088 6 hard covers
ISBN 0 521 31745 2 paperback

CE

Contents

v

129436

Preface

MY PURPOSE in the present volume, as its subtitle indicates, is to examine certain aspects of the Romantic movement of the early nineteenth century as it expressed itself in the philosophical and religious thought of the period. Although romanticism's most celebrated achievements were in literature and the arts – especially music – that side of it which I shall be concerned with is of more than marginal significance, since its most representative figures all favoured a religious interpretation of the cosmos, or at any rate such a spiritual view of life and the world as to leave room for the preservation of religious attitudes, though the forms of Christian orthodoxy might have to be radically modified or even abandoned. Thus the word 'God' could be used symbolically for the Absolute, or the World Soul, or the Power of Nature, or Providence, or perhaps only a scarcely articulate 'sense of something still more deeply interfused'. Romanticism differed fundamentally therefore in outlook and aim from the sceptical and rationalist doctrines of the eighteenth-century Enlightenment. In philosophy this reaction took shape in the great idealist metaphysical systems of Fichte, Schelling and Hegel and the theology and religious philosophy of Schleiermacher, all of whom opposed the abstractions of Newtonian 'reason' with a new appeal to experience – the apprehension and appreciation of life in all its range and variety, its accomplishment and promise. And the centre of such experience was of course man himself. Nature and humanity could not be sundered, the former having of necessity to be viewed from the standpoint of the human understanding as historically situated and determined.

Nor, however, could the advance of science be gainsaid: Newton might be hated but he could not be ignored. The Romantics were, if in some respects anti-rationalist, nevertheless not obscurantists. Except in a few instances the reaffirmation of religious values did not mean a straight return to the theological orthodoxies of pre-Enlightenment days. 'Rational theology' was not, as such, a thing to be repudiated. In the first flush of the romanticist fervour a contrary impression might have been created, but it did not last. 'Reason' in the form of the sciences had come to stay as a main component in the structure of human knowledge. But the concept of reason needed to be enlarged and refined, made more flexible and sensitive. Science, that is to say, had to be adapted to a wider and more various subject-matter requiring more overtly experimental methods. Hence concern for religion did not imply a refusal to submit it to rational scrutiny. Rather, as itself a vital mode of human experience, it fell within the scope of a philosophy which recognized that the life of humanity, emotional as well as rational, affords the only possible approach for a comprehensive intelligence of the world. In this sense idealism was the natural and typical way of conceptualizing the Romantic attitude to reality.

Romanticism unquestionably drew much of its inspiration from historic Christianity. But the lessons of the age of reason could not be unlearned. Those lessons may not seldom have been mistaught, yet in their essentials they were necessary and salutary, and it was no longer feasible to present Christian doctrine, as the eighteenth-century apologetic had done, in the guise of pseudo-scientific propositions. To sustain its authority in the new age religion had to be reassessed as itself part of the fabric of human experience. In the process it was both objectivized – i.e. seen as a historical and social phenomenon – in a manner hitherto unconsidered, and subjectivized – i.e. its primary 'objectivities', the content of an alleged divine revelation, interpreted with reference to the psychological needs and moral aspirations of the believer himself. Thus dogmatic theology could appear either in its more usual role as an elucidation of faith in a logically ordered scheme, or alternatively as a symbolic figuration of principles inherent in – to use Hegelian language – the self-determination of *Geist* or Mind. Another view – with an appeal, it seems, particularly Gallic – was that religion may find its principal justification as a socially cohesive force, its 'truth' lying first and foremost in its use.

But as the nineteenth century got under way romanticist sentiment had to come to grips with a new wave of rationalism created by the empirical sciences, natural and humane. It did not willingly relinquish its 'egoistic' values, at times indeed clinging to them in plain defiance of the positivism and realism which the ever-widening province of 'objective' knowledge might appear to demand. But some kind of accommodation with change was inevitable and forms of theological liberalism and modernism were adduced to safeguard ethical freedom against a system of 'nature' subject to the fixed patterns of uniform law.

In the chapters which follow I have chosen for my subjects a number of thinkers who, after one manner or another, reveal the tensions which resulted from the Romantic attempt to synthesize religion and reason. They represent markedly differing viewpoints and aims, ranging from that of Catholic orthodoxy – or what its proponents claimed to be such – through forms of liberalized or speculative Protestantism to free-thought and overt rejection of any sort of traditional creed. Yet each, I submit, is in character with the period, in which the urges to conserve and to change were both potent. In one or two instances their influence is still to be felt, but the intrinsic interest which all of them retain is what really attracts the historian of thought.

My actual choice of subjects, the reader will at once observe, is limited to continental European authors. My decision not to introduce British representatives – although, in addition to Coleridge, Carlyle and Matthew Arnold would have competed for selection – was in part a practical one (I did not wish to enlarge the present volume to the extent which their inclusion would have necessitated), but partly also theoretical. English romanticism is especially difficult to characterize in any very positive manner. Far more than its continental parallels it lacked definition, being eclectic in its outlook, distrustful of intellectual schematisms and with no taste for manifestos. Moreover, in recent years Coleridge, I venture to think, has received attention enough.

A word, finally, concerning my use of the terms 'Romantic' and 'romanticist'. Exact differentiation is not always possible, but in general I apply the latter to an attitude of mind which has revealed itself in European thought and literature more or less continuously over the centuries but which attained its clearest and most self-conscious manifestation in the early nineteenth century. The former I restrict to this precise historical reference, as in 'the Romantic movement' and 'the Romantics'.

Thanks are due to the Society for Promoting Christian Knowledge and the editor of *Theology* for their kind permission for use to be made in the first chapter of this book of material previously published in that journal.

BERNARD M. G. REARDON

Romanticism, idealism and religious belief

I

WHOEVER sets out to discuss the Romantic movement will soon be faced with the problem of definition, for romanticism, like religion itself, is notoriously difficult to define. It has even been argued that the very word 'romantic' has come to mean so many things 'that, by itself, it means nothing. It has ceased to perform the function of a verbal sign.'[1] This, no doubt, is an extreme view, and it has not gone unrefuted.[2] Yet to discover any single principle of unity in romanticism still defies ingenuity. As Kierkegaard declared: 'I must first protest against the notion that romanticism can be enclosed within a concept; for romantic means precisely that it oversteps all bounds.' Negatively, it is opposed to classicism, but the essence of classicism likewise cannot easily be encapsulated in a phrase.[3] On the other hand, as with many other things that tend to elude exact definition, classicism and romanticism are almost always clearly distinguishable in practice. To take some obvious instances in literature, we know that Dryden or Pope and Racine are 'classicists', whereas Shelley and Lamartine or Victor Hugo are 'romanticists'. But when it comes to naming the special qualities shown by either pair of authors in contrast with the other we feel less sure about an answer. It may well be that classical and romantic are not mutually exclusive; that classical art has not seldom exhibited a romantic vein, and that romantic art by no means repudiates the virtues we are wont to think of as classical. Thus no one surely will deny that Shelley's *Adonais*, or – to cite an instance from the sister art of music – Berlioz' *L'Enfance du Christ*, is lacking in classical chastity of form as well as of temper. Nor will mere chronology help us out; it has been claimed, for example, that St Paul's 'irruption into Greek religious thought and Greek prose' provides an essential case of a romantic movement, and even indeed that 'the first great romantic was Plato'.[4] August Wilhelm Schlegel, himself unquestionably among the romanticists of his time, characterized the entire Christian era as romantic. So might it not fairly be said that 'classical' and 'romantic' are simply convenient labels to apply to differing outlooks and attitudes of mind that coexist in all ages and frequently in the same individual? Nevertheless, one or other of these differing attitudes and outlooks will tend to preponderate in certain persons and during certain periods; and it is then that we become most vividly aware of the antithetical qualities on which the seemingly perennial debate usually fastens.

There can be no real question but that the first four decades of the nineteenth century constitute a 'romantic' era in this special sense – the Romantic era *par excellence* – although its time-span may quite properly be extended backward into the preceding century to include pre-Romantics like Rousseau and Herder, and again forward to the neo-Romantics, symbolists and 'decadents' of the later nineteenth. In truth, the whole of the nineteenth century exudes an aura of romanticism to a greater or lesser degree, the twentieth itself having got under way before new and anti-romantic intellectual stances and aesthetic ideals made their sometimes abrupt appearance. On the European continent philosophical romanticism, in the shape of the existentialist movement, enjoyed a remarkable efflorescence as late as the Second World War and after. But, however we assess such anticipations and continuations of Romantic beliefs and sentiments, the thought and art of the early nineteenth century possess in the aggregate an immediately recognizable identity resting on a fundamental congruence of outlook, aspiration and style. For the Romantic age is the age of Goethe – for all the classicism of his 'Hellenic' period[5] – of Byron – the archetypal Romantic figure, as Europe was quick to decide – of Chateaubriand, of Lenau, of Leopardi; the age of Wordsworth and Coleridge, of Shelley and Keats, of Novalis and Jean Paul Richter, of Schumann, Chopin and Berlioz, of Delacroix, Turner and David Caspar Friedrich, of Schleiermacher, Hegel and Schopenhauer; the age also which, in its lingering Indian summer, witnessed the diverse achievements of Kierkegaard, Baudelaire, Liszt, Wagner and Nietzsche. In genius and creative energy, therefore, it superabounded. What, within its tight limits, I shall attempt in this introductory chapter, will be to distinguish some leading characteristics of the mind of the Romantic movement so far as they may be seen to relate to religious feeling and belief. It may well emerge that romanticism is in some respects a religion in itself, however far removed were its forms and standards from those of religious orthodoxy.

The task of making such a discrimination is, again, no easy one. The variety and multiformity of Romantic thought and art are manifest. The Romantic scene, historically speaking, is immensely colourful and invariably fascinating to observe; but it is appallingly cluttered – a treasure-house in disorder. Can we venture to say that behind all this teeming confusion there are principles which, when grasped, yield us coherence, a true pattern of consistency? Could it possibly be that there is even, after all, a single principle which is the source and spring of all romanticist sentiment? The nineteenth-century French literary critic, Émile Faguet, wrote that 'the basis of Romanticism is a horror of reality and a desire to escape from it ... [a desire] to liberate oneself from the real by means of the imagination, to liberate oneself again through solitude and by retiring into the sanctuary of personal feeling'. There is an element of truth in this. The stress here laid on the rebellious or fugitive character of the individual imagination, the yearning for solitude, the cultivation of private emotions, is unmistakably romanticist: Romantic literature and art are full of these features. All the same, Faguet has not gone, I think, quite to the root of the matter, seizing only on the more obvious negative side of the Romantic attitude. It is more likely that 'the horror of reality' of which he speaks is rather dissatisfaction with the supposed reality of the surface of things, a reality which in the age of the Enlightenment was too readily taken for the whole. We might then say that the essence of romanticism — if determination of its 'essence' be possible at all — lies in the inexpugnable feeling that the finite is not self-explanatory and self-justifying, but that behind it and within it — shining, as it were, through it — there is always an infinite 'beyond', and that he who has once glimpsed the infinity that permeates as well as transcends all finitude can never again rest content with the paltry this-and-that, the rationalized simplicities, of everyday life. As William Blake puts it:

> To see a world in a grain of Sand,
> And a Heaven in a Wild Flower,
> Hold Infinity in the palm of your hand,
> And Eternity in an hour.

Again and again in Romantic thought we encounter this sense of the coincidence of the finite and the infinite. In all things finite the infinite is present, latent, and the part is meaningless without the whole. August Wilhelm Schlegel, contrasting romantic art with classical, found the latter 'simpler, cleaner, more like nature in the independent perfection of its separate works'; but the former, in spite of its fragmentary appearance, to be 'nearer to the mystery of the universe'. That phrase, 'the mystery of the universe', is significant. The heart of Wordsworth's *Tintern Abbey* is reached when the poet speaks of

> a sense sublime
> Of something far more deeply interfused,
> Whose dwelling is the light of setting suns,
> And the round ocean and the living air,
> And the blue sky, and in the mind of man:

> A motion and a spirit that impels
> All thinking things, all objects of all thought,
> And rolls through all things.

The same 'sense sublime' finds utterance again in *The Excursion* –

> For I must tread on shadowy ground, must sink
> Deep, and aloft ascending breathe in worlds
> To which the heaven of heavens is but a veil

– as likewise in the 1805 version of *The Prelude*, though here with a theistic turn –

> The Feeling of life endless, the great thought
> By which we live, infinity and God

– lines which in the later (1850) version, when the poet had returned to Christian orthodoxy and the Church of England, become more theological –

> Faith in life endless, the sustaining thought
> Of human being, eternity and God

– a distinctly different notion. The one voices a sense of the infinite, the other affirms belief in immortality.

It is this idea of the infinite in the finite which furnishes the basic motif of German romanticist philosophy, in which nature and human history alike are conceived synoptically as forms or manifestations of one infinite Life. We also have it, very signally, in Schleiermacher, whose *Reden über die Religion* gave it such telling expression. These – undelivered – discourses of his, addressed (as he worded it) 'to the cultured despisers of religion', mark a characteristically romanticist reaction against both rationalism and orthodox dogma, with their common assumption of a duality of worlds, the natural and the supernatural, the here and the hereafter, the realm of humanity and the realm of God. For Schleiermacher the divine is not, as in the usual type of apologetics, an *inference* from the phenomenal world of experience. He uses turns of phrase like 'World' and 'Universal', 'the One and Whole', 'the lofty World-Spirit', 'the divine Life and Action of the All' more or less interchangeably. The universe, as he sees it, is divine – divine, that is, *as* the universe, *as* the totality of being, with religion the vividly sensed apprehension or 'feeling' of this Whole upon which the individual is completely dependent:

> You lie directly in the bosom of the finite world. In that moment you are its soul. Through one part of your nature you feel, as your own, all its powers and its endless life. In that moment it is your body; you pervade, as your

own, its muscles and members, and your thinking and forecasting set its inmost nerves in motion.

Genuine religion, true 'piety', as Schleiermacher understands it, consists basically in an awareness of man's limitation,

> ... of the fortuitous nature of his life as his being runs its course and silently disappears in the Infinite ... It is to live in the endless nature of the Whole, to perceive and divine with quiet reverence the place assigned to each and all. It is to have sense and taste for the Infinite, to lie in the bosom of the Universe and feel its boundless life and creative power within your own.

The pantheistic tendency of all romanticism is undeniable, and in the metaphysics of the great idealist thinkers it becomes all-pervasive. Hegel himself, however, was no advocate of romanticist 'feeling' or 'intuition', as his criticisms of both Schelling and Schleiermacher as well as Jacobi prove. On the contrary, he was an intellectualist. One might have said an intellectualist through and through, but although speculation was as the breath of life to him there is a further quality in Hegel's metaphysical thinking that may not inappropriately be described as mystical; a *mystique* albeit of the intellect, almost a Spinozan *amor intellectualis dei*, and this does betray his romanticist kinship. For to Hegel the whole is assuredly present in the part, just as the part is unintelligible save as seen in relation to the whole: to take any single concrete instance of the dialectic is to hold the key to all reality. And when, as in the reflective mind of man, reality at last becomes conscious of itself, of its own inner and essential nature, you have that which for Hegel is God. Hegel's idealism is, in its loftily intellectualist way, actually a religion of redemption inasmuch as the self-comprehension of the Absolute requires the reconciliation of all oppositions. Or, as a genial cynic might observe, 'tout comprendre, c'est tout pardonner'.

However, although the Romantic spirit longs for ultimate reconciliation and peace – the Wordsworthian stillness subsisting at the heart of endless agitation – it is won only out of ceaseless striving and struggle. Thus Schlegel, again, can contrast ancient poetry – 'a harmonious promulgation of the eternal legislation of a beautifully ordered world' – with its romanticist counterpart as 'the expression of a secret longing for the chaos which is perpetually striving for new and marvellous births, and which lies hidden in the very womb of orderly creation'. That indeed is why Romantic poetry brings us nearer to 'the mystery of the universe'. Classical art, we may say, looks to a perfection of balance, a harmony of proportions, which ideally exclude effort and conflict; whereas for Romantic art effort and conflict are of the very stuff of life. Reality it sees not as static but dynamic, ever in

5

movement and always aspiring. And here, we may all agree, it finds its metaphysical self-interpretation in romanticist philosophy. Just as for the artist the essential aesthetic problem is to discover the form of forms capable of receiving the overwhelming richness of an experience which in itself seems to have no limits, so for the philosopher the reality he contemplates is not simply an immobile *structure*, but rather the ceaseless *process* of man's spiritual evolution as his history unfolds it. The real, in other words, is always in the making and never finally achieved. Accordingly – and this we are bidden to recognize as a central truth – the process is itself the reality, at any rate not less so than the ideal end towards which it is continuously moving. Hence the significance which the Romantics – and following them the entire tradition of nineteenth-century scholarship – saw in history. For history is not merely the past – the largely hidden and chaotic work-shop from which the perfectly fashioned products of modern enlightenment have at last emerged. It is the ongoing here and now to which men have always belonged and which inexorably shapes them into what they are perpetually becoming. Hence too the valuation put upon experience as such. Because we cannot see the ultimate goal of the process, nothing in its actual course is to be dismissed as irrelevant or forbidden. All is grist to this eternally grinding mill.

Despite the emphasis of Hegel in particular upon history and the historical and the great influence he exerted upon the *savants* as well as the philosophers in the generation immediately following him, it was not until much later in the century that the philosophical view of history which we now call historicist came into its own. It is above all associated with the name of Wilhelm Dilthey, who died in 1911. For historicism the individual person, event or object is always unique. In the words of a modern defender of the historicist position, 'Everything in history now' – i.e. as seen by the Romantics – 'took on a different appearance from before; things no longer lay in the same plane open to uniform scrutiny; they stood in perspective with a background that could not be fully measured, as had formerly been supposed, but as an eternal process of newborn, unique and incomparable events.'[6] In this 'abyss of individuality', as Friedrich Schlegel termed it, all things are justified as and in so far as they exist. Nothing therefore is to be discarded, even though all things are inevitably relative. For the result of this way of looking at life is likely to lead in the end to a total relativism. It is true that historicists usually do their best to avoid such a conclusion, with its clear implication that their philosophical doctrine also must be subject to its own law.[7] For where all is flux there can be no fixed point, no supra-historical anchorage, and every doctrine, any opinion, is no more than transient. But during the nineteenth century the historicist view became a widely prevalent assumption. Lord Acton, although himself sharing it to some extent, was alive to its dangers. 'If, with Hegel,' he wrote, 'we considered history as all reason, as the expansion of reason, we should probably be tempted to ignore evil and to deny morality.' And he directly linked this with the romanticist approach. The Romantic prefers 'imagination and constructiveness' to 'analysis and criticism', and teaches 'the appreciation of every standpoint' and 'sympathy even with that which repels'. He judges a man 'by his time' and the time 'by its degree of advancement and knowledge'. The Romantic chooses to see things '*im Werden*', studies their genesis and approves each of their successive stages by the standard of progressive 'insight'. All this was understandable and even necessary if history were not merely to provide themes for moralists. The Romantic school 'was to make distant times, and especially the Middle Ages, then the most distant of all, intelligible and acceptable to a society issuing from the eighteenth century'. Thus in romanticist eyes the men who in the first fervour of the Crusades 'took the Cross, and after receiving communion, heartily devoted the day to the extermination of the Jews', were not simply to be condemned. 'To judge them by a fixed standard, to call them sacrilegious fanatics or furious hypocrites, was to yield a gratuitous victory to Voltaire ...' Thus the historicists, Acton avers, would leave us with 'no common code; our moral notions are fluid; and you must consider the times, the class from which men sprang, the surrounding influences, the masters in their schools, the preachers in their pulpits, the movement they obscurely obeyed, and so on, until responsibility is merged in numbers, and not a culprit is left for execution'.[8] In our own days Karl Barth has similarly protested against the spiritual perils of a historical relativism parading under the name of science. Moreover, this sense of the endless flow of things was to be a main cause of what, apparently, was an endemic malady of the Romantic soul – its pessimism; a pessimism somewhat too histrionic perhaps in Chateaubriand or Byron, a little too self-consciously reflective in Alfred de Vigny, but deeply moving in Leopardi and articulated with a high degree of philosophic insight by Schopenhauer. The *mal du siècle* – the vague and indefinable melancholy of *Werther*, *René* and *Obermann* – was a mood, certainly, in no small measure induced by the feeling of the mutability and transitoriness of life. Chateaubriand voiced it rhetorically but faithfully:

> On est détrompé sans avoir joui; il reste encore des désirs, et l'on n'a pas d'illusions. L'imagination est riche, abondante et merveilleuse; l'existence pauvre, sèche et désenchantée. On habite, avec un cœur plein, un monde vide, et sans avoir usé de rien on est désabusé de tout.

The same note is heard again, though with a more mordant pathos, in the lyrical verse of the Austrian Lenau.

If, then, the individual is unique it can only be from the standpoint of the individual himself that the world is ever beheld. It could even be said that for the Romantics the ego is the measure of reality; and among systematic thinkers it is Johann Gottlob Fichte who most readily comes to mind here. Reflecting on the subjective element in the critical philosophy of Kant he asked himself why, if the ego plays so great a role in the determination of experience, any limit at all should be placed upon it. What we call the 'objective' world exists, it seemed to him, only as the realm of the ego's freedom. Consciousness translates this objective world into the subjective, the non-ego into the ego. No doubt for Fichte, or for any of the great idealists, consciousness is not to be equated simply with the finite consciousness of the individual. But the Romantic poets of Fichte's generation brushed aside metaphysical distinctions of that sort and discovered the basic creative principle in the personal imagination. The Italian poet and novelist Ugo Foscolo went so far as to declare that 'all that exists for men is but their own imagining ... We fabricate reality after our own fashion.' For Wordsworth, too, imagination

> Is but another name for absolute power
> And clearest insight, amplitude of mind,
> And Reason in her most exalted mood.

After all, had not Fichte himself said that 'all reality is produced purely by the imagination'? But given the creative power of the empirical ego – my imagination and yours – boundless egotism, in some instances amounting to egomania, was the sure consequence. A case of it is Novalis' 'magic idealism': the thinking, or rather imagining subject can do anything; he is a sorcerer, a miracle-worker. 'To destroy the principle of contradiction is perhaps the highest task of the very highest logic.'

Yet in its endless creativity the personality itself loses its inward identity and so belongs nowhere. The true Romantic hero is an exile, a wanderer on the face of the earth. He has no real place in society, and society in truth alienates him. He is Chateaubriand's René, Byron's Childe Harold. Rousseau, the *promeneur solitaire*, found that the company of his fellow-men diminished him. 'I long', he said, 'for the moment when, delivered from the fetters of the body, I shall be *myself*, without contradiction, without division, and shall have need only of myself in order to be happy.' Senancour believed that the real life of man is 'within himself'; and Novalis, that 'the way to all mysteries leads inwards. Eternity, with all its worlds, all past and future, is either within us or nowhere.'

An obvious outcome of this Romantic egotism was an intense emotionalism. But the emotionalism of the Romantic movement is to be seen in proper focus. The eighteenth century had by no means been devoid of emotion, but its own brand of it had served only as a kind of condiment to reason. It could therefore more aptly be described as sentimentalism. The English novelist Samuel Richardson provides a nice example of it. The soft feelings, the tears, were a necessary emollient for an otherwise hard-hearted world. But Romantic emotionalism had an altogether deeper function. We need not deny that romanticist literature offers a good many instances of its own variety of sentimentalism – Constant's *Paul et Virginie*, for one – but these are only occasional lapses. The real significance of emotion is cognitive; it is through the power and penetration of feeling that *knowledge* is attained. Perhaps, as in the case of Schleiermacher, we would do better to call it intuition, akin at times to that questing, conative urge that Plato assigns to *eros*. In Romantic art and much romanticist philosophy it is not reason – intellect or the logical faculty – which is the means to truth: to suppose that to be so had been the cardinal error of the Enlightenment. It is the emotionally stimulated imagination that has the real revelatory power, a principle stated by no one with greater clarity than by Samuel Taylor Coleridge in his famous distinction – unoriginal though it was – between Reason and Understanding. The former he takes to connote the very opposite, to all intents, of what the previous century had meant by the word. In his usage it is 'the organ of the supersensuous', so contrasting with the Understanding, which is simply 'the faculty of judging according to sense'. The one is 'the science of phenomena', the other 'the Power of Universal and Necessary convictions, the Source and Substance of Truths above sense, and having their evidence in themselves'. And Reason, thus defined, is not far in Coleridge's mind from what he designates 'the primary Imagination', which he holds to be 'the living Power and prime Agent of all human perception and as a repetition in the finite mind of the eternal act of creation in the infinite I AM'. It was of course on this conception of imaginative reason that Coleridge based his apologetic interpretation of Christianity. Religion is not science and ought not to be treated as such. His comments on rationalist evidence-theology are well-known. 'I more than fear', he wrote, 'the prevailing taste for books of Natural Theology, Physio-Theology, Demonstrations of God from Nature, Evidences of Christianity, and the like. Evidences of Christianity! I am weary of the word. Make a man feel the want of it; rouse him if you can, to the self-knowledge of the need of it; and you may safely trust to its own Evidence.' Make a man *feel* the want of it: the real evidence of truth is in subjectivity, to

9

borrow Kierkegaard's phrase. 'I am certain of nothing', stated Coleridge's younger contemporary Keats, 'except the holiness of the Heart's affections, and the truth of the Imagination.'

Hence also the aestheticism of the Romantics. It not only stamps their attitude to the Christian religion, as in Schleiermacher, for whom faith may look like a synonym for the aesthetic imagination; aesthetics itself becomes a religion, with art as its dogma and liturgy. For Schelling, at one period of his career at least, art was a 'Miracle', the supreme miracle of life: through art we have the truest revelation of the ultimate. Accordingly it was the philosophy of art which afforded the most comprehensive method, the 'single and eternal organon', of all philosophy, 'the keystone of the entire vault'. So too with Friedrich Schlegel: the goal of philosophy is much less knowledge and truth than beauty and aesthetic satisfaction, and especially the satisfaction of art. And art, in the world of romanticist feeling, had perhaps its essential, or most typical, expression in music – one recalls Schumann's remark that a specifically romantic *school* in music can hardly be formed, since music is romantic in itself. 'Music', pronounced Goethe's friend and admirer, Bettina von Arnim, 'is a revelation of a higher order than any morality or philosophy.' Schopenhauer, who wrote more penetratingly on aesthetics than probably any other thinker of his time, judged that, whereas other arts speak only of 'the shadow', music does so of 'the thing itself'. But in any event the reason why art as a whole possesses this revelatory power is that it comes from *within*. Once again we discover that the real life of man is that of his soul. As Novalis says, 'The way to all mysteries heads inwards.'

It would be surprising, then, if this insistence on inwardness were not vital to the Romantic view of religion. Religious truth is not an objective datum; it exists in subjectivity. The medium of revelation is the ego, with its individual needs, hopes and imaginings. 'We fabricate reality after our own devising', said Foscolo. Such is the consistent claim of the Romantic poets, to be articulated systematically by the Romantic philosophers, who resolve the problem of objectivity – the whole enigmatic and embarrassing world of the Non-ego – by identifying both subject and object in an all-encompassing unity.

What, therefore, pre-eminently distinguishes the Romantic understanding of Christianity is its subjectivization of all religious truth, and this new attitude may, I think, be said to mark the beginning of that process of immanentizing religious reality which was characteristic of the nineteenth century in general and which, despite the neo-orthodox reaction, has continued through the present century as well. For the modern theologian, however orthodox he may wish to appear, finds the thought of *two* worlds worrying. Somehow or other eternal life has to be seen to be lived here and now, eternity itself to be a dimension of the present order of things, the basic Christian values rooted in this world, Jesus Christ to be the man in whom all men may see their own idealized reflection. Romanticism was as decisive a revolution in ideas as were the events of 1789 in politics. We are still tossed about in the wash of both. Mediaevalism – which the Protestant Reformation of the sixteenth century only perpetuated in a revised form – with its hierarchically structured system of truths and values grounded in objective certainties was itself, paradoxically enough, to become a romanticist dream.

It nonetheless was a paradox which the Romantic poets and thinkers readily accepted. For one outstanding feature of the Romantic movement and an unmistakable badge of its identity was its entirely new regard for the past. The age of the Enlightenment did not appreciate the historically distant; or rather, in its own estimation it could appraise it only too well. For the past happily was past, and best forgotten except in so far as it might provide awful warnings. What it stood for was oppression, ignorance, superstition. Such at least was supposed to be true of the middle ages. Classical antiquity of course was different and was wont to be idealized as an earlier era of enlightenment. Did not the French revolutionaries glorify the example of ancient Rome by seeing themselves as latter-day Catos and Catilines? But the long, monotonous centuries after the fall of Rome were the dark night of civilization. Hence Lessing, when looking back over what he interpreted as the education of the human race, could congratulate himself and his contemporaries on that victory of reason which they, at last, had been vouchsafed to witness. But for the Romantic mind the infinite was present not only in every form and particle of the finite, but in every period and moment of time. No age was without its intrinsic significance and typical excellence. Civilization, like life itself, was felt to be organic and continuous. In other words, no single phase of the historical process was to be discarded or discounted, because the process in its totality carries meaning. Break into the continuum of history at any point and you will discover the virtue of the whole. 'Is Time, then, not ordered, as Space is?' asked Herder. 'Both indeed are twins of one Fate. Space is full of wisdom, Time full of apparent disorder; and yet man is obviously so created as to seek order, to survey a spot of time so that the future may build upon the past.' The historical therefore is all-important and must be taken with commensurate seriousness; which explains how it was that the nineteenth century witnessed the birth of historiography as a science. Yet to begin with it was not scientific history which caught the Romantic imagination, but traditional. Tradition embodied the sense of continuity, manifested the truth of permanence in fluidity. Thus one of the forms of Romantic longing was to surmount the barriers of time, and the mediaeval world in particular acquired force of attraction through its sheer remoteness and strangeness. The very things that had repelled the eighteenth-century intelligence captivated romanticist sensibility; not only the picturesqueness of the Catholic middle ages – a newly-discovered 'Gothic' wonderworld – but faith, dogmatic religion, hierarchy, unalterable law. 'Those', urged Novalis, 'were beautiful, brilliant times, when Europe was a Christian country, and a single Christian faith dwelt in this humanized region of the world.' It was this old, feudal, Catholic order that Chateaubriand extolled with such panoplied eloquence and of which Sir Walter Scott became the recognized high priest.

It is thus understandable that the Romantic movement should have produced so remarkable a revival in Catholicism. As Chateaubriand wrote, on the morrow of Bonaparte's concordat with the Vatican: 'There was a need for faith, a desire for religious consolation, which came from the very lack of that consolation for so many years ... People hurried to the house of God, just as in time of plague they would to the physicians!' In Germany there were many notable conversions among the intellectuals, hitherto either conventional Protestants or sceptics (see below p. 118), whilst in France, following the restoration and under Chateaubriand's pervasive influence, Catholicism acquired a new social vitality and resourcefulness, by no means entirely dependent on the reactionary policies of the new government. Its prophets were Bonald, Maistre and above all Lamennais – that brilliant but impulsive and temperamental Breton, one of the outstanding religious personalities not only of his age but of the century. And the continental revival had its counterpart in England with the Oxford Movement under the leadership, pre-eminently, of John Henry Newman. The striking thing – the essential paradox of the situation in view of the Romantics' sometimes unbridled individualism – is that this aspect of the movement takes the form of a deliberate and calculated glorification of authority and dogmatic traditionalism. Joseph de Maistre was the most authoritarian thinker of his time, a man for whom the French Revolution and all it stood for were anathema, although it is only fair to bear in mind that he himself had suffered grievously under it. But he is a true Romantic when he sees society as an organism and religion as the life-blood of that organism. 'Religion and political dogmas, mingled and merged with each other,' he writes, 'should together form a general or national mind sufficiently strong to repress the aberrations of the individual reason, which is, of its nature, the mortal enemy of any association whatever because it only gives birth to conflicting opinions.' A man's proper attitude is one of submission and belief. A far cry, this, from the fervent libertarianism of Byron and Shelley; but Romanticism was multiform, and in any case the two English poets were, in politics at least, men of the Revolutionary era and its ideals rather than of their own day.

The Catholic renaissance on the European continent was, one may think, less a religious revival in the true sense than a social movement reacting against both rationalistic and pietistic individualism. Thus to Maistre the arch-enemy was Voltaire, while Lamennais's contempt for Protestantism was unqualified; indeed Protestantism was no more than rationalism in a religious guise. 'Who', he inquires, 'does not see that the authority of Scripture becomes the authority of reason alone? ... Everyone ought to believe what his reason clearly shows him to be true, which is precisely the principle of the deist and the atheist.' For Lamennais society needs authority, otherwise its very cohesion is threatened. But the authority he postulates is that of tradition, embodied in the *sensus communis*, or 'common reason', of mankind, although ultimately a matter of divine revelation or implantation. In content it comprises belief in God and the fundamental truths of morality. Such things cannot be proved, they have to be assumed. 'The universal, absolute doubt, to which a severe logic condemns us, is impossible to men ... All men, without exception, believe invincibly thousands of truths which are the necessary bond of society and the foundation of human life.' What man needs is not proof, in the strict meaning of the word, but certitude, and speculative reason destroys certitude. Hence to prefer one's own reason, one's personal judgment, to the general authority is madness. Nevertheless tradition must have a focus and a voice. Lamennais himself began by being an ardent royalist, but the restored Bourbon monarchy disillusioned him and, breaking with the Gallican traditions of the French church, he turned to the papacy. He must therefore be reckoned among the creators of modern ultramontanism, although the actual pope to whom he appealed did not thank him for his pains. But the point to observe is that for Lamennais religion is essentially a social force, not a personal sentiment. The form of society might be monarchical, papal or democratic, and Lamennais's own view favoured all three in turn, but in any form of it religion remained the animating spirit. In the end, as it happened, he was disappointed in all his hopes. Abandoning Catholicism and even Christianity, he died, what probably at heart he always was, a romantic individualist.

In England the Oxford divines of 1833, under the increasingly forceful leadership of Newman, disclose a similar tendency. They not only denigrated the Reformation heritage and deplored the contemporary evangelicalism in the name of Catholicism and tradition, but, above all, opposed everything that could be covered by the opprobrious name of 'liberalism'. Liberalism, as Newman saw it, was the 'anti-dogmatic principle'. It comprised such notions as that no religious tenet is important unless reason shows it to be so, that no one can believe what he does not understand, and that it is dishonest in a man to exercise mere faith in default of proof. Against this subversive doctrine must be set the historic creed of Christendom, not in its diminished, compromising, Protestant shape, but in its original integrity as handed down from the Fathers of the early church, unsullied however by Romish accretions and perversions. Once more we have the typical Romantic appeal to the past, to tradition, to the continuing organic life of the community, as against the atomistic individualism brought about by the irresponsible use of critical reason; once more the invocation of miracle, mystery, faith and dogma as against rationalism, utilitarianism and the 'march-of-mind' philosophy generally.[9] For Newman the private judgment meant doubt, loss of certitude, and eventually corrosive scepticism inimical to life itself. The only assurance lay in authority; and not only in authority but in an infallible authority. It would seem that in Newman's many-faceted personality there was a gnawing element of doubtfulness, the counterbalance, one might suspect, to a rather self-conscious credulousness. To cite his own words from the famous *Apologia*:

> The Church's infallibility is the provision adopted by the mercy of the Creator to preserve religion in the world. Outside the Catholic Church all things tend to atheism. The Catholic Church is the one face to face antagonist, able to withstand and baffle the fierce energy of passion and the all-dissolving scepticism of the mind. I am a Catholic by virtue of my belief in God.

To which he adds these significant words: 'If I should be asked why I believe in God, I should answer, because I believe in myself.' *Because I believe in myself*: back we come again to the Romantic ego and the *sentiment du moi*, that ultimate self which is the truly creative principle and necessary clue to the understanding of all things.

This thought brings us – somewhat strangely, as it might seem – to the last characteristic of the Romantic movement that may be considered here, namely its negative, destructive, even demonic side. Romanticism, as we have seen, has a strong tendency to introversion. The sense of the self is obsessive and inescapable. Its shadow falls across every experience. The result can be morbid, a persistent inward suffering – *Weltschmerz, le mal du siècle, tristitia*, worldly sorrow, whatever the name given to it – from which there seems no relief except in death. The mood was well expressed by Chateaubriand in the passage quoted above. Doubtless there was an element of pose in it: Byron, for instance, was a good deal less melancholic than he affected to be in *Childe Harold's Pilgrimage*. As he himself confessed:

> Let us have Wine and Women, Mirth and Laughter,
> Sermons and soda water the day after.

Yet, for all that, the Romantic soul was painfully aware of the burden of existence; or rather, it felt human existence to be a burden in a way that the preceding century assuredly did not. 'Amaro e noia la vita, altro mai nulla; e fango è il mondo', is Leopardi's bitter cry. For Schopenhauer man is the hapless victim of his own ceaselessly striving will, an unquenchable spiritual thirst; when he gains his objective satiety brings only boredom, *ennui* and an ever-deepening disenchantment.

In all this, however, the Romantic thinkers did at any rate begin that serious probe of the 'abysmal deeps of personality' which the age of Enlightenment, with its easy optimism, did not comprehend or even realize existed. Thus emerged the concept of the unconscious, of which Freud was not the inventor. But the unconscious appeared to throw up impulses and drives that sometimes take on a violently irrational form, sexual and even satanistic. This is an area of romanticist thought, and indeed behaviour, widely explored if not altogether adequately explained by Mario Praz in his well-known book *The Romantic Agony*,[10] though much of what Praz describes belongs more to the later, 'decadent' phase of romanticism. But even Kant was awake to what he called 'the radical evil' (*das radicale Böse*) in the human soul. Romanticism, in fact, overthrew the idea that man is an essentially rational creature in whom an improved environment and a sound education will produce fully regenerative results. Not indeed that it destroyed it; 'Benthamite' notions were soon to have their confident exponents once more. Romanticism perceived that the mind of man, although cultivated in one part, is a wilderness in another – a wilderness, some suggested, to be enjoyed for its own disorderly state, regardless of reason or morality. The Marquis de Sade was one such, the author of *Les Fleurs du mal* another. Yet in this respect romanticism did anticipate our modern understanding of the human *psyche* whilst retaining, if in a perverted way, its characteristic sense of the infinite in the finite, the eternal in the temporal. Below or beyond reason lies the non-rational, phantasmagoric twilight world of the haunted imagination, the world of E. T. A. Hoffmann and the paintings of Caspar David Friedrich. Hence the seemingly plausible comment of Goethe: 'Classisch ist das Gesunde, Romantisch das Kranke.'

2

In truth no 'world', no consistent ordering of experience, was for the Romantics possible apart from such subjectivity, with the consequence that when the nature of experience is thought through, object and subject are apprehended as ultimately one. There is of course much in the idealist doctrine which bears the imprint only of its own time, and this quickly turned out to be transient. But much also has proved its capacity to last and has contributed substantially to the outlook of our century. This conspicuously is the case with regard to the social philosophies which still loom large on the contemporary scene, especially in so far as they articulate the swell of nationalist feeling and the right as well as the capability of the state to organize the economic life of society as a whole. Thus romanticism did not by any means disown the achievements of the *Aufklärung*. While abjuring the abstractly 'critical' spirit of the preceding age, it did not reject the scientific method as such. How could it have done? But the scientific *ideal*, in the eyes of the Romantics, was too narrow, too restrictive. It left out of account altogether much that gives human existence its depth and vitality. Science, they recognized, yields knowledge, but not necessarily or readily wisdom.

However, was not romanticism politically and socially reactionary? If Wordsworth could have said, casting his thoughts back to the heady early days of the French Revolution, 'Bliss was it in that dawn to be alive, / But to be young was very heaven', there were others who took a different view, and for them surely Maistre would have spoken up in his remark that of all monarchies 'the hardest, most despotic and most intolerable is King People'. In part, then, the charge is true; after the Napoleonic wars there was throughout much of the European continent an emphatic reassertion of the attitudes and values of the Old Régime, along with a restoration, as far as conditions allowed, of its institutions. Moreover, the religious revivals of the period, Catholic and Protestant alike, were, as I have said, a repudiation of the standpoint of the Enlightenment, whether sceptical, rationalist or materialist. At the same time traditional orthodoxy was apt to look with suspicion upon, when it did not openly censure, romanticist interpretations of Christian belief. The idealist philosophies were monistic and allowed little room for supernaturalism of the traditional kind, and as the century advanced, bringing in its train a vast increment of knowledge both scientific and historical, the objectivism and this-worldly humanism of these systems were to give rise to types of theology which to a greater or less degree parted company with the old orthodoxy.

Nineteenth-century liberal theology, at any rate in Germany, varies according to the prevalence within it of the Kantian or of the post-Kantian influence. It is very relevant to make this distinction. The post-Kantians – Fichte, Schelling, Hegel – were not preoccupied simply with the philosophical problem of how to transform the critical philosophy into a metaphysic. Each of them had a marked personal interest in theology, and all of them actually started their careers as theological students – Fichte at Jena and Schelling and Hegel at Tübingen – and, although none of them subsequently became a theologian *de métier*, their respective philosophies reveal a strong undercurrent of theological concern, even when religion is not explicitly under discussion. For Hegel, quite expressly, the subject-matter of philosophy is the same as that of religion, which he sees as 'the eternal truth in its objectivity, God and nothing but God and the unfolding (*die Explication*) of God ... Philosophy unfolds only itself when it unfolds religion; and when it unfolds itself it unfolds religion.' Nietzsche in fact objected that all three thinkers were, as he put it, 'concealed theologians', and there is enough truth in the observation to obscure its equal measure of falsity.

The difference in method as in temper between Kant and his successors is the more readily appreciable when one recollects the diversity of their early work. Kant addresses himself to scientific subjects: for example, the retardation of the earth through the tides (1754), the causes of wind circulation (1756) and of earthquakes (1755–6), and the concepts of motion and rest (1756); though of these scientific treatises the fullest and most important is his *Universal History of Nature and Theory of the Heavens* (1755), which adumbrates a nebular hypothesis to explain the formation of the solar system. It was this scientific bent that gave direction to his philosophical thinking not only in the pre-critical period but subsequently. Hegel's early writings, on the other hand – they were first published only at the beginning of the present century (see below pp. 61–5) – are deliberately theological in their choice of theme. He begins, that is, not with questions of what then was known as 'natural philosophy' but with the relations of finite and infinite, of God and man, and his approach was historical. His first theological essay of significance was actually a 'Life of Jesus', in which the gospels are made to expound the Kantian ethic, while in the most considerable piece of writing in this group, and one to which its modern editor accords the title 'The Spirit of Christianity', the young philosopher attempts to show that the unity of finite and infinite is realized by love, in the sense of wholeness or harmony, a quality revealed in the teaching and example of Jesus. 'To love God', he says, 'is to feel oneself in the "all" of life, with no restrictions ... In this feeling of harmony there is no universality, since in harmony the particular is not in discord but in concord.' Nevertheless Hegel is still unsatisfied; love is, intellectually, inchoate, a 'holy innocence', an undeveloped unity, with the subjective aspect of consciousness always uppermost. Something more, therefore, is required – such a synthesis of subjective immediacy and objective form as is offered, he thinks, by religion. In other words, at this stage in his philosophical development he believed that it is the religious consciousness which can best express the elevation of the finite to the infinite. Later of course he finds that only speculative thought can effect this, in the Concept, the Idea; with the result that, in the end, religion has to cede to philosophy as the highest form of the understanding. But the key-place of the theological writings of the 1790s in the building up of Hegel's mature thought is undeniable and accounts for the importance which modern Hegel study assigns to them.

With Fichte the relation of infinite and finite is less in evidence, at least in his earlier work, where he concerns himself more with the development of Kant's deduction of consciousness. Later the religious aspect assumes a larger place in his philosophy, and, although in his own day he was charged by his critics with atheism, his conception of absolute Being is equated by him with the divine, albeit not as yet personalized. But his *Guide to the Blessed Life* (1806) marks the culmination of his religious musings, and in it, under the inspiration of St John's gospel, he arrives at a sort of Christian Platonism, in which 'knowledge transcends faith and transforms it into vision'. Schelling's view of the religious dimension of philosophy brooks no doubt; for him the relation between the infinite and the finite is the central metaphysical issue. In his *Philosophy and Religion* (1804) he insists that faith and knowledge are one and that the aim of both is the restoration of man's lost union with God, conceived of as creative living force, or rather 'eternal Will' who reveals himself in 'free autonomous beings, for whose existence there is no ground but God, and who yet are even as God is'. In his later religious philosophy the idea of the divine as *personal* emerges still more clearly. On the whole, however, the idealists had difficulty in reconciling infinity with both transcendence and personality: a transcendent infinite seemed a *contradictio in adiecto*, while a personal deity was simply an anthropomorphism. If the infinite is one with the Absolute as the sum of reality, God becomes either the non-personal or at any rate supra-personal equivalent thereto, or else merely a personalized symbol of it. In neither case will Christian theism have any logical standing. But, although the idealists might conceive of the Absolute as the all-encompassing totality, they had no desire to deny the reality of the finite. But how was finitude to be given its place in the infinite without calling its reality in question? It was a problem not easily solved and the resulting metaphysics tended to oscillate between theism and pantheism, with the word 'God' as the most ambiguous term in its vocabulary. Yet it denoted a concept with which they could not dispense, and the theological issue is a shade which haunts all idealist thinking.

The name Romantic idealism is in common use, but were it taken to mean that the idealist systems were simply romanticist sentiment in its most philosophic mood it would certainly be misleading. Idealism does not stand to romanticism as effect to cause. It could as plausibly be argued that the Romantic movement in Germany was in part the creation of Fichte and Schelling themselves, although whereas the latter may well be cited as the intellectual typification of the Romantic spirit Fichte was by no means uncritical of attitudes prevalent in his day, and Hegel likewise had scant sympathy with the romanticist outlook if it meant, as it too often did, an excess of emotionalism. In any case those writers who could most readily be grouped together as *die Romantik* – the brothers Schlegel, the poet Hölderlin, a fellow-student of both Schelling and Hegel at Tübingen, Novalis and Schleiermacher (the last-named joined the 'Romantic' circle in Berlin in 1796) – were not without a philosophy of their own, an *aesthetic* idealism, although none of them, with the exception perhaps of Schleiermacher, could be said to have fashioned it into a fully articulated scheme of thought.

Yet there can be no doubt that a genuine affinity existed between the Romantics and the great speculative systems of their time. For what lay behind these systems was a certain disposition of mind, a desire to compass life as a whole. To the idealist philosophers as to the Romantics all experience entered into their purview; nothing was irrelevant, and the life of thought and imagination was no less real than that of the body itself. Critical analysis was to be accepted, but in order to render synthesis possible. The difference between them – again, notably so in the instance of Hegel – lay in their respective views of the roles of speculative reason and of intuition. 'The universe', said Friedrich Schlegel, 'we can neither explain nor conceive, but only contemplate and reveal.' Philosophy itself he saw as 'logical beauty', and the way to knowledge therefore as through art. The artist is himself a mediator of truth, aesthetic truth, with the power at his command of reconcilation and unity:

> Through the artist mankind becomes a single individual, since he unites the men of the past and of posterity in the present. He is the higher organ of the soul, where the living spirits of all outer humanity meet and in whom the inner man acts immediately.

In all this Schlegel had an eager disciple in Schelling, whose *Philosophy of Art* appeared in 1804. For him the creative genius of the artist was nothing short of a revelation of the Absolute. For Novalis, too, art or poetry *is* philosophy. 'Poetry', he tells us, 'is the truly absolute reality. It is the kernel of my philosophy.' So understood philosophy is for him 'the science of sciences' – a phrase reminiscent of Wordsworth's acclamation of poetry as 'the image of man and nature ... the impassioned expression which is in the countenance of all Science'. And it is so because of its power to strike through to the heart of all reality. 'The outer world becomes transparent, and the inner world manifold and meaningful.'

The correlation in Germany between romanticism and idealist metaphysics, between speculative thought and the arts, is scarcely intelligible until it is placed in its social context. The late eighteenth and early nineteenth centuries were an era, in the German-speaking lands, of an astonishing cultural efflorescence, one of the richest moments, aesthetically, in the history of Europe; and this in its turn cannot be explained without reference to the intellectually and socially emancipating forces to which Germany had now become open: libertarian individualism – in itself the product of the *Aufklärung* and of French revolutionary faith and fervour – the declining authority of conservative-minded religious institutions, the breakdown of a narrow and puritanical provincialism in morals and social habits with the spread of cosmopolitanism in ideas and manners. And with social change and cultural innovation came a new disposition to query, to doubt, to challenge, especially on the part of the young. When the old certainties were no longer to be relied on, a reassessment of values, as always in such circumstances, was inevitable. Wherein does the vocation of man really lie? Has life, individually or socially, an overall meaning? Does history conform to any rationally apprehensible pattern? Such were the questions to which the intellectually alert of an entire generation were moved to address themselves. The predominant interest was humanistic. Scientific problems would continue to be wrestled with, but not with the same arrogant confidence in the all-sufficiency of scientific method as formerly. The priorities had shifted. Man now was much more obviously problematic to himself, whether in his essential nature, his social and political self-determination, or his ultimate destiny. It was with these large issues that the idealists were preoccupied.

It is a mistake therefore to approach the post-Kantians only from the standpoint of the critical philosophy and the principles and procedures of Kant himself. The Königsberg master had sought to demonstrate the impossibility of a theoretical knowledge of ultimate reality. The idealists, however, believed that such knowledge is possible, and Hegel's imposing system is the most audacious rebuttal of all anti-metaphysical arguments. Technically, that is, the Kantian theory of knowledge had to be shown to imply, when submitted to close scrutiny, the very thing which the *Critique of Pure Reason* had stated to be unattainable. The enterprise meant that the *noumenon*, the unknown and unknowable thing-in-itself, is an otiose notion, by the elimination of which the world becomes in all its aspects the manifestation of thought or reason, and Kant's distinction between the *a priori* and the *a posteriori* ceases to be final. In consequence the categories are no longer subjective forms of the human understanding but are intrinsic to external reality itself. In the same manner teleological judgment forgoes its purely subjective character, for if nature, as the expression of reason, appears to exhibit purposiveness then it is appropriate to conclude that the natural order is itself teleological, moving towards an end which thought can anticipate. But this bold advance beyond the limits imposed by the critical philosophy was brought about by something more than a dialectical attempt to resolve difficulties which Kant himself, in pursuing his own tentative and cautious methods, seemed almost deliberately to have left in the path of his successors. For the fact is that the post-Kantian idealists would in all probability have reached their positions independently of the Kantian critique of knowledge, their intellectual interests being quite other than his. Unfortunately the dominance of his presence on the German philosophical scene at the turn of the century meant that all the younger men felt obliged to involve themselves with the sort of theoretical problems which he, with his scientific bias, deemed of first importance, but which for them, with their very different concerns, occasioned only a rather unprofitable digression. Kant's great achievement was an impressive philosophical interpretation of the world of the Newtonian physics. But it did not provide the atmosphere in which the idealists could naturally breathe. The great *Critique* was thus no better than an obstacle in their way which, despite their evident incompetence for the task, they struggled to remove rather than simply disregard. They belonged to a new age, one repelled by the idea of mechanism as a model for order, turning instead to organism and the reconciliation of diversity in 'purposive' development. In this respect the idealists were Romantics to the core.

Romanticism was a fervent reaffirmation of human values on the strength of what was seen as the immense potential variety, vividness and depth of experience. The concrete rather than the abstract, the particular rather than the general, gave access to the realms of living truth. As Mephistopheles told the young student in Faust's study:

Religion in the Age of Romanticism

Grau, theurer Freund, ist alle Theorie
Und grün des Lebens goldner Baum.[11]

A remark attributed to Spinoza – who in other regards was a fount of inspiration to the Romantic mind – was that 'the purpose of Nature is to make men uniform, as children of a common mother'.[12] Universalization, standardization, the definable and the uniform had been extolled by the age of Reason, which strove to render life explicable in terms of its simplest components. Only so could it be sufficiently rationalized and hence improved. Diversity meant disparity, confusion, anarchy – in the end the triumph of unreason and the forces of destruction which this would unleash. For the Romantics the principle was reversed. Difference evidenced vitality; the prodigal multiformity of nature demonstrated it. So far from diversity spelling confusion, excellence assumes many shapes, the very abundance of differences being itself a condition of excellence. It was the function of art to reflect the variety of nature and to create whatever forms might be necessary for depicting it. The idea of the *single* ideal, the perfection to be attained by restraint and restriction, had no appeal. Human experience was rather to be accepted as it is or, better still, deliberately stimulated to ever greater diversity, discovering men's latent capacities and prompting their response to life in all its aspects. So the *étalage du moi* becomes a goal in itself. Experience must always be more various, more intense. The vocation of man is to know and enjoy the sheer plenitude of existence.

But the philosophical Romantics were not content merely to contemplate the fact of the inexhaustible wealth of experience; they sought to bring to it the orderliness of rational comprehension. Nature as such, or at any rate the scientific understanding of it, might engage their attention less, but humanity presented a compelling field of study. Indeed it was through humanity that the universe itself was to be explained. For when we speak of the *cosmos* we presuppose the perspectives of the human intelligence. Or, as Hegel expressed it, 'The real is the rational, the rational the real.'

Because of the idealists' belief that the world-process is the self-unfolding of reason, the importance they attached to *system* is easy to see. If philosophy is the reflection of Being as apprehended by rational thinking it could complete its task only with the systematic interpretation of Being as a whole. Anything in more abrupt contrast with Kant's view of what philosophy can accomplish is hardly to be imagined. With Hegel, above all, confidence in the reach and power of the speculative mind to encompass the entire range of being is almost without parallel in the history of thought. In that sense he is the prince of rationalists and only Aristotle can be compared with him. For the Hegelian logic purports to offer nothing less than the self-portrayal of the universe, the self-identification of the Absolute. It occupies the topmost rank in the hierarchy of knowledge, surpassing the spiritual insights even of religion, if not in actual content then certainly by its method of speculative self-comprehension.

Looked at from the angle of a sober criticism, the sweeping claims of the idealist metaphysics would appear to be only the final pretence of romanticist megalomania. But for all its presumptuousness one should judge the idealist venture fairly. This philosophy, as I have said, is basically a humanism. Its fundamental principle is the perspective of humanity; it does not try to bypass the human standpoint in order to arrive at some non-human 'objective' truth according to which all things are what they are simply in and of themselves. The idealist contended that it is useless to talk of knowledge and truth apart from that reasoning faculty by which man himself knows and lives. The world, inescapably, is *his* world, and if he is to understand the setting in which his life is passed it can only be as it is presented to his own consciousness. Interpretation of it must be such as to give meaning and direction to his personal existence. To understand it he has to be its focal point, the significance of the world being its significance for him.

The emphasis of the human factor in cognition accounts for the attention paid by the idealists, as by the Romantics in general, to man's historical experience and that high estimate of the importance of the work of the historian which led eventually to historicism. To the nostalgic romanticist interest in and reverence for the past I have already alluded. This reverence was not by any means purely antiquarian; it recognized that the present is the product of the past and that only from a sympathetic knowledge of the past will come the wisdom necessary for a better future. A sympathetic knowledge, be it noted, not that patronizing and moralistic 'mirror-for-magistrates' attitude to former times which had characterized the age of Reason. Such a knowledge called for the use of the imaginative powers: the past, to be understood, needs to be brought to life again. As the French historian Jules Michelet put it:

> I have given to many dead that assistance of which I myself shall be in need ... I have exhumed them for a second life. Now they live with us, and we feel ourselves to be their relations and friends. Thus a family is formed, a common city between the living and the dead.

Augustin Thierry likewise claimed that 'for the imagination there is no past, and the future belongs to the present'.

This attempt imaginatively to relive days long gone by, combined with the typically romanticist sense of the infinite variety of individual existence, meant that the writing of history acquired, in addition to a new interest, the sort of prestige hitherto reserved for science. This view of it, without doubt, was the creation of the nineteenth century, and as we already have observed, it was the Romantics who began the work. Back in the 1780s Johann Gottfried Herder had pointed out that history must be seen as the continuous development of all the diverse potentialities of human nature. Schlegel took the same view, but at a more subjective level: the study of history is a vital part of man's quest for self-understanding. Not that romanticist historicizing was without its perils. Imagination in this field is a much-needed servant, but as a master it can all too easily confuse and delude. To the Romantic mind the facts of history tended sometimes to lose themselves in the mists of sentiment as well as of metaphysical or theological interpretation: Chateaubriand's 'aesthetic' treatment of historic Christianity springs to mind. As he himself admits of the *Génie du christianisme*: 'It was necessary to summon all the charms of the imagination and all the interests of the heart to the aid of that religion against which they had been set in array.' So history becomes propaganda: 'The faithful felt themselves saved, there was a craving for faith, a thirst for religious consolations.' Most obviously it could become a form of escapism – to use a glib modern expression – a refuge from the present and its problems: or in Jean-Paul Richter's phrase, 'the paradise from which we cannot be expelled'. Sentimental longing for the past might thus replace religion in seeking the consolations of another world.

But, if historiography as a science was the creation of the nineteenth century, to what extent was romanticism really a contributory factor? About this opinions have differed keenly, the maximizers attributing almost everything of lasting value in the century's cultural achievements to romanticist influence, the minimizers, on the other hand, going so far as to deny outright that in the matter of historical *science* the Romantics' preconceptions and lack of objectivity were anything but a positive hindrance to its growth. The truth would seem to be that while the Romantics' enthusiasm for the past brought to the study of it the fructifying power of the imagination, the impressions they actually formed of the past were often wrong. Nevertheless once history had acquired interest for its own sake the need to treat it seriously soon became evident, and love of mere anecdote and picturesque detail yielded to a deepening sense of its relevance to an understanding of man's place in the world. This conviction is most forceful in Hegel, whose attempt to view world-history in a unified perspective – and his personal knowledge of it was truly remarkable – clearly prepared the ground for a genuinely scientific treatment of the historical past. The work of one of Hegel's disciples, Ferdinand Christian Baur, on the early history of Christianity well illustrates this, whatever has to be said of the manner in which Baur's philosophical principles impaired his objectivity.

The method of scientific historiography, as distinct from either the vagaries of romantic curiosity or the distortions of metaphysical prejudice, was the gradual accomplishment of professional historians, themselves a new class of men. Historiography became academic in Germany, with the introduction of history as a subject taught in schools and universities. Detached as it now was from other concerns, it learned to be impartial in its handling of data as well as gaining increasing skill in the techniques of research. It was now possible to make an informed and objective assessment of a distant age or an alien civilization. An impetus to historical study was of course – and to no small degree – the political cause of German nationalism, but in the main the German school of historians prided itself on the impartiality and accuracy of its procedures. Herder, in dismissing the notion that history is a mere panorama of happenings, maintained that the historian's business is to reconstruct the past as it was. His contemporary, Friedrich August Wolf, in a 'Prolegomena of Homer' (1795), had called for a new critical awareness in dealing with historical texts, although Wilhelm von Humboldt, who was largely instrumental in the founding in 1809 of Berlin university, urged that the historian's true task was to disclose the ideas behind events; to which end he considered that both religious beliefs and the idea of the national state were of prime importance. But the idea of historiography as exact scholarship had its most noted apostle in Leopold von Ranke, who occupied a professorial chair at Berlin from 1825 until 1871. Hailed by Acton as 'the Columbus of modern history', he adopted what for him was the fittest of mottoes: *Labor est voluptas*. Details, he believed, must always be exact and sources used with a tireless scrupulosity. 'From history', he wrote, 'one has the duty of judging the past, to serve the needs of the world for instruction concerning the future.' But his own investigation, he feared, would not serve so lofty a purpose: 'It simply explains what really happened (*wie es eigentlich gewesen*).' Since his time the historiographical aim of total objectivity has been much criticized as both impossible and undesirable. Be that as it may, the new and rigorous methods which Ranke demanded were necessary then and they remain necessary still. He himself had a sharp eye for the individuality of a given epoch or historical situation, and especially for what he saw as its 'idea' – the spirit or principle which it embodied. Ranke also was a deeply religious man who ultimately saw in history nothing less than the hand of God; and, in holding that all individual historical manifestations are, as he averred, 'immediate to God', he voiced an assurance which led him to reject any idea of a recurring secular 'pattern' in events. To discover 'what really happened' seemed to him at once more reasonable and more pious. Hence the need to go back to the original documents, using secondary material as little as possible and always with an eye to its *Tendenz*. The facts should be allowed to speak for themselves, in all their variety and individual uniqueness. If history is to be understood strictly in terms of the relativities of time and place then Ranke was probably the greatest of all historicists.

3

The nineteenth century witnessed an *intellectual* rekindling of Christianity, both Protestant and Catholic, without parallel since the high middle ages. In great part this movement was indeed a reaffirmation of traditional belief, and the impulse behind it was to conserve, not to change. Even so, the traditional faith itself, in the much-altered conditions which the post-Revolutionary period had brought about, came to be looked at in a new light, not always consciously but nonetheless certainly. The apologetic need of explaining Christianity to a generation that had widely lapsed from that faith could really do nothing other than appeal to the contemporary viewpoint and exploit the current mood. More was wanted, that is to say, than could be provided by the old rationalism whose dry abstractions made little impression on the younger men. At the same time the body of Christian beliefs inherited from the past could scarcely be hoped to win positive response from more sophisticated minds without taking account of the Enlightenment's solid achievements. 'Proofs' of divine existence drawn from the mediaeval natural theology had, since Hume and Kant, lost their cogency, and in any case seemed misguided. Miracles, formerly the mainstay of divine revelation as presented by orthodoxy, had themselves become a stumbling-block which the apologist now found embarrassing. For not only had the scientific principle of the uniformity of nature rendered 'miracle' more or less inconceivable, the historical problem of authenticating any alleged instance of miraculous intervention was all too obvious: credulous hearsay could hardly be accounted evidence. And merely to reassert the authority of the ancient creeds while ignoring the objections which the sceptical intelligence raised against them would be profitless.

Yet romanticism stood primarily for a religious interpretation of the universe, not only in terms of pantheism and nature-mysticism, but in those often enough of the received Christian teaching, Catholic or

Protestant. Converts from unbelief were plentiful. The idealist philosophies, however, sought a middle way, in a reconstructed rational theology or philosophy of religion – the latter phrase now being used for the first time – the approach to which could vary, from the intellectualism of Hegel to the emotionalism of Schleiermacher or the moralism – if at a rather later date – of Lotze and Ritschl. But the influential precursor of this religious reconstruction was Jean-Jacques Rousseau, whose 'Profession de foi du vicaire savoyard' in the fourth Book of *Emile*, although its actual content was no more than a *réchauffé* of the prevalent deism, laid stress on the individual's personal feeling of relationship with the divine. Religion must appeal to the heart and even the passions, whatever the effect on moral conduct. In fact, after Rousseau and *pace* Kant, mere reason had to give room to the emotions. To the romanticist even morality should be spontaneous, personal and affective. 'The first stirring of the ethical (*Sittlichkeit*)', wrote Schlegel, 'is opposition to positive legality and conventional righteousness, and a boundless sensitivity of spirit.'

But, despite its repudiation of bare abstractness and dogmatism both in morals and religion, the Romantic philosophy had no intention of avoiding the way of reason in pursuit of understanding. Experience may be immediate, but comprehension of it is reflective. Science, so far from being abandoned, was to be developed, widened in range and made more flexible in its methods. Moreover religion itself was now deemed to need the corroboration of speculative philosophy, even though it had to be appreciated in its own proper nature, as something grounded in a living experience – *religious* experience as such. *Vernunft* was distinguished from *Verstand*, while Schleiermacher, in exploring the religious consciousness, was to locate the essence of religion in a '*feeling* of absolute dependence'. But as the century wore on and the sciences commanded ever-greater areas of knowledge a readjustment to 'scientific' reason was bound to follow. No philosophy, no theology, could be judged sufficient which lacked adequate analyses, especially of man's psychological and cultural experience in its many forms. The development of the disciplines of anthropology and the social sciences meant that philosophy too sensed the need to become 'scientific': positivism was the outcome. Nor could theology remain unaffected: a crop of liberalisms and modernisms sprang up, all endeavouring to preserve what was of tried experiential value in religion while at the same time conceding the necessity of squaring it with the irreversible advances of modern science. The aim was sound, but success was no more than partial; contradiction was not always resolved, nor tension eased.

Yet to the historian the course of modern religious thinking can be plotted in fairly clear relation to its point of departure in Romantic idealism. At times, as with Kierkegaard and Ritschl, it veered sharply away from the metaphysical doctrines of the great idealists themselves; at times again, as in France and Britain, with Cousin, Vacherot, Renan, Carlyle, T. H. Green, the Cairds and Bosanquet, the glow of its idealist past lingered on. That it should have moved far beyond the limits of theological orthodoxy is immaterial. A philosophy of religion may now assume many guises, and naturalism and humanism are not necessarily foreign to it. It suffices that it should recognize the place which religion occupies in the cultural life of man, who does well ever to remember that nothing human is finally alien to him.

The chapters which follow comprise a series of studies of continental European writers who may be said to embody or reflect romanticist attitudes to religion generally and Christianity in particular. Obviously theirs are not the only names that might have been chosen, even leaving aside writers in English – whom I have decided to omit but of whom Coleridge, without doubt, would have been the most appropriate in this setting. But the selection is not, I think, in any wise an arbitrary one and it pursues the principle that each author or group of authors should be seen to offer a distinctive perspective on nineteenth-century romanticism in its bearing on religious thought. Schleiermacher, Hegel and Schelling – all three in the Protestant tradition – are (with Fichte) the salient representatives of idealism, while the German Catholic theologians – and notably those of the Catholic faculty at Tübingen, who in certain instances came under the direct influence of Schelling[13] – disclose their romanticist affinities in their attempt to reform and revive the study of theology under the guiding concept of the continuity of history. The sixth chapter, dealing with ontologism in Italy, seeks to illustrate how the effort could be made to meet the intellectual challenge of the times by recourse to the Platonism – not without its pantheistic leanings – by which the ideas of some of the Romantics were unquestionably inspired. The subjects of the remaining chapters – Lamennais, Comte and Renan – all crossed the divide (the latter two quite early in life) between Catholicism and non-belief, Protestantism for them being no second option. Lamennais and Comte, each after his own fashion, stand for the utopianism of which their era was so productive, Renan for the scholar-aesthete's ideal of man's liberation through knowledge. Although their several responses to the demands of the age thus differed widely, the characteristic ethos of the Romantic movement – its subjectivity and personalism, its humanitarianism, its aestheticism and pantheism, its pervasive sense of history and continuity – surrounds them all, I would claim, in varying ways and measures, and constitutes the unity beneath the diversity.

2

Schleiermacher on the religious consciousness

T HE FAILURE of rationalism in religion was first signalled by the eighteenth-century revivals of traditional religious faith, notably in German pietism and English evangelicalism. Romanticism, however, was not for the most part content simply to direct its gaze back to the past or accept traditional dogmas on the presuppositions of the old supernaturalism. 'Natural theology', after Hume and Kant, could no longer stand its ground, but 'revelation' itself was much less to be taken at its face value than read in the light of human experience, in which feeling and volition are elements more potent than the critical intellect. Further, the *ipse dixit* of an external authority, ecclesiastical or biblical, having been undermined by rationalism itself, was now no substitute for the sense of personal need and inner conviction by which the self was held to achieve its own identity and affirm its autonomous right. Thus a fresh interpretation of the very nature of religion was to become a main feature of romanticist thought with the dawn of the new century. The way to the understanding of religious reality was seen to lie rather in an analysis of consciousness, a probing examination of the life of the emotions. Religious experience, it might then appear, would show itself to be a matter of the deeper sensibilities, of an inward awareness much closer to the aesthetic sense in its passivity and receptivity than to the pert operations of logical reason. Romanticism, whatever else the term may be used to cover, marked a re-evaluation of religion as an experience the authenticity of which must be sought within itself. If such authenticity could not, primarily at least, be found there it would be found nowhere. Abstract argument, as essentially extrinsic to the experience itself, was unavailing. Faith has its roots in feeling and intuition, of which theological doctrines can never be more than an imaginative symbolism, historically determined.

No religious thinker of the nineteenth century was in this respect more typical of the attitude and temper of romanticism than was Friedrich Daniel Ernst Schleiermacher (1768–1834), who, at any rate for the Protestant tradition, has remained *par excellence* the theologian of the movement in its emphasis on subjectivity and inwardness as the mirror of the infinite. With his no less characteristic belief in the significance of the individual consciousness it followed that for him every man, once awakened to the presence of the infinite within him, will experience God in his own unique way.

On leaving his first post, that of tutor in the household of a Prussian landowner, Count Dohna von Schlobitten, he was ordained to the pastorate and served for a time as his uncle's assistant in the latter's parish at Landsberg-am-Warthe. Two years later, in 1796, he moved to Berlin to take up duties as chaplain at the Charité hospital – for him a consequential step, since it was in the Prussian capital that he got to know Henriette Herz, the beautiful and cultivated wife of a physician whose house was a regular meeting-place for some of the most distinguished figures in Berlin political and cultural society, including men whose names have come to symbolize the characteristic ideas and sentiments of early-nineteenth-century romanticism. It was here that, for instance, in the autumn of 1797, he first met Friedrich Schlegel, with whom he was soon on terms of intimacy, as it was here too that he made the acquaintance of Novalis and Ludwig Tieck, and joined the circle of 'The Athenaeum', contributors to a critical magazine of that title devoted to philosophical and literary matters and hostile to the standpoint and principles of the *Aufklärung*. In fact it was as a new recruit to *The Athenaeum*'s band of authors that Schleiermacher, at Schlegel's insistence, entered upon his own career as a writer.[1]

The intellectual climate in which he now found himself, after his upbringing in Moravian pietism – he had attended school at Niesky and the Moravian seminary at Barby – followed by a 'reactionary' period of rationalism which impelled him to give up his seminary training and enrol at the university of Halle, was conducive to a further shift in his opinions, the expression of which was the book that remains his best-known literary work, his *Reden über die Religion*, begun in August 1798 and published in the summer of the next year.[2] It has been described as a 'veritable manifesto' of romanticism, not least in 'its love of opposition for opposition's sake, its disregard of the strict discipline of the schools and its use of original intuitions, analogies, and fantasy-filled combinations' in preference to the intellectually more rigorous attack in the thinking of the older generation.[3] Not only is Schleiermacher's whole conception of the nature of religion, as set forth here, in complete antithesis to that of the preceding age, his literary style is shaped to match it. Emotionally charged and highly rhetorical, even though the discourses were never intended for oral delivery, the book is throughout intensely personal, and occasionally 'poetic' to excess. Indeed for a prime example of German Romantic prose one need look no farther, whatever difficulties its mannered and effusive utterance may pose for the modern reader.[4]

However, the *Reden* are no mere historical curiosity. Schleiermacher, together with Kant, Herder and Hegel, is a founder of the philosophical study of religion as we know it now, broaching as he does the intellectual questions raised by religion in and of itself, and although he had no immediate disciples to propagate and develop his teaching his influence on theological thought has been so pervasive as to have won him the designation 'the father of modern theology', and there can be little doubt that with him Protestant theology entered a new era. His mind was truly creative, and his *oeuvre* as a whole, with the *Christliche Glaube* of 1821–2 as its centre-piece,[5] is probably the most original re-exploration of the Protestant theological position since the Reformation. To cite the judgment of his most searching twentieth-century critic, Karl Barth: 'Positively or negatively, we can draw lines from everywhere leading to Schleiermacher; from every point we can come to understand that for his century he was not one among many others, with his theology and philosophy of religion, but that it was possible for him to have the significance of the fullness of time.'[6] Moreover, while the man and his work have by no means ceased to be of historical importance, the issues he discussed are still of moment in the field of theological debate.

The fundamentals of Schleiermacher's religious philosophy are contained in the *Reden* and it is with this that I shall be mainly concerned here, although reference to his later writings, the *Christliche Glaube* in particular, will be necessary in order to clarify certain points. That Schleiermacher's thought should have undergone development in course of time is only to be expected, given a mind so alert and questing as his. But it is very doubtful that he ever departed from the basic views adopted by him in earlier life. In after years he was willing enough to explain his meaning and even to change his terminology, as the subsequent editions of the *Reden* show. Nevertheless his language is frequently ambiguous, leaving precise interpretation open. It has even been said that he 'takes both sides on every question'. But there was no radical break in the continuity of his doctrine, no sudden about-turn or even retractions of previous statements. He himself felt assured of this, holding against repeated objections that his opinions had remained consistent. They therefore who persist in charging him with inconsistency are under obligation to prove their case.

While at Halle Schleiermacher began to read Kant, the permanent effect of whom on his own thinking has to be recognized. That the Königsberg master should have been the first real stimulus to his youthful speculations is not surprising, although even then Schleiermacher was not in full accord with his ideas: one of his earliest essays, first printed in the appendix to Wilhelm Dilthey's *Leben Schleiermachers*, was a criticism of Kant's moral philosophy. *Religion within the Limits of Reason Alone* had not at that time been published, but the great *Critiques* seemed to restore religion to a place on the map of human knowledge from which, since the close of the seventeenth century, it had so often been ousted. A reductionist 'rational' theology may have survived in deism, but Hume, deftly using his sceptical empiricism to exclude religious assertions from any kind of rational acceptability, had scornfully consigned religious belief to a nebulous region of 'faith' entirely outside reason's province. Kant's doctrine, on the other hand, not only permitted but emphasized the part of the moral reason and the will in reaching a comprehensive understanding of human existence. The true evidence for religion, that is, lay in the moral consciousness. In his last major work Kant upheld Christianity, if not – as is plain – on the terms by which orthodox believers sought to justify it, then certainly on those required by man's experience as a moral being. Science and religion alike could thus be freed from the embarrassment of resting their authority upon claims neither of which was in a position to sustain. But in re-establishing the authority of religion by bringing it once more within the realm of the rational Kant had virtually equated it with morality. 'Even the Holy One of the gospel', he declared, 'must first be compared with our ideal of moral perfection before we can recognize him as such.'[7] The rational consciousness, not the incidence of miracle, provides the credentials of divine revelation.

Thus for Kant religious belief was to be construed in the language of moral duties, albeit described as 'divine commands'. To contend that it is more, that it demands something over and above what the moral consciousness itself propounds, would be, he argued, to introduce a new and heterogeneous element into experience that would inevitably impose limits on man's autonomy and to that extent lower his spiritual status. This was not at all a heartening idea to the religiously-minded, and it is possible that Kant himself came to have second thoughts about it. He could not in any case have been unaware that ordinary Christian believers would not welcome it, since it excludes what is usually thought to be integral to religion, namely sentiment and worship. Yet the principle of autonomy, for the world of the Enlightenment, had gained such complete endorsement that it could not be overthrown by an arbitrary return to the spirit of either mediaeval Catholicism or Reformation Protestantism. If the post-Reformation era had demonstrated anything it was that not ethics alone but every other area of human experience and culture – science, art, philosophy, political theory, even religion itself – was a part of the human domain, and hence measurable by human standards and referable to human needs. The day of modern secularism had already dawned.

To maintain this principle and at the same time to account for and justify the place of religion in human life was the task undertaken by the thinkers who came after Kant. On the one hand man's self-sufficiency in all the works of his civilization had to be conceded. Indeed by the time of the outbreak of the French Revolution he was deemed to have the power to control his own destiny and to need no succour or enhancement that he himself was not able, potentially if not actually, to command. It was an image of humanity magisterially enshrined in the writings of Goethe, in the light of whose Olympian worldliness a realm of ultimate transcendence or supernature seemed more or less irrelevant. The earlier phase of rationalism, which could still pay at least verbal tribute to the 'Beneficent Author of Nature', was now giving way to a self-confident humanism. The question for many was thus whether religion in any form, traditional or deistic, could meet the Promethean ambitions which in Western Europe were firing the imaginations of the educated young as they entered upon the new century. Many were content with a negative answer, but among those who sought to present religion to its 'cultured despisers' under an altogether fresh aspect was Schleiermacher. In attempting this he himself had the advantage of sharing their viewpoint to a considerable degree, but without their prejudices. He too was awake to the inadequacy of much that had passed under religion's name ˙ and had carried no brief for those 'theologians of the letter who believed the salvation of the world and the light of wisdom are to be found in a new vesture of formulas, or a new arrangement of ingenious proofs'.[8] Nor would he, in the manner of rationalist theologizing, plead for it as 'the faithful friend and useful stay of morality'.[9] For he too believed fully in man's spiritual autonomy, although in a way less abstract than that of Kant's formal ethicism. In any event Kant's own argument lacked consistency. For to resort to 'postulating' God as a demand of practical reason in effect compromised the principle of autonomy itself. Kant had argued that the morality of an action is not determined by the interests of the doer in any way whatsoever, but solely by the criterion of duty; its motive must be entirely pure. Yet he also contended that if man is to attain the *summum bonum* happiness and duty must be coincident; and such coincidence God alone can secure. The concept of divine existence thus becomes necessary if the nature of morality is to be rationally comprehended.

Schleiermacher, in response, points out that this only has the effect, postponed though it be, of detracting from that very purity of ethical obligation on which Kant is otherwise so insistent. 'If the desire for happiness is foreign to morality, later happiness can be no more valid than the earlier.'[10] Furthermore, Kant wishes to set religion firmly within the sphere of the rational – of the 'practical' reason if not of the speculative – whereas Schleiermacher himself would ground it in something beyond, or rather *before*, rationality, in a phase of consciousness which must be thought of as preceding any such distinctions as those which Kant drew. This primal, pre-reflective consciousness, that is, is anterior to either knowing or willing, as these are commonly understood. 'Fix your regard', he says to his sceptical readers, 'on the inward emotions and dispositions.' For the pre-rational consciousness is the world of *feeling*. It is here, Schleiermacher contends, in this region of our mental life, that the essence of religion is to be looked for.

That religion is essentially feeling was a notion that at once exposed Schleiermacher to criticism and even ridicule, as it still perhaps does with those who have not taken sufficient care to examine what he actually is affirming. Its apparent implication is that religion is no more than a subjective condition, a state of the emotions unrelated to any object and therefore literally meaningless. Should this in fact be what Schleiermacher implies then it is idle to talk about religious *knowledge*. Emotion in itself is unintelligible unless it can be traced to a cause or assigned to an object. But on Schleiermacher's definition no object or cause would seem to be posited. According to one of his severest modern critics, Emil Brunner, Schleiermacher maintained that 'everything conceptual, every thought, is alien and accidental to religion as such',[11] and he cites Goethe's words 'Gefühl ist alles, Name ist Schall und Rauch.'

The force of this objection depends, however, on what Schleiermacher himself meant when using the word 'feeling'. It may be that his choice of it was not altogether happy, especially if he wanted to avoid misinterpretation. But that he used it deliberately to exclude all reference to objectivity is not sustained by the *Reden*. It is clear enough from the text of at any rate the first edition that he employs the terms 'feeling' and 'intuition' (*Ansicht*) interchangeably. Thus religion may be described either as an 'intuition of the whole' or an 'immediate feeling of the Infinite and Eternal'.[12] On the other hand religion emphatically is not knowledge or science, of either the world or God, even though it of course recognizes that knowledge, science, has its place in association with it. In itself religion is an 'affection' which is also, Schleiermacher says, 'a *revelation* of the Infinite in the finite'. The contemplation of the pious is 'the immediate consciousness of the universal existence of all finite things in and through the Infinite, and of all temporal things in and through the Eternal.'[13] What else can these assertions mean but that religious feeling has a correlative object, however little specificity is at its primal stage to be attached to it? It is this implicit relationship of subjectivity to something at the very least *sensed* as objective which calls for elucidation if Schleiermacher's position is to be rendered intelligible. For what he is alluding to is a phase of consciousness in which differentiation of subject and object has not yet occurred.

A fully developed consciousness arises with and is dependent on such a differentiation – a fact which Schleiermacher no more questions than does Kant. But differentiation of subject from object, or of object from subject – let alone the conceptualization which is consequent upon it – are subsequent to that 'timeless moment' in which subject and object are one. Consciousness at that point may be characterized as 'pure' consciousness, or consciousness *per se*, before it has become a consciousness of anything in particular; a *pre*-consciousness, that is, if consciousness be taken, as in its usual meaning, to involve a specific awareness. But although, as Schleiermacher allows, such consciousness can scarcely be experienced directly – because with any degree of reflection it will already have passed – it can be realized, or sensed, indirectly.

> You must apprehend a living moment. You must know how to listen to yourselves before your own consciousness. At least you must be able to reconstruct from your consciousness your own state. What you are to notice is the rise of your consciousness, and not to reflect upon something already there ... Your own thought can only embrace what is sundered. Wherefore as soon as you have made any given definite activity of your soul an object of communication or contemplation, you have already begun to separate.[14]

The contents of such consciousnes cannot be instanced since to pinpoint it upon *this* or *that* would be to destroy it. 'Did I venture to compare it', he continues poetically,

> seeing I cannot describe it, I would say it is as fleeting and transparent as the vapour which the dew breathes on blossom and fruit, it is as bashful and tender as a maiden's kiss, it is all this. It is the first contact of the universal life with an individual. It fills no time and fashions nothing palpable. It is the holy wedlock of the Universe with the incarnated Reason for the creative, productive embrace. It is immediate, raised above all error and misunderstanding. You lie directly in the bosom of the infinite world.[15]

Schleiermacher's wording in these passages should be carefully observed. It is evident that he sees the process of growth to full consciousness as gradual. The original though fleeting unity or identity of subject and object – an idea which in some form or other permeates all Romantic philosophy – is sundered and the distinctiveness of each becomes apparent. Both may not be equally manifest at the same time: either the object will occupy the foreground of consciousness, or else the subject. In the former case our awareness moves on to cognition; in the latter to a sense of freedom and activity.

> Both knowledge and activity are a desire to be identified with the Universe through an object. If the power of the object preponderates, if, as intuition or feeling, it enters and seeks to draw you into the circle of their existence, it is always knowledge. If the preponderating power is on your side, so that you give the impress and reflect yourselves in the object, it is activity in the narrower sense, external working.[16]

Schleiermacher is, however, emphatic that religion in its proper nature is neither knowledge nor moral action. Cognition relates to specific objects as these are encountered in the world of finite experience, whereas religion is, to repeat his own phrase, immediate consciousness of the Whole. The believer indeed claims that knowledge of God is possible at the theological level, but this is not to be confused with religion itself, as a basic mode of *experience*. 'If ideas and principles are to be anything, they must belong to knowledge, which is a different department of life from religion.'[17] Creeds and dogmas, therefore, are not themselves religion and ought never to be mistaken for it. But, while agreeing with Schleiermacher that theological formularies may be assented to without real depth of conviction, an objector could well reply that a claim to knowledge is a normal element in religion, in that experience is not merely a subjective state but always implies relatedness, an awareness of something apart from which it would not have happened. One has a religious *experience*, that is to say, because one already entertains some idea of a religious *object*. Schleiermacher admits the argument to have force, but only up to a point. Religion, he concedes, never appears quite pure, its outward form invariably being determined by something else. In 'the sources and original writings of religion', for example, a great deal of theological and moral teaching is to be found. But this is not the issue, for what Schleiermacher is concerned with is not religious experience in its articulate expression but what it is *in itself* – a question, he thinks, seldom if ever considered. His whole purpose in composing the *Reden* is to repair this omission. When such enquiry is pressed it becomes clear that abstract or speculative knowledge is not of the essence of religion. In this regard theology and philosophy stand together, theological science forming part of the total scheme of human knowledge when this is extended to include theism. In what is called 'natural theology' the idea of God is treated abstractly; it is not introduced as a direct means of communicating religious experience but simply as a token signifying the first cause, or the ultimate condition, of phenomena. In other words, its only aim is to demonstrate the rationality of the content of religious faith, not to create that faith. No doubt the Christian theological tradition would in general agree with this, holding that faith itself is not the product of discursive reasoning. Nonetheless the theologian does use reason to explore and develop the implications of faith in the manner indicated by St Anselm's *fides quaerens intellectum* or by Karl Barth's 'analogy of faith' – which Barth himself did not regard as at all inimical to reason. What the theologian strives for is understanding *within* the area of faith, and to this end reason is indispensable. Schleiermacher's contention, however, is that the vital spring of the religious experience is not something mediated, but rather immediate apprehension, 'feeling', inner contemplation, and that as such it is sufficient of itself. At heart it is not an explanation of anything; for explanation takes us beyond the 'pure' experience into another mental realm altogether. In its essence, therefore, religion is not rational understanding, even in a rudimentary way, but an experience in which the self is transcended, self-lost, as it were, in the totality of being. One could say that it is 'taste and sense for the Infinite'.[18]

And what is true of knowledge is no less so of moral conduct. Not that Schleiermacher intends for one moment to deny the intimate connection between religion and morality, or the extent to which, historically, they have exerted a powerful mutual influence. But he insists that religion and morality are in themselves intrinsically different, the one being active, the other passive.

> While morality always shows itself as manipulating, as self-controlling, piety appears as a surrender, a submission to be moved by the Whole that stands over against man. Morality depends entirely on the consciousness of freedom ... Piety, on the contrary, is not at all bound to this side of life. In the opposite sphere of life, where there is no properly individual action, it is quite as active.[19]

Schleiermacher is not suggesting that the passivity of the religious life is not without a moral dimension or that the act of self-surrender will not itself have significant moral consequences. But the inherent disparity between the two is shown in the fact that morality relates always to the self. God, for the moralist – should he invoke the concept – is in the final resort the *ground* of moral action, not its object. Even man's love of God is, from the moral angle, to be seen only as the basic, or ultimate, condition of man's own perfection. The aim of religion, however, is not human perfection but union with God.

Thus the core of the matter, according to Schleiermacher, is neither cognition nor action, neither ethics nor science, but 'to have life and to know life in immediate feeling'. 'It is life in the infinite nature of the Whole, in the One and in the All, in God, having and possessing all things in God, and God in all.'[20] But is not this constant emphasis on 'feeling' and 'life' pretty clear indication that Schleiermacher's real concern is with the purely subjective or psychological side of religion? On first acquaintance with the *Reden* it is, as I have said, easy for the reader to gain this impression. Nevertheless I believe it to be an erroneous one.

Let us at the risk of some repetition glance back for a moment to Schleiermacher's account of the growth of consciousness. It has its beginning, he tells us, in the undifferentiated unity of subject and object, its development proceeding thereafter as subject and object are by degrees distinguished from and juxtaposed to each other. Full consciousness is reached only when knower and known, action and what is acted upon, become separately identifiable. To explain the origin of the religious attitude Schleiermacher's interest focuses on the intermediate stage of this process, that in which subject and object, although sensed as different, have not yet acquired distinctiveness; a stage therefore at which it would be premature to speak of the subject's actual *knowledge* of the object. For what has so far emerged is only a vague awareness of the distinction between the self and the not-self, with the sense of their unity stronger than that of their diversity. In the growth of consciousness, that is, the objective is already a component, but not to the point where objects are discriminated as such. And the same is true of the subject; what we have is an apprehension of subjectivity rather than of a subject individually aware of himself as knower or doer.

Yet Schleiermacher recognizes that there is here at least an incipient antithesis of subject and object. If the balance tilts, as it were, towards the subject we may, he suggests, call such self-consciousness 'feeling'; if toward the object, then 'intuition', although of course both sides must be sensed if consciousness is to emerge at all.

> Either the intuition displays itself more vividly and clearly, like the figure of the vanishing mistress in the eyes of her lover, or feeling issues from your heart and overspreads your whole being, as the blush of shame and love over the face of the maiden. At length your consciousness is finally determined as one or other, as intuition or feeling. When, even though you have not quite surrendered to this division and lost consciousness of your life as a unity, there remains nothing but the knowledge that they were originally one, that they issued simultaneously from the fundamental relation of your nature.[21]

Schleiermacher, be it noted, is not expressly contrasting feeling with intuition; on the contrary, he sees them as virtually one and the same; all he is saying is that in so far as they are distinguishable feeling describes the subjective factor, intuition the objective. They are in fact mutually dependent and complementary. This is very clear in the first edition of the *Reden*, where he states that 'intuition is nothing apart from feeling; it has neither the right origin nor the right force; nor is feeling anything apart from intuition. Both are real only when and because they are originally one and unseparated'.[22]

2

It is, then, this second stage of consciousness which Schleiermacher regards as the matrix of the primal religious experience – 'the immediate feeling of the Infinite and Eternal', a phrase describing the experience in at any rate its original and relatively pure state: relatively pure, because the balance of its components is always less than perfect, since the external object begins at once to make its presence known *as* external, while the subject likewise becomes aware of its personal individuality. In the later editions of the *Reden* Schleiermacher chose to use the term 'feeling' exclusively to designate religious experience, dropping 'intuition' altogether. Whatever his reason for so doing it has unfortunately led to misconception of his meaning. It has been assumed that he ultimately saw no more in religion than emotion, but it seems clear from what he says again and again that for him feeling was itself an inchoate form of cognition, and if in deciding between *Gefühl* and *Ansicht* he opted for the former it was evidently because he thought it better expressed the subjective unitariness of religious experience.

In the *Glaubenslehre*, however, Schleiermacher uses 'immediate consciousness' with exactly the same reference, and for further light on the way he comes to associate the immediate or pre-reflective consciousness with the religious we need to move on from the earlier work, where his view is assumed rather than argued, to the more discursive account in the later one, although we should bear in mind the probability that during the intervening years his ideas underwent some development and perhaps modification. At the outset (section 3.2) he is careful to distinguish between immediate self-consciousness or 'feeling', and self-consciousness as usually understood: i.e. 'that consciousness of self which is most like an objective consciousness, being a representation of oneself, and thus mediated by self-consciousness',[23] this latter, obviously enough, implying an element of cognition. But, if feeling as a form of consciousness is anterior to thinking or willing, it nonetheless accompanies these when they appear.[24] As he explains in a passage occurring in the *Dialektik*:

> In so far as thinking is also willing, or willing is thinking, the immediate consciousness must at every moment be present. Whether that moment is

predominantly one of thinking or of willing, we find it always attended by feeling. It seems indeed to disappear when we are wholly occupied with thought or activity, but in fact it does not do so. At the same time, however, it is never more than an accompaniment. Now and then it may seem to occur on its own, obliterating all thought and action. But again this is only apparently the case; for always there attend it some vestiges or seeds of cognition, no matter how faint.[25]

Within self-consciousness Schleiermacher discerns two more elements, the one a self-caused, or relatively *active* (*ein Sichselbstsetzen*), the other a non-self-caused, or relatively *passive* (*ein Sichselbstnichtsogesetzthaben*); or alternatively, a 'being' (*Sein*) and a 'by-some-means-having-come-to-be' (*Irgendwiegewordensein*). The latter of these, he says, presuppose another factor besides the self which is the source of the particular determination and without which the self-consciousness would not be precisely what it is. But this 'other' is not objectively given to the immediate self-consciousness, with which he is just now concerned. 'For though of course the double constitution of self-consciousness causes us always to look objectively for an "other" to which we can trace the origin of our particular state, yet this search is a separate act with which we are not at present concerned.'[26] Schleiermacher goes on to define the 'active' or assertive factor as a feeling of *freedom*: here the not-self, the 'other', is determined by ourselves. The 'passive' or receptive factor, on the other hand, is distinguishable as a feeling of *dependence*, inasmuch as the predominating sense is one of being ourselves determined or constrained by the 'other', the not-self. Not indeed that either may be described as absolute. The former certainly is not, 'for if the feeling of freedom expresses a forthgoing activity, this activity must have an object which has somehow been given to us, and this would not have taken place without an influence of the object upon our receptivity'.[27] A feeling of absolute freedom would be possible only if the object came into existence through our activity, which is never the case absolutely, but only relatively.

So too with the feeling of dependence: it also is relative, for even though the object be in some way *given* to us there is always a degree of counter-influence, voluntarily to renounce which would again induce a feeling of freedom. We may go still farther and maintain that the universe itself is not enough to create a feeling of *absolute* dependence, since at least the possibility remains that man in his turn can at any point influence it by reacting to it. But in the end, urges Schleiermacher, it is the self-consciousness which accompanies all our activity – necessarily determined as it is and hence precluding absolute freedom – which itself gives rise to a consciousness of absolute dependence. For this consciousness is the consciousness that the whole of our spontaneous activity comes from a source outside of us, in just the same way that anything towards which we should have a feeling of absolute freedom must have proceeded entirely from ourselves.[28] To put it otherwise, our apprehension of the self's relative freedom and of its relative dependence – in short, of the entire order of contingent being, of self and not-self alike – is as such a new determination of consciousness, namely a feeling of *absolute* dependence. And this feeling of absolute dependence (*Gefühl der schlechtinnigen Abhängigkeit*) is to be identified with the primal religious consciousness, with religion in its essence – 'the self-identical essence of piety'.

But if religion, or the religious consciousness, is to be defined after this manner, does not the definition necessarily postulate a transcendent object, such as is expressed by the word *God*? Schleiermacher's answer, in the *Reden*, is that there is no original *concept* of God and that what this term denotes is no more – if no less – than this unique feeling of total dependence. A specific idea of God, whether as a particular reality within the cosmos or even the cosmos as a whole, is not in itself an indispensable part of the religious experience, because religion in its primal state is not directed towards any conceived object. At this stage, therefore, the claim to knowledge is an irrelevance. If we are to speak of God at all it is in the sense merely of 'the Whence of our receptive and active existence'. For such indeed is the proper and original sense of the word. 'God signifies for us simply that which is the co-determinant in this feeling [of absolute dependence] and to which we trace our being in such a state; and any further content of the idea must be evolved out of this fundamental import assigned to it.'[29] To acknowledge this is not to question the legitimacy of the idea of God as a subsequently derived objectifying concept; but it does so only as a symbol of the original experience, which in itself has no direct objective focus. The relation of symbol and experience thus needs to be clearly grasped; otherwise the latter's true nature will be misconstrued. 'The transference of the idea of God to any perceptible object, unless one is all the time conscious that it is a piece of purely arbitrary symbolism, is always a corruption, whether it be a temporary transference, i.e. a theophany, or a constitutive transference, in which God is represented as permanently a particular perceptible existence.'[30]

The reason for Schleiermacher's insistence on feeling as the essence of religion thus becomes more positive. Not that he regards all feelings as religious; on the contrary, it is only 'the highest grade of immediate self-consciousness', i.e. the feeling of absolute dependence, which partakes of this quality or character, because it points to the transcendent ground of all consciousness – that wherein consciousness and being are one. Only in the realm of feeling is the discerned opposition between self and environment overcome. This transcendental ground is apprehended therefore as the supreme and ultimate Being, or in philosophical language, the Absolute. Herein, then, lies the objectivity of the religious experience, the condition which prevents it from being a mere unoriented emotion. Schleiermacher's analysis of consciousness thus discovers a 'moment' of revelation in which the 'absoluteness' of Being is sensed by us; and it is precisely at this moment, when consciousness of self and not-self are alike transcended, that religion discloses its true nature or *Wesen*, as the experience in which 'the whole soul is dissolved in the immediate feeling of the Infinite and the Eternal'.[31]

It is important to realize, however, that the feelings of both partial freedom and partial dependence are themselves the condition without which that of *absolute* dependence would not continue or even come into being. Although, that is to say, they do not and cannot constitute the religious consciousness as such, they do impart to it its determinate character.

> Being related as a constituent factor to a given moment of consciousness which consists of a partial feeling of freedom and a partial feeling of dependence, it [the religious consciousness] becomes a particular religious emotion, and being in another moment related to a different datum, it becomes a different religious emotion; yet so that the essential element, namely, the feeling of absolute dependence, is the same in both, and thus throughout the whole series, and the difference arises simply from the fact that it becomes a different moment when it goes along with a different determination of the sensible consciousness, i.e. the consciousness which is in part one of freedom, in part one of dependence.[32]

From this it is plain that Schleiermacher sees the two levels of consciousness, the sensible and the religious, as standing to each other in a reciprocal relationship. Each is a determinant factor in respect of the other, the religious consciousness taking its colour and tone, so to speak, from the sensible while at the same time imparting to the particular feelings – whatever they may be – associated with the latter a character which brings them too within the sphere of the religious. Apart from the sensible consciousness the religious, if it could arise at all, would bear no relation to our emotional life and would thus be of no relevant significance. But by being a component of our *total* consciousness it acquires meaning by being specific. Nevertheless it is only as a feeling of absolute dependence that it reveals, or points to, absolute Being. To that extent trans-subjective, it is an intuition of ultimate reality and not merely – *pace* Schleiermacher's critics – a purely subjective state.[33] It also suggests that when Schleiermacher tells us that the religious consciousness is never pure he means that what is intuited – the transcendent ground of both being and consciousness – is only partially apprehended, since full apprehension is impeded by opposing elements within the sensible consciousness.

If Schleiermacher is right in his analysis it is to be inferred that the religious experience is something native to man in that his religious consciousness is intrinsic to his whole mental constitution. Schleiermacher says so, in fact, quite explicitly: 'If the feeling of absolute dependence, expressing itself as consciousness of God, is the highest grade of immediate self-consciousness, it is also an essential element of human nature.'[34] Man is distinctively a religious animal. Starved of religion his humanity is deficient; with it he becomes truly himself. Whence also the necessity of religion alike for true science and genuine morality; although it requires no certification from them, they are defective without it. In this respect the prejudices of religion's 'cultured despisers' could not be more egregiously wrong. 'To wish to have true science or true practice without religion, or to imagine it is possessed, is obstinate, arrogant delusion, and culpable error.'[35] For what can a man accomplish worth speaking of in either life or art that does not arise within him from this deepest sense of the infinite?

However, as the religious consciousness is always a determinate and never an indeterminate consciousness there is no such thing as religion *sans phrase*, and attempts by rationalist thinkers to reduce it to a supposedly 'uncorrupt' condition based on the alleged principles of universal reason have been wholly beside the mark. This so-called 'natural religion', says Schleiermacher, 'is usually so much refined away, and has such metaphysical and moral graces, that little of the peculiar character of religion appears.' Religion as it actually is is always and necessarily positive. Speaking abstractly, all religions presuppose the feeling of absolute dependence; it is their common differentia. But the historically determinate forms of religion vary in accordance with those of the sensible self-consciousness.[36] The feeling of absolute dependence cannot, as we have seen, persist by itself; specific religious feelings take their identity only from the union of the sensible and the religious consciousnesses. This explains the manifoldness of the varieties of religious feeling, which so far from being arbitrary conform to certain definite laws or principles. 'That the religious sense of one person is moved in one way, and that of another in another, is not pure accident, as if the emotions formed no whole, and as if any emotions might be caused in the same individual by the same object. Whatever occurs anywhere, whether among many or few, as a peculiar and distinct kind of feeling is in itself complete, and by its nature necessary.'[37] And given the fact that religion, like other basic forms of human experience, manifests itself in social groupings and propagates itself through social contact, the rise of the positive or historical religions becomes explicable.[38] It explains too why these religions lay so much stress upon their origins, asserting their historic character by grounding their authority on particular historical claims, upon the maintenance of which their unity depends. This is of course very notably the case with Christianity, where historical events are the medium through which religious feeling is determined by the facts of the sensible consciousness.[39] For it is in the founder or authoritative teacher of a religion, Schleiermacher argues, that we are confronted with one or another of the possible types of felt relationship with the divine expressed in concrete historical shape.[40] And the founder, again, has disciples who in a measure at least share his experience – one moreover which must be kept alive within the religious tradition as handed down to posterity, although the chances of its being corrupted or becoming petrified are many: dogmatism and conventionalism, which can mortify the spirit of a religion, are recurrent in history, the true spirit being found only among those 'who live in it as their element, and ever advance in it without cherishing the folly that they embrace it all'.[41]

What, then, is the truth in the charges against Schleiermacher that he is guilty of reducing faith to feeling and of eliminating all thought of the object of experience by fixing attention solely on the condition of its subject – in a word of offering not theology but only a phenomenology of the religious consciousness? If, his critics say, you remove the cognitional element from religion and concentrate instead entirely on the state of mind of the 'believer', what are you left with but an aesthetic emotionalism, so that the religious man's experience is assimilated to that of the artist? Also are not Schleiermacher's references to 'consciousness' (*Bewusstsein*) often inconsistent? For if at times he does seem to imply cognition – for consciousness presumably has to be consciousness *of* something – does he not at least as frequently use it to indicate feeling only, without cognitional overtones? Does it not therefore remain a matter of doubt with him whether religious doctrines are an expression of feeling alone or of feeling *relative to* an object, with the result that the reader begins to suspect that whatever plausibility Schleiermacher's argument has really turns upon the dubiety itself?[42]

I do not think one can dismiss such criticisms out of hand. Schleiermacher is all too often unclear. But it has to be remembered that he stands by the principle that God is not an *object* of knowledge at all, since he is the transcendental ground of all knowledge as of all action. Accordingly, our awareness of this ground cannot be mediated directly through the rational faculty but through something more fundamental, something which he saw rather as constitutive of the unity of the self as a whole. And it is this, the very root of the human personality, which he designates *feeling*. But although feeling is not a source of cognition in the way that conscious reason is it is not without a certain cognitive capacity. The substance of religion, that is, is not to be equated with the concept of God as 'a single being outside of the world and behind the world' – for that would be no more than an imaginative objectification of the divine – but our immediate consciousness of deity 'as he is found in ourselves and in the world'.[43]

This view is elaborated by Schleiermacher in his *Dialektik*, where he argues, more fully if not always very luminously, that all knowledge presupposes a transcendental ground as the basis of unity of thought and being, of real and ideal, and that as such it cannot itself be the direct object of thought by forming the predicate of a judgment.[44] Although it is questionable whether 'being-itself' may or may not, in Schleiermacher's mind, be synonymous with deity, he is clearly convinced that God cannot be known by us *in himself* and that feeling alone provides that means by which his reality can become accessible to us.[45] And, since the feeling of absolute dependence is itself determined by the sensible consciousness, it follows that there can be no awareness of deity apart from our awareness of the universe:

> There is no isolated intuition of the Deity, but we intuit it only in and with the entire system of intuition ... Our knowledge of God is completed only with the intuition of the world. As soon as there is a trace of the latter we discern the outlines of the former. In so far as the intuition of the world remains incomplete, the idea of God remains mythical.[46]

But does this not mean that the world and God have to be conceived as correlates, standing in a relation not simply of compresence but of mutual implication? That Schleiermacher repudiates sheer pantheism, the equation of God with the universe, cannot surely be questioned:

> The deity is always regarded in thought as unity without plurality, the world as plurality without unity. The world fills space and time; God is spaceless and timeless. The world is the totality of antitheses; God is the real negation of all antitheses.[47]

Or still more succinctly:

> God is the unity excluding all antitheses; the world is unity including all antitheses.[48]

God and the universe are, then, not the same, but neither can they be conceived apart from one another; if there is no complete identification of the two ideas, nor is there a complete separation. Take away the God-concept and the universe is inadequate to our intellectual demands; yet take away the universe and the God-concept becomes meaningless.[49] But this implies that God is not, as in orthodox Christian teaching, the creator of the world, of his own will bringing it into existence *ex nihilo*, for were he ultimately independent of the world the latter would have to be regarded as accidental or fortuitous.[50] Indeed to speak of a 'free' act of God is conceptually to subject him to the antithesis of freedom and necessity.[51] Even to represent God as determining matter would be to render him as in some sense conditioned by matter.[52]

On the face of it these ideas are not easily reconcilable with the biblical view of God as free and sovereign Personality. And the impression is reinforced when we turn to Schleiermacher's notion of divine providence as a uniform causality operative throughout nature and human history:

> The equivalence of divine causality with the whole content of the finite enables every act to excite the religious consciousness; every act, that is, in which we take up into ourselves a part of the natural order to identify ourselves with such a part, every moment of our self-consciousness as it extends over the whole world. And thus whenever a person either moves or is moved, he is also drawn to a conscious apprehension of the power of the Highest directly near to him in all finite causality.[53]

But Schleiermacher did not believe that in so stating his doctrine he was in any essential respect departing from traditional Christianity, and assuredly not from Reformation teaching:

> It has always been acknowledged by the strictest dogmaticians that divine preservation, as the absolute dependence of all events and changes on God, and natural causation, as the complete determination of all events, by the universal nexus, are one and the same thing simply from different points of view, the one being neither separated from the other nor limited by it.[54]

Perhaps the two perspectives are not basically contradictory, but Schleiermacher's, with its pantheistic suggestions, is typical of Romantic immanentism.

The reason for this is that Schleiermacher, as a true Romantic, approaches all religious belief not by the traditional route of a revelation objectively mediated through events but by way of the believer's consciousness. It is almost inevitable therefore that the sheer 'givenness' of divine truth seems to lose itself in the mists of personal subjectivity. Thus he tells us in the *Glaubenslehre* that 'all attributes which we ascribe to God are to be taken as denoting not something special in God, but only something special in the manner in which the feeling of absolute dependence is to be related to him',[55] a proposition which, he himself points out, in general denies the speculative character of the content of the various divine attributes affirmed in Christian doctrine. More than that, however, all propositions, he insists, which the Christian doctrinal system sets before us are to be regarded as descriptions of personal states of mind, even though they may appear in a different guise as metaphysical statements about the divine being and action or as statements as to the constitution of the world; and although he admits that all three forms have subsisted alongside each other he contends that these guises are misleading and that ideally all theological propositions should be seen as conforming to a common type. Propositions of the latter two kinds are permissible only so far as they can be developed out of propositions of the first kind, since only thus can they really be authenticated as expressions of religious emotions, which is what theological doctrines essentially are.[56]

How this restatement of Christian doctrine in all its interrelated areas is to be carried through is Schleiermacher's task in the *Glaubenslehre*, although he recognizes the difficulty facing him in practice, in view of the historic conditions under which dogma has taken shape: the result, he fears, 'would lack a really ecclesiastical character' and so, as a presentation of Christian dogmatics, fail of its purpose to communicate the Christian experience. This is a serious admission indeed, but Schleiermacher is in no two minds about what for the sake of consistency needs to be done. Let us therefore consider for a moment how he treats the basic doctrine of God.

Unfortunately for the reader, Schleiermacher breaks up his discussion of the divine attributes into three separate sections widely removed from one another. The 'metaphysical' attributes of eternity, omnipresence, omnipotence and omniscience appear early on in the second section of part one, where they are connected with the religious consciousness inasmuch as this is expressive of God's general relationship to the world. The divine holiness and justice, however, are dealt with a good deal later, in connection with man's awareness of sin. Finally, discussion of God's love and wisdom is deferred until very near the end of the work, and then only in relation to the divine causality interpreted in terms of redemption. By this procedure the Christian's 'God-consciousness' is divided between feelings of a general and abstract kind and those which have arisen from historical conditions. To some this is a fault, but methodologically it may be held justifiable. Clearly Schleiermacher prefers to approach so fundamental a doctrine in accordance with what he sees as differing aspects of the religious experience itself. The standpoint is subjectivist, admittedly, but as touching, I would say, the manner of his thinking rather than its actual content. What is more important is whether the several divine attributes, as Schleiermacher treats of them, are self-consistent and body forth into a coherent doctrine. Obviously this is a large subject and anything like a systematic examination of it here would necessitate an unacceptably lengthy digression. But some comment on Schleiermacher's account of the metaphysical attributes may be offered.

The question that at once prompts itself is whether the feeling of absolute dependence in which Schleiermacher finds the core of the religious experience implies that the Whence of this feeling, the That in regard to which existence is felt to be wholly contingent, stands in no reciprocal relationship at all to the consciousness which apprehends this total dependence. The self as conscious both of a relative freedom and a relative dependence is certainly contingent. But can we *logically* pass from the recognition of contingency, our own and that of all other finite entities, to the affirmation of a reality which is absolutely non-contingent? What, it seems, Schleiermacher is really doing is to assume without argument the claim of traditional theism that God the creator is himself absolutely unconditioned. At any rate to say that such a concept can be derived from an analysis of the believer's self-consciousness is to beg the question. It is, as we have well noted, a basic principle with Schleiermacher that it is not possible to claim knowledge of what God is in himself. To posit the existence of a wholly non-contingent reality on the grounds of the *sense* of contingency is therefore to go beyond what self-consciousness warrants. Moreover, it does not follow from the creature's own feeling of utter dependence that the Creator himself is completely unaffected by his creation; at the least he has knowledge of it, and he may well – Christian theology indeed teaches emphatically that he does – have a determinate purpose in regard to it.

As to the attributes themselves, Schleiermacher looks on them not as speculative *a priori* notions but concepts derived from the divine causality manifested in the universe. It is a view that has been deemed to give still further substance to the charge that his general outlook is pantheistic, despite his clear assertion in the *Dialektik* that the concept of the universe is a *Grenzbegriff*, a limit of thought, and not the transcendental ground of thought, to which alone the term God is applicable.[57] But his repeated insistence that these ideas are also not to be separated and that they are in fact correlative, since it is only in seeking to give completeness to our idea of the universe that we arrive at the concept of God as a presupposition, does not even today altogether disarm his critics.

A particular element in Schleiermacher's theology which they fasten on is his doctrine of creation, or rather that of *preservation*, to which, as they maintain, the former is reduced. Indeed he takes the chief purpose of the doctrine of *creatio ex nihilo* to be an underlining of the conviction – implicit in the feeling of absolute dependence – that nothing exists which does not have its origin in God. Strictly speaking, however, the doctrine, referring as it does to an event in the inconceivably distant past, is not, on Schleiermacher's understanding of it, directly related to the immediate self-consciousness, so that its real function is the negative one of excluding the claim that the universe or any part of it is self-existent. But on its positive side we are told that the religious consciousness coincides with the view that all things are conditioned and determined by the interdependence of nature.[58] But is this sufficient to distinguish between divine and natural causality? Or does it not after all merely blend God indissociably with nature? When, later, Schleiermacher goes on to discuss the divine omnipotence these misgivings are likely to be intensified. In this attribute, he states, two ideas are comprised. The first is that 'the entire system of nature, comprehending all times and places, is founded upon divine causality, which, as eternal and omnipresent, is in contrast to all finite causality' – a principle which takes us little farther than those already propounded in explanation of the attributes of eternity and omnipresence.[59] But the second is more challenging. For this alleges that the divine causality, as affirmed in our feeling of absolute dependence, is 'completely presented in the totality of finite being, and consequently everything for which there is a causality in God happens and becomes real'.[60] On such a view it is hard to avoid the conclusion that God's creativity is wholly expended in the causality of the universe and that there are no reserves of power available to him. Schleiermacher's own words leave no room for ambiguity here: 'The idea of potentiality outside the sum of the actual has no validity even for our minds.'[61] Hence the world could not be other than it is, an idea which brings Schleiermacher exceedingly close to his beloved Spinoza. For what becomes, it may be asked, of the doctrine of the divine transcendence? Nor does Schleiermacher allow any difference between 'can' and 'will' in God, any more than between the actual and the possible: the entire omnipotence, undivided and unabbreviated, is what does and effects all things. So too with the divine knowledge: whatever God knows he wills. There is nothing left in his mind to which there is no correlative in existence.[62] All this is not to be put down to the limitations of human knowledge. On the contrary, for although Schleiermacher says plainly that man's knowledge is limited he commits himself at least in this matter to quite categorical statements.

The upshot is that it is not at all easy to discriminate in Schleiermacher between God's action and the causal interdependence of nature. To be conditioned by the natural order is to be conditioned no less by the supernatural and *vice versa*; the descriptions are interchangeable and either may be chosen, depending on the standpoint adopted. Perception of God in nature in no way implies that nature's uniformity need be qualified. 'The human soul is just as necessarily predisposed towards a knowledge of the world as towards a consciousness of God.' It is only a false science that would dismiss religion, as likewise only a mistaken religion which would impede the progress of natural knowledge.[63] So too with human activity; providence itself operates through it. In the divine causality there is no division or opposition anywhere; the order of the universe is unchanging, inasmuch as in God himself there is no change, and no possibility of it. The notion of a 'special providence' therefore is completely ruled out.

> We cannot avoid affirming the independent existence of the particular as an element within the whole; but we instantly leave the right track when we assume for this particular a special divine causality in any way separate from connection with the whole, and thus view the particular in question as the special object or result of divine government, to which other things therefore are subordinated as a means.[64]

That Schleiermacher has no use for the traditional belief in miracles is – need it be said? – a matter of course. Miracle is to be excluded on theological no less than scientific grounds. It does not demonstrate the divine omnipotence; to maintain that it does requires that an act which suspends the order of natural causation reveals omnipotence more truly than does the original and no less divinely ordered course of nature itself. While, as for empirical testimony of miracle, how could any single instance of it be recognized with certainty by us, seeing that the progress of science has proved that the unusual is not the same as the inexplicable? An event – any event – rather is a miracle that inspires feelings of religion.[65]

3

I pass now from Schleiermacher's account of the religious consciousness in general to what he has to say of the Christian consciousness in particular, but of this, the content of the *Glaubenslehre*, our survey can only be the most cursory. Christianity he defines, somewhat technically, as 'a monotheistic faith, belonging to the teleological type of religion, and is essentially distinguished from other such faiths by the fact that in it everything is related to the redemption accomplished by Jesus of Nazareth'.[66] This definition rests upon Schleiermacher's classification of the historic religions into two main groups, either of quite distinct types, or else of developments more or less complete of the same type.[67] But if religion is at the root a feeling of utter dependence, then monotheism, of religion's diverse forms, must be deemed the highest, and to it, in the end, all others must conform.[68] Yet in itself the designation 'monotheistic' is not sufficiently precise. Monotheism represents the final stage in the development of religion, but it is a category under which a number of otherwise differing religions can be subsumed, and it is necessary to discriminate between them. A sub-classification therefore will distinguish them as either 'natural' or 'moral', according to whether the natural in human life is subordinated to the moral or the moral to the natural.[69] By *teleological* Schleiermacher denotes religions which are predominantly ethical in their stress, whereas those in which the ethical element is lacking or minimal he describes as *aesthetic*. Such an arrangement is obviously schematic, and although useful up to a point needs to be supplemented by considerations of a concrete and historical order, harking back to a religion's origins. Christianity then emerges as both teleological and monotheistic but as differing from all others of the kind through its explicit connection with the redemption wrought by Christ.[70] It will be observed that, in consonance with this reasoning, Schleiermacher remains faithful to the procedure he has all along adopted, namely the 'internal' approach which classifies religions by the types of experience they embody. In this respect Christianity, in contrast with Judaism, which conceives man's relation to God to be determined by 'universal immediate retribution' for wrongdoing, is marked by the 'more glorious intuition' of 'the universal resistance of finite things to the unity of the Whole, and the way the deity treats this resistance'. Hence Christianity's message is essentially one of reconciliation and the overcoming of alienation.

> Corruption and redemption, hostility and mediation, are the two indivisibly united, fundamental elements of this type of feeling (*Empfindungsweise*), and by them the whole form of Christianity and the cast of all the religious matter contained in it are determined.[71]

The Christian religion, then, is *par excellence* the religion of redemption; and as such it is at once related to and distinguishable from all other expressions of the religious consciousness. This appreciation of it is reached, not, as with the supernaturalists, by a review of its dogmatic content, nor, as with the rationalists, by reducing it to a few supposedly self-evident truths. Instead, the criteria are those of experience and history. The method combines the empirical with the speculative in a manner which surely justifies Schleiermacher's claim to a unique place in modern theological thought.

Now if God is apprehended in the immediacy of self-consciousness it follows that theological doctrines must be understood accordingly.

They are not to be taken as objective accounts of some divine realm of being. To imagine that God 'as he is in himself' could be adequately described in the language arising from and appropriate to finite relations would be to bring him, *per impossibile*, into the order of the finite himself. Rather has theological terminology to be 'relational', explicative of the affections of the believer's consciousness. Nothing can be affirmed of the divine 'in excess of the immediate self-consciousness'.[72] Christian theological statements are simply expressions of the Christian's religious feelings 'set forth in speech'. Every proposition, says Schleiermacher, which can be an element within the Christian proclamation (*kerygma*) is also doctrine, inasmuch as it 'bears witness to the determination of the religious consciousness as inward certainty'.[73] It is legitimate to speak of 'revelation' in the sense of the *originality* of the experience upon which a religious communion is founded, in that the individual content of the religious emotions that characterize the communion's life is not to be explained 'by the historical chain which precedes it'. But this original datum is not, Schleiermacher insists, to be thought of as doctrine and addressed to man purely as a cognitive being – a principle that applies to the Christian revelation no less than to the constitutive faith of any other religion. What cognition pertains to is the articulated disciplines of the religious consciousness itself, and these it is the responsibility of dogmatic theology to enunciate. Rightly speaking they are indicative of the self's awareness of utter dependence and so necessarily refer back to the self as its own interpretations of experience of the divine, although in the process poetical and rhetorical language has to be translated into that of formal concepts.

The central point of the Christian experience, the fulcrum upon which its whole doctrinal scheme turns, is for Schleiermacher man's consciousness, on the one hand, of sin and, on the other, of the grace and blessedness flowing from the redemptive work of Christ. Realization of sinfulness springs from the weakening of the sense of the divine by the downward pull of our lower, sensual nature. It is thus a universal human condition. It does not result from any divine disclosure but is a fact of human nature. Sin impairs and diminishes God-consciousness, for the power of the flesh being such as constantly to hinder the advance of the spirit, the latter is always at a disadvantage. Inner conflict therefore is inevitable, heightened by the fact that we recognize the good long before we command the strength of will to attain it, so that the essence of sin is the disorder and confusion within our humanity brought about by the antagonism of contradictory ends. Further, the freedom to choose and the sense of responsibility this entails carry with them feelings of guilt and wretchedness. But sin is not only an individual matter, it also has a social dimension in that man is a communal being and his life is largely dependent on his communal existence. Thus sin has causes in society as well as consequences for society. This state of affairs Schleiermacher does not, however, attribute to any moral 'fall' of man in the distant past, and the doctrine of original sin, any more than that of creation, is not to be explained by reference to some primaeval event. Original sin is properly interpreted as the sinfulness which is present in an indivudual 'before any act of his own, and which is grounded outside his own being'. Its mark is an incapacity for good. In this respect 'the first human pair' were situated no differently from mankind in all ages. What we have to deal with is the 'simple idea of an absolutely common guilt identical for all' and a 'timeless original sinfulness always and everywhere inhering in human nature and coexisting with the original perfection given along with it'.[74]

But, although sin is the universal condition of our humanity, an intrinsic property of human nature as we know it, the energizing spiritual force which enables us to overcome it is imparted to us by Jesus Christ. Herein lies the true meaning of his redemptive action. For, since relief cannot spring from the sin-permeated life common to the human race, redemption must be looked for from a source outside man, in the person of one having a uniquely intense God-consciousness – a consciousness nevertheless communicable to man. Precisely who or what Christ was *in himself* is not a pertinent question, for we know him, as the Reformers so often remind us, only through his benefits towards us. Jesus' God-consciousness controlled his entire being, to the extent that we can rightly speak of his complete sinlessness and moral perfection. He is in fact not only the *Vorbild*, or example for humanity, he is its *Urbild*, its very archetype or ideal. And as such he is one who can *effect* man's spiritual and moral renovation, an idea expressed by Schleiermacher under the figure of the Pauline 'Second Adam', the head of a new race of mankind – a point, I would say, that should be borne in mind by critics who have charged him with offering a 'reduced' Christology of pure exemplarism. Thus he sees Christ as a fount of grace which man of his own resources could not supply or even conceive of. Here Schleiermacher reveals himself to be nearer to orthodoxy than was Kant, in whose *Religion within the Limits of Reason Alone* Christ has no other role than that of exemplary symbol. Indeed Jesus is for Schleiermacher a 'miracle', in the sense at least of not being explicable simply as the product of that historical continuum to which of course his humanity as such belonged, but as a new creation of God. It is this which justifies the ascription to Christ of the title Redeemer. The completeness of the God-consciousness which constitutes this unique phenomenon in human history is what in fact we mean by Christ's divinity and his power to mediate salvation.

It should at the same time be noted that the figure of Jesus, fact of history though he be, is treated by Schleiermacher under the heading 'of the state of the Christian, inasmuch as he is conscious of divine grace', and not, as one might have expected, among those doctrines which he categorizes as assertions about the constitution of the world. The reason is that, consonant again with Schleiermacher's whole method in dogmatics, he sees Christ as the differential reality to which the Christian consciousness must at every moment be related. To say that Christianity signifies 'the redemption accomplished in Jesus of Nazareth' means that the new God-consciousness conveyed to man by him is essentially a 'God-consciousness *through* Christ'. The Christ-reference is the indispensable element in the Christian experience of regeneration and sanctification, of grace triumphing over sin.

But the Christian religion is a historical religion in that the experience of grace has in Jesus of Nazareth a specific historical ground. Schleiermacher's Christology is rooted in his appreciation of the historicity of Christ's life and mission. Apart from his historical existence we cannot begin to understand him. It is the incontestable 'given' on the basis of which alone theological speculation can proceed. Yet it has to be admitted that Schleiermacher's estimate of Jesus' historicity is little determined by considerations of historical criticism, the beginnings of which, by the time the first edition of the *Glaubenslehre* made its appearance, were already evident, and the exalted view he takes of Jesus' 'ideality' (*Urbildlichkeit*) draws largely, one cannot but observe, on the 'mystical' Christ of St John's Gospel.

But the order of grace and blessedness, although founded in Jesus' historic mission, is mediated to the individual believer only through the community of believers, the church – those who, in whatever measure, greater or less, partake of Jesus' own God-consciousness in a new and invigorated spiritual life. In other words, it is by contact with the religious community that the individual's faith is created and sustained. Schleiermacher's emphasis on the place and importance of the church is striking. Eighteenth-century individualism, which was content to regard it as an aggregation of independent human units, is altogether eschewed in preference for the Pauline conception of an organic whole of many members with diverse functions. Nevertheless Schleiermacher's understanding of the church as the inspired medium through which, over the ages, Christ's redemptive work becomes effective for the believer, along with his dismissal of what he calls 'magical' views of redemption, means that Christ's action is radically historicized and subjectivized. Once more it is a matter of the determination of the believer's consciousness by the experiences into which he enters. Even the doctrine of the Holy Spirit is to be interpreted as the 'vital unity of the Christian fellowship as a moral personality' or, more simply still, as 'the common spirit' of the members of that fellowship.[75] Thus in the end it is through the church's perpetual remembrance of Christ's saving mission that the individual finds reconciliation and blessedness.[76] The divine energizing of the Christian fellowship is to be experienced through the shared faith of its members, even if, as it might seem, at the expense of the individual's sense of a personal relation with God.

The significance of Schleiermacher for modern religious thought can scarcely be overestimated. What the Kantian criticism is to the history of philosophy so is the content of the *Reden* and *Glaubenslehre* to that of post-Reformation theology. Not only does Schleiermacher's achievement signalize a fresh start after the inertia which had gradually settled upon the religious spirit in the later eighteenth century, but the issues which he raised were to be of commanding interest for the generations to come, nor have they yet ceased to exercise the theological mind. But Schleiermacher was representative and typical of his own age in so far as he gave utterance, in the theological realm, to the romanticist ideas and ideals of that time. He left behind him, however, no distinctive 'school' of disciples, in the sense of followers who could be said to have perpetuated his personal spirit and procedure. The truth is that Schleiermacher, by virtue of his singular disposition and manifold talents, stood alone. Perhaps the nearest he had to an immediate successor was the Swiss theologian Alexander Schweizer (1808–88) of Bremen, whose *Christliche Glaubenslehre nach protestantischen Grundsätzen* (1863–9) recalls the master's work by its speculative range and underlying philosophical monism. But the liberal Protestantism of later years stands under his shadow. Individual liberals, like Albrecht Ritschl, may at times be somewhat cool in their appraisal of him – the moralistic Göttingen pundit was especially critical of Schleiermacher's 'aestheticism' – but what they owed to him cannot be gainsaid. Towards the end of the nineteenth century and during the first decades of the present, in the writings of Auguste Sabatier, Ernst Troeltsch and Rudolf Otto in particular, something of Schleiermacher's spirit was to live again.

It was with the resurgence of Protestant orthodoxy after the 1914–18 war that Schleiermacher and his whole liberal inheritance came under attack. Karl Barth stigmatized the entire liberal era as 'Schleiermacher's century'. 'After describing all sorts of curves, both great and small, it nonetheless always returned to him.'[77] But for all his acknowledged greatness – and Barth insisted that unless his greatness is acknowledged criticism of him is misplaced and impertinent – his overall influence on theology has to be judged as baneful. Schleiermacher, he thinks, made the fatal mistake, out of his concern to render Christian belief intelligible to the educated modern man, of putting himself, as it were, above it. Paradoxically for the author of the *Glaubenslehre*, the authority of neither the Bible nor the ecclesiastical tradition of doctrine was of paramount importance; under the necessity which he felt of restructuring Christian theology he was prepared to play fast and loose with both. Not that he omitted to recognize the normative force of the New Testament for the Christian consciousness at all times, or the pedagogical value of Christian doctrine as an expression at any time of the actual state of the Christian consciousness. Rather, he placed dogmatic theology itself within a strictly historical perspective as the intellectual reflection of that consciousness in the church as it is modified from one age to another. However, in neither the Bible nor the doctrinal tradition does the ultimate authority reside, but in the vital momentum of religious experience itself. In principle at least he considered that no man need look beyond his own self-consciousness for living contact with the divine. He who, out of the fullness of his personal experience, might conceivably have written the scriptures has no need of a sacred book, any more than he who possesses the living truth within him has need of a doctrinal confession. Such external guides and props may well be, as they so often manifestly have been, a practical necessity, but the value they have and the function they serve derive from the life of personal religion and are confirmed experientially. Karl Barth was probably right in seeing here the effect of the influence upon Schleiermacher of his Moravian upbringing no less than of the individualistic romanticism into which religious sentiment could so readily be translated. Little wonder is it that in his eyes theological metaphysics was of slight account, since such argumentation does little to endorse or promote the essentially affective response in which the religious experience consists. Intellectual verification is the procedure of philosophy, but for Schleiermacher, as Barth very aptly says, 'truth in the ultimate, decisive, but also ineffable sense is reserved for mute feeling, the feeling which in the best event sings' – 'Singing piety', Schleiermacher himself averred, 'is the piety which ascends most directly and gloriously to heaven ... and only as a last resort, and then inadequately, speaks'.[78] Thus the entire realm of religious reality would seem to have its ground within the world of self-consciousness itself, the world of man's own hopes, aspirations and fears, and one which the assaults of a sceptical rationalism left unscathed. Romantic psychologism could, it would seem, go no farther.

On the other hand it would be a sad misrepresentation of Schleiermacher's position to suppose that he identified the religious consciousness only with the self-consciousness of the single individual. For him the Christian community was integral to Christianity itself, to the extent that the Christian consciousness is to be defined with reference to the Christian communal consciousness, by which in fact the individual believer is always instructed, guided and supported. Without its mediation the knowledge of salvation in Christ, the faith and love for which the gospel stands, is beyond the individual's reach.

But from the orthodox standpoint Schleiermacher's philosophy of religion inevitably gave rise to other misgivings as well. The recurrent charge of pantheism can be dismissed if it is meant literally. Schleiermacher himself consistently repudiated it. He stressed that pantheism has never been the confession of actual historical religion, and that use of the term is really no more than 'a taunt and a nickname'. Were it to be confined to the formula 'One and All' God and the world would even so be distinguishable, at least as regards function, and the so-called pantheist, inasmuch as he looks upon himself as part of the world, will feel himself to be, along with the *All*, dependent on that which, correspondingly, remains the *One*. But Schleiermacher immensely admired Spinoza, and there is no denying that Spinozistic echoes are to be heard again and again in his pages, not only in the *Reden* but in the *Glaubenslehre* also. To conceive of God as the unity correlative with the multiplicity phenomenally present as the world, or the equating of the divine omnipotence with the totality of natural causes, is a doctrine of radical immanence, a close parallel to the Spinozan *natura naturans* and *natura naturata*. It might even be contended that Schleiermacher's account of the divine attributes reproduces Spinoza's concept of substance if God is to be thought of as utterly simple in his unity and operation to the exclusion of all differentiation and determination, these being but the refraction, so to say, of the unity and simplicity within the human consciousness.[79]

One might go on to list the more detailed objections which critics, in defence of the integrity of orthodox belief, have levelled at Schleiermacher's doctrine. But overall the impression he leaves in the mind of the reader is that of a theology subtly transformed into a philosophy of idealist monism. How precisely it has been done tends to elude him, however. The traditional landmarks are all there: revelation, the Bible, the articles of the faith, the church. Yet all show up in a perspective new and somehow altered. Their objectivity has become less palpable, their meaning more equivocal. The viewpoint has shifted, that is, from a theocentrism to an anthropocentrism, so that what really has happened, one begins to suspect, is that Christian dogmatics has been covertly translated into a philosophy of the religious consciousness, for which a variety of elements have been drawn upon. The change, in important respects, undoubtedly had a liberating effect on all subsequent theological thinking. The old deistical conception of transcendence, along with the arid intellectualism of so much post-Reformation orthodox as well as rationalist theology, became a thing of the past. Immanentism brought the divine into the world-process itself, God, man and nature coming together in a cosmic harmony in which each blends with the other in the soul of the believer. Nevertheless the philosophy of identity was to find a yet more thorough-going and influential exponent in the thought of Schleiermacher's illustrious contemporary at the university of Berlin, his colleague and rival, Hegel. To him, then, we may now turn.

3

Hegel and Christianity

IF Schleiermacher, reflecting here the Romantic temper in what perhaps was most characteristic of it, discovered the essence of religion in feeling, his great contemporary and, in later years, colleague at the university of Berlin, Georg Wilhelm Friedrich Hegel (1770–1831), found it in *knowledge*, elevated to the status of total rational comprehension. In this regard the philosopher was a legitimate son of the eighteenth century, for the justification of reason as the proper expression of mind he never questioned, provided that reason be interpreted speculatively in the all-embracing manner he himself envisaged; for the *Aufklärung*, he judged, had been in error not in what it saw but in what it failed to see. Here indeed the insights of romanticism – above all its sense of the unity of finite and infinite, of objective and subjective – went far beyond the grasp of rationalism as commonly understood. For Hegel, therefore, the problem of religion remained primarily intellectual, although one the solution of which required to be stated in terms very different from anything the deists, or even Kant, had essayed. A new synthesis had to be attempted; grounded it might be in Spinoza, but, following Herder, apprehending reality in its indispensable historical dimension. To Hegel history is the realm of truth in which Spirit achieves its final and absolute manifestation, and his profound respect for the historical as unending process is what, more than anything else, obliges us to place him among the Romantics of his period. Some other features of the movement, especially its tendency to emotional excess, he like Goethe deplored. But that his own metaphysical system – or logic, as he preferred to call it – could have been devised at any other time than the early nineteenth century is scarcely conceivable.

Hegel's influence on Protestantism has been large, although not always readily acknowledged or even recognized by those subject to it. For it was not only Hegel's immediate theological disciples who fell under his spell; others, who have rejected and scoffed at his method and the grandiose structure of thought built on it, have often quite clearly established their own position in reaction to his, and to that extent in dependence upon it. Thus it can fairly be claimed that Hegelianism, when examined with the care which its intrinsic interest and historical importance alike demand, yields us some fundamental categories by which doctrines and attitudes that appear to be in conflict are all in greater or less degree governed, and it is only from its study that these latter can, I believe, be rightly correlated. The days are past when it was assumed, with an arrogance which few at the time had the temerity to challenge, that Hegel is not worth the trouble of reading.

But quite apart from any direct influence of his on the theological thinking of his century, Hegel's assessment of the overall philosophical bearing of Christianity and his interpretation of its inner meaning constitute a landmark in the history of the modern Western mind. He himself was not a theologian, nor did he pretend to be; but as a philosopher his rationalizing treatment of Christian dogma raised the entire issue of religious faith and reviewed its difficulties in a new light. After Hegel the question had to be faced whether religion as intellectual assent may not become redundant when set beside philosophy. Hegel professed to be a Lutheran and his personal sincerity in doing so there is no ground for doubting. He certainly did not repudiate orthodox Protestant doctrine – on the contrary, he rather prided himself on upholding it – but his way of expounding it is not orthodox, and those who, like Philipp Marheineke in Germany and J. H. Stirling in this country, hailed him as the church's ally in its struggle with modern unbelief had clearly not taken the full measure of his thinking or pondered the depth of its ambiguity. When a neo-Hegelian like J. M. E. McTaggart saw Hegelianism in its relation to Christian teaching as 'an enemy in disguise – the least evident but the most dangerous', and tells us that doctrines which seemingly have been protected from external refutation are found, in the crucible of Hegel's mind, 'to be transforming themselves till they are on the point of melting away', he is not, it well might seem, very far from the truth. Hegel's immediate successors among the Hegelians of the 'Left' – D. F. Strauss, Bruno Bauer, Ludwig Feuerbach, the young Karl Marx – realized this quickly enough and used the master's ideas, as they themselves construed them, to launch the most seriously damaging assault on the tradition of Christian faith which until then it had ever sustained. It was something, let us grant, which Hegel himself did not intend, nor, so far as we can surmise, did he at all foresee. His own aim was one of reconciliation, *Versöhnung*, on the widest possible scale. He sought not to destroy – the negative rationalisms of the *Aufklärung* he despised – but to construct. The Young Hegelians, however, were perceptive enough to understand that Hegel's *philosophy* of religion was much more searching, questioning and ultimately subversive of belief than any criticism at the more usual theological level could ever be. Its implications indeed were so far-reaching as to pose the entire issue of truth – itself a tribute to the range and penetration of the Hegelian logic. Hegel took Christianity – I repeat – with the utmost seriousness, judging its doctrinal content to be no mere temporary phase in the process of man's advance to self-knowledge, but to have universal significance even though it had to wait for the full maturation of the philosophical understanding for that significance to be declared in universal terms. The conclusion to be drawn from this insight is that the problem of Christianity is the problem of humanity itself, no less.

I have just said that Hegel's preoccupation with Christianity was lifelong. In 1788, at the age of eighteen, he entered the theological seminary at Tübingen – the *Stift*, as it was commonly called – with the intention presumably of becoming a Lutheran pastor. He never perhaps entertained the idea with any great seriousness, but it so happened that his university education was to a very considerable degree theological. 'For three years', observes a recent commentator, 'he must have read Lutheran theology of a distinctly conservative type.'[1] It has to be said, however, that this theological training left him dissatisfied; his teachers did not stimulate him – although G. C. Storr, who lectured on dogmatics and New Testament exegesis, was a man of some intellectual standing.[2] Nevertheless what is perhaps the earliest of Hegel's writings, unpublished till the present century, begins with the sentence: 'Religion is one of the most important concerns of our life.'[3] He never really qualified this opinion, and in his maturity considered that religion was the foundation of his whole philosophy, and that his interpretation of Christianity in particular was integral to it.

In his early theological writings, dating from the years when he was a private tutor, first at Berne and then at Frankfurt, this former seminary student showed himself all the same to be highly critical of Christianity as he knew it. He could not but contrast it unfavourably with the natural and unified social-religious consciousness of the ancient Greeks. The divided and artificial consciousness of modern civilization was, it seemed to him, in no small part the product of a religion rooted in Jewish legalism. The influence of Kant's *Religion within the Limits of Reason Alone*, which Hegel must have read soon after its publication in 1793, is obvious. At the same time he is not himself satisfied that religion is a matter solely of reason. On the contrary, it appeals powerfully to the heart and feelings, as well as giving a new and sublime impulse to morality and its motives; but not least because 'the image (*Vorstellung*) of the sublimity and the goodness of God towards us fills our hearts with wonder and the sense of humility and gratitude'.[4] But if Kant's *Vernunftsreligion* would not suffice, Hegel, in a 'Life of Jesus' written in the early summer of 1795, was still clearly committed to Kant's moral doctrines.[5] At all events Jesus is represented as expounding them in recognizably Kantian language. Exactly what Hegel's purpose was in composing it is not altogether obvious, but the explanations he provides for – one may assume – not very well-informed readers suggests that it was intended for publication and not simply as an exercise in articulating his own impressions. Probably after his then recent attempts to sketch out a *Volksreligion* on the classical Hellenic model[6] it was an effort to provide for it 'scriptures' of fittingly Christian inspiration.[7] Certainly Hegel does not approach the gospels in the spirit of a critical historian, and no attempt is made by him to explain how a religion stemming from the rational moralism of its putative founder could have developed into something so 'statutory' – in Kant's term; Hegel's is 'positive' – as is the Catholicism, or for that matter the Protestantism, of history.

But this question of 'positivity' was dealt with forcefully in 'The Positivity of the Christian Religion' which Hegel completed, more or less, by the end of November 1795.[8] Historic Christianity comes in for some drastic handling. The church is said to offer truth like a commodity in the open market, or, by a different metaphor, it 'gurgles noisily in every street and any wayfarer may take his fill of it'.[9] The ecclesiastical institution has in fact become an oppression, flouting the rights of reason and tyrannizing over the laity. All this is good, knockabout 'Enlightenment' vituperation. But Hegel states his real purpose at the outset:

> Wholly and entirely in reference to the topic itself I remark here that the general principle to be laid down as a foundation for all judgments on the varying modifications, forms, and spirit of the Christian religion is this – that the aim and essence of all true religion, our religion included, is human morality, and that all the more detailed doctrines of Christianity, all means of propagating them, and all its obligations ... have their worth and their sanctity appraised according to their close or distant connection with them.[10]

Kant himself could have asked for no more.

Christianity arose, Hegel maintains, because classical religion, a religion for a free people, had collapsed with the loss of that freedom, for reasons economic and political. 'Loyalty and liberty, the joyous participation in a common life', disappeared. Instead, men's attitude and aim became purely individualistic. Activity for the sake of a totality, for an Idea, was now a thing of the past. Of this spiritual void Christianity was able to take possession. But Christianity had its roots in Judaism, a legalistic religion of command and obedience, in which autonomous reason had no part. This condition it was, in fact, Jesus' personal intention to change in order 'to restore to morality the freedom which is its essence'. He introduced no new moral teachings, but he did seek to give a new inwardness of meaning to those already established. He did not believe that slavish observance of the Mosaic law was the source of virtue. His mission, however, was in vain as regards all but a few of his co-religionists, and in the end he was sacrificed to 'the hatred of the priesthood and the mortified national vanity of the Jews'. Even the few who did accept his teaching did so only through a misunderstanding. The Jews looked for a Messiah, and Jesus' disciples believed in him as such, imbibing the truth of what he said not for its own sake but for the personal authority with which he said it. Thus the 'positivism' of Judaism, instead of being abolished, passed over into Christianity. To create a sect was assuredly not in Jesus' mind, but his followers achieved this. Herein the effect of his teaching differed widely from that of Socrates, whose hearers as citizens of a free state listened to him only for his wisdom. But Jesus' disciples, lacking the political interest such citizens take in their native land and its welfare, confined their loyalty to the person of their master. And to this must be added their belief in his miraculous deeds. 'Nothing', observes Hegel, 'has contributed so much as these miracles to making the religion of Jesus positive, to basing the whole of it, even its teaching about virtue, on authority.'[11] The great transformation came about with the preaching of the resurrection, which turned the disciples' personal conversion into a movement, and eventually even a mass-movement that became in time part of the fabric of civil society and a force for the maintenance of public morality. Thus Christians declined to the same status as that of the Jews – 'slaves under the law'. The lesson which the young author drew from all this was that the Protestant church, at least, must teach that all religious observance should be voluntary: 'the faith of every individual Protestant must be his faith because it is his, not because it is the Church's'.[12]

What is of interest in this early account of Christianity is Hegel's *historicist* approach to the problem. He rightly remembers that Jesus was himself a Jew and that his mission must be placed in the context of the contemporary Judaism, whatever may be thought of Hegel's notion of what Judaism was. And he distinguishes the belief of Jesus himself from that of his followers. Again Hegel is right in relating the rise of Christianity to the circumstances of the age. That he could not have made use of the knowledge both of late Judaism and of primitive Christianity which nineteenth-century critical study was eventually to bring was not of course his fault. The essay's defect is that the author still tries to assess historic Christianity by the yardstick of Kantian ethical presuppositions.

By the time Hegel came to write the series of pieces which make up the essay entitled 'Der Geist des Christentums und sein Schicksal' ('The Spirit of Christianity and its Fate') his viewpoint had shifted very considerably,[13] and the atmosphere of the *Aufklärung* has changed to that, more nearly, of *die Romantiker*. Even the literary style is different. It opens indeed with a discussion of Judaism no more flattering to the religion of the Old Testament than was the previous essay. The embodiment of the Jewish spirit is Abraham. In separating himself from his kinsfolk and so breaking the bonds of communal life and love he committed an act of self-estrangement which made him the 'progenitor of a nation' itself likewise estranged from both man and nature, exhibiting always 'the spirit of self-maintenance in strict opposition to everything'. 'The whole world Abraham regarded as his opposite; if he did not take it to be a nullity, he looked on it as sustained by God, who was alien to it. Nothing in nature was supposed to have any part in God, everything was simply under God's mastery.'[14] The same characteristics are observable throughout the biblical history; the Mosaic legislation simply codifies them. The very Sabbath symbolizes the Jews' slave-mentality: a day of idleness after six days of labour. The truth writ large in the scriptures is that God is all and man nothing. Jesus however, though himself a Jew, rejects this view. His opposition to Judaism is the opposition of love in the spirit of *reconciliation*; indeed the essence of Jesus' morality, on Hegel's showing, is that of love as the transcendence of penal justice and the reconciliation of fate. Mere punishment may be withheld, but the retribution brought by life itself cannot. No man is able to evade or escape his fate; he has to learn through love to be reconciled to it. The rediscovery of life, the picking up again of its threads, is, according to Hegel, the work of love, which is nothing less than the principle and spring of all virtue.

> To complete subjection under the law of an alien Lord, Jesus opposed not a partial subjection under a law of one's own, the self-coercion of Kantian virtue, but virtues without Lordship and without submission, i.e. virtues as modifications of love.[15]

The motive of Jesus' own action was pure love, which is why his virtue is unique.

This phase in Hegel's thinking has been called, not inaptly, a 'pantheism of love'.[16] The young philosopher sees in Jesus' teaching the means or principle whereby man's estranged existence is restored to its original unity through a love which transcends Kant's — and Judaism's — antithesis of duty and inclination. Later he came to think that love is a kind of 'holy innocence' – that it cannot achieve simple reconciliation and the return to natural immediacy, since estrangement, fundamentally, is the emergence of the discriminating intellect. Instead immediacy must assume an objective form in *religion*. 'Love is a divine spirit, but it falls short of religion.' Itself a feeling, i.e. a subjective condition, 'it must be fused with the universal, with something represented in idea'.

> The need to unite subject with object, to unite feeling and feeling's demand for objects, with the intellect, to unite them in something beautiful, in a God, by means of fancy, is the supreme need of the human spirit and the urge to religion.[17]

Thus did Hegel come to see that his earlier view of Christianity was too narrow and negative, insufficiently appreciative of the significance of its historicity. A life-enhancing faith held by millions over centuries could not be dismissed as blatant error. The positivity of the Christian religion was now to be seen not as an accidental deformation but as its necessary strength. Historical Christianity was a revelation of truth, but in concrete, representational shape. It had so to be. 'The universal must pass into actuality through the particular.' To understand Christianity in 'idea' it has to be examined in its historic life; but only when the idea itself is comprehended does the rational necessity of its historical positivity become intelligible. As he was to say later in his Berlin lectures, the mind must grasp in *thought* what first has been exhibited to Spirit (*Geist*) in feeling and representation (*Vorstellung*).

2

For a full exposition of Hegel's mature view of Christianity we must have recourse to the text of these famous discourses.[18] His general theory of religion, as there presented, is that all its differing types are in their way and degree expressions of 'the nature of Spirit which has entered the world to bring itself to consciousness'.[19] Before and apart from Christianity these expressions are but partial and fragmentary. They contain elements of the truth, but none of them, not even all of them taken together, yield us that total concept (*Begriff*) of religion in which, as Hegel puts it, 'it is the Idea itself that is its own object' – exists, that is to say, 'in and for itself' (*in und für sich*), totally self-apprehending and self-understanding. Or, in theological language, if in one aspect religion is man's consciousness of God, in another it is God's own consciousness of himself in man.[20] As the mediaeval mystic Meister Eckhart says, 'The eye with which God sees me is the eye with which I see him; my eye and his eye are one.'[21] Man can know God as Spirit, however, only because Spirit has manifested itself – has appeared 'in itself', 'for itself' and 'in and for itself' in history. In truth this is precisely what is meant by speaking of God as 'Spirit'. The perfect or *absolute* religion, therefore, is that in which the divine self-consciousness is fully attained; it is absolute because it is here and here alone that Absolute Being finds its complete reflection. When we look for the absolute in history – because it is only in history that we shall find it – we see, Hegel claims, that Christianity, and no other religion but Christianity, embodies the ideal. It is the perfect religion because it is the religion 'which represents the being of Spirit in realized form', the religion which *religion itself* has become, objective in relation to itself. Christianity is thus to be understood as the expression and representation of the timeless, supra-spatial dialectic intrinsic to God's own being as it manifests itself under the conditions of time and space. As the knowledge which Spirit has of itself *as* Spirit it is in the full sense of the word *revealed* (*offenbare Religion*): God reveals himself to himself. 'Revealed religion is manifested (*geoffenbart*) religion because in it God has become wholly manifest. All here is proportionate to the Concept, i.e., what God is in himself; no longer is there anything secret in God.'[22] The terms 'revealed', 'revelation', are correct because they refer to the work of the divine Spirit and not to any mere discovery of man. God, so the reason comes to realize, exists in his self-realization, by means of differentiation and determination. Thus the religion of revelation is necessarily *positive*.

But the speculative reason does not simply acquiesce in such positivity, taking it only as and for what it is. A truth becomes in the proper sense intelligible only when it ceases to be accepted in its mere externality and is apprehended internally in its rational necessity. Christian doctrine, as given in its biblical sources, is clearly external and positive, and as such it can be readily appropriated through the imagination and feelings. It is in this way that a genuine, 'felt' conviction arises. Yet because man is a rational being he cannot rest content with a purely imaginative and emotional acceptance of religious truth; he has to lay hold of it with the full strength of the reasoning intelligence. The biblical imagery and language may suffice for the simple believer, but the quoting of biblical texts does not make the theologian. Any serious attempt to elucidate the meaning of scripture takes the student into the region of inference, of reflection and thought, and here personal presuppositions relating to the thought-forms of the age to which he himself belongs are likely to colour the resulting exegesis. It is here therefore that the clarifying and corrective function of philosophy is required. If, however, theology rejects the aid of philosophy, unaware of the extent of its own reliance on what in fact are philosophical categories, or from conscious but surreptitious use of notions that are idiosyncratic and arbitrary, it resigns itself to a positivity which is false and misleading. In Hegel's view it is in the speculative Idea alone – in philosophical thinking at its most penetrative and constructive – that the true interpretation will be found. Only so can the thoughtful believer come to 'possess' the truth, to have it and to know that it is his own. He must see for himself the 'reason' in it, and the necessity for it. Then alone does consciousness of the truth, along with consciousness of holding the truth, become the determinant of full self-consciousness. To use the word which beyond all other is the key to Hegel's dialectical thinking, the 'positivity' of biblical thinking must be *aufgehoben* – at once affirmed, denied and sublated.[23] This speculative interpretation of Christian doctrine will disclose not only the 'concrete' necessity or actual providential ordering of the whole process of *Versöhnung* or reconciliation, but the logical coherence which renders it rationally comprehensible. Whereas the one calls only for faith, the other demands the higher response of fully rational persuasion.

Hegel's detailed account of Christian dogma in speculative or philosophical terms is elaborated in the third part of the *Religionsphilosophie*, but should be supplemented and illustrated by his lectures on the philosophy of history, which likewise belong to his Berlin period.[24] The *Religionsphilosophie*, that is, continues to treat its subject in a mainly speculative and abstract way, since Hegel's immediate interest there is in the inherent *logic* of Christian doctrine, and not the historical conditions under which it took shape or the institutional forms in which it received expression. Indeed for Hegel, in this regard conspicuously unlike Kant and numerous 'liberal' theologians of the post-Hegelian era, the essence of Christianity is to be sought in its dogmatic structure, and to empty it of its theological content is to de-nature it completely. The 'absoluteness' of Christianity as 'the religion which represents the Spirit of God in a realized form' is thus, he thinks, to be apprehended under a plurality of aspects – a threefold plurality, in fact, the historic symbol of which is the dogma of the trinity. In the first place – i.e. logically – God is to be understood as he is in himself, as the absolute and eternal Idea, unrelated to the natural world of the creation or the historical world of humanity. Secondly, however, the created order itself has to be seen in relation to its 'Creator' under the forms of both physical nature and finite spirit. For in Hegel's system the universe not only objectifies or 'dirempts' God, but in a necessary sense alienates him from himself, such diremption being the necessary precondition of that final reconciliation in which the universe knows itself in God as God knows himself in the universe.

Thirdly, the actual process of reconciliation may be described in Christian theological terms as the unifying and sanctifying work of the Spirit. But we have to recognize that these three aspects or modalities of truth are not simply a schematization devised by the abstract intelligence; rather are they the determinate stages or 'moments' in the evolving reality of *Geist* itself. Analytic thought (*Verstand*) does no more than reflect and record them. The first stage may be conceived of as 'outside' time, the second as falling within time, the third as appearing within time but also as extending 'beyond' time into an eternal present. Or to use terms closer to the language of religious discourse, the *locus* of the unfolding divine reality is, first, 'heaven', then the world we know, and finally the world 'lifted up' again – *aufgehoben* – to the eternal.

Stated philosophically, on the other hand, these successive moments are those of universal, particular and individual – the universal undergoing diremption into the particular, and the particular restored once again to the universal in the individual.[25] But the philosophical interpretation has in the Christian doctrinal scheme its appropriate, and in the process of understanding no less necessary, representation or *Vorstellung* in the trinitarian dogma, in which the *Begriff*, as we have seen, is portrayed as the relationship of Father, Son and Holy Spirit – a 'childlike relation', says Hegel, a 'childlike natural form'. 'The *Verstand* has no category, no relation, which in point of suitability for expressing the truth can be compared with this.'[26]

When viewed at the level of understanding, the doctrine of the trinity would seem to be no more than a conundrum, since if the three 'moments' be thought of as *persons* how conceivably can they be one or one three? Yet on the face of it this is exactly what the dogma asserts. To interpret it speculatively, however – i.e. by way of 'reason', *Vernunft* – is to penetrate to its inner rationality, where the essential meaning of the spiritual at last becomes clear to us. For this doctrine, through its interior differentiation of God's eternal being, affords the clue to what is affirmed when it is said that God is Spirit. His nature is thereby revealed to us.[27] In the 'Son' God the 'Father' objectifies himself, but in remaining thus objectified, differentiating himself from himself, he simultaneously 'annuls' the difference, therein showing his love for himself by restoring his own self-identity, such love being the 'Spirit'. Indeed Hegel is here simply treading in the footsteps of St Augustine, who similarly interpreted the dogma as Father/Lover, Son/Beloved and Spirit/Love Itself.[28] The tritheism involved in an assertion of three separate 'personalities' – taking the word 'personality' in something resembling its modern sense – is thus avoided. The speculative concept of the Idea makes it plain that the differentiations really represent simultaneous 'moments' or modalities within the unity of God's essential being.

Clearly, then, the dogma of the trinity is for Hegel no mere appendix to the Christian doctrinal system, no speculative extra for the declaration of those who prefer the abstruse to the simple. Rather is it the fundament, the necessary ground, of the entire structure – a fact which brings him into unexpected contiguity with such an 'unphilosophical' theologian as Karl Barth.[29]

Nevertheless, although Christianity is as the 'absolute' religion the complete revelation of God's nature, it conveys this revelation in the form of a knowledge of the divine providence and plan in world history, by which *Versöhnung*, reconciliation, is fulfilled. The process must be historical, since the universal, Hegel insists, has always to pass through the particular. The positivity of Christianity, so far now from being an obstacle to rational comprehension, is the natural and determinate 'concrete' means or mediation of eternal truth. We start, therefore, with the doctrine of the fall of man, where the estrangement or alienation (*Entzweiung*) of creation appears at its most urgent, in the stark antithesis or 'otherness' of revolt against and separation from the love of God.

The reconciliation of human and divine is not, however, a mere contingent possibility. It is an end that has to be achieved and can be achieved, the achievement being possible because it also is necessary. In other words, the principle of *Versöhnung* is not an abstraction, an option to be entertained by the reflective intelligence; it is realized and manifested concretely in time and place as the determinate movement and goal of history. *Geist* is actualized in the historical, in the life of man, Absolute Spirit existing only in so far as it progressively attains self-reflection in human consciousness. The implicit (*an sich*) becomes explicit (*für sich*) when human history is accomplished.[30] To put it crudely, man does not make up his mind to become one with God; it is not a decision open to him, a choice that lies before him. Indeed he does not even recognize the possibility of it, at least not until after the course of his history has revealed to him its inherent movement and direction.

The facts of human history and experience – all too much a tale of sin, suffering and misery – assuredly do not themselves suggest man's unity with God. The utter estrangement of man from the principle of his existence is sadly obvious. The Christian *mythus* attributes this condition to a 'fall', which Hegel describes thus:

> Man, created in the image of God, lost, it is said, his state of absolute contentment, by eating of the Tree of the Knowledge of Good and Evil. Sin consists here only in Knowledge: this is the sinful element, and by it man is stated to have trifled away his natural happiness. This is a deep truth, that

evil lies in consciousness; for the brutes are neither evil nor good; the merely Natural Man quite as little. Consciousness occasions the separation of the Ego, in its boundless freedom as arbitrary choice, from the pure essence of the Will – i.e. from the Good. Knowledge as the disannulling of the unity of mere Nature, is the 'Fall', which is no casual conception, but the eternal history of Spirit. For the state of innocence, the paradisaical condition, is that of the brute. Paradise is a park, where only brutes, not men, can remain. For the brute is one with God only implicitly (not consciously). Only man's spirit has a self-cognizant existence. This existence for self, this consciousness, is at the same time separation from the universal and divine Spirit. If I hold to my abstract freedom, in contraposition to the Good, I adopt the standpoint of Evil. The Fall is therefore the Mythus of Man – in fact the very transition by which he becomes man. Persistence in this standpoint is, however, Evil, and the feeling of pain at such a condition and of longing to transcend it we find in David, when he says: 'Lord, create for me a pure heart, a new steadfast spirit.' This feeling we observe even in the account of the Fall; though an announcement of reconciliation is not made there, but rather one of continuance in misery. Yet we have in this narrative the prediction of reconciliation ... profoundly expressed where it is stated that when God saw that Adam had eaten of that tree he said: 'Behold Adam is become as one of us, knowing Good and Evil.' God confirms the word of the serpent.[31]

I have cited this passage at length because it expounds a theme in which Hegel detected the deepest significance. The biblical myth of the fall is the 'Mythus of Man' in that it symbolizes a truth vital to man's self-understanding, indicating as it does the process by which he becomes man in assuming full human responsibility. His childlike innocence has to be transcended and lost if he is to enter upon the life of Spirit. Mere innocence is a negative state; it implies 'the absence of will, the absence of evil, and consequently the absence of goodness'.[32] But through the fall man *knows* good and evil, he does not simply know about it; he has perforce, in order to fulfil his destiny, to *live* it. Thus it cannot but be that knowledge is *per se* evil, or at any rate the source of evil, having as its inevitable consequence separation and estrangement. 'For knowledge or consciousness is just the act by which separation, the negative element, judgment, division in the more definite and specific form of independent existence, or Being-for-itself in general, comes into existence.' Yet it is this same knowledge which also reveals to him the fact of his sinfulness, his 'Unhappy Consciousness', as Hegel calls it. He is sadly aware of his alienation, the difference between what he actually is and what he is in his essential nature, i.e. what he *ought* to be. Nevertheless this state is 'the condition of contrast to which man, because he is Spirit, must advance'. The evil is therefore necessary; it cannot be bypassed, being an integral element in humanity's spiritual development. But, says Hegel, here also is the point which is the ultimate source of reconciliation. The positive is latent in the negative, for if the fall supplies the principle of man's divisiveness it also involves 'the promise and certainty of attaining the state in which man is once more the image of God'.[33]

This de-mythologized account of the fall cannot be said to be that of orthodoxy. Yet orthodox or not it has had a substantial influence on Protestant thought about the matter ever since Hegel's day. For, as soon as a more or less literal reading of the myth has been abandoned, the sin of Adam is bound to be construed as in some manner an elevation, or at any rate a broadening and enrichment, of his nature, a condition of things which, however deplorable in certain aspects – and man's sinfulness is the greatest cause of his suffering – was not the less necessary if he were to become fully himself and so fitted for a higher destiny than that of 'dreaming innocence'. Liberal theology's debt here to Hegel is however not often acknowledged.[34]

An obvious reason for Hegel's great interest in the fall-myth is that it provides a copy-book example of how a religious idea can be translated into a speculative one. Adam is simply historical man, his 'sin' being, with whatever further consequences, an advance in his knowledge and understanding. On this view the 'fatal' act was not an accidental yielding to a temptation from without. Man had to grow, develop, live out his destiny.

Thus Hegel endorses the principle of the doctrine of original sin by explaining it not indeed as a kind of genetic defect but as an inevitable and thus 'natural' condition, by showing that man's sinfulness is something which he is unable to escape, since he cannot be human without sin. But does this not mean that the evil in man – Kant's *radicale Böse* – is either God-created or else represents a residual element in things which God cannot overcome – that reality, in fact, is dualistic? Hegel does not concede either alternative: not the latter, certainly, because God and man are essentially one, as the paradise-myth indicates; nor yet the former, since the 'sinfulness' – as we rightly judge it to be – is a concomitant of his finitude, being dependent on it; for when the meaning of finitude is thought through we see that it necessarily entails the partiality of view, the onesidedness, the self-concern, the persistent self-interestedness from which sin issues. In the fall man's uncomprehending state of harmony with his environment is replaced by the 'knowledge of good and evil', an awareness of his limitation, individuality and self-wilfulness.

But the meaning of his destiny – his strangely paradoxical fate, he may think – is revealed to him 'in the fulness of time'. What to the Hegel of mature years gives the Jewish people their world-historical importance is their profound sense of man's estrangement from God and the sorrow which this brings with it. 'For from this state of mind arose that higher phase of which Spirit becomes the absolute self-consciousness – passing from that alien form of being which is discord and pain, and mirroring itself in its own essence.' In the Genesis story God's words, 'Adam is become as one of us, knowing good and evil', by confirming those of the serpent, convey the truth, explicitly no less than implicitly that 'man through Spirit – through cognition of the Universal and the Particular – comprehends God himself',[35] even though the actual joy of reconciliation is still distant from humanity. But it was approaching.

> The recognition of the identity of the Subject and God was introduced into the world *when the fulness of time was come*: the consciousness of this identity is the recognition of God in his true essence. The material of Truth is Spirit itself.[36]

And the nature of God as pure Spirit is manifested in the Christian religion.

What does Hegel mean by these oracular phrases? He quotes from St Paul's Epistle to the Galatians (4:4): 'When the time was fulfilled, God sent his Son'; adding: 'When the need for spirit came into existence, Spirit manifested the reconciliation'. Stated otherwise, when the consciousness of humanity was ready for the revelation of reconciliation to occur God acted, i.e. when the historical circumstances were ripe. And what these inherently pointed to was the *incarnation*.

For it is in the incarnation, in the appearance of the god-man, that the truth of the principle of *Versöhnung* is not only manifested but historically realized. The divine–human unity, that is to say, although implicitly true, has to be consciously affirmed, has to be recognized as true, and so enter into human knowledge. It is man's *destiny* to become aware of the identity of his own nature with God's; a destiny, however, to the achieving of which his condition of sinful finitude stands seemingly in invincible opposition. For can he, contemplating himself as he is, admit not merely the possibility of such identity but its reality? So the scales must drop from his eyes; he must be able to behold the truth in concrete demonstration. And this he can do in Christ, whose advent, as Hegel magniloquently phrases it, was 'the axis on which world history turns'. For in Christ the implicit truth becomes explicit. *Versöhnung* is at once proclaimed and actuated in a historical fact. Moreover, this concretization of truth was not 'privileged' in the sense of available only to the relatively few who were favoured by time and circumstance. It must be universal, at least potentially – of a nature such that all men may grasp its signification. There is no other way, Hegel stresses, for the essential unity of God and man to become known to mankind except by manifesting itself in a completely temporal, utterly common appearance in the world, in a particular man, in the person of one who comes not simply as a teacher nor even as a being of a generally higher plane than common humanity, but 'as the highest, as God's Son', the divine Idea itself.[37] 'Christ has appeared – a Man who is God – God who is Man; and thereby peace and reconciliation have accrued to the world.'[38] Thus the absolute singularity of Christ is in the fact that he not only proclaims the things of God with unique authority, but that he *is* God. He is divine as the very embodiment of divine truth. Or as Hegel states it, more abstractly, in his *Geschichte der Philosophie*:

> In the world what has come to pass is that the Absolute has been revealed as the concrete, and further, not only in thought in a general way as intelligible world, but because it has itself proceeded to its ultimate point of intensity. Thus it is an actual self, an 'I', the absolute universal, the concrete universal – that is, God; and also the absolute opposite of this determination, the clearly finite determined in unity with the eternal as self.[39]

Christ is the 'immediate certainty and presence of the divine' on earth and among men, not indeed as the very Idea itself, Hegel is careful to point out, but as 'the form under which truth appears'.[40] 'The appearance of the Christian God involves, further, its being *unique* in its kind; it can occur only once, for God is realized as Subject, and as manifested Subjectivity is exclusively one individual.'[41]

Hegel, in claiming that Jesus Christ is the perfect and therefore unique embodiment of the divine Idea, is asserting the difference between him and all other men who have received the ascription of divinity. They may be regarded as precursors, shaping men's thoughts for readiness to accept the fact of the full incarnation of the divine Idea. The concrete reality of Christ is to be seen as in all respects adequate to the Idea.[42] But not, be it said, merely on the strength of historical–critical investigation. For while Hegel is emphatic that the truth of the divine–human unity is given not simply as a philosophical principle, but in history, under the specific conditions of time and place, the incarnation is itself a *symbol*. What historical investigation can or cannot do in presenting that symbol purely as a historical event does not touch its intrinsic significance. 'Make of Christ what you will, exegetically, critically, historically – demonstrate as you please how the doctrines of the Church were established by Councils, attained currency as the result of this or that episcopal interest or passion – let all such circumstances have been what they might – the only concerning question is: What is the Idea or the Truth in and for itself?'[43]

The advent of Christ is an event in the life of both God and man on account of which history itself has been changed. The abstract and universal has passed into the realities of time, the Kingdom of God is focused and manifested in Christ – for the concept is one thing, its realization quite another.[44] That is why the teaching of Jesus is not sufficient in itself to establish his divinity; it is his *life* as a whole which does so. For there we see God revealed, God existing in history, indeed entering into the state of alienation of all existing persons and things. But this does not mean, as it cannot mean, that Christ is a supernatural prodigy.[45] Himself in and of history, Christ is truly man, living a natural and ordinary life. Yet again, not merely the life of a particular individual, although a particular individual Jesus undoubtedly was. What, rather, Hegel sees in him is the divine Idea translating itself into the history of mankind as such, which thereby enters into the existence of Spirit.[46]

But, as every Christian believes, the life of Christ is significant beyond all others because of his passion and death on the cross. The meaning of the crucifixion is for Hegel the truth that the Spirit when united with the finite must itself assume all the conditions of finitude, involving an estrangement that has its ultimate or highest point in death, since only in death is the full truth about finitude disclosed. Did God not so humble himself to the extent of enduring everything that genuine finitude cannot escape, his historical and human manifestation would be incomplete and reconciliation unattained.

> Christ's death primarily means that Christ was the God-man, the God who had at the same time assumed human nature, even unto death. It is the lot of finite humanity to die; death is the most complete proof of humanity, of absolute finitude, and Christ in fact died the aggravated death of a malefactor ... In him humanity was carried to its furthest point.[47]

The death of Christ, like that of any other man, marks the yielding up of 'all that is peculiar to the individual, all those interests and personal ends with which the natural will can occupy itself, all that is great and counted as of value'.[48] It thus is the completion of the pattern of all finitude: Spirit, that is, passes over into its opposite, becomes wholly externalized and limited. Yet, were it not so, Spirit could not achieve self-fulfilment, since if the life of Spirit demands self-estrangement the latter must be total before reconciliation can commence and atonement be gained, for only when Spirit is completely actualized in the finite, taking on all its characteristics, all its limitations, does the finite become one with Spirit. And this means – paradox of paradoxes – that Spirit must itself 'die'. Or more vividly, and in the words Hegel himself uses, '*God* has died, *God* is dead – this is the most frightful of all thoughts, that all that is eternal, all that is true, is not, that negation itself is found in God.'[49] So 'the temporal, perfect existence [*Dasein*] of the divine Idea ... becomes manifest only in Christ's death', the 'highest abnegation' (*Entäusserung*) of the divine Idea – the 'deepest abyss' of estrangement,[50] on which Hegel expatiates with such remarkable feeling and eloquence, and in a manner that inevitably recalls the great Protestant tradition of the *theologia crucis* in which he himself as a Lutheran stood, however widely different the intellectual outlook of the romanticist speculative thinker from that of the biblicist Reformers.[51] I would call attention here too to the way in which Hegel dwells on the dishonourable form of Christ's death – 'the death of a malefactor, the most degrading of all deaths, death upon the cross, it involves not only what is natural, but also civil degradation, worldly dishonour'. Except that in that death the cross is transfigured and 'what according to the common idea is lowest, what the state characterizes as degrading, is transformed into that which is the highest'.[52]

But if in the death of Christ we have the unique symbol of the destruction of finitude, that same symbol bespeaks the emergence of Absolute Spirit. When Hegel tells us that 'God dies' what he means is that the individualized personal God of the traditional theism has ceased to be. As he expresses it in the *Phänomenologie des Geistes*: 'Death then ceases to signify what it means directly – the non-existence of this particular individual [i.e. God] – and becomes transformed and transfigured into the universality of Spirit, which lives in its own communion, dies there daily, and daily rises again.'[53]

The resurrection following the cross is the sign that God's death is not final; it is only 'the death of death': the crucifixion is but one aspect of a twofold event. 'God comes to life again, and thus things are reversed.'[54] The complete negation of Christ's negativity is in fact what constitutes his resurrection and ascension into heaven. They are the pictorial representation (*Vorstellung*) of the truth that Spirit's particular embodiment is sacrificed, yielded up, and the negative itself negated, thus making way for the coming Absolute Spirit, holy and universal. But the finitude of God in the man Jesus was no more than a transitional phase, although an essential one. In other words, the real meaning of Christ is to be found in his universality, not in his particularity. In this whole story, Hegel explains, mankind has reached consciousness of a profound truth: namely, that 'the Idea has come to be a certainty for them', a reality immediate and present; indeed the actual representation of the process of the evolution of man as Spirit. With the death of God 'what has potential or essential Being returns to itself and by this act first becomes Spirit'.[55] Only by Christ's self-abnegation and self-nullification was the necessary step taken whereby his particularity, his human individuality, was transcended in order to attain fulfilment in the universal Spirit. Herein lies the vital meaning of Christ's glorification which Hegel discloses in a sentence:

> It is with the consciousness of the Spiritual Community, which thus makes the transition from man pure and simple to a God-man, and to a perception, a consciousness, a certainty of the unity and union of the divine and human natures, that the Church or Spiritual Community begins, and it is this consciousness which constitutes the truth upon which the Spiritual Community is founded.[56]

Although Hegel is clearly quite happy to use the traditional language of Christian theology, he dwells but little on the actual mission of Jesus as recounted in the gospels. What he is concerned with is rather the faith of the church, for which the death–resurrection event was all-important. Only after his death was Christ exalted to heaven to sit at God's right hand, for in this way alone did he become Spirit.

> Not till the feast of Pentecost were the Apostles filled with the Holy Ghost. To the Apostles, Christ as living was not that which he was to them subsequently as the Spirit of the Church, in which he became to them for the first time an object for their truly spiritual consciousness.[57]

The followers of Christ who unite on this principle, seeking to make their own the spiritual life he inaugurated for them, are those precisely who constitute the church, which is nothing other than the Kingdom of God. In it the universal reconciliation of divine and human implicit from the beginning is recognized, understood and accepted. The exalted Christ thus becomes the Spirit which animates the Christian community. Here again Hegel's own words may be quoted in full, for their perspicuity is such that they need no further explanation or commentary:

> It has already been remarked that only after the death of Christ could the Spirit come upon his friends; that only then were they able to conceive the true idea of God, viz., that in Christ man is redeemed and reconciled: for in him the idea of eternal truth is recognized, the essence of man acknowledged to be Spirit, and the fact proclaimed that only by stripping himself of his finiteness and surrendering himself to pure self-consciousness, does he attain the truth. Christ – man as man – in whom the unity of God and man has appeared, has in his death, and his history generally, himself presented the eternal history of Spirit, – a history which every man has to accomplish in himself, in order to exist as Spirit, or to become a child of God, and a citizen of his kingdom.[58]

Faith, that is to say, is not simply the recollection of Jesus' own words, still less a mere piecing together of biblical texts, but an inward conviction generated by the spiritual society itself.[59] The Christian religion is life truly in the Spirit, reconciliation as *lived*. For by a seeming paradox Spirit can make the occurrence of evil *not* to have occurred. 'In the death of Christ man's finitude has been destroyed for the sake of the true consciousness of Spirit ... the finite, indeed evil in general, is annihilated.' It is not a matter simply of a knowledge of what once happened in history; the subject himself is drawn into the process. 'He feels the pain of evil and his own alienation, which Christ in assuming humanity has taken on himself. But through Christ's death this is abolished.'[60] The victory of Christ over finitude and evil is thus universalized in the thought and experience of the Christian church, by whose members it is individually appropriated.

But it is necessary again to stress that Hegel does not see this, after the fashion of much liberal theology later in the century, as little more than a continuing moral influence. *Versöhnung* is in Christ an accomplished fact, to be realized by all men who acknowledge that in him God has appeared and acted on earth. The church's existence is in its 'continual becoming' – its continuously developing, Spirit-guided historic life and its power to be freely productive of those 'finite flashes of light' by which the individual consciousness is recreated and brought to an ever-deepening comprehension of itself. In this way, the Christian self-consciousness becomes divine consciousness, under forms of progressing adequacy. 'Out of the ferment of finitude ... Spirit rises like a vapour.'[61]

The church, then, is the community (*Gemeinde*) of those awake to their life in the Spirit through the relation of Christ. The 'sensuous history' of the gospel was the necessary point of departure for Spirit, namely perception and realization of the divine–human unity; for what appeared, so to say, paradigmatically in Christ has to be actualized in the life of each and every man. This community, in which the Absolute Religion has its historic embodiment, is to be recognized therefore as the goal of the entire historical process. Spirit, *Geist*, is not an abstraction, not something 'wholly other' and transcendent, but rather the ongoing movement of history itself. 'It is movement, life; its nature is to differentiate itself, to give itself a definite character, to determine itself.'[62] The church, being imbued with the Spirit which Christ revealed, is itself Christ's promised Kingdom, having its existence *here and now*, and not only in the future. Its authority rests on the fact that it establishes its members in a corporate life based on the common possession of a recognized truth. The life of the individual is drawn into and made to share a tradition, both doctrinal and ethical, which completely transcends his own individuality, and within which idiosyncrasy and personal wilfulness are controlled. But the church's exercise of authority must not become a cause of petrification: the Spiritual Community cannot, as spiritual, remain static; there must always be change in continuity as well as continuity in change. The Protestant principle, *ecclesia semper reformanda est*, is one of progressive purification, in contrast with the Catholic principle of *semper eadem*, representing the instinct to preserve and consolidate whatever past human experience has discovered to be of permanent value. The two principles are correlative and coordinate. If either is dropped the result is sectarianism, inimical to the spirit of universality.

The significance of the historic Christian community for Hegel will go far to account for the importance he attaches to the Christian doctrinal tradition. Dogma is the formalized articulation of the church's faith and experience, and without it the church could not subsist or even achieve self-identity. The doctrinal tradition must therefore be maintained in all essentials, confessed and taught as objectively valid truth, resting on the principle of reconciliation. It is this latter, presented in a 'pictorial way', which discloses in 'an absolutely completed form what ought to be accomplished in the individual as such'.[63] And in order to raise it above the mere flux of personal opinion it has to be enshrined in verbally fixed formularies. For thus the potentiality of the human spirit is 'brought into consciousness as something objective' and 'developed in such a manner as to know what to be the truth wherein it exists'.[64] But the purpose of the outward is to stimulate and develop the inward. So the truth becomes identical with the self, with the will of the individual, becoming his will, his spirit.[65]

The church's experience of Christ as the realization of Spirit has its most vivid expression in its worship, and especially its sacramental rites. Thus baptism shows the child as having been born into a sphere essentially different from the sin and misery of a hostile world – now 'the Church is his world'. The child through natural birth is Spirit implicitly, but only implicitly, being not yet *realized* Spirit. It is only with his sacramental entry into the church that the truth comes to explicit recognition. 'Otherness', alienation, is then overcome.[66] So too in the eucharist; for here man enjoys in a sensible, immediate way the consciousness of his reconciliation with God and of the Spirit directly within him. Hence the Lord's Supper is central not only to the corporate Christian life but to theology as well, since from it, Hegel judges, 'all the differences in Christian doctrine get their colour and peculiar character'.[67] On the real presence he adopts a remarkably positive and traditionalist position. While rejecting the Roman doctrine of the mass for its 'externalism' in teaching the presence of Christ to be in the consecrated host alone, he criticizes the Reformed theology for regarding the rite as a bare commemoration – 'an unspiritual and merely lively remembrance of the past'. There is no divine presence, no really spiritual existence, according to this view; the truth 'has been lowered to the prose of the enlightenment'.[68] Hegel himself believes the right doctrine to be the Lutheran, one nearer to the Catholic than the Calvinist in holding that Christ is an actual presence 'in faith and in Spirit'.[69]

It is clear from all that Hegel says about historic Christianity that in so far as the Christian religion is 'absolute' it is in consequence of the purificatory process which it underwent in the sixteenth century. The Reformation, he tells us, resulted from the mediaeval corruption of the church, which, however, was no accidental phenomenon in the simple shape of an abuse of power and dominion. The corruption rather was native to its growth, in which the combination of spiritual with temporal authority created an ecclesiastical (geistlich) realm within the spiritual (geistig) Kingdom of God. This historic development was in the circumstances unavoidable, and probably even salutary. True freedom of the spirit has not yet been attained. Or, as Hegel himself phrases it, 'Speculative conviction does not yet rest on a basis of its own, but is content to inhere in the spirit of an extrinsic authority.'[70] Thus the priesthood becomes a caste, and the hierarchy – whose powers reached their summit in the middle ages – an ecclesiastical aristocracy, leaving the laity 'alien to the divine'. The latter had simply to believe, their duty being that of obedience, the obedience of 'faith' without on their part insight or inner certitude. But with the Reformation this spiritual servitude was broken. The mediaeval system had not indeed been without value as an educational discipline, but with its decline men were ready to enter upon the inheritance of freedom which is theirs by right. Truth could become all men's possession, should they so desire, and the work of reconciliation be accomplished in every man's soul. 'Subjective Spirit had to receive the Spirit of Truth into itself, and give it a dwelling-place there.'[71] That absolute inwardness of soul which pertains to religion, and the freedom of the church as an institution, were thus both secured. The secular life, life in the world, was moreover no longer held to be an alien sphere inimical to the soul's health, but one in which, on the contrary, man could at last realize his potentialities as a free being. This accounts for the Reformers' emphasis on faith, not as certainty respecting mere finite things but as an inward assurance of the reality of the eternal being and truth of God.

Yet the freedom inherent in the Reformation ideals of the Germanic peoples was not achieved at once. Protestantism itself tended to slip back into the externalism of the old Catholic system. This retrogression was to some extent halted by the Pietist movement, with its attention to what is felt inwardly and its dislike of neo-scholastic intellectualism, but both came under fire from the rationalism of the

Aufklärung, a new and revolutionary era in European thought and culture brought about by the growth of science and the development of the critical spirit. That movement Hegel sees as French in origin, but it had passed over into Germany to create there a new world of ideas. The absolute criterion now replacing all authority based on religious belief and positive laws was the verdict pronounced by mind itself on what was to be believed or obeyed.[72] Its effect, on the negative side, was of unquestionable value; but on the positive its limitations soon became obvious. A narrow and constricting 'reason' fails to satisfy the living spirit and readily leads to agnosticism and pessimism; and in religion at all events sceptical rationalism and its orthodox counterpart, dogmatism, had overmuch in common. Both misconceived the true nature of the Christian religion by supposing it to stand or fall by the reality or otherwise of a 'supernatural' order attested by miracle. Neither of them understood 'faith' for what it really is and so wasted its efforts on futile inquiries and controversies.

3

It is clear that in Hegel's mature thinking his general view and philosophical assessment of Christianity had changed radically from the opinions set out in his earliest writings, his interest in it and the ultimate importance he attached to it having, as the years passed, waxed rather than waned. For he came to see the Christian religion not merely as a stage or phase, intermediate and temporary, in the spiritual evolution of mankind, but rather as its climactic point, as an absolute in anticipation of which all other manifestations of Spirit are but relative and transitional. As such it is possessed of a finality which the speculative form of thought, the vocation of philosophy both at its most comprehensive and most penetrating, can now interpret, explicate and, in fully self-conscious rationality, justify. The question therefore that enters the mind of the reader who has sought, with whatever difficulties by the way, to follow Hegel on his long intellectual trek, is whether the content of truth at its highest level was not in fact already given to the philosopher by the Protestant faith in which he was nurtured, which he at no time renounced, and which, in the lectures delivered at Berlin at the apex of his fame, he extolled and expounded as a revelation of the Absolute; in short, whether his whole vast philosophical scheme did not turn upon a problem – that of *Versöhnung*, the resolution of all antitheses – which both first and finally presented itself to him in religious terms, so that one can say of Hegel's philosophical logic that its inspiration can be seen to be, at its heart, Christian. Yet with it the question also arises whether in this logical universalizing of the meaning of a single historical phenomenon Hegel does not translate the Christian gospel into a rarified metaphysic, the methods of which were bound to result in the disappearance of its concrete positivity and historic 'once-for-allness' in a fog of abstract notions. For thus it is that orthodox theologians have usually seen the matter.

This of course is the issue of Hegel's alleged *Aufhebung* or 'sublation' of the Christian religion into a philosophy, or at any rate the eventual transcendence of religion by philosophy. It is an issue, let it be said, far from easy to resolve satisfactorily. To begin with, Hegel unlike Schleiermacher does not locate the essence of religion in *feeling*, which he saw as belonging only to the animal side of man's nature and to be confined to the individual, and subjective.[73] A religion purely of feeling could not properly be communicated to men, as it could hardly acquire any institutional embodiment. Yet Hegel was not in the least an intellectualist of the old-fashioned sort who imagined that the essence of Christianity could be encapsulated in a series of abstract propositions. He is firm in holding that religion must be 'in our hearts'. But at the same time there is no brooking the fact that religion is concerned with truth and that in the means it employs to convey truth the intellect is continuously active. For what religion purports to offer is, in Hegel's uncompromising words, *God as he is in himself and man in relation to him*. Yet inasmuch as it has its own modes of expression – imaginative, that is, rather than formal – its utterance is less exact than that of the higher reason of philosophy. In some respects it is closer to art. For art, too, as Hegel understands it, is a form under which the Absolute is cognized, though only in the shape of *objects of sense*. It must needs be that a higher level of cognizance is one at which Spirit is apprehended *as* Spirit, spiritual things being in the end spiritually judged. Religion deals directly with the things of the Spirit, but it at once becomes apparent from a study of its phenomenology that its characteristic mode of cognition is the *Vorstellung*, in which truth is expressed, not conceptually, but through representative symbols. The word *Vorstellung* is used indeed by Hegel sometimes with a narrower connotation, sometimes with a wider; in the former case, as we have seen, it is equivalent to 'pictorial thinking', while in the latter it becomes virtually synonymous with the entire process of our ordinary rational mental activity – sense-experience, memory, imagination, understanding. But in either usage the *Vorstellung*, we should note, is not simply an *individual* mental impression or picture (*Bild*), but one which through the understanding has received the form of the universal.[74] Its transition from sense to imagination and from imagination to thought is a continuous process. In the special sciences this process advances from sensuously-given phenomena to the abstract general 'laws' which are framed to explain them, although the sensuous element is never completely disposed of by the intellectual explanation. In religious experience it has a somewhat different function, for here the starting-point is not mere sense-data, to be taken up through imagery into the abstract understanding, but rather sensuous feeling in which, as with Schleiermacher, the divine is already implicit, even if at a level at which the God–Self distinction has not yet emerged. It is within this matrix that the pictorial image, the myth, comes to birth.

And it is the Christian myth in all its complex theological structure, as enshrining the primal truth in regard to God, the world and mankind, which in Hegel's mind requires to be explicated and re-presented at the speculative level appropriate to philosophy. For it is the proper task of philosophical thinking to transport us beyond the mental world in which images, myths, *Vorstellungen* will suffice. As such their purpose has been a necessary but still a limited one, and imagery, figures and metaphors must for the ends of pure thought be replaced by concepts, *Begriffe*.[75]

It has to be appreciated, however, that it was by no means Hegel's intention, from what we know of him personally, to suggest that religion should be or can be superseded by philosophy. In the first instance there is that vast majority of persons for whom the philosophical account of reality will always be elusive; they lack both the training and the aptitude. Many in any case will prefer the 'pictures' of religious thinking as not only more emotive and stimulating but as actually more instructive; for them the language of metaphysics says little. But in Hegel's mind there was no question but that the task of philosophy is explicative – finally and sufficiently – and that its scope admits no bounds; all things are compassed by it, religion last and most fittingly of all. But explication, especially at the highest level of speculative thought, is not nullification. On the contrary, Hegel urges, the actual content of philosophy, its interest and its aim, are wholly consonant with religion. His own statements are emphatic and clear:

> The object of religion as well as of philosophy is eternal truth in its objectivity, God and nothing but God, and the explication of God … Philosophy explicates itself when it explicates religion, and in explicating itself it explicates religion … Thus religion and philosophy come to be one. Philosophy is itself in fact worship (*Gottesdienst*); it is religion inasmuch as it renounces subjective notions and opinions in order to occupy itself with God.[76]

Hegel of course is no less concerned to show wherein philosophy and religion also differ, and how each fulfils its function in its own particular way. Philosophy is certainly not religion *per se*, but neither is its content or its method such as to transport us into some further realm of knowledge beyond religion in a manner that comes to us as a revelation of new truth. In this sense, I think, we must accept Hegel's assurances that philosophy is not the *Aufhebung* of religion but rather its *Beglaubigung*, the demonstration of its essential truth by methods which philosophy alone is in a position to use. In this respect it is doing what religion as such is unable to do; it is intellectually ahead of it, so to speak, and thus can look back upon it with total understanding as upon any other realm of being and thought. Thus if ultimately the status of philosophy is the more honourable — at any rate by the criterion of pure intellection — Hegel as a philosopher cannot but accord the fact his nod of satisfaction. The only form of thought that is finally adequate is, he again would remind us, that of the all-penetrating, all-comprehending speculative reason. Religion cannot itself draw a rational map of its place within the universe of being and thought, cannot of itself attain to the Idea. Nor can it understand, of itself, its relation to any part of that universe; whereas it is at once the privilege and responsibility of philosophy that it and it alone can disclose the true nature of Spirit, can declare the Idea.

The advantage, therefore, which philosophy has over religion is not that it opens up any fresh realm of knowledge but that it can grasp the truth concerning God and man's relation to God in a way that may be said to take us above religion, or at least above all the historic forms of it — even that 'absolute' form which is Christianity and with which, in its traditional or popular shape, most believers will ever remain content. As a consequence a believer who also is a metaphysician, one who understands the intrinsic logic of faith, is in a superior position to one who is not and cannot qualify intellectually to become so. The superiority, that is, lies in his understanding; as a believer he cherishes the symbols of faith, but as a speculative thinker he will be able to resolve the contradictions and ambiguities from which these symbols, because of their inevitable limitations as images of the finite, are never free. This privileged standing of philosophy Hegel himself indicated in a few magisterial sentences at the close of his *Religionsphilosophie*. Philosophy, he there says, forms a sanctuary apart, and those who serve in it constitute an isolated order of priests, who must not mix with the world and whose work is to protect the possessions of truth.[77] Religion, one has to conclude, should rejoice to have its authenticity certified by so august and exclusive a fraternity. But we may be sure that Hegel did not utter these words in any ironical spirit. His attitude towards Christianity was entirely positive and benevolent. In the past its doctrines, as he recognizes, had been the object of bitter and damaging attack, but this was because it had been misunderstood; its symbolism, taken in a narrow and literalist sense, could not withstand critical analysis. But the *Aufklärung* was in this regard itself naive. It knew only of 'negations, limit, determinations', whereas the *Begriff*, to which speculative thought is able to raise the whole content of faith, represents that 'higher element which also embraces within it different forms and allows their right to exist'.[78]

But for this metaphysical aid and enhancement theology has a price to pay. And the extent of the cost has been repeatedly pointed out by theologians who have not, unlike certain of Hegel's contemporaries and immediate successors, succumbed to the obvious attractions of his doctrine. Central to their objections is Hegel's account of the incarnation. As we have seen, he appears to attach great weight to this historical manifestation of the truth of the divine-human unity. Yet his actual references to the historical Christ are curiously a-historical. Not the individual as he lived, subject to all the restricting circumstances of time and place – the 'Jesus of History' whom the liberals of a later generation were so earnestly to seek: it is a striking fact that Hegel rarely if ever refers to Jesus by name – but rather the symbolic Christ of the church's theological dogma, moving indeed in a broad historical setting but not in any precisely factual manner a part of it. Why this particular figure should have been selected as the singular embodiment of the eternal God–man relation is never quite apparent. One is to understand presumably that Spirit 'finds' itself historically in the Christ-event, becoming manifest to itself and to mankind in the faith which it creates. The principle of *Versöhnung*, however, is not, as in orthodox teaching, itself dependent on the redeeming act of him who reveals it. There can for Hegel be no question of God – in Johannine language – 'sending' his Son into the world; the whole process of the life of Spirit is immanent *in* history. The Christ-figure, therefore, does not bestride history but falls wholly within it, and his significance accordingly would appear to be simply illustrative of what in principle the historic evolution of mankind can *at any point* be perceived to mean, if we have but the 'speculative' eyes to see it.

The same may be said of Christ's death and exaltation. They are vividly imaginative symbols of ideas whose import is likely always to be present to the mind of the philosopher. They express the inescapable finitude of life when looked on only in its finitude; but when finitude itself is viewed *sub specie infinitatis* they assume an altogether different aspect, pointing to the truth that the destiny of man is fulfilled only in conscious unity with the being of God, of the Absolute. Indeed it is *in* man, thus one with the infinite, that God comes to know himself as God. Christ's death and resurrection are not, therefore, in themselves the crucial events which the traditional faith has ever taken them to be, but glimpses, fleeting disclosures of a truth which no event, no single element within the continuum of history, can of itself be sufficient to establish. For the paradox is that Hegel, supreme historicist as he may seem to be, in the end attaches little importance to the concrete realities of history. The process, as such, is all. The sheer facticity of things does not, I concede, escape Hegel – and the range of his own historical knowledge was astonishing – but he does not contemplate the historical after the manner of a scientific historian intent on the accumulation and assessment of specific data within a selected area. Rather is it that he looks *through* history more than at it. Hence no historical event or period commands his attention for more than a short while and he once more passes on, always in quest of the eternal Idea. The divine is manifested in history, but the ever-changing historical vesture has no ultimate and lasting import. To a religion like Christianity, which has made it its distinctive claim that God has acted decisively in certain *unique* happenings, an interpretation such as Hegel propounds would appear to be fatal.

However, yet another paradox awaits us as we tread this strange Hegelian path. And it arises from what many see to be a final and irresolvable ambiguity in Hegel's thought. It has indeed been said of the great philosopher that ambiguity was of his essence – 'sein Wesen war Zweideutigkeit' – and the question of whether his absolute idealism left any room for theism continues to be debated. Does the statement that 'without the world God is not God' (*ohne Welt ist Gott nicht Gott*) mean that God has no reality apart from the world? Those who would reply in the affirmative – and today, I fancy, they would be much in the majority among students of Hegel's works – cannot but conclude that the real *Aufhebung* of religion, according to his thinking, is not metaphysics but history itself: that in the end the Idea does not take us beyond the space–time order but abandons us instead to the never-ceasing, ever-shifting historical process. On this view the truth of the gospel is entirely absorbed into the life of the Christian community. That is to say, the gospel does not stand *over* the church, distinct from and always judge of it; it *is* the church. Christ exists only in the dogmas of the faith and in the ecclesiastical institutions whose foundation they are. Moreover, as the gospel is to be equated with the church, so the church in its turn is to be seen as essentially one with Christendom, which for Hegel meant in fact the Germanic Protestant world as the culminating phase of Western culture. But this at once raises a further problem, and one again depending directly on the interpretation we make of Hegel – or better perhaps, on how Hegel saw his own philosophy. For, if the correct philosophical reading of history is possible only 'when actuality is ripe', then must we not suppose that the Germanic Protestant era will already itself have drawn to its close? And this can only mean that the 'absolute religion' in its historical embodiment will now be slipping away into the past and that a new, post-Christian era is in sight. In the oft-quoted words from the preface to the *Philosophy of Right* (*Grundlinien der Philosophie des Rechts*, 1821): 'When philosophy paints its grey on grey some shape of life has grown old and cannot by this unrelieved grey be made young again, but only known. The owl of Minerva takes wing only as the twilight falls.' Is this in truth what Hegel believed? It may very well be, good Lutheran as he chose to think himself, that he did not wish to believe so and that the Christian religion does reveal the 'absolute' and so must stand in perpetuity. But his doctrine, if one understands it aright, does not support this assurance. On the contrary, the dialectic of change is all-eroding and 'nothing continueth in one stay'. No manifestation of the Absolute can itself be absolute, since history knows only of relativities.

Assuredly Hegelianism itself soon proved to have no absolute validity. Within a decade or so of Hegel's death in 1831 the philosophy which, in the eyes of the master's immediate disciples, was to end all philosophies by having at last proclaimed the fullness of Truth was beginning to disintegrate under criticism. The reason for this, again, lies in its ambiguity of meaning. Hegel's religious philosophy, it has aptly been said, was from the start a *Janus bifrons*, and those who at first were drawn to it quickly perceived that very widely divergent ways opened up before them.[79] Some, like Karl Friedrich Göschel (1784–1861), were theological conservatives who hailed the new philosophy as a final vindication of Protestant orthodoxy at the bar of reason: Hegelianism was a light by which modern man could once more walk securely along an old road. Others, such as Karl Daub (1765–1836), Philipp Marheineke (1780–1846), and later Alois Emanuel Biedermann (1819–85), were prepared to follow what they took to be Hegel's own ascent to the metaphysical highlands: the historic Christ, as the realization of the divine ideal in a human individual, was one through whom humanity might discover its own divinity. But some also there were who were less complaisant. On the one side were traditionalists by no means ready to countenance the dissolution of dogma in a metaphysical logic. For them the support which Hegelianism claimed to give to faith was rather its betrayal. On the other side, in a group styling themselves the Young Hegelians – among them Bruno Bauer, David Friedrich Strauss and Ludwig Feuerbach – were men of a more sceptical outlook who objected to Hegel's retention of a dogmatic Christianity even under the mask of the *Begriff*.[80] In particular, Strauss's *Leben Jesu*, published in 1835, indicated a wholly new way. The inspiration here was still basically Hegelian, but the procedure was radically different. And this destructive criticism was carried to yet further lengths in Feuerbach's *Das Wesen des Christenthums* of 1841. In the outcome, 'speculative' Christianity showed itself to be unstable and its collapse in Germany was rapid, hastened, it may be added, by those very advances in scientific historiography to which Hegelianism itself had given impetus. In the light of history seen 'as it really was' the pretensions of *Geschichtsphilosophie* seemed less and less acceptable. But chiefly the cause is to be sought in the fecund diversity of Hegel's own thinking. The structure, immense as it was, contained too much to be enduring, and now it is long gone. Yet the profundity of Hegel's insights, the illumination he brings to everything he discusses – not least in the field of religion – have an abiding value and appeal, and, as modern Hegel research demonstrates, his work, probably the supreme intellectual achievement of his age, holds an interest which the lapse of time appears unable to quench.

4

The idea of God in the philosophy of Schelling

I

IF Hegel was primarily a rationalist and a Romantic only in certain aspects or nuances of his thought, in Schelling, on the contrary, German romanticism found perhaps its most representative voice. Indeed, at the philosophical level it can be claimed for him that he was the most typical Romantic of his age anywhere in Europe. Coleridge certainly owed much to him.[1] Yet for the English-speaking world, despite the familiarity of his name and the aura of intellectual brilliance which sustains his memory, his work has remained comparatively little known. Much the greater part of it is still untranslated and in the original he is, I fancy, seldom actually read. Historically he is associated with Fichte and Hegel, who now overshadow him: Fichte as the inaugurator of post-Kantian idealism, and Hegel as its great consummator, the master in whom it achieved its splendid culmination, but in whom also – in his native Germany at least – it reached its effective end. Metaphysical prodigy though Schelling was – he was appointed to a professorship at Jena at the age of twenty-three, his first notable publication having appeared when he was only twenty – he has left on posterity the impression of having changed his viewpoint rather too often – his work contains some five distinguishable systems – and, for all his speculative insight, to have dabbled in too many matters of which his knowledge was no more than sketchy. Indeed it was for only a relatively short period in his long career that he can be said to have occupied the forefront of the philosophical stage. In later life he experienced the mortification of being outshone and eventually more or less forgotten. Moreover, he who as hardly more than a youth was wont to publish a major treatise almost annually seemed in his maturity strangely unwilling to admit his thoughts to print at all. He evidently felt increasingly as the years went by that he had missed his mark. His Berlin lectures, among the most weighty of his writings, were published only posthumously.

Schelling's failure, if such we must deem it to have been, coupled with his personal reputation for self-interest, vanity and touchiness –

he quarrelled at some time or other with almost everybody he ever came to know – has established an unfortunate image, alike of the man and the thinker, which critics and commentators have been virtually unanimous in perpetuating. Further, at the time of his death in 1854, the style of philosophy which his early publications so vividly expound had gone out of fashion. In Germany, whatever its fortunes elsewhere, absolute idealism was by then in eclipse, shadows obscuring the fame even of Hegel. Hence anything like recognition of positive merit in Schelling's work was long retarded, and even today there is no real Schelling revival, at any rate of a kind like that which, since the Second World War, has been enjoyed by his successful rival. But some renewal of interest, and with it an increase of knowledge and understanding, there nevertheless has been, stimulated, one may suppose, by the republication of his collected works.[2] For Schelling has benefited not only from the mid-twentieth-century recovery of interest in the Romantic movement generally; he is now better appreciated, I surmise, on his own account. Thus he is no longer merely coupled, greatly to his detriment, with Hegel, while the personal animosities which he aroused during his lifetime and even afterwards have since passed into oblivion. The exuberant speculations of his early years have no doubt still not lost their intensely 'period' character – although they can be better appraised as type-instances of the Romantic attitude – but his mature thinking, the 'positive philosophy' of his Munich and Berlin phases – is today regarded as a remarkable anticipation of twentieth-century existentialism.[3]

One of the most interesting developments in the modern study of Schelling has been a move to qualify, if not wholly to dispel, the notion that the romanticist philosopher's doctrines were no more than a sort of metaphysical kaleidoscope, each following the other in quick succession with little continuity or connection. In spite of his unquestionable gifts, so it has usually been averred, the complex and even contradictory aspects of his personality were reflected in his ever-shifting ideas, none of which was adequately deployed before some fresh orientation of his thought took its place; Hegel, it is to be recalled, scornfully charged him with carrying on his philosophical education in public. Thus there is no really coherent system, no finally shaped interpretation of life and the world, which metaphysics, if it is to be pursued at all, should purport to offer. But, as I have said, more recent study, in taking a closer and more objective look at Schelling, finds in his successive philosophical stances a greater degree of coordination than hitherto suspected, and even to observe a guiding thread of principle supplying both direction and connection to what so easily may appear as a mere charivari of notions and problems. It has even been maintained that his whole career in philosophy is marked, in fact, by a consistent drive to discover the truth of life and a recognition that, if this should from time to time necessitate fresh starts, so it had to be. Only in this sense does Schelling's work in retrospect seem anything but fragmentary and inchoate.

So much revised a view of Schelling may by some be thought exaggerative, and possibly it is. But there had previously been an imbalance which called for correction. Prejudice as well had to be overcome, for no doubt as a man, in both his private and his public *personae*, he was difficult and often to be faulted. But personal defects such as his were not at all rare among artists and intellectuals of his time. In any case we today are in no position to be especially censorious on this account.

Friedrich Wilhelm Joseph Schelling was born on 27 January 1775 at Leonberg in Württemberg, where his father was a Lutheran pastor with a reputation as a learned orientalist. In childhood he was intellectually precocious, and he entered the theological seminary at Tübingen, the so-called *Stift*, when no more than fifteen years of age, two of his fellow-students being the future poet Hölderlin, and Hegel, the latter his senior by five years, though at this stage much less brilliant than he. His first studies were in theology, biblical exegesis and ancient languages. But he soon turned to what was to be his great passion – philosophy. His final year at the *Stift* saw his first publication, *Über die Möglichkeit einer Form der Philosophie überhaupt* ('On the Possibility of a Form of Philosophy in General'), quickly followed by *Vom Ich als Prinzip der Philosophie* ('On the Ego as Principle of Philosophy'), in which the influence of Fichte is obvious, and the first part of the *Philosophische Briefe über Dogmatismus und Kriticismus* ('Philosophical Letters on Dogmatism and Criticism'). Like Hegel he left the seminary with no apparent desire for an ecclesiastical career and took up a private tutorship at Leipzig, where he furthered his own education with an assortment of studies – law, medicine, physics and mathematics – whilst also composing articles on philosophical topics, all of them plainly Fichtean in inspiration, followed by two weighty treatises within a year of one another: *Ideen zu einer Philosophie der Natur* ('Ideas towards a Philosophy of Nature') and *Von der Weltseele* ('On the World-Soul'). It was in 1798, when the second of these appeared, that he got his chair at Jena, then the mecca of German intellectuals. He had already attracted the attention of Goethe and Fichte and won their commendations. He had, too, become personally acquainted with several of the leading Romantic writers of the day, including brothers Schlegel, Novalis and Tieck, and soon took his place among them as the movement's philosopher. The year after his arrival in Jena saw the publication of *Erster Entwurf eines Systems der Naturphilosophie* ('First Sketch of a System of the Philosophy of Nature'), in which there were signs already of a veering away from Fichte, although not as yet of overt disagreement. In fact in 1800 came the *System der transzendentalen Idealismus* ('System of Transcendental Idealism') which was clearly influenced by Fichte's *Wissenschaftslehre*.[4] In January 1801 Schelling was joined on the staff at Jena by Hegel, whom he partnered in editing a new *Kritisches Journal der Philosophie* (1802–3).

The first year of the new century was of importance for Schelling in that he now definitely broke with Fichte's 'subjective' idealism, drawing up a *Darstellung meines Systems der Philosophie* ('An Exposition of my System of Philosophy') in order to demonstrate that he had. In this the fundamental divergence between the two thinkers surfaced, although the breach was not to become complete until after an exchange of letters that in themselves constitute a remarkable philosophical document. By now Schelling felt himself to be a philosopher in his own right, with his face set towards fresh horizons. The outcome was the 'philosophy of identity', expressed first in a Platonic dialogue, *Bruno, oder über das göttliche und natürliche Prinzip der Dinge* ('Bruno, or On the Divine and Natural Principle of Things') (1802),[5] and more fully in *Fernere Darstellungen aus dem System der Philosophie* ('Further Expositions of the System of Philosophy') and *Vorlesungen über die Methode des akademischen Studiums* ('Lectures on the Method of Academic Study'). In the immediately preceding phase, represented by the *System of Transcendental Idealism*, Schelling's thinking had culminated in a philosophy of art, in which he propounds the view that the immanent but unconscious intelligence in nature which rises through the inorganic to the organic, and finally to the organism Man as the apex of the whole process, has its first completely self-conscious utterance in art, in which it at last realizes its infinite capability. Art, therefore, has to be seen as the goal towards which all intelligence moves, and which, as such, is the true philosophy in so far as it achieves the needed reconciliation of nature and history.

Now, however – about the time of Schelling's espousal of Caroline Schlegel, after the dissolution of her marriage with August Wilhelm Schlegel, when Schelling moved to the university of Würzburg – he began to direct his attention to questions of religion, under the influence of his reading of the early-seventeenth-century mystical writer Jakob Boehme. In 1804 he published *Philosophie und Religion*, in which he attempts to counter misunderstanding of the concept of the Absolute as pure identity by repudiating any idea of it as mere formless 'substance' – Hegel's 'night in which all cows are black' – and thus effectively indistinguishable from sheer vacuity.

But this is to look ahead; in embarking on the subject of the present chapter we must go back to Schelling's first major work, *Vom Ich als Prinzip der Philosophie*. The problem of the existence of a personal deity had occupied him since his student days. In correspondence with Hegel after the latter had left Tübingen he stated his opinion forthrightly. 'We have done', he said, 'with the orthodox conceptions of God. We go farther than the ideal of a personal Being.'[6] As he himself sees it, God is only the absolute 'I': 'Gott is nichts als das absolute Ich'. Already he had no use for the arguments for divine existence deployed by the theologians. In fact, contemporary apologetic was evasive and dishonest and at odds with any genuine theology.[7] He was especially critical of the moral argument of the Kantians which conceived God as an 'absolute Object' altogether external to the thinking subject. With all a young intellectual's brash confidence he regards himself as Kant's true successor and his own idealism, based on the concept of *das absolute Ich*, as the natural and proper outcome of the critical philosophy. But what did he mean by the phrase?

Schelling's dissatisfaction with the *Critique of Pure Reason* centred on the difficulty, as he saw it, that the various forms under which the mind is there represented as conceiving objects failed to point to a unitary underlying principle.[8] Unless such a principle were to be disclosed, philosophy as essentially the unifying interpretation of experience could make no progress. Happily Fichte, in his *Wissenschaftslehre*, had shown the way forward. The ego is the experiencing subject, over against which is set the non-ego, the world of 'objective' realities present to the experiencing subject's mind. Inasmuch, though, as ego and non-ego stand in reciprocal relation to each other, the one being conditioned by the other, neither can be considered as absolute and so is unable to serve as the wholly unconditioned principle from which philosophy must start.[9] At the same time the absolute principle is to be sought neither in the mere fact of the relativity of subject and object, nor in 'self-consciousness'. Indeed, self-consciousness has to be distinguished from it.[10] What Schelling does therefore is to go beyond subject–object relativities to Fichte's *absolute Ich* or Ego, which not only has absolute causality in itself but is the precondition alike of the ego and the non-ego. The completed system of knowledge, he affirms, has to begin here, with the absolute Ego.

In the light of this principle Schelling faults in turn the theologians of his day, the philosophy of Spinoza and even a post-Kantian like K. L. Reinhold (1758–1823), whose reinterpretation of Kant he otherwise can describe as 'the morning light that precedes the noonday'.[11] The first of these, taking their cue from Kant, introduce God as a moral postulate, but straight away transform him into a moral Being. While, that is, they rejoice in stressing the limitations of the speculative reason they play up the 'thing-in-itself' on moral or 'faith' grounds. Philosophy is thus meanly reduced to the requirements of the pulpit.[12] But to conceive God as an absolute Being, in the way orthodox theology does, is inadmissible.

> Let us posit God as object and assume him to be the real ground of knowledge. Then, as object, he falls within the sphere of our knowledge. But if he is within the sphere of our knowledge he cannot be that whereon the entire sphere itself depends.[13]

God does not, however, exist as an object, he is 'pure, absolute Ego',[14] and to believe in an absolute, infinite object means the annihilation of the believing subject.[15] Objectivity implies the mind's complete grasp of what it knows.

> Inasmuch as the object is a representation in the mind of man, man himself giving the object its form and conditions, man rules it. He has nothing to fear from it; he himself sets its limits. If he abolishes these limits, if the object can no longer be represented in his mind, he finds himself lost.[16]

The error of dogmatism, as Schelling calls this mode of thinking, extends also to Spinoza, admire him as he so much does. Although 'the quiet intuition of rest in the arms of the world' has a profound appeal to many minds – something which the talkative moralism of the theologians lacks[17] – Spinozism spells the end of freedom by identifying subjective causality with objective, since here again the personal ego is annulled. 'Spinoza has set up as the first principle of all philosophy a proposition which could be established only at the end of his system and as the outcome of the most painstaking proof.'[18] He has also made the mistake of absolutizing what is in truth only an intuition of his personal ego, whereas, so Schelling himself maintains, 'everything that exists does so in the ego, outside of which there is nothing'.[19]

Schelling is certain, furthermore, that 'consciousness', the empirical ego, cannot provide an adequate basis for philosophy. The empirical ego is, so to say, only our ordinary, everyday self – a finite experiencing being through whom the true self, the absolute Ego, never achieves total expression. Schelling thus infers that the empirical ego exists through a limitation of the absolute; it is, he would say, an inchoate or fragmentary expression of it, i.e. our ordinary self is in part, but only in part, identifiable with the true self. Hence the causality of the empirical ego is quantitatively but not qualitatively different from that of the absolute.[20] The important difference between the two, however, is that although in everyday experience personality depends on the unity of the consciousness, 'the infinite *Ich* knows no consciousness, no personality.' Yet if we are to speak of God at all it is to the absolute Ego alone that the word can be applied. For the latter is at once the real and the ideal – both that which basically is and that towards which 'reality' is ever moving.[21]

But how is the absolute Ego known? All ordinary knowledge, Schelling replies, derives in the last resort from 'immediate experience'.[22] In the case of the Absolute, on the other hand, that experience is a matter of intellectual perception.[23] Intellectual perception or intuition, but not logical deduction, since logical deduction itself presupposes it. In other words, knowledge of the Absolute is not discursive reflection, it occurs where the perceiving self is one with the perceived self – a moment at which the 'pure absolute eternity is within us'.[24] This intuition of ultimate reality – reminiscent as it is of Schleiermacher's *Gefühl* – is for Schelling, I think, fundamentally religious. He says that Friedrich Heinrich Jacobi, a man of deep spiritual insight, had well described it, but admits nevertheless that it is something extremely difficult to express intelligibly in words, although it has much in common with what in the language of religion is called faith. To have this intuitive knowledge of the original and ideal unity is a state of blessedness; to fall away from it is to decline into sin.[25]

The Absolute, therefore, is to be characterized first and foremost as the ultimately *real*.[26] It is pure Being, as distinct from the specific entities that subsist under the categories of general law, which to it is inapplicable.[27]

> Were there for the Infinite Self mechanism or purpose in nature, for it purpose would be mechanism and mechanism purpose; that is, both would coincide in its absolute Being. Hence even theoretical investigation must consider the teleological as mechanical, the mechanical as teleological, and both as comprised in one principle of Unity.[28]

If God were to exist as object he would be a particular being, even though unique, whereas as absolute he is beyond the categories of being as we know it. The truth of this is brought home to us in a flash of intuitive certainty; we inwardly recognize the Absolute to be 'substantial' in a sense that renders all else accidental. But the absolutely real is also the absolutely *one*. It is not a species nor an individual, but is completely homogeneous, pure self-identity, that wherein being and thought wholly coincide.[29] Finally, it is the ultimate causal principle, of knowledge as of being.[30] 'In the Ego, philosophy through its struggles now gains the highest laurels of its strife; it has found the all-embracing unity.'[31]

But, given the concept of the Absolute, how should the world be thought to have come into existence? Or, as Schelling himself phrases the question, How did the Absolute come out of itself and oppose the world to itself?[32] This is the ancient and residual problem of all metaphysics, that of the one and the many, the transition from the infinite to the finite. The truth is, says Schelling, that as posed it is unanswerable. Thus we have to adopt the opposite procedure, that of starting with the finite but transcending it in a move towards the infinite.[33] For finite and infinite are not juxtaposed as contingent, mutually exclusive entities; the finite is itself an aspect of the infinite. Spinoza understood this in regarding the self as no longer its own (*Eigentum*), but as belonging to an infinite reality.[34] Yet the approach of the finite to the infinite demands never-ceasing effort. If the absolute Ego is theoretically the beginning of the quest, in practice it is its far-distant goal, to be reached only after an arduous journey.[35] But this difficult and toilsome advance is preferable, because more rewarding, than the too-easy assurance offered by the 'moral' God of orthodox theology. As Schelling wrote to Hegel in the letter from which I have already quoted: 'There is no personal God, and our highest strife is to destroy our personality, passing over into the sphere of absolute Being, which however is something not in eternity *possible*; therefore only a drawing-near to the Absolute in action (*praktische*); and therefore – *immortality*.'[36]

To the extent, Schelling concludes, that the infinite Ego is represented schematically as the ultimate goal of the finite ego – and thus external – God can be represented in practice as likewise *external* to the finite ego, but of course only as identical with the infinite Ego.[37] Philosophically, he is saying that God is really to be conceived as the unity anterior to any separation of subjective form and objective content, and that it is only in terms of the absolute Ego that he can rightly be portrayed.

The second stage in the development of Schelling's thought has until fairly recently been the best known and the most influential, the 'philosophy of nature', the first important expression of which was the *Ideen* of 1797. What we observe in this work is a distinct movement away from Fichte's predominantly subjective, ethical position, and an emphasis now on the non-ego. The world of nature, that is, is felt to be as important as the world of the self. In Fichte's *Wissenschaftslehre* the knowing and willing subject was the focal point of existence, but Schelling has become increasingly disposed to stress the self-existence of the objective world. Nature, however, is not to be understood simply at the level of empirical observation and scientific theory, the truth being that it has a deeper significance of its own which it is the function of speculative or intellectual intuition to penetrate and interpret. Basic to this conception – and astronomy, physics, biology and psychology, although separate sciences, require coordination – is the principle of a dualism of forces in polarity.[38] These opposing forces may be described as, on the one side, positive, active and productive, and on the other as negative, restrictive and limiting. Matter, in truth, *is* force, its properties being repulsion and attraction.[39] In each individual body, so Schelling argues, the forces of attraction and repulsion are in equilibrium, and apart from them nature is not intelligible.[40] But dualism as such being foreign to his mind, Schelling seeks some dynamic, underlying reality, an 'absolute' unity, which the opposition of the forces must itself imply and from which they in fact emanate. But exactly how can the absolute One be conceived of as thus 'going out of' itself? It is a problem, Schelling saw, not easy to solve.

But to go back to the question of these forces – are they really equal? Schelling proceeds to show that they are not, although they are mutually necessary. The former, the 'positive', as we may call it, is of its very nature superior; for it is the positive which determines the fundamental character of reality as conditioned, while the negative simply provides the conditions without which there would be no reality. In other words, the positive is that by which alone the facts of existence can be explained, whereas the negative determines the form of reality through the limitation of those facts. In a sense, therefore, the positive is 'living', the negative 'dead'. Or to put it in another way, the positive can be thought of as a unity, the final condition of all things, whereas it is the function of the negative to break up the unity into multiplicity, imposing the specific conditions which determine what things are. Yet again, the positive may be associated with the organic, the negative with the mechanical. Nature is primarily an organism; though, as Schelling phrases it, the organic does not mean the absence of mechanism, but rather that mechanism obtains where no organism exists.[41]

Thus for Schelling the positive is the ultimate force, the absolute One. It is, he says, 'the age-old idea of a primal "matter", which opens itself out into innumerable phenomena like the many single beams of light broken up in an infinite prism'.[42] A not unfitting designation of this absolute One is *Weltseele*, 'World Soul', a term originating with the ancient Greeks, though here connoting not 'Mind' but physical force, describable variously as 'matter', 'ether', or 'light-ether'. Nor is it to be identified with the actual world-process, since this, as we have noted, involves duality and opposition. It is the 'organic' character of the Absolute, however, that explains life. Dead matter could not produce it. Life and spirit, in other words, are latent in nature, reaching self-consciousness in man. Reality has to be conceived therefore as evolving.

Viewed thus – not as mere 'object', that is, but as 'subject' – nature is essentially dynamic: *natura naturans*, productivity.[43] Being *a priori* it cannot itself be known; we know *of* it only through its products. In a sense indeed product and productivity are mutually opposed, since every product signifies to some extent the limitation, or even the negation, of productive force.[44] Yet this limitation is not purely negative: 'Universal duality, as a principle for explaining nature, is as necessary as the concept of nature itself.'[45] It alone accounts for empirical or 'objective' nature – *natura naturata*. 'Nature as object is that which emerges from an infinite series', though what Schelling is here referring to is nature as a whole, not particular natural objects, inasmuch as 'absolute activity can be represented not by a finite product but only by an infinite one'.[46] Thus empirical nature is never completely achieved or fulfilled; it is always a 'becoming', never, finally, a 'being'.[47] If we ask 'What is the earth?' the answer is that 'its history is woven into that of nature as a whole, and this proceeds upwards from the fossil through inorganic and organic nature to the history of the universe – a single chain'.[48] But the story can never be told in its entirety. 'Our science itself is an infinite task.'

The dialectical method so far adopted by Schelling was still that of Fichte, but applied not, as with the elder thinker, to the active consciousness of the ego but to the process of the non-ego, the external world. In the *System of Transcendental Idealism*, his most schematic work, he offers his own version of the philosophy of consciousness, bringing to the philosophy of nature insights derived from the critical theory of knowledge, to yield 'speculative physics' and 'transcendental philosophy'. The former, dealing with the objective world of nature, shows how intelligent consciousness arises; the latter, beginning with the subject or ego, how it is possible to attain to a knowledge of the 'objective' world of nature.[49] What unifies them is the Absolute as identity of subjectivity and objectivity, so that both inquiries are, as it were, opposite sides of the same coin. But clearly the break with Fichte's thoroughgoing subjectivism is now approaching. The absolute Ego has become Nature. 'The Ego appears subjectively as infinite productivity; objectively, as eternal becoming.'[50]

In tracing the growth of knowledge Schelling distinguishes three stages: from sensation to perception, from perception to reflection, and from reflection to volition. Sensation is simple awareness of the non-ego as limit: self-consciousness passes outward, so to speak, only to encounter the pressure of the non-ego upon it. So for the ego an objective world in *space* comes into being, and therewith immediate consciousness of the self as living and active in *time*, the relation between them being one of *causality*. This perception of the external world gives rise in turn to reflection, while from reflection on the interiority of the self as distinguishable from the not-self comes will, in which the ego takes account of itself as free, active power. Thus we pass from the first and theoretical part of the transcendental philosophy, intended to explain the inner world of the self, to the second and practical part, dealing with the free determination of the self through volition. But the will has to realize itself in terms of moral action – among individuals, in the state and in history. The end of the historical process is for Schelling the gradual realization of freedom under law, a movement towards the perfect state and even, ultimately, 'an Areopagus of peoples, made up of all civilized nations'.[51] But more is wanted, Schelling thinks, than the light of a moral ideal to ensure that the end is attainable. Freedom has to become necessity, and necessity freedom.[52] 'I demand', he says, 'something absolutely objective which, entirely independent of freedom, secures and, as it were, guarantees its highest goal.'[53] Thus within human freedom we must suppose a 'hidden necessity' to be operative, the outcome of which will inevitably be something rational and harmonious. What we have to understand is the fact of an absolute identity between freedom and necessity, although of course it is not present to consciousness. Subjectively, and for inner experience, it is we who act; objectively, however, it is not we but something acting through us. In other words, the whole movement of history must be conceived as a revelation of the unconscious Productivity underlying all things, the Absolute in which real and ideal are one. Thus a perfect moral world-order is the *telos* of the entire historical process, so that we can speak of progress as assured. But because the Absolute is infinite the progressive movement must be unending, never finally complete. Or, to use religious language, God never *is* but gradually and continuously comes to be. His existence therefore cannot be given a logically conclusive demonstration; it can only be divined in the progressive march of history.[54] For this reason God is not an object of *knowledge* – in the strict sense of the word – but only of *faith*, 'the eternal presupposition of action'. True religion is a 'system of Providence'.

The division of the transcendental philosophy into theoretical and practical parts completes an obvious parallelism with Kant's three *Critiques* when a third part introduces a philosophy of art. In neither the theoretical part nor the practical does reason, in Schelling's view, arrive at its highest realization, whereas in art, as he claims with true Romantic fervour, the human ego becomes one with the productive energy of nature. For here at last the self is aware of the cosmic creative power working through its own free acts. What the mind was unconsciously striving after, what the will was consciously seeking without ever fully realizing, art, we are told, actually achieves. Indeed the philosophy of art is 'the true organon of philosophy',[55] and aesthetic idealism the coping-stone of the entire idealist system. 'The work of art reveals to us the identity of the conscious and the unconscious', its fundamental character being 'an unconscious infinite, a synthesis of nature and freedom'.[56] Through his aesthetic sensibility the artist vouchsafes to mankind nothing less than a vision of the ultimate nature of reality, for what 'Providence' is for religion 'Genius' is for art: 'Genius is for aesthetics what the Ego is for philosophy, namely the highest absolute Real, which, while it never becomes objective, is yet the cause of everything that is objective.'[57] Thus it is not ethics but aesthetics which signifies the final stage of the dialectical development of self-consciousness. Necessity and freedom, the unconscious and the conscious, the real and the ideal, nature and spirit are here wrought together in ultimate unity. To understand this is 'infinite satisfaction'. God, it may truly be said, is revealed as Beauty, with the inspired artist as his prophet. The unconscious, impersonal forces present but concealed in man's conscious acts in history have their counterpart in the emotional experience of the artist, in whom something greater than his conscious self flows through him to create what is infinite and eternal.[58]

2

By the year 1800 Schelling had completed the earlier phases of his system. In the first he had worked out a doctrine of the 'Object' or Nature, balancing this, in the second, with one of the 'Subject' or Spirit. He also had devised a philosophy of art to explain how in aesthetic experience Nature and Spirit are fused in concrete identity. It remained, however, to elicit and examine the metaphysical implications of that experience and to determine precisely how Nature and Spirit accomplish the union which is thus intuitively discovered. The *Darstellung meines Systems der Philosophie* of 1801 marks the beginning of the third phase of the scheme, the 'philosophy of Absolute identity', as Schelling fittingly calls it. The dialogue *Bruno*, which appeared in the following year, provided further detail, but it is in the *Vorlesungen über die Methode des akademischen Studiums*, published in 1803, that he explores its themes at length.[59] The principle which this new form of the doctrine embodies is that the Absolute is neither Subject nor Object, neither Ego nor Nature, but an original unity which expresses itself in both. This absolute identity of nature and intelligence, of knower and known, is to be found in their common 'neutral' source, reason. 'All philosophy', states Schelling, 'consists in the recollection of the condition in which we were one with nature', and in recognizing the truth that knowledge, as a 'reproduction' of nature, is nature's highest expression.[60] Hence an appropriate name for this philosophy would be 'objective idealism', in contrast to Fichte's 'subjective idealism' in which the ego is all, philosophy now being seen as the systematized knowledge of this 'neutral' absolute.

In setting out his doctrine Schelling draws on Plotinus, Giordano Bruno and Spinoza. He follows Spinoza's geometric method, that is, while Plotinus' *nous* suggests the concept of pure rationality; but Bruno's vitalistic pantheism – along with some hints from Herder and Goethe – supersedes Spinoza's materialistic determinism. The absolute Reason he defines as reason from which the rational intelligence of the individual has been abstracted. It is distinct therefore from any actual process of thinking; as Schelling himself phrases it, it is 'reason in so far as it is thought of as total indifference of the subjective and the objective'. It is equivalent to absolute knowledge, compassing both the 'form' and the 'essence' of the universe. And as the Absolute itself there is nothing outside it.[61] It is the authentic *Ding-an-sich*, the sole 'thing-in-itself'. Accordingly, philosophical understanding is a knowledge of things as they are in themselves.

The problem, however, is to explain the existence of the finite world, the derivation of the many from the One. There can on Schelling's view be nothing 'outside' the Absolute. If the infinite real *contains* all that is then it cannot be the external cause of the universe, and to suppose otherwise has been the cardinal error of almost all philosophies in the past. The absolute Identity cannot 'step outside of itself';[62] indeed the whole of existence constitutes the absolute Identity. But if the Absolute is pure identity all distinctions must be external to it: as Schelling says, qualitative difference is possible only outside the absolute Totality.[63] To resolve the crux any distinction of subject and object must be deemed illusory except from the point of view of empirical consciousness. The Absolute, that is, produces nothing 'out of' itself; it is not the source of things nor their ground; it is essentially *what they are in themselves*. The usual idea is that nature and spirit proceed from the original unity, so becoming mutually opposed as object and subject. Schelling, however, in his own philosophy of nature, has sought to show that nature, while material and unconscious as 'object', is as 'subject' spiritual and conscious. The transcendental philosophy had similarly demonstrated the same to be true of spirit. Thus everything that is represents the identity of subject and object. Each and every finite entity is the Absolute inasmuch as *in itself*, or at the level of absolute Reason, it is infinite. Ultimate reality is one, qualitatively undifferentiated.

How the empirical consciousness is able to take quite another view, and what status this view has ontologically, Schelling does not inform us, although the obvious fact is that whatever the residual unity which a monism like his may demand, empirical distinctions do remain. Qualitative difference Schelling disallows, as I have just said, but quantitative difference between subject and object he acknowledges, holding that in all things the subjective and the objective are in varying degree mingled. An excess or preponderance of one or the other he calls a 'Potency' or 'Power' (*Potenz*). In nature there is a preponderance of objectivity; in spirit, of subjectivity. The Absolute, however, is the identity of all such Potencies; in other words, were we capable of beholding all things in their totality we would recognize a perfect equality. On the side of nature the first of these Potencies, Schelling thinks, is weight, with light as the second. The third, organism, is the common product of both. And what we find in the material world is present also in the ideal, where the Potencies are knowledge and action, with reason as the union of the two. In the order of 'values' these latter represent the true, the good and the beautiful respectively. The symmetry is thus complete.

We see, then, that although the Potencies are conceptually differentiated there is no real multiplicity within the One. Such multiplicity as appears is only an aspect of the unity, not something produced by it or generated from it. Empirically there is a process of evolutionary self-expression and self-recognition in the Absolute, but it is not creation *ex nihilo* as Christian theism teaches; it is simply an actualization of what already exists potentially. Nevertheless the Absolute as Subject-Object can exist only in differentiation. Resorting, as Schelling himself frequently does, to religious language, we may say that God has his existence in and through his progressive revelation in human experience, so that man is himself the cause or ground of God's being. But, since the process occurs only *in* the Absolute, and is in fact identifiable with the Absolute, it is no less true to say that God is *self*-caused, arriving at self-knowledge by the actualizing of his inherent potentiality.

In his last years at Jena, Schelling was wont increasingly to speak of the Absolute as divine. He did not indeed simply equate God with the Absolute; rather did he think of him as *natura naturans*, the primal unity of the unconscious World-Self. But this, it is to be noted, is a more static concept than his earlier one, for deity now is less an eternal activity or energizing will than 'rest and inactivity'; activity is to be found in the process of the finite. Hence God is an aspect of the Absolute rather than the whole of it. In himself he is beyond rational comprehension, but he is revealed in human history, in which Schelling distinguishes three successive epochs. The first is that of Nature: the ancient world, with its naturalistic religions, signifies the preponderance of the natural; its finest product was the religion and art of Greece. The epoch of Fate, which follows next, is that of late antiquity, characteristic of which is the mechanical legalism of Rome. But with Christianity the epoch of Providence commences. God became 'objective' for the first time in Christ, although the incarnation is not to be looked on simply as a unique temporal event: it is an eternal act. Christ represents in his own person the sacrifice of the finite in order to make possible the advent of the Spirit as the light of a new world. Thus Christianity's basic dogma is that of the trinity, an admission which should not obscure the fact that Schelling's theological views are nonetheless a good way from orthodoxy. He certainly sets little store by the Bible; replete as it is with legend and superstition, it is an obstacle to reason. A regenerated Christianity will depend on the triumph of speculative knowledge, in which religion will unite with poetry to form truth of a higher order.

Schelling's Würzburg lectures mainly re-explore the ground of the transcendental philosophy, adapting it to the needs of his students, but his one new work of importance, that on philosophy and religion, develops some elements in his teaching more fully than previously. He had been challenged by a friend, Carl August Eschenmayer, to supplement his philosophy by an avowal of religious faith, which the latter regarded as a necessary advance on abstract philosophical thinking and a safeguard of morality against pantheism.[64] In reply Schelling affirms that God, the Absolute, is to be apprehended not by any special religious faculty or endowment – 'faith', 'feeling', 'devotion', call it what you will – but in immediate knowledge. In other words, faith and reason are one; or at most faith is only 'a particular aspect of that general relation to the Absolute which exists in fullest form in knowledge through reason'.[65] It is the aim of both faith and reason to restore to man his lost unity with God. To describe the Absolute as pure identity does not mean that it is an amorphous and featureless 'substance', nor mere vacuity, but that it is an absolutely simple infinity. Conceptually, however, it can be approached only negatively, by the entire elimination from our thought of every finite attribute. Hence it can be known only by intuition: it is, says Schelling, the composite alone which can be known by description – the simple must be intuited. 'To describe the evidence which lies in the idea of the Absolute human speech is too weak.'[66] But the soul is capable of intuitive knowledge of the Absolute because of its own fundamental unity with the divine. It is this intuition which is the starting-point of philosophy. 'All philosophy begins and has begun with the idea of the Absolute quickened into life.'[67]

Nevertheless the problem of the origin of differentiation within the

Whole, of the world (so to speak) 'outside' God as distinct from the world 'inside' him, has to be tackled. Schelling goes back to the precedents set by Plato and ancient Greek philosophy, as possibly also to the early Christian doctrine of the Logos. 'All ideas', he tells us, 'are one Idea' – which is itself to be understood as the immediate and eternal reflection of the Absolute and which, as such, represents the divine self-knowledge. But we still have not passed from *natura naturans* to *natura naturata*; ideas do not themselves produce objects. So what of the empirical order? That 'ideas' of it exist eternally is no sufficient explanation of the concrete reality we know. Schelling had of late immersed himself in the writings of Boehme and at this point was minded to introduce the notion of a cosmic Fall (*Abfall*). The world, he contends, originated in a falling or breaking away (*Abbrechung*) from God; one might even say a 'jump' (*Sprung*): 'From the Absolute to the real there is no continuous transition; the origin of the world of sense is conceivable only as a complete breaking away by means of a leap.'[68] This presents difficulties, but we must try to grasp Schelling's meaning; he is not thinking of an actual breaking-off, as it were, of a part of the Absolute, still less of anything like an event in time. The Fall is non-temporal, eternal and necessary, inasmuch as, being a rupture with or a separation from the Absolute, it must itself possess the character of 'aboluteness'. It cannot, that is, be equated with a contingent happening and so cannot be assimilated to the fall of man as depicted in Christian theology. It is rather that 'fallen' being resembles a reflection of, or shadow cast by, a body – the Platonic theme is obvious – and, in so far as what the finite entity reflects is itself but an 'idea' within the Absolute, the entity *per se* is no more than an image of an image. Yet as an image of an idea in the infinite Idea it partakes of infinitude itself. The 'real' world, therefore, has a double aspect, an infinite and a finite, but in its finitude it is alienated from its true centre in the infinite and thus cannot be other than, in some measure, a negation of it. The empirical universe has genuine being – that cannot be questioned; but finitude and particularity signify the negative and so 'distance' themselves from the Absolute. This however implies that, as in the gnostic systems of Christian antiquity, no finite thing is to be looked on as of immediate divine causation and must therefore be referred for its explanation to the unending chain of causes and effects that constitute the world of sense-experience. That world, as we behold it, is a unitary nexus of finite entities relatively independent and self-subsisting. But this appearance is confined to our 'fallen' viewpoint. Its true relation to the Absolute, resulting from its fallenness and alienation, emerges only in a metaphysical and religious perspective.

But does not the empirical world itself, on Schelling's theory, exist necessarily if it is in some sense an image of the Absolute? This the philosopher will not allow. Finitude, he insists, is not deducible, and there is no properly rational explanation of it. The possibility of the world's existing must, then, depend on freedom.[69] Whence, though, is this freedom? Schelling's argument here, it has to be admitted, is somewhat tortuous. In one sense the Absolute is not 'free', it is necessary; yet the Idea as the self-reflection of the Absolute – a 'second' Absolute, or, as we might say, the divine Logos – has 'existence in itself', or is self-related. 'Along with the essence of itself the Absolute bestows upon its counterpart independence also. This "in-itselfness" (*Selbstheit*) is freedom.'[70] It is 'pure', evenly-balanced freedom, without bias either way. If it chooses its own 'egoity' or follows its centrifugal urge then it 'falls away' from God, to become the differentiated unity of the world we know. Thus God, the Absolute, has himself no responsibility for the way taken; nor, on the other hand, is the world responsible for its own existence. This accounts for at any rate the possibility of finite things existing, but what of their actuality? Schelling's answer is that 'the empirical world is produced only through and for itself', meaning presumably that there is no real explanation at all of finite things as such: 'The falling-away cannot be explained', as he expressly states.[71] Their ultimate origin occurring 'outside' of all time they are not causally explicable after the manner that conditions within the finite order are. The world was, in principle, possible, and the world *is*: freedom implies potentiality. That is really all we can say!

This, though, is not the end of the story. The Absolute is not only *alpha*, it is also *omega*. If the balance of the eternal order has been disturbed by the actualization of a possibility, rectification is likewise possible. The finite ego indeed is 'the point of furthest alienation from God', and it suffers the guilt of the fall's unhappy consequences.[72] But it longs for reconciliation with the infinite – a longing which is destined not to go unrequited. For 'the grand intention of the universe and its history is nothing other than the restoration and perfect reconciliation with absoluteness'. To cite Schelling's own often-quoted words:

> History is an epic composed in the mind of God. Its two main parts are, first, that which depicts the departure of humanity from its centre up to its furthest point of alienation from the centre; and secondly, that which depicts the return. The first part is the Iliad, the second the Odyssey of history. In the first part the movement was centrifugal, in the second it is centripetal.[73]

When at last the individual has liberated himself from the desire for and constriction of what is merely finite – a condition which itself is a punishment – he has achieved immortality, the eternal blessedness in which his individuality is lost.[74]

Thus was Eschenmayer's challenge met. Schelling in *Philosophie und Religion* had sought to show, if in a somewhat rhapsodic manner, that religion is not a necessary addition to or supplementation of speculative philosophy, but that the latter, as a means to the knowledge of God, can stand on its own; nay more, that unless philosophy in itself can do so religion will not. The two are linked together in 'an eternal bond'.[75]

3

In 1806 Schelling moved to Munich to take up an appointment as general secretary to the Academy of Fine Arts, and he was to remain in the Bavarian capital until 1841, although from 1820 to 1827 he gave lecture-courses at Erlangen as well.[76] His much-loved wife Caroline died in September 1809 – a grievous loss to him[77] – but three years later he married a friend of hers, Pauline Gotter. A less passionate union than the former, it did bring him the stable happiness which a man of his eruptive temperament wanted. For by now he had definitely broken with both Fichte and Hegel. The latter's *Phenomenology of Mind* had been published in 1807, and although it did not mention Schelling by name it was sharply critical of the 'philosophy of identity' with its – as Hegel judged – indiscriminate *mélange* of subjective and objective. Schelling took the criticism personally, his resentment being further heightened with Hegel's increasing displacement of himself in the public eye. For as his rival's star rose his own waned. The astonishing outburst of creativity which had marked his early years was never to be repeated, and in fact but little more of his work was published during his lifetime. He did not at once shift from the main positions of the *Identitätsphilosophie*, but he had come to realize that other aspects of human existence needed to be taken into account, resulting in modifications of his doctrine as hitherto presented. For what, he now asked himself, of the irrational element in things? What of evil? And most imperative of all, what of human freedom? Was it compatible with the determinism of the Absolute? An answer to these questions was attempted in his *Philosophische Untersuchungen über das Wesen der menschlichen Freiheit* ('Philosophical Inquiries into the Nature of Human Freedom'), which appeared in 1809, a short treatise but arguably his most masterly.[78] Further, he had already begun to perceive, from the cloud of metaphysics in which he had been living, that 'the real point about which the inert mass of men moves, and at which the lever must be fixed to move them', was 'religion, the public faith, and life in the state'.[79]

The *Philosophische Untersuchungen* continues to maintain that God and the world are identical, but only in the sense that antecedent and consequent may be said to be identical. Schelling is seriously concerned, that is, to rebut the charge of pantheism. The visible world, *natura naturata*, is not itself God, as pantheism in its common meaning supposes. Nor on the other hand does his philosophy imply an acosmism in which finite entities are somehow absorbed and dissolved in the Absolute. His own view is a form of immanentism, holding that all things are contained in God, who is their creative and sustaining principle. Importantly for the personal and moral life, it is an idea that allows room for human freedom. Indeed the paradox is that 'that which is not free is necessarily outside God'.[80] But if God himself is free then the soul of man, which is God's image, is likewise free. 'In the final analysis', Schelling states, 'there is no other existence except Will. Will is original Being – groundlessness, independence of time, self-affirmation are applicable only to Will.'[81] From our standpoint the essence of freedom is in the choice between good and evil, and the fact that we can and do choose between them. But if this is true of the consequent we may presume that it is true also of the antecedent. In which case are we not to deduce that the power of evil, because of his freedom, resides in God himself?

In answering this question guidance comes from human experience and personal introspection. Personality is not simply a 'given', it is an achievement. We emerge, as it were, from darkness into light. There is in our nature an impulsive, urge-driven side, rooted in psychological obscurity, in the subconscious. And it is on this foundation that our personality is built up. But in the process sense contends with spirit, instinct with reason. A man may allow himself to be dominated by sensual desire, or he may submit himself to the control of rationality and the moral law; yet even if he chooses the way of reason his life will not be free of moral conflict and strife. He never succeeds in liberating himself entirely from the pull or the pressures of his darker, subliminal self; the upward path is always hard-going. The power of *choice*, however, is his distinctive quality: 'Man is set on that summit where he has in himself the authority of self-movement towards good or evil. The bond of the principles in him is not necessity but freedom. He stands at the point of decision.'[82] For of course freedom cannot but mean the possibility of evil. Are we, though, to say the same of God? Stimulated by his reading of Boehme, Schelling is prepared to attempt a conceptual analysis of the divine Being himself.

Ultimately, as we have seen, God has to be thought of as sheer unity, the 'absolute indifference', the undifferentiated Ground of all differentiation. As such he is not personal, since personality implies consciousness and self-integration.[83] Yet this original unity, or 'Unground', as Schelling terms it – 'a will in which there is no understanding' – divides itself into two equally eternal beginnings.[84] What he intends to affirm by this is, seemingly, that God, being *causa sui*, his own cause, is to be distinguished both as existing and as caused, in such a way that we may conceive of the cause 'as not being itself God'. As Schelling expresses it: 'Since there is nothing before or outside of God he must therefore have the ground of existence in himself',[85] but at the same time there is that 'in God which is not God himself' – i.e. 'that which is the ground of his existence'. But as this is no *temporal* relation of antecedent and consequent the two must be alike eternal. Thus the Absolute, we are to understand, is not simple but complex, distinguishable as simultaneously existence and ground of existence. Yet this original 'grounding' power or 'Will' of God, although inseparable from him, is in itself an irrationality, eluding all understanding. His irrational or unconscious 'volition' can even be described as 'the egoism in God'.[86] But out of it, Schelling maintains, comes a rational Will, loving and self-communicating: 'God himself is begotten in God.'

Thus God's being, from its very complexity, is dynamic and creative. 'The first beginning of creation is the yearning of the One to manifest itself; it is the Will of the Ground.'[87] Nevertheless it is in this creative though irrational 'Will of the Ground' that the principle of evil lies – the divisive and alienating principle which is the opposite of Reason, since Reason *unites*. These two principles coexist in tension in all things. To summarize Schelling's argument in the words of a modern commentator:

> Inasmuch as an original unity obtains between what is embodied in the Ground and what is embodied in the Reason, and inasmuch also as the process of creation is simply an inner transmutation or elevation of the original Dark Principle (*der dunkler Prinzip*) into Light, both being united in every natural existent, if in a limited degree.[88]

In men the Dark Principle subsists as self-will – an appetite and impulse contrary to the universal principle of Reason which thus separates him from God. Yet when this same principle is raised to the Light something higher draws upon him, namely Spirit. In so far as the soul of man is the living identity of both principles it is Spirit, and Spirit is 'in' God. However,

> ... if the identity of the two principles were as indestructible in the human spirit as it is in God there would be no distinction between God and the human spirit. In other words, God would not manifest himself. Therefore the unity which is indestructible in God must in man be capable of being destroyed. Hence arises the possibility of good and evil.[89]

But although the possibility of evil is grounded in God himself, its realization occurs only in man. The divine personality – if I interpret Schelling aright – is basically a unity, an integrated whole, whereas the human personality is not; its constitutive elements are separable, and in fact are separate, only too obviously. The Dark Principle, the egoistic drive, tends to dominate it, with resulting discord within and disorientation of man's nature. Yet it has to be recognized that without this latent destructive power there would be no order of existence and therefore nothing which could be called good. The potentiality of the one is necessary for the actuality of the other.

Man's freedom, however, does not depend on absoluteness of choice, because it is not completely indeterminate. For his choice is grounded in what he constitutionally is, a rational being – a case, once again, of antecedent and consequent. But there is that also in him, Schelling holds, by which he can dirempt himself from the universal reason and will of Love and follow the dark, 'natural' and egoistic will of the Ground: 'Man has from eternity attached himself to egoism and self-seeking, and all who are born are born under the influence of the dark principle of evil.'[90] Thus although a man's actions may be predictable he nonetheless is free; for here the determination is an inner one, created by the self's original choice – an act, Schelling thinks, which occurred below the level of consciousness, indeed outside of time and 'in the beginning of creation'. But this inner determination is itself freedom, in that a man's essence is inherently *his own act*. 'Necessity and freedom are mutually immanent, a single reality which appears to be one or the other only when looked at from different sides.'[91] For this Schelling finds an ultimate metaphysical basis, since the Absolute itself embodies that identity of necessity and freedom which is present also in man. It has, I think, to be admitted that Schelling's theory of man's primal, unconscious but determinative choice – the self-positing of the ego – is not easy to understand. For in what can we suppose it to have consisted? The idea presents much the same problem, surely, as does Kant's notion of the origin of the 'radical evil' (*das radicale Böse*) in man. Schelling is evidently concerned to avoid anything suggestive of Calvinistic predestinarianism, while at the same time disallowing the view that man enjoys the liberty of complete indifference. The *tertium quid* he proposes, though, falls a good deal short of clarity.

Of the two conflicting principles in man's nature his own history furnishes the ample record. Without freedom he could have had no history, a condition which provides us with the key to a philosophy of history. From an original state of innocence in unconscious indifference and through increasing struggle and conflict, man's historical

Odyssey moves onwards to that final 'Kingdom of God' in which evil, creative though it is, is at last subdued to good. History, that is to say, strives towards unity in a way which reflects the similar drive in nature itself. 'As the plurality of things in nature strives after a unity, and only in such unity reaches completion and the feeling of blessedness, so is the plurality of the world of man.'[92] Schelling's *Weltalter*, had it ever been completed, would have purported to show this; but although he repeatedly announced its forthcoming appearance he never saw the work through to the end.[93]

Yet, as I have just indicated, it is Schelling's contention that, apart from what from our viewpoint is identifiable – paradoxically no doubt – as the principle of evil, there would be no finite creation, and thus neither human consciousness nor personality. But also, Schelling points out, no deity either.

> Consciousness begins the moment we become aware of the two principles within us, when we subdivide ourselves, when we set ourselves against ourselves, when with the better part of us we raise ourselves above the lower ... The same holds true of God ... The life of God has the closest analogy with the life of man.[94]

Evil, then, it might well be said, is misdirected good, discord mixed with concord, but thereby composing an ultimate harmony. Good, in fact, is the true face of evil in so far as evil has a proper and probably necessary role in the process of the universe. It is in this sense that we can say of evil that it is divinely 'permitted', because God is not simply static Being but Becoming, Life. All life involves process, of which suffering is an inevitable concomitant. In order to become personal God himself entered into process, when he divided the light from the darkness. Being has to express itself in Becoming because it realizes itself only through opposition. Being is achieved *in* Becoming: God 'makes' himself – and suffers in consequence. Yet without the concept of a humanly suffering God, an idea, Schelling believes, common to all the spiritual religions of antiquity, the course of history would be incomprehensible.

Thus is the divine life realized and manifested in the world-process: cosmogony is theology. The divine consciousness has its beginning in the creation of the world; 'nature' is God's nature, God's 'natural' being. For it is that which is determinate in God: 'The necessity of God is what we designate as the nature of God.'[95] When, however, the 'creative Word' triumphs over the Dark Principle, Spirit emerges, in which the darkness and the light are united, both principles being subordinated to its own self-substantiation as personality. Yet even Spirit is not the cosmic process's highest achievement. The supreme place is reserved for Love, in which the being of God has its final expression and the universe attains the goal of its development. But it is man, we have to recognize, who in Schelling's system stands at the apex of creation. In him 'God first rests; in him is his main end reached'.[96] All else in the natural order is peripheral; man it is who is at the centre of God's being, since he alone, for all his finite existence, is free. Placed, though, as he is between nature and spirit he commands a power that is capable of misuse; and, sadly, he has misused it. But, as the embodiment of the divine, salvation also was in his power.

At this stage, then, of Schelling's philosophical thought God is still described in terms of a thoroughgoing immanentism, or near-pantheism, with man as deity's ultimate means of self-identity and self-articulation. As such the doctrine is altogether characteristic of romanticist feeling about the universe. In *Die Weltalter*, where the influence of Boehme and Eckhart is plain, Schelling continues its exposition, but with a greater anthropological and historical emphasis. Why he left this book unfinished it is perhaps idle to surmise, but even in its incomplete state it is of great interest as marking a turning-point in his philosophical development. For it ushers in the last, and as many now would say the most significant, phase of all his metaphysical thinking, covering the years from 1821 until 1854 and set out in lecture-courses given on repeated occasions and constantly revised. Schelling had every intention of publishing these and shaped them accordingly; but as with *Die Weltalter*, he delayed and the work never saw print in his lifetime. The success of these lectures with his audiences, since from all accounts he was a very effective speaker, was unfailing and should have given him the fullest confidence. Procrastination, for whatever reason, got the better of him, however. But it should be remembered that this new 'positive' philosophy, as he liked to call it, was of an impressive scope and amplitude and we may readily believe that in his almost obsessive envy and fear of Hegel and the Hegelians he could not contemplate offering it to the world in anything less than a fully systematic and well-rounded form. With the years also his power of concentration declined and the great project remained still uncompleted at the time of his death. Schelling's son Karl saw it through the press.

Although conceived as a whole, this *Spätphilosophie* is far from constituting a properly organized scheme. It is often repetitive and there are notable gaps in the logical design. The two main parts are the *Philosophie der Mythologie* and the *Philosophie der Offenbarung*,[97] but accompanying these are treatises which are more or less independent, such as the *Einleitung* to the *Mythologie* and an important course on 'Monotheismus' that is really central to the entire scheme. Also to be included are his Munich lectures on the history of modern philosophy. It was Schelling's aim to coordinate the 'positive' philosophy with the 'negative' of his earlier years – to create a metaphysic with, as it were, two different but mutually necessary wings. How far he succeeded in this continues to be a matter of some dispute among recent commentators.[98] The attempt to run two contrasting styles of philosophical thinking in harness may pose more problems than it solves, and I would myself say that the later philosophy is best judged on its own merits and without trying to align it with what had gone before.

The meaning of the terms 'positive' and 'negative' in the present context is not self-evident. Briefly, it may be said that whereas the latter deals with ideas, concepts and definitions – in a word, with 'essences' – the former is concerned with the actuality of being, with 'existence'. Schelling had long been clear in his mind that from ideas ideas alone can be deduced; the world of things cannot be constructed by a process of logical inference, no matter how elaborate. A supreme Idea or Ultimate Essence, that is, may very well *define* reality but is unable to *constitute* it. This, Schelling insisted, was the underlying error of Hegelianism, and Hegel's personal brilliance and fame could not conceal it. After reading the preface to the *Phenomenology of Mind* he failed to discern wherein precisely the difference between himself and his former colleague at Jena lay. Had Hegel merely formed his impression from false reports of his, Schelling's, views?[99] But from all Hegel's subsequent publications it seemed clear enough to Schelling himself that Hegelianism's standpoint was really that of the *Identitätsphiloso-phie*. What the philosopher of the Absolute Idea had all along missed was that the ideal and the actual are not identical; that, to quote Schelling's own words,

> It is two wholly different things to know *what* an existent is, *quid sit*, and to know *that* it is, *quod sit*. The former, the answer to the question as to *what* it is, provides an insight into the *nature* of the thing, or it enables me to understand the thing, to have a conception of it, or to have the *thing itself* in the conception. The latter, however, gives the insight *that* it does not provide me with the mere conception but with something extending beyond the mere conception, which is the existence.[100]

Or to put it rather more succinctly, the *negative* conditions of an entity's existence – those apart from which it could not be what it is – are to be distinguished from its *positive* conditions, or those by virtue of which the entity exists. Thus purely 'negative' or 'essentialist' philosophy will not account for the existence of the world; it deals only with possibilities, not with realities, with defining attributes, not concrete instances. The philosophy of identity presented *in idea* the unity of the universal creative Reason with the rationality that constitutes human intelligence, of the objective and the subjective, of existence and thought. It only states what, if such and such is to be the case, is 'not *not* to be thought'.[101] Hence rationalist thinking can give us only one aspect or function of philosophy; logic cannot prove existence, for what it needs is the supplementation of experience, which alone can supply the *substance* of truth.[102] The Hegelian domination was in Schelling's opinion a 'dismal episode' in the history of philosophical thought, at best serving to show only 'that it is impossible with the pure reason to reach actuality', as Kant's criticism of the ontological argument had sufficiently demonstrated.[103]

In 1840 Schelling was invited to occupy a chair at the university of Berlin, with the object, he was to understand, of 'rooting up the dragon's teeth' of Hegelianism – a commission, on royal authority, which must have given him satisfaction over and above that simply of academic preferment. Nevertheless the obnoxious doctrine continued to hold its own in the Prussian capital and Schelling's lectures were poorly attended.[104] Disappointed and disgruntled, in 1845 he gave up teaching and the last decade of his life was passed in more or less valetudinarian retirement. Against the new thrusts in religious philosophy and scholarship signified by the names of Bauer, Vatke, Strauss and Feuerbach, Schelling's speculative treatment of the themes of mythology and revelation offered no effective resistance. A title of nobility was conferred on him by the king of Prussia in 1851, but in the late summer of 1854 he died while on holiday at Ragaz in Switzerland.

To return to his Berlin lectures. Assuming his claim to be justified that the negative and positive philosophies are not merely juxtaposed but intelligibly related, how is the passage from the one to the other to be effected? As we have seen, it is not for Schelling by any means a purely logical proceeding. The central issue in positive philosophy, he holds, is that of God and fallen man, and to affirm God's existence demands a motion of the will, an act of faith. For once we leave the contemplative realm of intellect and understanding and enter that of will and personal commitment, God ceases to be just a metaphysical principle. Man does not inhabit a world only of ideas and ideals, but one of personal experience and history, in which the consequences of the fall are all-pervasive. But the self as fallen and alienated needs not only to comprehend but to be delivered from its condition. And what can accomplish this but divine action? The conclusion that God must be a personal Agent is thus irresistible. The thought of a Fichtean 'moral order' or Hegelian 'Absolute Idea' will not meet the needs of the troubled soul. God must be felt as living, creative and redeeming. Not even Kant's practical reason will serve here, for the 'faith' to which the critical philosophy purports to make room does not rise above the negative plane of thought, and for the Königsberg teacher God is scarcely more than a dialectical expedient, a bare 'postulate', not a Person. But the religious consciousness cannot be satisfied with any such abstraction. 'A person', Schelling urges, 'seeks a person'. Reason and law do not love, only personal beings can do so: 'The self, as itself a personality, desires personality; it demands a Person who is outside of the world and above the universal, and who understands – a Heart that is like unto our own.'[105] The religious consciousness, therefore, calls for a God who is purposive and responsive to human need. '*Him, him* will it have, the God who acts, in whose keeping is a Providence, him who as real himself can oppose the reality of the Fall – in short, him who is the Lord of existence, not only transmundane but supramundane.'[106] Only in such a God does the self behold the real, the supreme good. The historical fact of religion is itself evidence of man's want of God – a God, that is, who acts, whose providential purpose determines history and with whom the individual can enter into a personal relationship. It is with God in that sense alone that the positive philosophy is concerned; for what negative philosophy describes is possible not actual religion.

Hence the traditional natural theology is of no help in securing the transition from negative to positive, since it is itself confined to the negative. But this does not mean that the act of will which we call faith is without rational support. The rationality must however be grasped empirically, in the experiential evidence available to us that God is self-revealing and redemptive in human history. In other words, to show that God exists in the sense which positive philosophy demands we have only to survey the development over the ages of the religious consciousness itself. For Schelling sees the world's religions as comprising an organic whole, the various components of which are of mutual implication and whose actual historical occurrence follows – as he would believe – a pattern shaped by the dialectic of his metaphysical thinking. What in this last phase of his speculative quest Schelling offers us therefore is essentially a philosophy of religion. This explains both his choice of subjects for exposition – myth and revelation – and the order in which he expounds them as indicating the historic process of the divine self-disclosure and redeeming action.

But the fact should be emphasized that these final works of Schelling's are not empirical in the sense of attempting an objective phenomenological study of the historic development of the religious consciousness. On the contrary, Schelling is determined to retain the content of his negative philosophy, the function of which is to 'unveil the inner organism of reason'.[107] Thus we have to accept the rational deduction of God in his three 'potencies' as the first principle of philosophy. The absolute 'That' – as distinct from the 'What' – the Self-existing considered apart from all relations, is not itself God, but only the *'prius* of the Godhead'; God himself is the union of the Self-existing and the Existing. In denoting the pure 'That' of self-existence the word 'God' would be void of meaning, as beyond thought. The substance of the concept is provided only by existing reality, the 'what' of things in their total possibility, including thinking.[108] And to this metaphysical deduction the idea of the cosmic fall, and thereafter the return to God, must be added. What the lectures purport to do by following a supposedly 'empirical' method is therefore to confirm a speculative concept already fully elaborated. But this clearly suggests that what Schelling is offering us is less a philosophy *of* religion than a religious philosophy coupled with a historical commentary. The question to be asked is whether the historical component retains any empirical value when forced into a preconceived metaphysical framework. The answer is probably to be inferred from the fact that Schelling's philosophy of myth and revelation had practically no influence at all on the scientific study of the history of religion later in the nineteenth century.

It is important for an understanding of Schelling's religious philosophy to be clear on his distinction between mythology and revelation. Mythology is first in order, both logically and chronologically, but is to be thought of only as 'unfree' and 'unspiritual' religion. What this means, seemingly, is that while myths are not simply arbitrary creations of the human imagination they are not to be taken as in any proper sense a freely given disclosure of the divine. At bottom they are unconscious, although they are capable of conscious development and are themselves the outcome of a necessary process. For what they signify is a natural and spontaneous apprehension of the divine under various forms corresponding to Schelling's Dark Principle of God. With this unwitting apprehension of God his own deliberate self-revelation stands of course in complete contrast, since in revelation we have God's free impartation of himself to mankind. But both are rightly classifiable as *religion*, the mythical no less than the revealed. Indeed it may be said that in religion God comes to a second birth, the historical development of the religious consciousness in man being, as it were, a reflection of the eternal in time. Viewed thus the mythological stage represents a necessary 'moment' in the divine life itself, preparatory to the free revelation which is to come. And being free it cannot be pre-determined by mythology. In revelation God shows himself as at once infinite, personal and creative, but myths do anticipate revealed truth, as philosophical insight will readily discern.

It is clear that Schelling himself believed that the history of religion is an index of God's self-disclosure, but the problem for him was, while recognizing this, to maintain the Christian religion's uniqueness. His solution of it would appear to be that Christianity manifests in all its fullness the *inner* truth of religion and that it does this not by some implicit logic governing the evolution of the religious consciousness but by God's chosen purpose of free decision. It is this which in Schelling's view constitutes the all-important difference between mythology and revelation, the truth which religion in all its forms seeks to embody being that which is made known, whole and perfect, in Christ. By what means, though, is this distinction and evaluation to be effected? Is Schelling in fact saying that the religious consciousness is 'blind' until philosophy intervenes to interpret it to itself? This certainly was not his intention, nor did he propose to submit revealed religion to criteria of judgment outside itself. Rather did he see his philosophy as articulating a process whereby religion arrives at full *self*-comprehension. A Christian philosophy, that is, will go beyond mere recapitulation of the doctrines and principles of the Christian faith and life by serving as a reasoned elucidation of them. The former are accepted in the first instance on authority, whereas a religious philosophy, as a work of discursive thought, is 'free'. As Schelling himself puts it, 'free religion is only *mediated* through Christianity; it is not immediately *posited* by it'.[109] Basically it is the old scholastic principles of *fides quaerens intellectum*, and there is no suggestion now of an *Aufhebung* of theology by philosophy.

Schelling also has an account to offer of the actual history of Christianity. He distinguishes three main periods, beginning with a 'Petrine', the features of which are law and authority as associated with the Latin peoples and the Roman church. Its theological root is God as the ground of being and identifiable with the First Person of the Christian trinity. The second period he classifies as 'Pauline', although it is not regarded as having properly commenced until the Germanic Protestant Reformation of the sixteenth century. Its keynote is freedom. 'In Paul the principle was at hand through which the church could be freed, not from its unity but from its blind uniformity.'[110] Theologically it relates to the Son. The third period, styled the 'Johannine', is yet to be, but will be recognizable by the convergence of the preceding periods and the reconciliation of authority and freedom in an organically unified Christian community. This will prove to be the age of the Holy Spirit, with the divine love as its energizing power. History then will have reached its goal and God will be all in all.[111]

In Schelling speculative romanticism achieved its most florid expression. To find the One in the All, the infinite in the finite, was with him a passion. Consistently it was the Absolute that lay at the end of his philosophical pilgrimage – beyond the finite consciousness, beyond all empirical inquiry, including the entire range of the special sciences, and, although his thought progressed through a succession of stages, in themselves of sufficient diversity to render it well nigh impossible to speak of his 'system' as though it were a unity, the central conception persisted virtually unaltered. In early life he turned away from Christianity, only to return to it in after years, albeit slowly and tentatively. In the end he arrived at a kind of theism, indeed at a semblance of Christian trinitarianism, but it still was a curiously gnostic or theosophical and quasi-pantheistic religion which for him bore the Christian name, as the young Jakob Burckhardt was one of the first to point out. The reason could have been the presence in his mind of influences, too many and disparate, which he failed properly to assimilate and integrate. Mentally he was highly receptive, but despite his dedication to metaphysics he was without either analytical rigour or the gift for truly architectonic thinking. He could readily systematize, but seemed nonetheless incapable of achieving a firm structure of reasoning. In this he contrasts strikingly with Hegel, who soon learned to know his own mind with commanding certainty. Schelling, for all his precocity and unquestionable fertility in ideas, displayed throughout his life something of the intellectual *flâneur*, the dilettante, even the dabbler. Trained in the sciences, for which he persuaded himself he had an aptitude, his outlook was not scientific; he had over-many interests, with few of them grounded in thorough knowledge. Thus his speculations lost touch with reality, although his conviction of being able to speak on the deepest matters with vision and authority seems never to have been shaken.

It is not surprising therefore that his fame and influence rapidly waned. Already in his last years metaphysical idealism had become *vieux jeu* in Germany, and the philosophy of mythology and revelation appeared merely fanciful in the days of Strauss and Baur. Schelling founded no school – indeed he had no real disciple, if we except his influence on Catholic theology at Munich and Tübingen – and at the time of his death he was all but forgotten by his fellow-countrymen.[112] In France he had an admirer in the eclectic Victor Cousin, while features of his doctrine recur in Ravaisson and Bergson, as they do also in the Russians Solovyev and Berdyaev, and although Kierkegaard wrote disparagingly of him it could hardly be denied that Schelling's positive philosophy left its mark upon him. In Germany in the present century, however, he has again attracted interest and even some genuine esteem, as the opinions of Heidegger, Jaspers, Tillich and the Catholic Erich Przywara testify, all of whom have found in him anticipations of their own 'existentialist' themes. And it would not be unwarranted, I think, to trace Schelling's general line of thinking in Teilhard de Chardin and the 'process' philosophy of A. N. Whitehead and Charles Hartshorne.

5

German Catholic theology in the Romantic era

IN GERMANY the response of Catholic thinkers to the challenge of Enlightenment rationalism assumed a markedly different form from what it did in France. In the latter country its effect had been to produce a wave of anti-rationalism, culminating in the traditionalism of Joseph de Maistre, Louis de Bonald and Félicité de Lamennais, according to which all knowledge of truth in the religious and moral order rests on an original divine revelation transmitted from age to age in an unbroken tradition.[1] Under this doctrine human reason has no intrinsic power of reaching such truth, which can be received only by an act of faith in the nature of an intellectual assent. In Germany, on the other hand, rationalism was answered by rationalism, if of a modified kind, a 'semi-rationalism'. The veracity of the Christian religion, that is, was to be demonstrated by appeal to its rational foundations. It could then be shown that theology, as itself a science, had no interest in resisting progress in any area of knowledge and that Catholicism could retain its rightful place in modern culture unembarrassed by the charge that its teachings had no support beyond that of an authoritarian and reactionary institution. In the circumstances of the time it was a bold claim, but those who maintained it were unabashed when confronted either by the negations of sceptics or the misgivings of their ecclesiastical superiors.

By the close of the eighteenth century the views of the *philosophes* in France had to a great extent lost credit, their superficiality, their anti-metaphysical prejudice and in certain instances – Holbach, for example – their professed materialism were increasingly out of harmony with educated opinion, and *idéologues* like Destutt de Tracy were now on the defensive. Rousseau's cultivation of *sentiment* and the primitive – albeit in an idealized shape – was more to the taste of the younger generation than was the trite sophistication of their fathers' day. It is of little surprise therefore that the Catholic reaction in France did not turn to speculative philosophy for intellectual support, though the need was beginning to be felt for something better than the text-book apologetics taught in the seminaries. Hence the impact made by Lamennais's *Essai sur l'indifférence* of 1817. In Germany, however, the scene was quite different. Here the prestige of philosophy stood high indeed, despite the anti-intellectualist tradition of evangelical pietism and fideism. It is this fact, I suggest, which goes far to explain why the Catholic revival of the early nineteenth century in German Catholic academic institutions should have turned naturally for guidance and encouragement to an intellectual movement that had become the admiration of Europe. That such a revival was timely is apparent enough. In many respects the Roman Catholic church in Germany was in a debilitated condition. All but three of the Catholic universities – Freiburg, Würzburg and Münster – had been suppressed, and even these were no longer reserved for Catholic students exclusively. At a deeper level the popular rationalism had affected Catholic thinking itself, alongside the encroachments of Protestantism, against which Catholic interests frequently had difficulty in holding their own. Thus for the more venturesome among Catholic intellectuals there seemed but one recourse, at a time of widespread cultural change, in order to recover the standing and credibility of their religious principles: namely to show not only to the faithful but to the German-speaking public at large that Catholicism had a firm basis in reason and could rightly solicit the adherence of their country's forward-looking youth. There was, moreover, evidence of a mood abroad more sympathetic to Catholic ideas and practice, testified by the number and the prominence of individual conversions or re-conversions. The most signal perhaps were those of Friedrich Schlegel and his wife Dorothea – in her case from Judaism: she was the daughter of the Jewish 'enlightened' philosopher Moses Mendelssohn – Adam Müller the social philosopher, who became a Catholic in 1805, Count Friedrich zu Stolberg, author of a voluminous history of Christianity, Princess Gallitzin, founder of the Münster circle of Catholic intellectuals, Zacharias Werner – later, in Vienna, to win fame as a preacher – the jurist C. L. Haller, Johann Görres, the so-called 'Nazarene' school of painters in Rome with their leader Friedrich Overbeck, and Clemens Brentano, the poet and novelist, as well as others only a little less distinguished.[2]

The times, then, required a new enterprise in the defence and explanation of the faith. The spirit of the *Aufklärung* was far from dead and its negative attitudes had to be countered. It is an indication of the renewed confidence of believers that the energy and resolution necessary for it were not lacking, at least in certain quarters. For some of course the only proper answer to free thought was a reaffirmation of traditional orthodoxy. Of such were J. R. Rothensee (1795–1835) of Speier, a stout defender of the papacy,[3] and the Benedictine monk Maurus Hazel (1780–1842), author of *Der Katholizismus und die*

Philosophie.[4] Others, however, were prepared in some measure to adopt the standpoint of their opponents in order to meet their arguments: for example, Matthäus Fingerlos (1748–1817) at Ingolstadt, a convinced Kantian,[5] and Franz Josef Seber of Bonn and later Louvain, a disciple of Schelling.[6] But better known by far than either of these, though falling into the same category, was Georg Hermes. Born at Dreierwalde in Westphalia in 1775, Hermes studied with the Franciscans at Rhiene, his first teaching post being at the Münster *gymnasium* (1798). In 1807, after his ordination to the priesthood, he was appointed professor of dogmatics at the university there. His marked ability as a teacher made him popular with his students, particularly through his courses on philosophical introduction to theology, planned to demonstrate the inherent reasonableness of Christianity, even if his methods did not go unquestioned by his fellow-clerics, among them Clemens zu Droste-Vischerung, afterwards archbishop of Cologne but always Hermes' most vigorous critic, and J. T. Katerkamp, a church historian and a member of Princess Gallitzin's group.[7] On the strength of his rapidly growing reputation he was summoned in 1820 to the university of Bonn as its professor of dogmatic theology, having already received a doctorate from Breslau following the publication of the first volume of his *Philosophische Einleitung in die Christkatholische Theologie.*[8] It was at Bonn that he attained the summit of his influence, with a now distinctively 'Hermesian' school of disciples to rally round him; and this not only in the university itself but in Catholic seminaries as far afield as Breslau and Braunsberg.

Hermes had encountered personal difficulties in religious belief back in the days of his youth, especially from his reading of Kant and Fichte, and it was in trying to solve them that in 1794 he embarked on the systematic study of Catholic theology. Unfortunately he derived less profit from the teaching imparted at Münster than he had hoped – few of the lecturers possessed any notable competence – and his doubts were at first intensified rather than alleviated. But he did not give up, resolving to grapple with the problems of faith at their most basic level. In this respect his years at the *gymnasium* proved fruitful. The conventional type of Catholic apologetic certainly did not satisfy him, with the result that, like Descartes, he was more and more thrown back upon his own cogitations; he had, he felt, to discover for himself where the real foundations of human knowledge lay. The quest eventually succeeded. At any rate it was with the appearance of his *Untersuchungen über die innere Wahrheit des Christenthums* in 1805 that he came to be recognized as a Catholic philosopher with fresh ideas. The then archbishop of Cologne, Ferdinand von Spiegel, thought so highly of him as to nominate him to an honorary canonry as well as appointing him his examining chaplain and a member of the episcopal council.

Hermes' followers included P. J. Elvenich (1796–1886), who taught philosophy first at Bonn and subsequently at Breslau, and the theologians J. W. J. Braun, J. H. Achterfeld, editor of Hermes' posthumously published *Dogmatik*,[9] and J. B. Baltzer, afterwards professor of theology at Breslau. Another concern of his was that of raising the educational standard of the clergy, regarded by many as a pressing need. His premature death in the spring of 1831 was a loss not only to the Catholic church in Germany but to Catholic theology generally, in spite of the eventual condemnation of his views by the Vatican.

Hermes was not interested in shortening the list of what a Catholic should be expected to believe, but he insisted that a man could properly believe only what he recognized as true by the light of reason. His study of Kant had not been in vain, for what is distinctive about his theology is the method by which it is worked out. Kant's own philosophy indeed seemed to him to undermine Christian doctrine, but he was persuaded nonetheless that Kantianism could be outflanked by making use of its own procedures. Further inquiry therefore was necessary into the nature of human knowledge: truth had to be tested by subjecting it to rigorous doubt. In this respect his scepticism was deliberate, though tempered by his own experience. As he states in the preface to the *Philosophische Einleitung*:

> Throughout this work I have been scrupulous in maintaining my resolution to doubt everything for as long as possible and to accept nothing as being determinately the case until I have been able to show the absolute rational necessity of admitting such determination. On this principle I have threaded my way through a great number of doubts, something which will appear only a waste of time and effort to one who has never in fact encountered a grave doubt.[10]

And the discipline he himself pursued he imposed also on his students. It might normally be wrong, he would tell them, expressly to provoke a sense of need where none already existed, but this did not hold for those whose responsibility it would be to teach religion, especially to such as wished to grasp it intelligently. In this field ignorance was not bliss, for where one was in the position of having to help others with their doubts it was a duty first to explore the possibilities of doubt to their farthest reach.

In the second part of the *Einleitung*, where Hermes broaches questions of Catholic dogma, he states that no religion, or at least no system of theology, should be embraced unless its truth be clearly perceived. Here all religious teaching must be treated in the same way. It is not enough to accept Christianity, and Catholic Christianity in particular, merely because one has been brought up in it. God-given reason ought as a matter of conscience to be one's guide. 'We must be ready to submit to the judgments of our reason regardless of their bearing on our settled opinions or religious beliefs.'[11] Quite simply, a believer should challenge his own faith to the point where it is plain to him that to relinquish it would itself be an act contrary to reason. The hardest rationalist could not, it would seem, ask more.

Soon after Hermes' death the question was raised as to whether his doubt was methodical only, or whether it was not in fact substantial, an actual failure of faith.[12] Probably no decisive answer is possible, one way or the other. As a young man his doubts were certainly real. It is in no sense strange therefore, given his manifest sincerity and warmth of temperament, that he should, whilst earnestly striving to believe, have known the difficulty of attaining full intellectual assurance. His aim was to discover whether faith could after all rest on a secure foundation of reason. What he seems not to have considered is the eventual implication of this for the principle of an external authority, to which Catholicism is emphatically committed.

Hermes' starting-point is the nature of certitude. Absolute certitude on any matter, he thinks, is not really reached until belief in it is seen to be unavoidable, and that a residual element of doubt would destroy it. One has to feel that one's judgment corresponds in all essentials with what actually is the case.[13] A subjective and emotional assurance is insufficient; one must have confidence that one's belief can be put to the most searching test without its being in any way shaken. Only when it becomes a rational necessity does it amount to an objective certainty. But Hermes maintains that certitude has a twofold source, since he follows Kant in distinguishing between the speculative and practical reasons, which he sees indeed as virtually separate faculties. The speculative reason, whose subject-matter is logical and metaphysical, may be said to affirm a truth when it demonstrates the impossibility of holding the contrary. The practical reason operates in the field of empirical reality, especially matters of historical fact; but it does so also, and very importantly, in that of moral principles. Its demands accordingly are not as exacting as those of speculative reason, looking only to a free and voluntary adherence to truth. For here the constraint of logic is not to be expected, but rather the acknowledgment of moral obligation. The criterion of such a truth is that it should conduce to the maintenance of human dignity, because it is the practical reason which shows what is necessary for the life of man if he is to achieve his full moral worth and status ('die reine Darstellung und Erhaltung der Menschenwürde'). In the former case we are bound to *hold* something to be true (*fürwahrhalten*); in the latter only to *concede* it as true (*fürwahrnehmen*). In the sphere of the practical reason moral responsibility carries us forward when purely rational argument stops short. Speculative reason cannot demonstrate a contingent fact, since doubt about it always remains a possibility. But practical reason can adduce good grounds for accepting it on the evidence open to us. Completeness of knowledge is not necessary to justify rightness of action, the testimony of general experience being enough.

Clearly, for Hermes, the practical reason would have a vital role in apologetics, the object of which was to show both that Christianity is divinely revealed and that the Catholic religion is the one true form of it. He held that the pure reason could not yield certitude on the *facts* of revelation, but only a degree of probability, however high. More particularly, the doctrine that revelation is confirmed by miracles was obviously impossible of proof. For in the case of miracles one cannot know for certain whether an extraordinary event, even if authenticated, was divinely caused or is simply an instance of natural causation operating according to a law as yet unknown. In fact the whole history of redemption, resting as it does on contingent occurrences, lies beyond the scope of demonstration, so that the veracity of the gospels has no firmer – if no weaker – a basis than reasonable likelihood. Belief in the truths of the Christian revelation, therefore, must be seen as a moral decision, whatever objections the pure reason may raise against it. If for the practical reason, that is, the *principle* of a divine revelation is to be allowed then so too are the contents of that revelation.

This view of reason bears directly on Hermes' account of faith, which he defines as

> a state of certitude or conviction respecting the reality of something known, a state to which we are brought either by the necessary assent of the theoretical reason or from the voluntary consent of the practical reason, since apart from the 'holding as true' of the former and the 'conceding as true' of the latter there is no other way of guaranteeing truth or reality.[14]

The definition applies to faith in general, the end of all knowledge being certitude, but it applies with special relevance to theology. In this realm, although certitude is primarily of moral force, conviction must be rational as well as personal. To accept theological doctrines on the authority of another is to evince only a superficial degree of faith. Belief in God does not itself depend on the authority of God, since we have first to assure ourselves that he exists; nor does it depend on the authority of men, for how can they guarantee his existence?[15] It is no doubt frequently the case that to accept something as true is for practical purposes a matter of relying on the word of others, but to ground belief *in* authority is really, Hermes thinks, to void faith of its inner content and hence to render the existence of God, as indeed of much else, altogether questionable.[16] Faith resting on authority is not the only form of faith, nor the truest. It must in the end be taken as a response of the practical reason to the promptings of the moral consciousness.

Hermes understood well enough what he was maintaining, and was not to be put off by talk about the need for a 'humble faith'. Between such and the way of affirmation through doubt there is no essential opposition. Rational demonstration, one rather could say, is the root and condition of faith, just as faith itself is the root and condition of virtue. Is it really 'pious' faith merely to believe what one is told? And how is one article of belief to be accepted and another rejected without some reasoned justification for so doing? There is no humility in blind choice. True humility, in this regard, is to submit to what reason demands, even though sensible evidence be lacking. And it is the function of consistent doubt to show what it is that reason does demand. 'Abandonment of the self to the guidance of reason is, as touching the rights of our sensible nature, no small act of self-denial.'[17]

However, if religious belief is an end-product of natural reason what need is there for supernatural grace for the act of faith? Or if reason compels assent what virtue is there in the mind's obedience? To Hermes' critics these questions were unavoidable. Yet Hermes himself insists that the affirmations of the practical reason contain a necessary *volitional* element and are not simply a matter of logic. Further, there must be, he urged, an essential distinction drawn between a 'living' faith productive of good works, for which divine grace is requisite, and a 'dead' or passive faith which only registers assent – Newman's distinction between a real and a notional faith.[18] 'Passive faith is the necessary outcome of the human understanding's purely natural constitution, and in this respect there can be no question of the need of an actual interior grace.' As such it gives rise to nothing beyond itself and is thus an inert faith and not an active one. But, as Hermes points out, if a purely intellectual assent is no more than *recognition* of its object it still leaves room for the will freely to cleave to that object. It is in this response that faith comes alive.[19]

It seems, then, that Hermes' rationalism is a good deal less uncompromising than might at first appear. The element of mystery in the actual substance of faith he never denied, and he scouted any attempt to bring Christianity 'within the limits of reason alone'. The sources of Catholic theology (*Erkenntnisprinzipen*) are scripture, tradition and the church's *magisterium*, and although none of these is established by purely rational means reason does accept them as the channels through which divine truth is communicated. In other words, although the principle of revelation is one which reason can readily accept, the content of revelation stands *above* reason – no slight restriction, surely, of the function which reason exercises in the life of faith. Hermes considered that some of the early Fathers as well as the mediaeval scholastics had gone too far in attempting to rationalize dogma.

The scope of theology Hermes defines as 'the body of doctrines which concern first God, and then the relation of the world, and especially of mankind, to God'.[20] In Catholic theology this knowledge centres on God's self-revelation in Jesus Christ, a revelation of which the church is the custodian. Theology is not therefore simply a deductive science stemming from a few basic principles; its subject-matter is *positive* in the sense of being historically conditioned, and to discover what it is we have no alternative but to consult the historic sources. The weakness of the scholastic systems – their excessively speculative character – lay precisely in their inattention to history. Philosophical procedures have in fact no business at all with theology except to examine the bases of the faith, to assemble its doctrines in due order and to defend them against attack. Beyond this the intrusion of philosophy is unwarranted and an abuse of its methods.[21] On the question of the relations of faith and reason generally, Hermes is satisfied that no contradiction can arise between truths divinely revealed and those of the natural understanding.

But if Hermes' views amount only to a semi-rationalism he holds nonetheless that where reason is operative it is effective in its own right. In the final resort it falls to it to judge whether any particular dogma of faith is actually to be found in the historic sources of faith, and to apply the way of methodical doubt consistently to the entire scheme of dogma.

At the time of his death Hermes was highly esteemed and his influence in academic circles was at its height. But his teaching was meeting with growing opposition, not least from his Bonn colleague Karl Josef Windischmann (1775–1839), whose own ideas seem to have been largely inspired by the idealists and especially Schelling.[22] All the same, Hermes' followers were determined to defend his doctrines and for this purpose founded a review, the *Zeitschrift für Philosophie und katholische Theologie*, which was to continue publication for some twenty years (1832–52). This in itself stimulated further controversy, to be sharpened by the appearance of Hermes' *Dogmatik* in 1834. A veritable warfare of articles and pamphlets ensued, the Hermesians urging their master's opinions more and more inflexibly, even though a frequent objection on their part was that while the views attributed to him by his critics were certainly erroneous he himself never taught them. But from the traditionalist point of view, as well as from Windischmann's 'fideist' angle, the basic fault with Hermes' teaching was that in purporting to be a 'philosophical introduction' to theology it rendered faith dependent on a preliminary rational assent. The debate, often acrimonious, reached a stage where authority was almost bound to intervene. In 1833 Pope Gregory XVI, at the instance of certain of the German Catholic bishops, set up a commission under Cardinal Raisbach, prefect of propaganda, and the Jesuit theologian Carlo Perrone, to examine the Hermesian teaching and report on it. On 26 September 1835 the papal brief *Dum acerbissimas* condemned Hermes' doctrines and placed both parts of the *Philosophische Einleitung* and the *Dogmatik* on the Index. (The remaining volumes received this distinction in 1836.) Meanwhile Hermes' patron Spiegel had died, to be succeeded at Cologne by the Bonn theologian's old adversary Droste-Vischerung, who at once forbad students at both Bonn and Cologne from attending lecture-courses in which Hermesian ideas were expounded. A lengthy statement by Hermes' disciples Elvenich and J. W. J. Braun, *Meletemata theologica*, aimed at vindicating their leader's orthodoxy, was despatched to Rome, but its publication there was refused. Finally, in July 1847, Pius IX confirmed his predecessor's verdict as a side-blow against those who had read his own earlier encyclical *Qui pluribus* (9 November 1846), directed against fideism, as in some way countenancing rationalist opinions. Pio Nono's actions, however, brought Hermesianism as a theological movement virtually to an end, although definitive judgment was to be pronounced by the 1870 Vatican Council in its Constitution *De fide*.

Achterfeld, one of Hermes' most faithful adherents and the last of them, died in 1877. But the demise of Hermesianism long preceded his. This was in the main brought about by the energetic action of the church authorities; but not wholly so. A profounder reason lay in its being out of touch with the times, of looking too much like an eighteenth-century survival at odds with the prevailing intellectual tendencies of the post-revolutionary age. Its concern in any case was only with the preconditions of faith, not with its content, of which it offered no new synthesis or constructive interpretation. In effect Hermes simply fell back upon a positivism of revelation, even though the conditions on which revealed truth as such is to be accepted had first to be tested by rational criteria. It failed therefore to satisfy the traditionalists inasmuch as it seemed to preclude the need of supernatural grace in the act of faith, as it failed also to inspire those who looked for a complete re-appraisement of the received theology in a more humanistic light. Hermesianism thus collapsed between two stools.

Nevertheless Catholic rationalism in Germany was not entirely extinct, even after the teachings of Hermes himself had ceased to have influence. This is evident from the writings of Anton Günther, who likewise assumed the task of defending the faith by appeal to reason whilst at the same time refuting the arguments of his rationalist critics. But, whereas Hermes' object had been to meet Kantianism on Kant's own ground, Günther's rather was the pantheistic tendencies of the contemporary idealist philosophy, in particular Hegelianism. The real difference between them was, however, that while the one had tried to secure faith upon a *basis* of reason the other sought to transform it into a fully rational *structure*.

The son of devoutly Catholic parents in poor circumstances, Anton Günther was born at Lindenau in Bohemia on 17 November 1783. Educated at the *gymnasia* at Haide and Leitmeritz and at the university of Prague, he developed an interest in philosophical studies – Herder, Kant, Fichte – which for a time shook his faith. But when in 1811 he moved to Vienna as tutor in the household of Prince Bretzenheim he came under the influence of the saintly Clement Maria Hofbauer,[23] through whose personal guidance he gave up the study of law, which he had intended to pursue professionally, and concentrated his mind on theology. Gradually his belief in Catholic Christianity revived and he started to train for the priesthood, to which he was ordained in 1820. Two years later he entered the Jesuit novitiate, but, soon realizing that he had no vocation to a life in the Society, he settled down as a secular priest to the bookish pursuits of a private scholar. These engrossed him until the end of his life, forty years on, although he gave some of his time both to private teaching and pastoral counselling and to the duties of a government censor of books. Over the years he received a number of invitations to take up professorships at universities in Germany, but he declined them all, hoping perhaps for the offer of such a post at Vienna, though this never came his way. He made a considerable name for himself as a writer, even though some of his books, under cryptic titles, were couched in a style of disconcerting opacity, while in none of them do his views receive systematic exposition. Although his influence spread abroad, not least through the teaching of disciples holding academic appointments, he increasingly met with criticism, especially on the part of the Jesuits and Redemptorists, with the result that his orthodoxy came under suspicion. Friends of his spoke up for him at Rome, but without preventing nine of his published works being consigned to the Index in 1857. He himself formally accepted the prohibition a few weeks later, but unwillingly and with some bitterness of heart.[24] He died in 1863.

Günther's success as an author was remarkable, however. *Privatgelehrter* though he was, he won for himself acclaim among German-speaking Catholic intellectuals as a man of obvious talent and distinctiveness of view. Like Hermes he set out to rebut anti-Christian rationalism by bringing Christian apologetics up to date, but he also entertained the further aim of infusing Catholic theology itself with new life. What was needed was a fresh style of Christian philosophy, capable of making theology sufficiently scientific to impress even unbelievers. If the old faith were to be preserved for the future it must come to terms with modern needs and speak with a contemporary voice. The support which Günther enlisted for his effort was notable for its fervour and the appeal it made to men like the historians Görres and Döllinger and even to Hermes' former opponent, the philosopher Windischmann.

But if reason was to be effectively employed in the defence of nineteenth-century religion the mediaeval scholastic use of it as still adopted in the seminaries – and in a debased form at that – would not do. Its methods and its terminology were antiquated. The old-fashioned natural theology, with its logical 'proofs' of divine existence, was no longer plausible. What was wanted was a philosophy embodying the modern spirit and utilizing modern approaches, and although it was Günther's professed intent to counter monistic idealism he was himself not a little affected by the idealist standpoint and outlook. What he envisaged was a far-reaching 'Christian philosophy' deriving from a unitary principle. But in order to avoid any suggestion of pantheism Günther resorts to a virtual dualism involving an antithesis of spirit and matter, soul and body. From this position he believes that the whole content of the Christian revelation can be shown to be not only self-consistent but necessary. This must mean that Christian doctrine harbours no 'mysteries', not even the dogmas of the trinity and the incarnation, which he believes are fully open to rational comprehension. His confidence springs from the assurance that the knowledge of God is an intelligible whole founded on a double revelation, first in creation and then in redemption.

The part of faith in Günther's philosophical theology is in recognizing the *fact* of revealed truths, as distinct from what reason perceives as their *necessity*. More specifically, the actual truths which Christianity teaches as revealed impose themselves upon the intelligence by reason, although the Christian religion itself issues from a historical event, and a historical event cannot as such be a rational necessity. The gospel has therefore to be accepted by an act of faith. Günther thus concedes that the necessary truth of Christian doctrine falls short of the total commitment which belief properly exacts, but what he does not very readily allow is the traditional distinction between truths accessible to reason and those that are not, i.e. truths known only by supernatural means. In so far as he leaves room for the latter at all it is only reluctantly and partially; they are, he says, 'relatively' supernatural, since on his principles no genuinely religious doctrine can really lie beyond reason. Günther is awake to a difficulty here, but tries to surmount it by enlarging the scope of revelation to cover not simply the original communication of truth but the entire work of redemption through Christ, which he designates a 'second creation' as counterpart and supplement to the first. The connection between the two has nothing fortuitous about it and the one follows logically from the other. The reason he adduces for this is that a primal revelation, in the form of a disclosure of specific truths about man, the world and God, was necessary if the first man, Adam, were to be brought to fully human self-consciousness. And this knowledge should have sufficed for Adam's posterity also, since the truths of the second revelation could have been inferred by them from those already in their possession. This they failed to do because of the sin into which Adam had wittingly betrayed himself. Hence the necessity for the second revelation, given by Christ; a contingent necessity, however, not an absolute one. Absoluteness belongs, in all strictness, only to the 'natural' truth of the primal revelation; that pertaining to salvation was conditional on the circumstances in which men found themselves. By a route of his own, therefore, Günther arrives at a quasi-deistic account of Christianity as in all essentials 'as old as the Creation'. All that man requires additional to his natural knowledge is a certain supplementation of truth relative to his actual state. This second revelation, accordingly, is intelligible only in the light of the first. Knowledge precedes faith, the latter serving as a temporary crutch, so to say, to enable the believer eventually to stand upright on his own two intellectual feet.

The faith is, then, rational through and through. Those who are unable to perceive its logical coherence will continue simply to 'believe'; but such as are capable of philosophical comprehension will arrive at knowledge. This scheme of a completely rational theology Günther sets out in his *Vorschule zur spekulativen Theologie des positiven Christenthums* (1828–9). On the strength of it he claims that it is impossible to hold up the doctrines of the Catholic church to any reasonable doubt.

Günther's dualism arises from the theory of knowledge from which he starts. Consciousness of one's *self* as a real being is his basic certitude. This however is not an immediate condition but is attained through the operation of the ego's faculties, namely its 'receptivity' and its 'spontaneity', or, in other words, through the understanding and the will, of both of which it is the foundation and explanation. By a process of deduction one reaches the concept of spirit (*Geist*) and thereafter that of nature – of a higher realm and a lower, the two being in fact antithetic. Human nature thus is a synthesis of two entities qualitatively distinct. From this ground Günther, as a rationalist, boldly attempts a conceptual reconstruction of the entire order of being, natural and supernatural. The existence of God is a matter of rational certainty. But Günther is not content with a re-stated natural theology, for the natural order is itself a reflection, as it were, of the relation of the divine Persons described by the 'revealed' doctrine of the trinity. Here Günther recognizes three 'egos', characterized in Hegelian fashion as thesis, antithesis and synthesis, or as absolute subject, absolute object, and absolute subject–object. Theologically these represent, in turn, the contemplating subject of the Father, the contemplated object of the Son, and the unity of contemplator and contemplated as the Holy Spirit. Moreover, since to create is an inherent necessity of the divine essence – creation, rightly speaking, is not 'free'– the consequence is that the trinitarian pattern is reproduced in the universe, which consists exclusively of spirit (thesis/subject), nature (antithesis/object) and man (synthesis/subject–object). So although its form is unitary – there is only one created world – its essential reality is threefold. In this respect the universe is a necessary though somewhat paradoxical contrast, or contraposition, with the divine being, in which there are three egos but a single substance.

Similarly, in Günther's anthropology we find pointers to a fresh understanding of the mystery of the incarnation. Human nature he sees as, again, composed of three elements: body, *psyche* or soul (*Seele*), and spirit (*Geist*), the second of which, like the first, is a product of nature and not a direct divine creation. Yet the soul is the seat not only of the imagination and memory but of the concept (*Begriff*)-forming intelligence also. Nevertheless it is the spirit alone that has the capacity to form ideas (*Ideen*), the latter being the means by which we arrive at the inner reality of things as distinct from their merely phenomenal representation. But between spirit and psyche there exists a 'hypostatic union', with a corresponding *communicatio idiomatum* ('communication of the idioms', to use patristic language); between, that is, the imagination, memory and intelligence, which pertain to the psyche, and the reason and will, which pertain to the spirit. The constitution of man's own nature, therefore, enables him to grasp the intrinsic rationality of the divine–human duality in Christ, where the human 'substance' is subordinated to and ordered by the divine substance of the Word.

Günther's religious philosophy is a thoroughgoing attempt to apply the Anselmic maxim *fides quaerens intellectum* to a point where the traditional distinction between natural and supernatural truth becomes blurred, or even, as his critics complained, disappears alto-gether, leaving only a unified 'divine science' wholly at command of the rational understanding. Yet it must in all fairness be said that Günther never held that such understanding could in practice be complete, realizing that even though reason may comprehend the 'why' of the mysteries of the faith it could not reach the 'how'. So far, however, he would have agreed that reason has unrestricted control. It follows also, given the scientific character of theology, that the role of speculative thought in the *formulation* of the church's belief is plenary; which means that dogma is to be seen as continuously developing in depend-ence on the actual state of human knowledge. Hence no particular formulary can have more than a relative permanence. It may be of service, and even necessary, for a time, but it is not immutable. Sooner or later it will have to be reconsidered – a view perhaps foreshadowing the Catholic Modernism of a later generation.

2

Rationalism, if in a modified form, was one aspect of the Catholic revival of the Romantic period in Germany, but it was less character-istic of the tendencies of the age than were the opinions of some other teachers and writers, even though the doctrines of Hermes and Günther be judged – as I believe they should – as less a throw-back to the ideas and ideals of the *Aufklärung* than an attempt to turn these to advantage in a new apologetic more in tune with current thinking. We now, however, must take a look at a different type of Catholic theological romanticism, one which was at times mystical and even theosophist in sentiment and deeply imbued with the sense of tradition and of the continuity of past and present, while also seeing in change and development a sign of vitality.

A centre of such romanticist thought was the newly established university of Munich, where Catholic scholars had been appointed to the principal chairs, although Schelling taught there as well, attracting large audiences by the sheer virtuosity of his lectures. One of his colleagues was Franz von Baader (1765–1841), likewise a striking personality and reputedly the most brilliant talker of his day – a sort of German Coleridge, one imagines, even if as a writer he was a good deal less illuminating. All who came in contact with him saw him as something of a prophet, with an ability to bring to Catholic doctrine the same rejuvenating vision that Schleiermacher and others had given to Protestantism and of putting anti-Christian rationalism out of countenance.[25] A *Muenchener* himself and the son of a distinguished physician, he studied medicine and general science at Ingolstadt and

Vienna. Later he turned to mining engineering, receiving his training at Freiburg-im-Breisgau but paying also a four-year visit to Britain (1792–6), where he acquired valuable practical experience. Incidentally, while here his concern was aroused by the social problems which, as he perceived for himself, the industrial revolution was already beginning to create. Returning to Bavaria he took up a career in the state department of mines, but a growing taste for philosophical questions – in England he had had an opportunity to study Adam Smith and Hume – led him by degrees into more abstract regions of reflection, and in 1826 he was appointed to the chair of philosophy and speculative theology at Munich. For by now the trend of his thinking had taken a theosophical direction, encouraged by his reading of Eckhart, Böhme and Saint-Martin. Christianity, he had come to believe, needed to be understood at a deeper level than was usually the case, the 'legitimate organs' of Catholic teaching having, he said, 'lost the key' thereto. The same disposition of mind precluded for him any affinity with the neo-rationalism of the Hermesian school.

Baader's philosophical ideas were first expounded in a work entitled *Fermenta cognitionis*,[26] and later in *Vorlesungen über spekulative Dogmatik*.[27] Aphoristic, not to say delphic, in expression, his views are frequently both cloudy and fanciful: August Wilhelm Schlegel dubbed him 'Boehmius redivivus', and a French commentator has described his doctrine, with perhaps more wit than justice, as 'a theosophical stew with Catholic sauce'.[28] Yet he caught the mood of the day as known to many of his Catholic contemporaries and his publications enjoyed a wide readership, even though the clerical world looked at him askance. In his social philosophy he was highly critical of liberal economic and political theorizing, but at the same time he had no liking for revolutionary ideas aimed at radical change of the existing social order. He believed in authority, hierarchy and status, and with Joseph de Maistre may be in some respects accounted a forerunner of modern fascism. He was one of the first to entertain the notion of the corporative state rendered familiar in twentieth-century political history.

But Baader's real interest for us today lies in his ecumenicism, for the reconciliation of divided Christendom had become for him a dream; a dream, though, for the realization of which he devised some novel schemes. One of these he set out in a pamphlet of 1815, which is reported to have caught the attention of Alexander I of Russia and actually suggested to him the idea of the Holy Alliance. At any rate Baader addressed his proposals alike to the Orthodox tsar, the Catholic Austrian emperor and the Protestant king of Prussia. His contention was that if there was to be lasting peace in Europe it would finally come about through religious unity. But religious unity would never be secured by the mere capitulation of the non-Catholic bodies to the Roman obedience. Rather would the main branches of the Christian church have to coalesce, each learning something from the others while contributing from its own tradition to a common inheritance, which one day he hoped would be given a supra-denominational form. This suggestion so impressed the tsar that Prince Gallitzin, procurator-general of the Holy Synod of the Russian Orthodox church and – after 1817 – minister of cults and education in the Russian government, asked Baader to organize an inter-denominational German group to visit Russia, he himself being invited to report regularly on the religious situation in Germany. Baader even drew up a plan for the founding of an inter-denominational academy at St Petersburg, the functions of which would include not only the bringing together of Christians of differing ecclesiastical allegiances but of promoting a deeper under-standing of the task of the churches in the altered social and cultural situation of the modern world. Catholic though he was he seems to have believed that Orthodoxy had a special potentiality and mission in this regard, having not been troubled by either the Protestant Reforma-tion or the rationalist Enlightenment. Unfortunately the St Petersburg scheme came to nothing. For reasons that are none too clear, a journey he was to have made to the Russian capital was interrupted at the frontier town of Memel, whence, after a delay of seven months, he was obliged to return to Munich. Prince Gallitzin had refused to receive him, probably on instructions from the tsar, who by this time (1822) had been advised by Metternich of the possibly subversive character of the latitudinarian pietist brotherhoods with whom in certain respects Baader was in sympathy. It is very likely too that reactionary elements in the Russian church had become suspicious of Baader's intents, whilst his Catholic critics back in Munich had their own doubts about his somewhat eccentric religious viewpoint and lack of authentic Catholic 'tone'. In the perspective of our own time he appears to have been a man of remarkable vision and breadth of outlook.

If Baader was a romanticist of large mind and generous disposition he also was impulsive and idiosyncratic, and his influence in the end was limited. However, a younger colleague of his at Munich occupying the chair of history was a man who might fairly be claimed to have been the outstanding figure of the whole nineteenth-century German Catholic revival – Johann Josef Görres (1776–1818). An untiring publicist, a most able teacher and a self-taught polymath, he is in some degree comparable with Leibniz in the range of his interests and erudition. Görres' career covers three phases, the first being that of his youthful dedication to the political and humanitarian ideals of the French Revolution, accompanied by a falling-away from the religion in which he had been nurtured. The period ended in disillusionment after a stay in Paris of some months from 1799 to 1800. He did not indeed abandon his hopes for mankind's ultimate freedom, but he was driven to feel, by what he saw as the Revolution's essential failure, that as yet it lacked maturity for so great a responsibility. In his second phase, lasting from the beginning of the new century until about 1819, he settled down to married life and academic pursuits, teaching natural science at the Coblenz *gymnasium* and from 1806 onwards history at the university of Heidelberg. By then German folklore had become his chosen field of research, signalized by the publication in 1807 of his *Teutschen Volksbücher*, although he was soon to extend his perspective to include mythology generally but especially oriental, his *Mythengeschichte der asiatischen Welt*, in two volumes, appearing at Heidelberg in 1810.[29] Yet his political concern was unabated, and in 1814 he founded a journal, the *Rheinische Merkur*, which, although it ran for only two years, at once established itself as the leading political periodical in Germany. Much of its content was the work of Görres' own hand and all of it reflected his inspiration, notably in its opposition of the growing force of reactionary opinion after the defeat of Napoleon. The publication of *Teutschland und die Revolution*[30] would have resulted in his arrest had he not fled to Strassburg, where he was free to continue his activities as a political journalist. But by this time his main interest had again shifted and he now identified himself openly with the cause of the Catholic religion and the Catholic church. An indication of this was his eager collaboration with Andreas Räss, a professor of dogmatics at Mainz, and Nikolaus von Weis, later bishop of Speier, in the review *Der Katholik*, which they had just launched at Strassburg.

In 1827 came the summons to a chair at the new university of Munich, a situation in which Görres' avocations became yet more varied. A redoubtable polemist ever on guard to defend the church's rights, he nevertheless shared something of Baader's ecumenical enthusiasm and was on good terms with the Protestants in this predominantly Catholic city and university. His house also was a meeting-place for some of the most cultivated minds in Bavaria, including Döllinger, Clemens Brentano, Johann Adam Möhler and Johann Michael Sailer, who in 1829 became bishop of Regensburg. In 1828 Görres' circle brought out the review *Eos*, which ran until 1832 when further issues were indefinitely suspended on government order. In the years that followed, Görres' efforts as a scholar were chiefly expended on a grandiose work on Christian mysticism. Otherwise his time was taken up with ecclesiastical affairs in the Rhineland, and in particular the Cologne controversy involving the archbishop, Droste-

Vischerung, who for a time (1837) was actually imprisoned by the Prussian authorities, an event which drew from Görres, under the title *Athanasius*, his best-known and most effective polemical writing championing the archbishop's cause in the vexed dispute over mixed marriages.[31] In the same year he lent his support to another controversial journal, the *Historische-politische Blätter*. He also defended Bishop Arnoldi of Trier when in 1844 the latter put on display in the cathedral a famous relic, the Holy Coat – allegedly the seamless robe of Christ – and was a good deal criticized for doing so.

Görres, it has to be admitted, was not in any true meaning of the term a scientific scholar, and his *Christliche Mystik*, a compost of history and legend, is now forgotten. Rather did he bring to historical studies the imaginative fervour of the early romanticists. But his zeal for justice and the frequent pungency of his literary style well qualified him as a political disputant.[32] Yet his ecclesiastical standing was not entirely unambiguous, since both ultramontanes and – later – the Old Catholics claimed him as their man. It would be fairer to see him as representing neither, but as holding a moderate, open-minded type of religion such as, on the whole, has characterized German Catholicism ever since his day. A society, the 'Görresgesellschaft zum Pflege der Wissenschaft des katholischen Deutschland', was founded at Coblenz in his honour by a group of German scholars and publicists in January 1876 to mark the centenary of his birth. Its aim was to promote Catholic historical scholarship, and not least to provide financial help for students. In addition it has aided the publication of the *Historisches Jahrbuch* (1880) and the *Philosophisches Jahrbuch* (1888), though probably the undertaking that has placed the world of historical scholarship most in its debt was its publication of the documents of the Council of Trent.[33]

3

However, it was among the members of the Catholic faculty of the university of Tübingen that the romanticist strain in German Catholicism attained its fullest and most characteristic expression and produced the scholarly achievements which carried the faculty's reputation beyond Germany, the two men who especially distinguished it being Drey and Möhler. The approach to the theological study favoured by both was the genetic, but not exclusively so. Although Catholic theology was very much a historical phenomenon, the real value of the historical perspective lay in the possibilities it offered for a fresh conspectus of the dogmatic and systematic fields. Moreover theology was to be justified by evidence of its relevance to life, and especially, it was felt, to contemporary cultural life. Thus the theologian's concern had to be existential – to use a modern word – and in this respect demanded a wider comprehension of the nature of apologetics. The spirit in which the Tübingen theologians pursued their objective was determined more by the ethos of Romantic idealism than by the traditional scholasticism, for which they had little esteem. They could with some justice indeed be described as the Catholic counterparts of the idealist tendency in German Protestantism. What they sought was, in a sense, a simplification of the Catholic dogmatic inheritance by ordering it according to its informing 'ideas', as these could be identified in the light of historical study. In its earlier phase the Tübingen school sounded a note typical of the Romantic movement in its tendency to an imaginative and somewhat sentimentally optimistic mysticism; but gradually this gave way to a more exact and specific notion of what theological *Wissenschaft* must involve, along with suggestions for practical reform.[34]

Johann Sebastian Drey can be regarded as the school's founder. Of Swabian peasant stock – his father was a shepherd – he was born at Killingen, near Ellwangen, in 1777. His theological studies were begun at Ausgburg, where he already showed considerable intellectual promise, and continued at the seminary at Pfaffenhausen until his ordination to the priesthood in 1801. After first serving in his home parish – his spare time was spent reading Kant, Fichte and Schelling – he taught at the Catholic *gymnasium* at Rottweil for a few years. In 1812 he was made professor of apologetics, dogmatics and 'theological encyclopaedia' at Ellwangen university, a new foundation. But with that institution's suppression five years later and the transference of its Catholic faculty to Tübingen his career centred on the famous Swabian seat of learning until his retirement in 1846. Only two years after his arrival at Tübingen he and three of his academic *confrères* brought out the first number of a periodical, the long-since famous *Tübinger Theologische Quartalschrift*, the intended purpose of which was to reconcile Catholic doctrine with modern knowledge.[35] In 1823 the Württemberg government nominated him for the see of Rottenburg, but Rome, for whatever reason, declined to give its approval. By way of compensation he was promised a prebendal stall in the cathedral, but this preferment too was abortive, and in 1838 ill-health obliged him to give up some of his academic teaching. He was publicly honoured by the king of Württemberg on his retirement, though his last years saw no slackening of his exertions as a scholar. His death in 1853 was sudden.

Drey's life-long aim was to work for the renewal of Catholic theological study. This first became apparent in an article of 1812, a plea for a thoroughgoing revision of theological science based on the view that theology is an organic unity, Drey's guiding principle being the romanticist idea of historical continuity.[36] Much of the argument was critical, directed against not only *Aufklärung* rationalism but the whole course of post-mediaeval theological development, and calling for a return to the mediaeval sources of scholasticism in order that church doctrine might once again draw inspiration from its golden age. Mediaeval theology had thrived because it was integrated with the Christian life, the wholeness of which it sought to express. In the middle ages Christian faith and piety had penetrated civilization in all areas because Catholicism then had been a religion of 'sentiment' (*Gemüth*) and not simply one of 'reason' (*Verstand*).[37] The true spirit of Catholicism Drey claimed was mystical, seeing the finite always in the context of the divine infinity and eternity. Protestantism's error had been to cast aside tradition and to base all authority on the Bible subjectively interpreted. At the same time Catholic teaching had tended to degenerate into an arid schematism in which thought was divorced from experience. Both Catholicism and Protestantism failed to appreciate the organic nature of the Christian religion as history reveals it.

The general tenor of Drey's thinking over the ensuing five years is recorded in his journal, 'Mein Tagebuch über philosophische, theologische und historische Gegenstände' (1812–17), in which the influence of Schelling is especially discernible. In 1819 he gave further publicity to his views in a pamphlet described as a *Kurze Einleitung in das Studium des Theologie*, in which his indebtedness to Schleiermacher's *Kurze Darstellung des theologischen Studiums* of 1810 is obvious.[38] In this he contends that Catholic theologians must equip themselves with a good general culture if they are to fulfil their vocation. Theological study derives a great part of its meaning and relevance from its historical background, which needs to be investigated with all available resources, including ancient philology, *Religionsgeschichte* and the history of philosophy. In other words, human knowledge constitutes a unity, and theological learning, to be properly deployed, must assume an intelligible place within it. Arbitrariness (*Zufälligkeit*) is to be shunned and the method adopted seen to be systematic, although system itself is very much more than a 'logical' stringing together of propositions. The key-word is 'organic',[39] the theologian's responsibility being to demonstrate the 'wholeness' of Christianity – especially by comparison with other religious systems – and therewith its proper nature or 'Idea'. In sum, historical theology will explain what Christianity is in the 'givenness' of its historical positivity, while systematic theology will coordinate its several elements by relating them to this central Idea, so displaying their natural coherence.[40] In this way it becomes possible to make a just differentiation between the essential and perdurable and the merely peripheral and transient, and point out a middle course between a reductive rationalism and crass conservatism.[41]

The first article in the *Quartalschrift*, entitled 'Vom Geist und Wesen des Katholizismus' ('On the Spirit and Essence of Catholicism'), was unsigned, but it is evidently from Drey's pen and is indicative of the whole drift of the Tübingen Catholic religious philosophy for the years to come. Divine revelation, as the author sees it, is embodied in the historic fact of the Christian religion, itself to be regarded as in process of development, continuity being sustained by the persistence through time of the gospel's essential nature. That nature is authentically realized, however, only in Catholicism, which, unlike the non-Catholic confessions, preserves contact through an unbroken tradition with the faith and life of the primitive church. But tradition is not a fixed and unchanging quantum; it is a complex thing evolving through the ages analogously to the individual's persisting sense of self-identity. For as a man is intuitively aware of his own existence as a person, so the Catholic inheritance continuously recognizes itself in the successive stages of its historic life. And like a seed divinely implanted in the soil of humanity it gradually manifests its inherent potentialities.[42] The continuity of tradition guarantees the survival of the original truth of revelation against the erosions of heresy, the hall-mark of which is the partiality and subjectivism which seize upon one aspect or component of the tradition and stress it in isolation from the self-cohesive whole to which it owes its life. That Catholic tradition maintains itself through all the vicissitudes to which it is exposed is the proof of its intrinsic vitality. For Catholicism alone can reconcile speculation and criticism with piety and devotion, and in its struggle with heresy reaches a deeper understanding of its own mission and witness.[43]

In this Drey's thought follows the current Romantic line of approximating the life of society to that of the individual. He likens the church to a personal self-consciousness and applies to its historic survival the biological test of the satisfaction of need. Catholicism is vindicated, that is, by its unique adaptability, and in particular its capacity to adjust reason to faith and love to obedience. Above all, through its liturgy and sacramental system it meets the human desire for the presentation of mystery in visible shape and in ways that signify the ultimate union of God and man.[44] The subjectivity necessary to the religious life is then balanced by the objectivity of the religious institution, whose interior unity in the Spirit has its exterior focus in the papal supremacy.[45]

The *Kurze Einleitung* in outlining Drey's plan of theological study again resorts to history. The Catholic religion, it repeats, is a living entity originating in the gospel of Jesus Christ, the sources of its dogma being scripture and tradition. Catholicism's organic character is re-emphasized: behind the church's faith and life as the historian observes them stands a single cohesive principle, apart from which there is only a heterogeneous collection of empirical facts – indication enough that theology is not simply historical and that it has a necessary relation with philosophy. A scientific theology, that is, is seen to turn upon a necessary and fundamental Idea, from which its other doctrines are dialectically deducible. The role of reason in systematizing the faith is of first importance therefore, and Drey is insistent upon it. The basic Idea, however, is not some abstract *a priori* but a datum of revelation: namely, the Kingdom of God. The Catholic church may appear rigid and unbending, but in fact she is infinitely supple, ever aware of the varying necessities of time and circumstances. So far indeed is she from constraining her members, it is only in her bosom that they attain true spiritual freedom.[46]

As touching method, then, Drey no less than Hermes and Günther is convinced that the internal coherence of dogma is what ensures its logical strength and its ability to meet criticism from without.

But Christianity is not simply a system of doctrine; as a historical phenomenon it is nothing other than 'God's eternal design manifesting itself in time'. The corollary of this is that dogmas are not so many discrete truths, each to be accepted on its own account, but rather the interdependent components of a unified whole none of which is intelligible apart from the vital relationship in which it stands to all the rest. This also is why doctrine cannot be understood in detachment from its complex matrix in the institutional unity of the church. For the spiritual bond, which is unseen, has its effectual medium of expression in the visible, historically conditioned organization wherein the development always inseparable from a temporal reality assumes its necessary and inevitable part.

Drey's research in the field of patristics we may pass over.[47] Unfortunately he published no comprehensive work on dogmatics and the outstanding product of his maturity is his three-volume *Apologetik*, in which he expounds his philosophy of revelation at length.[48] In his view apologetics should no longer be relegated to a merely ancillary place in theological science; the defence of Christianity and its teachings is an obligation which in the modern world has become more and more pressing. It has to be looked at as a discipline in its own right, with its proper ways of approach and procedure. He confesses in the preface that at the time of his first *Quartalschrift* article, when he was to some extent under the influence of Schleiermacher, apologetics and religious philosophy seemed to him one and the same thing, but that he since had changed his mind and he now believed that it is the object of the former to demonstrate Christianity's divine origin. The task of apologetics, it may be said, is that of providing theology with a philosophy of *revelation* – a justification of the Christian religion as viewed in the course and process of historical development, though what has also to be explained is the concept of revelation *per se*, and the manner in which Catholicism affords a concrete demonstration of it. Drey moreover draws largely on the history of religions generally for the working-out of his idea: only so can Christianity be given its appropriate context and a sound evaluation of it carried through. In this perspective it stands out as *par excellence* the religion of salvation; and as God alone can save mankind from sin and sin's consequences the idea of an actual Saviour appears necessary. Hence Christianity's origin in the incarnation, the miraculous event of God becoming man in Christ. Besides, since Christianity is a historic fact, and since by virtue of the incarnation God dwells in humanity, the religion of salvation which he imparted to mankind must take the form of an abiding historical institution, the Catholic church. To work out a satisfactory doctrine of the church is for the theologian, therefore, a main responsibility. This in fact is the subject to which the final volume of the *Apologetik* is assigned.

Drey's influence on nineteenth-century German Catholic thought was far-reaching, from both his writings and his personal teaching. Yielding in his early days to the appeal of Enlightenment rationalism, he was able by degrees to free himself from it under the inspiration of romanticism and idealism. With the example before his eyes of a re-invigorated Protestantism, he was convinced of the need for a like renewal of the spirit of Catholic theology, and was hopeful that this could be brought about by the assimilation of ideas already proving fertile in the realms of philosophy and literature. By contrast with the conventional seminary teaching, he turned enthusiastically to the prospects opened up by historical study and the new methods associated with it. In applying the concept of evolution to Christian doctrine he was ahead both of Newman and Möhler.[49] His lecture-course on the history of dogma antedated Döllinger's by some five years and supplied a model for such younger members of the faculty as Franz Anton Staudenmaier (1800–55) and Johann Kuhn (1806–87). He himself discerned clearly and also led others to see not only that theology has a history but that the historical form of divine revelation renders a historical interpretation of it necessary if its inherent rationale is to be understood. His later work on apologetics was scarcely less innovative. The apologist had to raise his sights from the pedestrian level of mere inter-confessional polemics to the higher borderlands of theology and philosophy, where he would confront the deepest problems of faith and reason, belief and knowledge.

But, although Drey was not only the *doyen* but, as I am disposed to think, the most original member of the Tübingen group, its most celebrated representative, as he certainly is one of the most outstanding Catholic theologians of his century in Germany, was Johann Adam Möhler, born at Igersheim in Württemberg in 1796. He too entered Ellwangen in 1814, where he studied philosophy and theology, moving to Tübingen when the former institution was closed. Ordained priest in 1819 he first did parish work at Weil and Riedlingen before returning to the university to equip himself for an academic career. In 1822 an opening was found for him as *Privatdozent* in church history. But before assuming his duties he made a tour of the German universities that included Jena, Halle, Göttingen and Berlin, thus acquiring first-hand knowledge of the trends in contemporary Protestantism. At Berlin he met Schleiermacher and Hegel's disciple Marheineke, and later expressed the opinion that his stay in the Prussian capital was the most important and decisive point in his life. But his contact with the newest Protestant thought, so far from shaking his belief in the Catholic religion, became 'in the hands of God, the means whereby Catholicism revealed itself in me in its robust and indestructible force, in its eternal elevation and dignity'.[50] Nevertheless he learned a good deal from Protestant teachers, and from Schleiermacher especially that 'religion has a social character, and that Christian thought is a social thought', so proving that it is possible to use Protestant arguments in support of Catholic doctrine, even the Catholic doctrine of the church.[51]

Möhler taught at Tübingen for some twelve years, much of that time as professor of ecclesiastical history. In 1835 he left Württemberg for Bavaria to occupy the chair of New Testament exegesis at the university of Munich, although he subsequently was to take over Döllinger's courses in church history as well. Unhappily, from 1836 to 1837 his work was interrupted by serious illness, and after only a brief resumption of teaching at the beginning of 1838 he died in the following April, a few weeks after his appointment as dean of Würzburg cathedral.

Möhler first and foremost was a historical scholar. Careful investigation of the original texts he considered indispensable, and like Drey he approached dogmatic and speculative questions always from the historical angle – in his own case that particularly of patristic study. But he is remembered less for his actual researches in ecclesiastical history than for the interest of the ideas to which his wide historical knowledge lent support. In this respect he was typical of the whole

Tübingen school, which believed that it is history which furnishes the proper basis for speculation. At the same time he held that facts take on life only when they are invested with a comprehensive meaning – Drey's 'Idea'. Möhler realized that the rationalist method, however, is abstract and in tendency reductive, and that if the true nature of Catholicism is to be appreciated its history and traditions are the sources upon which the theologian, whether dogmatic or apologetic, has to draw. The past, that is, must be looked on in its integrity – in its movement, its direction and its unity – if the 'spiritual bond' which holds it together is to be perceived. Thus alone will its inner significance become intelligible. But the key to this significance, so far as the great historic fact of the Catholic religion is concerned, lies in the idea of the church. In other words, Christian history becomes meaningful only in the light of the Christian *ecclesial* experience. It is this which gives it consistency and direction. The historian will recount the movement of events, but the theologian's role is to interpret them by a guiding principle.

Thus Möhler, as did Drey, came to see Catholic doctrine as the outcome of a process of organic development, except that he was less prone than the older man to rest his concept on speculative theory, preferring the data of history itself, data for which, as his knowledge of it grew, he came to have increasing respect. And, we may add, a deepening regard – especially following his studies of Athanasius (1827) and Anselm (1828)[52] – for traditional views. This meant that he also found it less and less easy to distinguish the process of doctrinal development – something he never quite succeeded in explaining – from the idea simply of the continuity of tradition.

Möhler's earliest publication, other than articles in the *Theologische Quartalschrift*, was his book on unity in the church: *Die Einheit in der Kirche*.[53] He confessed that, although his purpose in writing it had initially been that solely of a historian, he felt the need of a principle by which history could be seen as more than a mere succession of 'periods' and by which therefore any one such period could be organically related to the whole. The notion that presented itself was that of internal development. Throughout the centuries of their history the Christian religion and the church which Christ founded have, he was convinced, preserved their essential identity, Christ being the same yesterday, today and for ever. Indeed the basic theme of Möhler's argument is that there is no knowledge of Christ apart from the church. The church's bond of unity is the spirit of Christ at work within it, an energizing force which finds appropriate expression in the external institution and its forms – tradition, scripture, faith, worship and hierarchy. Accordingly the treatise falls into two parts, each of four chapters. The first seeks to demonstrate the church's unity in the Spirit: 'mystical unity', 'unity of doctrine', 'the many without unity' – i.e. the disruptive effect of heresy and schism – and 'unity in the many' – the fact that unity does not necessarily mean uniformity or the suppression of individuality. The second part deals with the church's hierarchical structure, represented in order of ascent by the bishop, the metropolitan of the province, the episcopate as a body, and finally the papacy as supreme. Wherever, says Möhler, forces of a certain kind manifest themselves they do so in conformity with that kind, and the Holy Spirit, in communicating himself to men and endowing them with power is bound to be productive of new external phenomena by way of natural response.[54] This idea of his was criticized at the time, as it has been since, for implying that the church as a visible, historically conditioned manifestation of the presence of the divine Spirit among men has no need to claim for its basic institutions a *specific* foundation by Christ and that the concept of the indwelling Spirit as employed here involves a general immanentism whereby all ecclesial forms are to be regarded as the spontaneous outcome of an intrinsic spiritual vitality rather than as of express ordinance. Möhler later insisted, however, that, although to his mature mind not a little that he had said in his book was the utterance of 'enthusiastic youth', he had no intention whatever of displacing the historic revelation of Christ by a doctrine of the creativity of the Spirit and that his thesis was in part an answer to certain pietist groups for which the notion of Spirit-illumination was a temptation to separatism. Nonetheless his basically 'mystical' ecclesiology and account of the outward as the historic and empirical articulation of the inward provided the core of a developmental theory not only in tune with the thinking of his own age, but, as it has been averred, one that distinctly anticipates the evolutionist views of the Roman Catholic Modernists, especially Loisy.[55]

Möhler's treatment of the papal supremacy also came under fire from conservatives. He admitted himself that at one time he had questioned whether the papacy as an institution really was of the church's essence, but that he no longer doubted it even though he considered it difficult to establish historically previous to the time of Cyprian. However, examination of the early Petrine tradition and his own reflections on the nature of a hierarchically organized society had persuaded him of the need of what the papacy stood for. What perhaps is not so clear from Möhler's avowal is whether he thought the papacy to have been of Christ's own foundation.[56] His belief in the *de facto* importance of it, on the other hand, never wavered, nor did his profound respect for ecclesiastical authority in general.

Whether from personal dissatisfaction with his work or in deference to his critics, Möhler never allowed *Die Einheit* to be reprinted. But the freshness and vigour of his writing place it among the most stimulating products of nineteenth-century Catholic thinking. He clearly wanted to break away from the merely static and juridical view of the church in favour of the Spirit-filled, Spirit-directed community, with the mutual love of its members as its bond and stay, and its external polity as the visible mark of its internal unity. To this extent he enunciates ideas which in our day have received the blessing of the second Vatican Council.

But the work of Möhler's that has done most to perpetuate his memory is his *Symbolik* – 'Symbolism' – published at Mainz in 1832.[57] The author discloses at the outset that the idea of the book was suggested to him by 'the adversaries of our faith' whose public university lectures on the doctrinal differences which divided European Christendom he himself much esteemed and that he now purposed to do something of the same sort from a Catholic angle.[58] Thus, rather than indulge in the usual polemical forays, he chose to offer a comparative survey of diverse systems of Christian doctrine with the aim of examining their inner consistency and discovering their central principle. The doctrines to which he especially drew attention were those of the fall and original sin, justification, the sacraments, the church and the rule of faith, all of which were matters of acute controversy between Catholics and Protestants. Their respective positions on each are aligned and compared with one another, Möhler's exposition being in every instance a model of clarity, although a certain polemical 'edge' is not lacking in so far as he shows how an erroneous assumption invariably leads to views which those who adopt it are reluctant actually to maintain and would discard if they could do so without self-contradiction. He fastens in particular on the cardinal Reformation doctrine of justification by faith alone and argues that Protestant exaggerations had resulted in schemes of dogma entirely at variance with Catholic teaching. In contrast the latter could demonstrate its own coherence and balance, showing that its informing idea, of which the dogma of the incarnation provides the authoritative statement, is the union of God and man, the visible and the invisible, nature and supernature, and that Catholic faith and Catholic life together are the idea's historic expression. It is something which, in Möhler's judgment, Protestantism with its doctrinal imbalance has signally failed to understand. Catholicism represents synthesis and unity, Protestantism partiality and division.

The sharpest antithesis, Möhler points out, between the Catholic and the Protestant systems is in their respective concepts of the church. He is especially critical of the Protestant idea of the church's essential 'invisibility'. In Catholic teaching the church is primarily the visible institution, its invisible character is secondary. In Lutheranism, on the other hand, the invisible is primary, the visible only secondary. The disparity may at first look inconsiderable, but when its implications are examined they are seen to eventuate in wholly antagonistic positions. The institution of a visible society, Möhler maintains, is a provision in conformity with the actualities of human nature, its weaknesses, needs and aspirations: for what the heart demands is a community of persons, not a disembodied idea. This necessity the historic Catholic church can be demonstrated to have met. For such is the meaning of the incarnation itself, when the eternal truth appeared in external and living form, because only thus could the divine message lay hold of the 'whole man'. Even so, had the incarnation been but a temporary dispensation the Christian revelation would have fallen short of its goal; whereas it continues in the church, which in a sense is an extension or prolongation of the incarnation – the image, as it were, of the Word made flesh. This aspect of the Word made flesh, made man, was something, Möhler declares, that Luther never understood.

> Jesus Christ desired the Church to be a manifestation of himself, of his abiding humanity, of his eternally living body. He conferred upon it the responsibility of teaching sound doctrine, and in order that it should not fail of its mission he imparted to it his Truth, his Wisdom, and his Spirit, which constitute the innermost meaning of the Church as his spotless bride.[59]

Möhler's idea of tradition concurs with Drey's. It is the inner consciousness of the Christian community, deriving ultimately from Christ and persisting over the ages. Fundamentally it is the divine Word eternally alive in the body of the faithful, by which scripture itself is to be interpreted and controversies about matters of belief are settled. It is embodied in the church's universal and abiding faith as this finds utterance in its official doctrinal formularies.[60] Tradition, in short, is the immemorial rule of faith, although it is the function of the church's teaching authority, its *magisterium*, to maintain, expound and defend it. A living voice, therefore, is necessary when decisive pronouncement has to be made; a voice, moreover, that speaks, when required to do so, infallibly, if the faithful are to be preserved from error. This function is fulfilled by the bishops, the infallibility which Möhler refers to being that, we should note, of the episcopate *as a body*; he does not commit himself on the personal infallibility of the pope as defined in 1870. Again, because tradition is a living force it must develop. Its effort in combatting heresy, the necessity of adapting itself to new needs and meeting new problems means that while in substance it remains the same its forms will inevitably change.

Möhler's *Symbolik* won for its author European and not only German fame. He was widely judged to have given the Catholic church a new polemical thrust, to have strengthened the faith of many questioning and perhaps wavering believers and to have gained converts from Protestantism. That it provoked controversy was to have been expected; such leading Protestant theologians as Marheineke, Nitzsch and Gösler at once answered Möhler, eliciting counter-replies from other pundits on the Catholic side. But Möhler's most formidable opponent was his Tübingen colleague in the Protestant faculty, the New Testament scholar and historian of the early church, F. C. Baur, to whom he in turn made a carefully considered rejoinder in 1834.[61] Möhler's theology, though, is in general mystical rather than speculative. Intuitive and synthetic, it relates easily to its period, the pervasive influence of which is apparent. In its way it is as characteristic of the romanticist outlook as Schleiermacher's, even though he came himself to view the great Protestant theologian's treatment of Christian doctrines as arbitrary and distorting, as well as disliking his subjectivism. From the Catholic standpoint, however, Möhler is likely to be regarded with greater sympathy today than at any time since his death. Both of his major constructive works are of obvious relevance to the modern ecumenical debate.

6

Italian ontologism: Gioberti and Rosmini

W E HAVE SEEN that the presiding aim of the idealist philosophy, following in this the general drift of Romantic
thought, was to apprehend, whether immediately or medi-
ately, the totality of things in their essential unity. It sought, that is, to
resolve the antithesis of subject and object, of spirit and nature, and to
discover the infinite in the finite, the eternal in the temporal. Any
dualism of subject and object, of finite and infinite, as in Enlightenment
rationalism no less than in the scholastic Aristotelian tradition of the
middle ages, had finally to be overcome if the metaphysical quest were
to attain its goal. From the standpoint of religious philosophy this
demanded a new approach to the problem of religious knowledge, an
approach which the leading Romantic thinkers saw as requiring, so to
say, the externalizing of the ego, the projecting of the self into the
world, either emotively, as with Schleiermacher and to some extent
Fichte, or intellectively, as with Hegel. In any case the world so
conceived was in some fashion to be identified with the self, subject and
object being given together in experience, thus making radical scepticism impossible. In religious terms, God and the soul are correlative:
one meets God in the soul, intuitively or reflectively. However, to a
number of religious thinkers of the period, brought up in the Catholic
church and deeply imbued with the sense of the 'objectivity' of the
Catholic creed, the way of post-Kantian idealism, although not by any
means wholly antipathetic to them, seemed nevertheless dangerously
subjective, tending to minimize what orthodox theism held to be the
vital difference between finite and infinite and obscuring the supreme
Object of belief behind a veil of 'psychologistic' thought and feeling.
They themselves, that is, while desiring to surmount the subject–object
dichotomy, sought to achieve this by discovering the subject in the
object, or rather by understanding subject and object alike in the
presupposition or postulation of Being as the ground of both. Such
were the ontologists, to accord them the name by which, taken more or
less as a coherent group, they came to be known. Indeed, throughout

much of the nineteenth century this ontologist type of thought had a considerable vogue among the Catholic clergy, especially in France, where it enjoyed the prestige of the Sorbonne and had its advocates among the Benedictines, the Jesuits and the Sulpicians, and in Belgium, where at the university of Louvain its adherents were strong enough to form a distinctive school. But in Italy also it had its signal representatives, claiming even that their country was its true homeland.[1]

Ontologism had its roots in the Platonism of St Augustine, its stem in the Augustinian tradition of the mediaeval Franciscans – notably St Bonaventura – and in the religious philosophy of the seventeenth-century French Oratorians whose principal ornament was Malebranche. The last-named, who in his *Recherche de la vérité* (1674) combined Augustinianism with the Cartesian philosophy in a kind of mystical rationalism, held that all men, through the reason they possess in common, have a vision of the infinite and indeterminate being – which he equated with God: *Deus est esse* – as the condition of all determinate thought. Similarly for the nineteenth-century ontologists man has a direct intuition of universal being – necessary, immutable and eternal – which again they appear to equate with God (*ens necessarium et reale*) and apart from which the contingent and particular are themselves inconceivable: what we know we know only in God, much as the sight of physical objects depends on the presence of light. The actual term *ontologism* seems to have been coined by the Italian thinker Vincenzo Gioberti, in order to distinguish his philosophy from that of Descartes, which he stigmatized as 'psychologism', despite the fact that the ontological doctrine has certain affinities with Cartesianism, as can be seen in Malebranche. But Gioberti was very much a man of the world, and not at all a mere wanderer in the abstract realms of metaphysics. He was a politician strongly influenced by Mazzini and passionately devoted to the cause of Italian nationalism, a commitment that provides the background to his entire life's work. In his youth he passed through successive crises of faith and unbelief until he at length opted for the philosophical views which for him were the way of reconciliation between traditional faith and modern scientific progress. In this regard he argued that his was an authentically Christian philosophy, recognizing the priority of revelation but also the role of reason in the adjustment of religious belief to the pressures of contemporary thought.

Vincenzo Gioberti was born at Turin on 5 April 1801, in circumstances verging on poverty. Orphaned in childhood, he was educated by the Oratorians who destined him for the priesthood, to which he was ordained in 1825. His intellectual abilities were evident from an early age. Taking his doctorate with a thesis entitled *De Deo et religione naturali*, he became a profesor at the Athenaeum theological college at Turin and was appointed chaplain to the royal Sardinian court. But neither his clerical functions nor his court connection deterred him from assuming an increasingly active part in the liberal and revolutionary political movement in northern Italy which sought freedom from the repressive force exerted by the Austrian occupation of Lombardy and Venice. He was the founder of a literary group whose interests were both philosophical and political, joined the Carbonari, a patriotic secret society, and formed ties with the Giovine Italia movement which Mazzini organized in 1830. In May 1833 he relinquished his court post, but his known political opinions caused his arrest and internment for some four months, after which he was exiled. He went first to Paris, but eventually decided to settle in Brussels, where he taught philosophy at an educational institution run by a compatriot of his. Intellectually the ensuing ten years or so were the most fruitful of his career, but he also used Brussels as a centre from which he tirelessly proclaimed the ideals of Italian independence and unity, as in *Il primato morale e civile degli Italiani* (1843), in which he propounded the idea of a reinvigorated papacy at the head of an Italian confederation.[2] Above all he exhorted his fellow-countrymen to draw inspiration from the Christian traditions of their fatherland. November 1845 again found him in Paris and following closely the course of events in Italy, especially after the election in June 1846 of Cardinal Mastai-Ferretti as Pope Pius IX, a man reputed at the time to have liberal sympathies. The events of 1848 resulted in Gioberti's return at last to Italy, where he was received with immense popular acclaim. The king of Sardinia, Charles Albert, even nominated him a senator, but he declined to accept the honour and stood, successfully, as deputy for Turin in the Piedmontese assembly (17 April). So great indeed was his personal popularity that a tour he made through northern Italy, ending up in Rome, became virtually a triumphal progress. The pope received him three times in private audience, taking him, it is said, in his arms and addressing him as the 'Father of his country'. The philosopher-politician was then at the height of his career, his speeches and other political communications being published in 1851 by his friend Giuseppe Massari under the title *Documenti della guerra santa d'Italia*. Back in Piedmont he was appointed minister without portfolio in the short-lived Casati government. As he himself, however, favoured outright war, he lined up with the opposition and presided at the federative congress which met at Turin on 10 October 1848. In December the king entrusted him with the responsibility of forming a government, but as president of the council he failed in his attempt to secure the intervention of France so as to bring about a union of all

Italians under the leadership of their sovereign princes against Austria. In the following February, after the Piedmontese defeat at Navaro, with the consequent abdication of Charles Albert and the accession of his son as Victor Emanuel II, he resigned. Although he was in good standing with the Launay–Pinelli administration, which sent him as Sardinian ambassador to Paris, he was in disagreement with official directives and he once more tendered his resignation, an act that terminated his political involvement. Thereafter he retired into private life, choosing to remain in Paris. He refused a state pension even though he had no financial resources of his own.

Gioberti was one of those thinkers whose ideas must be seen in relation to external events. In any case his personal course was determined by the vicissitudes of politics, its main phases being marked first by his exile and then by the revolution of 1848. He was always a convinced liberal and dedicated patriot, although his political stance underwent change. Thus when Lamennais's *Paroles d'un Croyant* appeared in 1834 he welcomed it with enthusiasm, yet he later criticized its author with some bitterness.[3] For him the *Risorgimento* of Italy, with its call for liberty, national self-consciousness and independence, became increasingly the cause to which his life was devoted. Nevertheless his vision was not simply political. He believed in freedom and in tradition, in liberalism and in monarchy, in Catholicism and the progress of knowledge. His neo-Guelphian concept of a national federation under the presidency of the sovereign pontiff but directed politically and militarily by the Piedmontese government – 'On the union of Rome and Turin', he declared, 'the destiny of Italy depends' – was a bold but far-seeing proposal, to which the hopes widely aroused in liberal breasts by Pius IX's supposed open-mindedness lent a certain credibility. But the opportunity for its realization which 'the year of revolutions' provided was lost through the failure of the necessary forces to concur. There was insufficient unity of purpose among the governments of the Italian states to strive effectively for independence, while the territorial ambitions of Piedmont awakened enough distrust to frustrate the chances of an Italian national confederation. Most disappointing of all perhaps was the pope's decision, conveyed in a consistorial allocution, to dissociate himself entirely from the war of liberation. Gioberti, by now disillusioned with neo-Guelphianism, brought out his *Rinnovamento civile d'Italia*, which henceforth looked to the Sardinian monarchy alone for the salvation of his country.[4] Going back to the ideas of his youth, he denounced the temporal power of the papacy, not necessarily as the cause of the reactionary attitude of Rome towards Italian nationalist expectations but more radically as the underlying cause of what he was coming to regard as the general deterioration within Catholic Christendom. In *Il Gesuita moderno* he attacked the Society of Jesus in particular.[5] His posthumous writings show that in his last years he had in mind a complete programme of church reform,[6] extending even to the questioning of basic principles of Catholic doctrine such as divine revelation, the nature of dogma, the church's *magisterium*, and the sacraments, in such a way as to place him, I would say, firmly among the precursors of the Modernist movement at the end of the century.[7] The rebuff to his political idealism, for which he was prone to blame the church, undoubtedly left its mark on his general attitude to religion and the institutions of Catholicism. The Vatican retaliated by putting *Il Gesuita moderno* on the Index (29 May 1849), a fate which its author lived to see overtake all his writings in January 1852.[8]

Gioberti's posthumous publications reveal the degree to which his philosophical views changed over the years.[9] The earlier writings fall squarely within the limits, if not too narrowly drawn, of Catholic orthodoxy, whereas the latter, with their pantheistic and rationalist tendency, betray the growing influence of Romantic idealism.[10] The question whether the course of Gioberti's thinking shows a gradual but consistent development, or whether at some point it veered sharply in a new direction, so that the later works represent a different position altogether, is one on which modern commentators diverge.[11] Gioberti was well aware that the primary issue for the modern philosopher is that of the nature of knowledge. How do we *know* that we know? By what means is certainty to be reached? Kant had recognized the role of the senses but in a way that led to scepticism, whilst the Cartesian doctrine of innate ideas could never free itself from subjectivism. The only escape from this dilemma, he believed, lay in *ontologism*: certainty is possible because there is a true correspondence between thought and being, between the logical and the ontological, by which the mind comes to possess a genuine intuition of reality. The human intelligence, Gioberti holds, has direct access to 'being-in-itself' – concretely, that is, and not as a mere abstract notion. The first and principal object of philosophy is the Idea as the immediate term of intellectual apprehension. This word, which since Plato has become an integral part of the philosophical language of Western civilization, is to be taken, he says, in a sense analogous to the Platonic, and thus used to describe, not some concept of our own, or indeed any particular thing or created property, but the absolute and eternal truth, in so far as it presents itself to man's intuitive grasp.[12] In other words, it is God himself, absolute and eternal Being, who is present to the human intelligence and received by us directly through reason. Enlarging on the meaning of the term Idea, Gioberti explains that he intends to denote by it the object of the rational understanding as cognized in itself, although to the notion of this object 'taken in itself' should be added also that of a relation between it and our knowledge.[13]

This is a large claim; how is it to be substantiated? By what means is the identity of idea and object to be proved? Gioberti's answer is that the truth of the statement must be accepted if either the sceptical or subjectivist pitfalls are to be avoided. Unless, he insists, the mind apprehends the object *immediately* there can be no logical certainty that reality is known.[14] Apart from the ontologist standpoint science is not competent to secure either truth or virtue, intellectual assurance or duty, on unshakeable foundations. Without complete conviction of the coherence of the intelligence with the order of being, scepticism is inevitable.[15] And he invokes the 'common-sense' philosophy of the Scottish school of Thomas Reid and others in support of the argument that our perception of the divine is exactly analogous to our perception of our bodies.[16] It preserves our representational ideas from radical doubt by affording them the basis of an immediate knowledge of being, the ultimate reality in which the archetypes of all things subsist. In regard to the problem of knowledge, therefore, the heart of the matter is the assurance that the immediate object of rational intuition – however imperfect in itself – is either God or else something other than God. If it is not God it must be a created thing, contingent and finite, in which case scepticism is unavoidable. The question that at once arises, however, is this: Why, if our intuition of being is a conscious one, is it possible to deny it, since denied it so often is? Alternatively, if it is not conscious, how can we affirm it? Gioberti's reply is that it certainly is a conscious intuition, but that it is not as a rule *perceived*, since comparatively few are capable of ontological reflection or possess any sort of 'ontological' sense. In its primal form it is only 'vague, indeterminate and confused', and so may be overlooked.

But for such as are capable of 'ontological reflection' – those, that is, who can pin-point their intuition and explicate its nature both to themselves and to others – it is evident that it contains a judgment: Being *is*. Moreover, the reality of being does not present itself to the mind as something merely contingent and relative, but as a reality that is necessary and absolute, such that to think the contrary is impossible. Consequently the judgment in question can be expressed in a proposition, *Being necessarily is*. This judgment is objective and in a sense divine, inasmuch as it is being-in-itself which confronts us, as it were, with the declaration *I necessarily am*. Knowledge of being thus comes as a disclosure, a revelation.

> The reiteration of this objective and divine judgment brought about by reflection is the first link in the chain of philosophical reasoning considered

as a human act. It likewise follows that philosophy has its basis in revelation – a revelation conveyed in the primal intuition – and that, strictly speaking, God himself is the first philosopher, human philosophizing being the continuation and repetition of the divine philosophy. God therefore is not only the object of knowledge, he is also the first teacher of it.[17]

But, if the intuition of primary Being (l'Essere primo) is initially no more than vague and confused, how is it so to be clarified as to become exact knowledge? In Gioberti's view this is the work of 'ontological reflection', which imparts to its object such distinctness and determinateness as to render it proportionate to man's apperception and the limits of his intelligence. This it does by giving it sensible form – something which in itself is, of necessity, arbitrary; but such arbitrariness is not just a matter of individual choice, it is socially determined; indeed it originates ultimately in the creative Idea, which manifests itself in a way that can be sensibly received. Its form, Gioberti tells us, is the Word, a key-notion in his philosophy. Language, he says, is 'the reflex revelation of the Idea', a succession of sensible modes by which the Idea discloses itself to the mind's reflective intuition, thus completing the direct intuition which must come first.[18] The Word, we may say, delimits and circumscribes the Idea in concentrating the mind on itself as on a determinate form through which it reflectively perceives the infinite ideal. Nevertheless it is the Idea, equivalent to primary Being, which is cognized in its infiniteness, even though it is brought to us under finite and sensible guise. Hence the Word which expresses the reality of Being must be the creation of Being itself. It is, Gioberti avers, a 'second revelation', or, more accurately, 'the primary revelation now given shape by the Revealer himself'.[19]

But Gioberti is also responsive to the challenge of the contemporary idealism to resolve dialectically the opposition between finite and infinite, real and ideal. This he seeks to do in terms of a philosophical 'first principle' (il Primo filosofico), itself unique and absolute, which would comprehend both a psychological first principle (il Primo psicologico) – the primary Idea that is the origin and source of all others – and an ontological (il Primo ontologico) – the primary Being that, again, is the source and origin of all things. This philosophical first principle, or Idea, may be stated in terms of a proposition or 'ideal formula' – a clear, simple and precise judgment; for, as man cannot think without judging, it follows that he cannot think the Idea unless he embodies it too in a judgment.[20] This ideal formula will have to be such as to cover everything that we cognize, however obscurely, in the primal intuition. Accordingly we may affirm that 'Being creates existence' (l'Ente crea l'esistente)[21] – produces freely and 'out of nothing' particular beings and finite substances. The intuition, Gioberti states, 'which in a primal act discovers Being, in a second such act realizes itself to be the effect of Being' and so mentally apprehends the entire sensible universe. In this way the mind finds itself 'in God', as in its creative cause, and then in turn finds the world within itself as in an energy endowed with perception and capable of cognition. This double order of existence is revealed to it by the intuition of creation that is inseparable from the intuition of creative Being.[22] Or to put it in slightly different terms: In the primal intuition we discern the three elements of the ideal formula which expresses the philosophical first principle – Being as absolute substance and first cause, particular existents as finite substances and secondary causes, and the act of creation as the link between the two. 'We apprehend existence as the work of Being and are able to contemplate Being itself as the principle and cause of all created things.'[23] Thus in Gioberti's view the Catholic dogma of creation is the foundation of all metaphysics and provides the sole explanation of the universe. Thereafter, however, philosophy pursues a rigorously scientific method in explicating whatever is implicit in the ideal formula.

In the field more particularly of philosophical theology Gioberti produced a remarkable apologetic treatise with his *Teorica del sovran-naturale, ossia Discorso sulle convenienze della Religione rivelata colle mente umana e col progresso civile delle nazioni* ('Theory of the supernatural, or Discourse on the harmony of revealed Religion with the human mind and with the civil progress of nations'), published in Brussels in 1838, the argument of which strikingly anticipates the *méthode d'immanence* propounded by Maurice Blondel in *L'Action* and other works around the close of the century.[24] In it Gioberti broaches his subject by way of the problem of human knowledge. The difficulties that present themselves when we try to understand cognition, including the recognition of the limitation of our human faculties, are sufficient to demonstrate that the claim to 'know' reality is far from easy to sustain. What essential connection is there between the intelligence and sense-objects? How can one 'take hold of' the other? Yet we are confident that there is a connection and that the sensible is intelligible. Precisely how, though? Can we be sure that Being and the relationships which constitute it do not elude the understanding? Gioberti is prepared to concede that in the last resort reality does lie beyond complete intelligibility, so far as the ordinary faculties of knowing are involved. But he goes on to postulate a further faculty, that of *super-intelligence (la sovrintelligenza)*, by which intuition of the essence of things is possible. For, as sensibility apprehends reality through the feelings and rational thinking through active intuition, the super-intelligence operates through an act of instinctive belief that goes beyond cognition as ordinarily understood. Gioberti argues, moreover, that corresponding to each of these cognitional faculties there is an active or practical one, sensibility implying instinct, intelligence free-will, and super-intelligence the desire of blessedness. This latter is a supernatural endowment, but one for which man is by his whole nature seen to be apt. In other words, because man possesses this third faculty he can become aware of, and therefore desire to reach, a profounder truth and a higher order of reality. What divine revelation does is to meet and satisfy this inherent need of the supernatural, bringing us the assurance that what our rational nature demands Being ultimately will require. Knowledge and faith thus find their reconciliation, while the seeming dualism of reason and sensibility, nature and spirit, is transcended.

Another interesting feature of Gioberti's apologetic is its affinity with the 'traditionalism' of Bonald and Lamennais. Revelation, Gioberti contends, was necessary for man even at the natural level if his life was to attain completion and fulfilment. Thus the gift of language was required in order to activate the rational faculty in him, since without language he would have remained only in an animal state.[25] Even more necessary was it for knowledge of the truths on which the moral life depends, but which, Gioberti holds, it would have been outside the power of reason alone to have attained to: ideas such as those of, for example, law, retribution and expiation. Finally, revelation was given not only to repair the great defects in human nature resulting from original sin, but that the true unity of nature and supernature might be realized. It is on this account, Gioberti considers, that there is no genuine philosophy apart from Christianity, because only there are reason and revelation synthesized and their reciprocity made apparent. For the rest, Gioberti's doctrine is theologically orthodox, with mystery and miracle as essential ingredients, miracle providing the 'sign' or credentials of divine revelation. But he was bound also to admit a sense in which philosophy is superior to theology in so far as it furnishes the latter with its interpretative categories. Gioberti's posthumously published writings, especially his *Filosofia della rivelazione* (1857) and *Protologia* (1857), reveal a clear development of his thinking in a direction for which he had already sustained criticism, most forcibly from the Jesuits of the *Civiltà cattolica* led by Matteo Liberatore.[26] The charges against him were those of pantheism and rationalism: he equated Being with God and maintained in effect that the knowledge of God is open to man's natural reason. These charges he strenuously denied, stressing his belief in the divine personality and in revelation, and he continued to urge his objections to the pantheistic and subjectivist positions of the German idealists. Nonetheless his phraseology, despite his use of the orthodox terminology, had dubious overtones for some Catholic ears, and his own attempts at explaining them away left his critics unconvinced. If, as he asserted, ideas are real in themselves, then it seemed to them that the distinction between God and his creatures disappears. If there is no difference, in Thomistic language, between act and potency, and therefore between essence and existence, it must be of the essence of all things to exist and there is but a single Being that includes all existence – a doctrine not easily distanced from idealist monism. When in 1861 the Holy Office condemned certain ontologist propositions as 'unsafe for teaching' ('tuto tradi non possunt') it was this feature of the doctrine which came in for particular censure.

In other respects Gioberti anticipated Catholic Modernism. It could be said of his Christian philosophy that one of its principal aims was to bring about a movement of reform in the Roman Catholic church which would enable it to align itself with modern culture. He disliked the scholasticism taught in the seminaries on the ground that it assumed a false dichotomy between the natural and the supernatural, which in turn reflected a separation of dogmatic theology from philosophy. What he himself envisaged was an integrated 'philosophical theology' embracing all aspects of thought and life. The traditional apologetic seemed to him especially unsatisfactory – 'externalist' in its approach to the problem of faith and thus unable to show the essential rationality of belief as consistent with human experience at large. He was also unhappy at certain forms of Catholic moral teaching, particularly in its asceticism and exaggerated 'other-worldliness'. But above all was he concerned for the rights of personal judgment: the church surely must teach with authority, but the individual's responsibility is to make that teaching his own through an act of critical apprehension. Hence the importance of understanding the true nature of dogma. Dogmatic definitions, he argued, are not precise and categorical statements, and their function is more negative than positive – to exclude error rather than to formulate truth, in that its positive affirmations can scarcely do more than indicate a direction or draw an analogy. In short, the plenitude of divine revelation cannot be enclosed in a single definition, which will present its content only in a limited and historically conditioned way. Dogma therefore is the servant of religious truth, not its master. Subsequent experience will bring further insight, to which the historic formula, however authoritative, must necessarily be subject. Absolute fixity of dogma is thus neither desirable nor feasible, since the exercise of reason is progressive. In fact Catholicism itself is not an unalterable magnitude, identical in all ages and circumstances; at least it is capable of a diversity of interpretations, none of which can be ruled out as in principle inadmissible. Only so will theology be a living pursuit, attracting original thought and opinion. Gioberti defends his view against the charge of subjectivism by arguing that each individual standpoint has its measure of objective validation in the ultimate and all-comprehending Idea. That he succeeded, however, in clearly distinguishing his own position from what his opponents saw only as an excuse for the vagaries of Protestantism and free-thought can hardly perhaps be claimed. In the intellectual climate of a time when ultramontanism was increasingly suspicious of any deviation from a tightly drawn orthodoxy, Gioberti's opinions were unlikely to win official favour, and did not.

Yet he was by no means without a following among his compatriots, to many of whom, both clerics and laymen, his ideas had considerable appeal. He himself maintained that ontologism was the authentic Italian philosophy, and he invoked it in the cause of Italian nationalism. Rosmini's attitude towards Gioberti's doctrines was, as we shall see, critical, but if, as has often been contended, the former's own views amount to ontologism then he himself is likely to be regarded as its most eminent Italian representative. Apart from him, though, the leading adherent of this teaching was the politician-philosopher Count Terenzio Mamiani della Rovere (1799–1885), a minister in the government first of Pius IX and then of Cavour in Piedmont, and author of *Il rinnovamento della filosofia antica in Italia* (1834), in which he sought to expose Rosmini's alleged idealism, although his later opinions, set out in *Dialoghi di scienza prima* (1846) and more fully in *Confessioni di un metafisico* (1865), differ somewhat from Gioberti's.[27] What, then, was Rosmini's own standpoint? On any rating he must be classed among the most original of nineteenth-century philosophers. But first we should take a look at the man himself, in his native Italy one of the outstanding figures of the century.

2

Rosmini is a thinker still relatively little known in the English-speaking world, in spite of the fact that a number of English translations of his works appeared between 1882 and 1888. Indeed, for all his high reputation, established during his lifetime among his fellow-Italians, his originality and depth of thought have even yet not won him any widespread recognition outside Italy. The literary genius of his contemporary and close friend, Alessandro Manzoni, have gained for the author of *I promessi sposi* international acclaim, but in his own way Rosmini – philosopher, moralist, patriot, political theorist, constitutionalist, educator, priest, pastor, and even, as some would aver, saint – was by no means a less remarkable man. As the president of the Italian Republic, Giovanni Gronchi, expressed it on the occasion of the Rosmini centenary celebrations in 1955: 'Profoundly Catholic, through his intellectual activity and through his personal sanctity which reached sublime heights, he drew the strength to restate Christian tradition in an organic system that included the claims of modern thought.'[28] Perhaps Manzoni's judgment, that 'he is a man whose smallest defects should be noted, lest you might think that he is more than human', should be read as the bias of strong personal esteem,[29] but it is far from uncorroborated. Nor was he predominantly an intellectual; the range of his practical concerns is scarcely less impressive, whether as the founder, in 1828, of two religious congregations – the Istituto della Carità for men, and the Suore della Provvidenza, both of them better known simply as Rosminians – or as an ecclesiastical reformer, or again for the political role he assumed during the 'revolutionary' years 1848 and 1849.[30]

The Rosmini family was noble and rich, with estates in the Trentino, where at Rovereto Antonio was born in March 1797.[31] But it was evident even in his childhood that the heir's natural inclination was for study rather than the life and responsibilities of a country magnate. From the first he read methodically as well as variously, his tastes extending from the classics to the moderns, although his ruling literary passion was for Dante and Petrarch. He early conceived the desire to become a writer himself, his poetic ambitions even embracing the composition of a great historical epic. But increasingly his thoughts took a religious turn; he read the Bible assiduously and applied himself to the study of St Thomas Aquinas, the greatest, he was convinced, of all Italian thinkers. The family library was of course available to him always, but somewhat precociously he soon began to amass a collection of his own, including manuscripts and rare editions. His schooling took place at Rovereto, though later he received private coaching to prepare him for entry to the university of Padua. His vocation to the priesthood may be dated not later than 1813, and in the following year he informed his parents of his decision, much to their disappointment, since they looked to him not only to continue the family line but also, rather than his less dependable younger brother, to carry on the management of its properties. But in spite of their opposition he stuck to his purpose and eventually, in April 1821, was ordained priest at Chioggia. In the same year he qualified for his doctorate. His first visit to Rome occurred in 1822, when he accompanied his bishop, Mgr Grasser, thither to attend the consecration of the patriarch of Venice, Ladislas Pyrcher. Besides being twice received in audience by the aged

Pope Pius VII, he met the Camaldolese monk Mauro Capellari, the future Pope Gregory XVI, as well as Cardinal Consalvi, later Pius VIII. Capellari in particular was always to hold him in high regard and personally befriended him. When Pius VII died in the summer of the next year Rosmini was invited by the clergy of the Rovereto district to deliver the panegyric in the town's main church, San Marco. In the event it made a deep impression on all who heard it. With a view to publication he enlarged it considerably, turning it virtually into a treatise on the relations of church and state. Its appearance, however, was delayed for some years by the Austrian censorship, suspicious of what it construed to be its excessive 'papalism', the Vienna censors even criticizing it, astonishingly, for its allegedly offensive remarks about Napoleon.[32] 'They treat me', he wrote to Bishop Grasser, 'as if I were a Carbonaro or worse.'[33] Meanwhile he had become parish priest of Rovereto, discharging the duties of his cure punctiliously, although not to the neglect of his studies, now focusing especially on St Thomas. He lectured the local clergy on the *Summa theologica*, a task he greatly enjoyed. 'It is', he told Grasser, 'nearly my sole recreation.'[34] What distressed him was the extent to which St Thomas – 'a genius as great, in my opinion, as Newton' – was so largely neglected, an omission partly attributable, he fancied, to 'the ill-repute of the philosophy of Aristotle', a prejudice he himself did not share.[35] In fact Rosmini's interest in Aquinas never faded, and he was for his period remarkable on account of the scholarly care he displayed for Thomist research.

In 1826 Rosmini left Rovereto for Milan, where he was appointed to a canonry at the cathedral. In the Lombard capital he was able to meet literary men and widen his social circle generally, for the first time making the acquaintance of Italy's leading Romantic, Manzoni, reconverted to Catholicism from enlightenment scepticism, who had already read Rosmini's little book on Christian education.[36] Each of the two men, it seems – Manzoni was twelve years Rosmini's senior – saw much to admire in the other, Rosmini finding in Manzoni true goodness of character as well as immense creative gifts, and Manzoni attracted by the younger man's brilliance of intellect as well as frankness and trustfulness. Indeed, while working on the second draft of *I promessi sposi* Manzoni sought Rosmini's criticism and advice, the latter for his part confessing to have been quite overwhelmed by this masterpiece of modern Italian literature. 'I think Italy', he wrote, 'will recognize something new; by this clear light now beginning to shine, she will feel that her perception has been enlarged.'[37] Not only was the young priest brought into closer contact with Italian romanticism – the effect of his upbringing had been a reverence for classicism – he profited by Manzoni's help in improving his own hitherto rather frigid literary style by adopting a more relaxed and familiar form, 'illustrating every passage by a light that could be understood by every type of mind'.[38]

But the great achievement of these early Milan years was the founding of the two religious congregations. His plan, which owed much to his friend the Marchesa di Canossa,[39] was submitted to Cardinal Capellari, who, whilst on the whole favourable, considered its aim – the inculcation of holiness – to be insufficiently precise, though he encouraged Rosmini in every way he could, and when he became pope he gave the foundation, at Domodossola in the foot-hills below Monte Rosa, his formal approval. The house of the Rosminian sisters was constituted a few years later, in 1832. The ascetic principles embodied in these institutions were set out by Rosmini in his *Maxims of Christian Perfection*.[40] The congregation's first mission to England took place in 1835, led by a young Roman, Luigi Gentile, in whom Rosmini had the greatest confidence.[41]

It was on a visit to Turin in June 1828 that Rosmini first met the Abbé Lamennais, famous as the author of the much-acclaimed apologetic treatise, *Essai sur l'indifférence* (see below Chapter 7) although it was Lamennais himself who sought the interview, having read Rosmini's *Opuscoli filosofici*, which had just then made its appearance.[42] Their discussion fastened on Lamennais's theory of the *sens commun*, but the Italian seems to have been somewhat disappointed by the Frenchman's rhetorical vagueness and doubted whether his ideas would suffice to give the church's teaching the kind of intellectual underpinning which he deemed to have become necessary. Where Lamennais was at fault was in not offering any criterion of certainty that would commend itself to the critical reason, since, although it is the individual who actually judges and always must do, the rational criterion itself is public and objective and not simply a matter of personal discrimination. Lamennais's doctrines, he even then suspected, contained the seeds of a dangerous, because ultimately irrational, 'populism' such as eventually bore fruit in the *Paroles* and *Les affaires de Rome*.

In spite of the demands of his growing pastoral responsibilities Rosmini yet found time for the series of philosophical works which had already begun publication. Of these the most important, and the work by which he is still best remembered, was *Nuovo saggio sull'origine delle idee*, an elaborate inquiry into the nature of knowledge and the origin of ideas.[43] This was followed a year later by *I principi della scienza morale*. Although the *Nuovo saggio* was sharply criticized by Gioberti, the latter was in sympathy with Rosmini's ideas generally and especially his political views: so much so, in fact, that he recommended the king of Piedmont to make use of his services. The outcome of this move was Rosmini's appointment as special envoy of the Piedmontese government to the Vatican, with a commission to negotiate a concordat with Pius IX as a step in the advancement of Italian unity. But Rosmini was himself in touch with the pope independently. Faced with the prospect of revolution the Italian princes were active in granting constitutions to their states, and the Holy See was no exception. For his part Rosmini believed that the pope ought not to act precipitately, and he let it be known through his agent in Rome that if his advice could be of any help he would gladly proffer it. 'If they take the very serious step of granting a constitution in Rome also', he commented, 'I should not like them to produce a poor one with the defects of all the others, which have been slavishly copied from abroad. Rome should either do nothing more than it has done .. or it should perform a really Roman work, original and worthy of the king-pontiff, an example to the world.'[44] The response to his inquiry was positive and he accordingly submitted, anonymously, his 'Plan for a Constitution',[45] which contained also an appendix on the 'Unity of Italy', proposing uniformity of government throughout the Italian states, as far as this might be possible, and the establishment of a permanent Diet at Rome, representative of the whole Italian nation under the presidency of the pope, which would have the power to declare war and peace. The pope was much impressed and asked Rosmini to become minister of public instruction in the papal government. Rosmini, however, refused, not wishing to have to collaborate with men whose views on some matters he certainly did not share. But with the outbreak of the revolution and the assassination on 15 November of Pellegrino Rossi, chief administrator of the estates of the church, Pius IX fled to Gaeta. Rosmini, whom the pope had intended to reward with a cardinal's hat, accompanied him into exile, but after the Austrian victories in Italy and the pope's own sudden change of heart about liberal reforms his influence waned.[46] Cardinal Antonelli, the new power at the Vatican, disapproved of Rosmini, who in any case had few friends at the papal court, even though he retained the pope's personal favour. In January 1849 he withdrew to Naples, where he was given hospitality at the Vincentian house, and applied himself to work on his commentary on the introduction to St John's gospel.

Like Gioberti, Rosmini had succeeded also in stirring up the opposition of the Jesuits. In 1835 he had attacked their well-known 'probabilist' casuistry in his *Trattato della coscienza morale*,[47] singling out in particular the views of a certain Father Segneri.[48] Rosmini in turn became the object of an anonymous diatribe circulated privately early in 1841 under the title 'Some affirmations of Antonio Rosmini, priest of Rovereto, with a few reflections written by Eusebio Cristiano' – an obvious pseudonym. Rosmini was accused of a string of heresies, including Lutheranism, Calvinism and Jansenism, and the book's whole tone was scurrilous. The mud thrown by its author was for the most part brushed off, but thereafter Rosmini's name tended to evoke suspicion. The Jesuits as the most conservative force in the Roman church could only look askance at a priest who seemed to identify himself with 'liberalism' both in politics and in doctrine and generally to exemplify the romanticist aim of coming to terms with contemporary culture and aspiration. When, therefore, in 1848 Rosmini published his *Costituzione secondo la giudizia sociale* ('Constitution according to Social Justice'),[49] followed by the even more widely read *Delle cinque piaghe della Santa Chiesa*,[50] he appeared quite definitely to have placed himself at the head of a 'reformist' movement, both political and ecclesiastical. He decided to publish the *Cinque piaghe*, which actually had been written as far back as 1832–3, because now that the church had evidently been blessed with a reforming pope the time looked opportune for him to make known his own opinions on what he believed to be wrong with the body ecclesiastic.

The burden of his message is a plea for the liberty of the church, as against Josephist and Gallican theories, for an improvement in the quality of the clergy, and for a liturgical revival. For his historical material Rosmini drew largely on the monumental *Histoire ecclésiastique* of Claude Fleury, despite the pronounced Gallican tendencies of its author.[51] The title of the book was suggested by an allocution of Pope Innocent IV to the Council of Lyons, in which he drew a comparison between the state of the church and the crucified Christ with his five bodily wounds. The church's present wounds, in Rosmini's judgment, were the separation of the people from the clergy in public worship, the inadequate standard of education among the latter, the disunion and isolation of the bishops, nomination to bishoprics by the state, and the enslavement of the church by its own wealth. The first of these was to be attributed to the general ignorance of the laity, partly through lack of any proper instruction, though partly also through the use of Latin, which in itself was a barrier betwen laymen and the clerical order. Rosmini believed that the people should have an active role in the liturgy instead of being mere hearers only, as 'passive as the columns and statues of the building itself'. It was the clergy's responsibility to teach the laity that they are themselves an integral part of the church, that 'to be a Christian is the first step in the priesthood'. But the pastors cannot enlighten their flocks without better training. Seminarians were taught to memorize rather than to think, their professors on the whole being too young and without much status. The actual writings of St Thomas were too little known, their place taken only by text-book summaries and commentaries. Even so, clergy training remained too theoretical; the pastoral side was comparatively neglected. As for the bishops, they were an order apart, having little contact either with one another, for they seldom met in synod, or with their priests. All too often they were subservient to the secular power; only in the United States of America were they free. Worse still perhaps, they were too much at ease in Zion; riches were an insidious source of corruption. Nor were their standing and influence enhanced by state nomination; the church should elect them, in accordance with ancient historical precedent. Although it might not be practicable for the people to have any direct say in such election they should nonetheless be consulted. Finally the church's extensive property had become a hindrance to its spiritual mission. Rosmini ends by expressing profound satisfaction that the invisible Head of the church should have set upon the chair of Peter a pope who seemed 'destined to renew our age and to impart to the Church that fresh impulse which will guide it into new ways, which although as yet unknown will be marvellous and glorious'.

The book was a great success, in so far as it was widely read and discussed. Pius IX himself read it and was evidently so well pleased by it that he invited its author to Rome.[52] All the same it was very far from winning universal approval. The idea in particular of electing bishops was not welcomed, and Rosmini had to go to considerable lengths to explain that he had meant nothing revolutionary by it. Indeed, with singular haste, and under pressure from Austria and Naples, the *Cinque piaghe* was placed on the Index (6 June 1849), although Rosmini did not himself hear of this until well into the following August. Not wishing to defy authority he accepted the condemnation – unlike Gioberti – without question.[53] Meanwhile his stay in Naples after quitting Gaeta was short. He had come under the surveillance of the Bourbon police and the good Vincentians found his presence with them an embarrassment; he was asked to leave. He also received a missive from the pope requesting further clarification of his views on the question of episcopal election *per clerum et populum* as a *ius divinum*. Rosmini at once replied, but it seems that his letter was never actually delivered to Pius himself. As however the pope had also suggested to him that he should write something forceful on the evils of the times, he responded by bringing out his book on communism and socialism,[54] as well as the *Operette spirituali* on which he was already working. The reaction of the anticlerical press to the news of the condemnation of the *Cinque piaghe* was of course foreseeable. Rosmini was personally blamed for what was seen as a feeble capitulation on his part, although he made it plain enough that he neither accepted censure nor wanted sympathy. Unfortunately the apparent disfavour that now surrounded him had repercussions for his Institute of Charity, causing a noticeable decline in the number of novices. He himself had nowhere to go except back to northern Italy, to settle at last at Stresa. But he gave no impression of personal resentment, despite the very obvious failure of his efforts in the ecclesiastico-political world. (In his spiritual fortitude he could only give thanks to 'that divine Providence which, disposing all things in love, has permitted this out of love alone'.)[55] The discharge of his priestly functions and the occupations of his study engrossed his remaining years. The two volumes of his *Psicologia* were finished in 1850,[56] followed in the next year by a new edition of the *Nuovo saggio*. In 1853 he wrote a series of articles for the Turin *Armonia* on a number of current issues in the field of religion and politics, while 1854 saw the publication of his *Logica*,[57] as well as further articles in the *Armonia* on freedom in education. At this time too he had the satisfaction of being informed that his published writings generally, which his critics had succeeded in getting delated to the Congregation of the Index, had been examined but not condemned, a *dimittantur* having been pronounced by the prefect of the Congregation on 3 July 1854.[58] The official statement declared moreover that in addition to the formal dismissal the examination itself 'in no way detracts from the good name of the author, nor that of the religious society founded by him, nor from his life and singular merits towards the Church'. Even so there were some who remained unconvinced by this exoneration and wanted him to give specific and *ex animo* testimony to his orthodoxy, possibly in the form of a compendium of Catholic doctrine. But this Rosmini would not consent to. 'If I were *ex abrupto* to publish a confession of faith ... in which I was required to explain *per summa capite* Catholic doctrine, and also promise to compose a volume of theological annotations to all my works, it would be evident that such a step was the result of the four-year examination of my works at Rome. Thus I should be condemned without any sentence of condemnation ... and the falsely accused would be the guilty party.'[59] It was a case of *quod scripsi scripsi*. In any event, although he was not yet an old man, his health was failing and he suffered a good deal of pain. His death occurred on 1 July 1855, his diocesan, the bishop of Novara, and his great friend Manzoni both being present. His elevation of character, and indeed, as a Catholic might view it, his personal sanctity, have never been in question. Pius IX himself declared that Rosmini was 'not only a good Catholic, but a saint', wisely adding: 'God uses his saints for the triumph of truth'.[60]

A large quantity of Rosmini's work was still unpublished at his death, the most important being his voluminous *Teosofia*, first published at Turin between 1859 and 1874.[61] The *Antropologia soprannaturale* appeared in 1884.[62] Noteworthy also is the book on Aristotle.

3

Rosmini's philosophy may be broadly classified as a form of idealism. In this respect he stood clearly aside from the empiricist school among his fellow-countrymen represented in Pasquale Galluppi (1770–1846), of the university of Naples.[63] His alleged ontologism is a matter of definition, since the philosophical doctrines to which that name has been attached vary markedly from one presentation of them to another. Rosmini was widely read in philosophy, and the sources of his thought, like Gioberti's, may be traced back ultimately to Augustine and Platonism. But he was also, as I have observed, a keen student of Aquinas, as well as being interested in the German idealists. His highly receptive mind thus was subject to a diversity of metaphysical influences, but the course he opted for himself was a middle one, neither absolute idealist nor empiricist. His overall aim was to devise a Christian philosophy that would serve the apologetic end of maintaining the essentials of Christian theism in a way that would meet the demands of the modern outlook. The task he set himself was therefore no easy one. Although the mould of his thinking was Augustinian, Kant's attempt to bridge the divide between rationalism and empiricism had to be taken into account, so far so in fact that some of Rosmini's interpreters have regarded his philosophy as little other than a form of Kantianism. Giovanni Gentile, for example, speaks of him as 'an Italian Kant', while a near contemporary of Rosmini's, Bertrando Spaventa, thought him 'more Kantian than Kant himself'.[64] It has to be admitted that Rosmini's ontologist idealism is a system of ideas that is complex, sophisticated and at times ambiguous.

The ground plan of the scheme is to be sought in what is usually judged his most significant work, the *Nuovo saggio sull'origine delle idee*, the inspiration of which is plainly Augustinian. Here the author's inquiry takes a threefold direction: the idea of being, the nature of intellectual perception, and the origin of ideas.[65]

Rosmini follows Kant in recognizing the double role of the *a posteriori* and the *a priori* in the process of knowledge, and grounds science in the latter. But he differs from Kant in reducing the *a priori* to a single category or form, namely the idea of Being, by which he means the residual common element in all knowledge and judgment – the sense, pure and simple, that *Being is*. By intuition or immediate perception we apprehend being as that which is primal, indeterminate (*l'essere indeterminato*) and universal. Such intuition is therefore antecedent to any specific judgment, of which indeed it is the precondition: 'L'uomo non può pensare a nullo senza l'idea del'essere universale'. Ideal being is primal in that it is the *prius* of all our experience, and indeterminate because not to be identified with actual existence in any form, since actuality is always only a *mode* of being, not being itself. At any rate one could say that it expresses no more than the potentiality of being. Further, the very indeterminacy of being entails that it also must be necessary and universal, and thus eternal, uncreated, infinite, unchangeable, absolutely simple, homogeneous, completely self-identical and indivisible. But what Rosmini especially emphasizes is its *objectivity*; the 'sense' of being precedes perception and understanding, is independent of them, and imposes itself on them. At the same time being is essentially relative to the intelligence; were it not so we could not cognize it. To this extent Rosmini is an idealist, in that being is always the object of *thought*; not necessarily our own, of course, as it is independent of the human mind, but certainly of God's. For in God being and thought are one.

Knowledge is possible because of certain forms of thought which are native to the human intelligence: substance, cause, number, truth, necessity. For objectivity of the idea of being ensures that our experience of particular entities is itself objective, experience consisting essentially in the perception of *things*. Rosmini, like Kant, sees it as the application of 'pure' or *a priori* ideas to sense-data, so giving rise to ideas which he describes as *mixed*. Of these mixed ideas those of mind and body, space, time and movement are fundamental. Being as a whole, and the particular beings which are the objects of our knowledge, are one and the same when brought within the concept of being-in-itself, being in its universality and indeterminacy. Where they differ is, as we have noted, in modality. Sense-experience, that is, furnishes us with the material of knowledge, the intuition of being with its formal constitution.

Both the intuitive idea of being *per se* and the sense-conditioned ideas of particular objects are, Rosmini believes, pre-existent in the mind of God, who eternally beholds, as it were, the entire creation and thus 'foresees' the way in which created entities become the objects of intelligent perception. Man accordingly must be thought of as the recipient of something which in itself is divine, inasmuch as the ideas which subsist in the divine mind are themselves of the divine substance. In and of God, they indeed *are* God. Rosmini's Catholic critics may here object – as they did – that if his argument is that the being we intuit is itself the substance of the divine mind then he clearly has committed himself to the express ontologism which Catholic orthodoxy frowns upon, and in fact long after the philosopher's death certain 'Rosminian' propositions came under Vatican censure (see below p. 174). His reply to this, however, was to urge the distinction between *ideality* and *reality*. In God the ideal and the real are identical, but from the standpoint of human knowledge they must be distinguished. For us to have an intuition of 'ideal' being as the pre-condition of all knowledge is simply to affirm that we necessarily see by the 'light' vouchsafed us by God, not to claim that we know as God himself knows. For if by the very constitution of our minds we have ideas which are the counterpart of God's it still does not follow that we discern God *as he is in himself*, since he is infinitely more than any human idea. Hence we can attach meaning to divine attributes such as God's goodness and wisdom without presuming that we know them as they are in God, who himself is far more than wisdom and goodness.

But to go back to Rosmini's theory of knowledge. Although he maintains that there is no knowledge apart from the immediate perception of being, our apprehension of the actual world in all its determinate forms depends, he recognizes, on sensation. Sensation and the idea of being are therefore coordinates. Without sensation we could know nothing of determinate reality, but without the idea of being sense-data would have no 'ground', no basis. The penetration or suffusion of sense by the intuition of being is what Rosmini calls intellectual perception. This occurs by virtue of what man is, as both sentient and intelligent. The act of knowing is a fusion of sensation and intelligence: pure sensation is no more possible than pure intellection. Only their simultaneous operation can give access to the real world in all its concrete variety. Knowledge is perceptive because it evokes this multifarious actuality, but it is also intellective because the idea of being already intuitively present to the mind receives from the mind such specific determinations of being as become, in cognition, ideas of particular objects. What has to be stressed, Rosmini contends, is the simultaneity of the factors in the cognitional process. Neither exists antecedently as a separate element. Man has an ordered experience of reality only because he is the complex sort of being the Creator has made him.

The origin of our ideas, other than the primal idea of pure being, arises, Rosmini holds, through abstraction. On a starkly empiricist or sensationalist view, like Galluppi's, sensation itself is the immediate raw material of ideas – sensation abstracted and reflected upon directly. This must be disputed. What reflection works on is not the bare sense-datum but objects apprehended and known as such by intellectual perception, which goes far beyond mere sensation. Given the object, that is, ideas are formed by abstracting from it certain features or qualities for attention, and disregarding others. In this way a whole sequence of ideas of increasing generality can be constructed. The sole exception is the most general idea of all, that of being *per se*, which is not reached thus since it is itself the precondition of all ideation.

In the *Psicologia* Rosmini investigates the 'self' in which the cognitional process takes place. A distinction must be drawn between the 'empirical' self and the soul proper. 'The self represents not the soul alone, but the soul as involved in a multitude of relationships by means of a whole series of mental operations that have to be performed before the monosyllable *I* can be meaningfully used.'[66] But the various activities by which the soul is self-identified necessarily presuppose the existence of a primary element anterior to its actual awareness of those activities. In other words, before we can consider the soul as conscious we have to recognize its interior reality; or, more simply still, we must allow that before the 'I' can be properly self-affirming it has itself to *be*. Thus to some extent at least 'selfness' (*meità*) is something other than the soul, which obscures its 'primitive and essential state' through the numerous relations with which the mind enfolds it. By removing this covering, so to speak, of relationships, we disclose at the root of the self a *sentiment* which precedes consciousness and constitutes the soul's 'substance'.[67] It is this 'fundamental sentiment' (*sentimento fondamentale*), something felt rather than demonstrated, that enables the soul to become aware of itself as an active agent by bringing to it, as with every other object of cognition, the 'ground' of universal being.[68] Moreover, this fundamental sentiment which we have of our selfhood, as both soul and body, is the underlying condition of all our perceptions, sensible and intellectual alike.

> If the soul did not feel its own existence prior to sensation, the latter would be nothing to it, since it would be no more than action upon a being which did not feel even itself, and which could therefore feel anything else still less.[69]

Also this fundamental sentiment need not be conscious.[70] Nor does it occur spontaneously, as it is always a matter of reflection. In order to become properly aware of it the mind has to grasp it intellectually, contemplate it for what it is.[71]

We may, then, characterize the fundamental sentiment as the permanent mode or aspect under which the self as a whole, the empirical 'I', is manifested. It is purely subjective and tells us nothing about realities external to itself. But its function in relation to sense is analogous to that of the idea of being in relation to each and every particular idea. It is thus the precondition of sense-experience, the forms of which are determinations of it, and so is both sensible and intellective.[72] Further, it does not exist in a void, but is always linked with specific sensations – heat, colour, and so on. By supplying the mind with the materials to which the idea of being is attached it makes possible the entire subsequent development of empirical knowledge. It is by means of it also that Rosmini is able to explain the union of soul and body. For the soul is in essence a sentiment, a feeling, and in all feeling the 'feeling' subject and the 'felt' object constitute a unity, like that of 'form' and 'matter'.[73] Accordingly man is to be understood as a unitary being, at once feeling and felt, the underlying duality however presenting itself as that of soul and body.[74] This 'corporeal sentiment', as Rosmini terms it, is characteristic of human nature.[75]

Unlike Kant, Rosmini does not confine purely rational knowledge to the phenomenal order. He himself is realist enough to believe that things in themselves are basically identical with things as apprehended by the mind. As an idealist, that is to say, he does not admit any essential dualism of nature and spirit. The world of spirit is reality as conceived by man, that of nature reality as it exists for God. Human thought is finite and therefore limited, but within its limits it is a true reflection of the divine mind. That is why it can be said to cognize things 'as they are in themselves'. Thus the Platonist element in Rosmini's philosophy becomes clear; the idea of Being – reality under its most general aspect – is not arrived at simply by abstraction; the essence of what is real is absolutely *a priori*, and known intuitively.[76]

In the *Nuovo saggio* Rosmini is concerned with the origin of our particular ideas, but the problem of the origin of the idea of pure being, being as such, is fundamental. Although he denies that it is a mere speculative concept, he does trace it back to what he calls 'theosophi-cal abstraction' (*astrazione teosofica*), an expression the meaning of which is certainly not self-evident. What Rosmini wishes us to understand by it would seem to be this. The idea of being is not that of things which are the object of sense, but rather of a Reality which is wholly and exclusively intellectual or 'spiritual', and therefore divine. Hence God himself is the origin of the idea of being. He it is who *abstracts* that idea by abstracting the ideal – his own attribute – from the real, *himself*. In order that created beings may have an existence apart from his own, God as Creator has to establish an identifiable distinction between himself, eternally one and unchanging, and the potentiality of being in all its diversity. For such is the condition of the existence of created things if they are to subsist with a reality of their own.

In Rosmini's view, then, the idea of pure being *is* produced by abstraction, but abstraction as effected by God, not by us, for whom it accords the possibility of all intellection, including the act of abstracting. Thus the idea of being depends on the reality of being, not indeed that of the objects of sense-experience, but the absolute Reality or God. So not only is the internal link uniting idea and reality not denied by Rosmini, he places it at the level of the creative act of God. Moreover, by grounding created reality in Being as creative, he seeks to make of human knowledge itself, in its primal, intuited form, a path that leads directly up to God. In opposition here to Kant, whose critical philosophy obviates all possibility of rational metaphysics, and therewith any supposedly logical demonstration of divine existence, Rosmini holds that, given the intuitively apprehended objectivity of the idea of being-in-itself, an idea rooted in the ultimate reality of God, divine existence is necessarily implied by the activity of reason itself. In other words, it is because man is able to think rationally that God's existence has to be seen by him as a rational certainty. For if, *per impossibile*, God did not exist man could not think rationally, since he would be lacking in that idea of universal being which is the light of reason itself. We cannot deny the existence of God without challenging the rationality which enables us to raise the question in the first place.

But in the idea of being a third form has to be distinguished: the *moral*, or the relation between the ideal and the real. Morality therefore has a place between theory of knowledge and ontology, as between subject and object. An intelligent being is a moral will, who loves being according to its degree. It is this love which constitutes the bond between the 'ideal' order of thought and the 'real' order of existence; or, as Rosmini himself phrases it, it is 'that which harmonizes the subject with the object, the perfecting of virtue, the fulfilment of the subject by means of its union with and adequation to the object; it is the beatitude of being'.[77] Morality comprises two constituent elements, the moral law itself as objective ideal, and the subjective reality of the individual will. Its purpose is to bring about a total, not merely a partial, coincidence of the subject (the real) with the object (the ideal). Thus the bases of morality, like those of knowledge, are objective. A morally good action is not one directed to the subject's personal happiness or advantage but to an objective good – 'the good in so far as it is viewed as and judged to be such by the understanding'.[78] Moral good, in short, is 'the good as recognized by the reason and desired by the will'. In acting morally the will cleaves to what the intelligence rationally affirms, and signifies the full agreement and harmony of a right mind with a right will, leading to an eased conscience and a mind at peace with itself. Rosmini's injunction, then, is: 'Love being wherever you encounter it and in whatever order it may present itself to your understanding . . . To be good the will must hate nothing and love all things according to their natural order.'[79]

Rosmini's contention is that there is no form of being unworthy of love, but each and every existing thing should be the object of love in proportion to its degree or measure of being. Thus he describes morality itself in terms of universal love, indeed approximating it to religion as the imitation of Christ. It culminates, that is, in the unconditioned love of God. Man cannot find salvation through self-fulfilment in the world, as modern thinking likes to suppose, but only in God and by freeing himself from the world – although not simply by denigrating and denying the world, for the world is God's creation. To imagine that man finds his own salvation in and through the world, as secular humanism maintains – on the principle that our humanity is self-sufficient – is in fact suicidal, destructive alike of true self-integrity and true world-possession. The fulfilment of nature is in Supernature. 'By his capacity for the closest union with the absolute Good, man identifies himself with that Good, wherein the supreme excellence of the creature surely resides.'[80] Only through a disinterested love of all creation, which also is love of the Creator and the gift of the self to him, do men really reach out to and make contact with each other, just as egoism and self-interest cut them off from one another. Love alone, Rosmini urges, is the way to understanding. Not to love is to forfeit the truth, to forfeit even one's humanity, for then one ceases to be a moral subject, a person, a free centre of actions authentically one's own and consonant with the dignity of a rational being. It is the truth only that frees and sustains freedom; which means that the scope of the moral law and of moral responsibility is all-comprehending.

And this is so, Rosmini insists, because the moral law is objective, eternal and necessary – given to man, not created by him. Were man himself the ultimate moral legislator there would indeed be no place for God, as much modern philosophy, in pressing the idea of man's complete autonomy, is ready enough to concede. It is Rosmini's conviction, however, that this is to cut at the root of civilization or any real progress in the rational ordering of life. In any case it does not follow that because the moral law is imposed by God man has no liberty and no autonomy. On the contrary, as a rational being he has 'nothing more authentically his own than his freedom of action'. But Christianity alone, with its doctrine of theonomy, can prescribe for human liberty an absolute end – something which the order of nature does not provide. Apart from Christ there is no freedom: 'Truth and charity . . . bear reciprocal witness to one another, because each inheres in the other, and neither is to be found outside the other.'[81]

Rosmini's claim is, in fact, that what he propounds is a genuinely

Christian philosophy, a properly Christian use of reason to show that reason is itself of and from God and that the intrinsic vocation of rational thought is to attain to the transcendent divine, without confusion of the natural with the supernatural. Being is reality in its wholeness, and truth can encompass it; but it is not known to us as a whole. To aspire to such totality of knowledge may be a natural and supreme aim for us, but it nonetheless is a goal beyond our reach. The being which spirit intuitively seizes is without limit because it is being's very essence and truth; but it is not absolute being. Intuition grasps the essence of being, that is, only as 'idea', not as it is in its unconditioned, unbounded reality. That an infinite Mind alone could contain. Yet it is the task of natural theology to treat of 'being as it is in itself'. As such therefore it is an inquiry into the absolute being of God. It is no mere flight of the speculative imagination, but an expression of reason's own intrinsic need, even when it is aware that 'being altogether surpasses anything which our minds can rise to'.[82] Natural theology, conceived of as the science of real and infinite being, is therefore a legitimate extension of philosophy. Man may not know what the absolute being is 'in itself', but he does know that *it is*, and is such that it must transcend the finite understanding.[83]

Rosmini describes this way of knowing God as *negative*, signifying thereby that man can have no direct knowledge of God. However, the intuitive apprehension of ideal or absolute being, of which the finite intelligence is capable, furnishes an intrinsic proof of God's existence, since by virtue of our rational nature there is within us an immanent divinity which imbues us with a sense of transcendent deity – a capacity which in itself affords rational testimony to the truth of theism. Moreover, awareness of the insufficiency of our human knowledge is likewise implicit evidence of the deep desire within us for the incomplete to receive completion. Thus are we disposed towards divine revelation. But revelation is something altogether beyond the attainment of speculative philosophy; on the contrary, it is a free disclosure pertaining to an order of understanding that is extra-philosophical and supra-rational. Our partial knowledge thus finds fulfilment only in an act of ultimate self-surrender to God. The possible objection that with this argument the 'philosophical' theologian, by abandoning any final appeal to the rational intelligence, takes leave of philosophy altogether, Rosmini counters by urging that nothing which touches the life and destiny of man is philosophically irrelevant. Philosophical inquiry should not set its sights too low; the problem of the existence of God and the great religious themes of creation and redemption are the supreme issues to which man as a rational being can address himself, a fact which no one with a knowledge of human nature is surely likely to deny or ignore.[84] To parenthesize man's 'existential situation' – if I may use a twentieth-century term to express Rosmini's meaning – is to disregard the practical implications of human finitude. Consciousness of sin, the sense of evil, cannot but tax the philosophical mind and so become a question for it. Philosophy will not simply eliminate the concept of the supernatural if it wishes to come to grips with the problem of what man is in his totality and what his spiritual vocation finally may be.

Thus Rosmini poses a question which the modern philosopher cannot easily evade, namely whether, if the range of human knowledge is as infinite as is the reality of experience itself, would not science be completely adequate and man have no need of God or revelation – in fact, whether or not positivism is the true philosophy. Rosmini's contention is, as a theist, that such an infinity of knowledge is not nor can be ours, so that of ourselves we are incapable of a knowledge which satisfies the demands of our nature as a whole. But this means that we will find ourselves set upon a spiritual quest the end of which is the only absolute goal – God. The Romantic philosophies of immanence try to circumvent this difficulty by an equivocation, seeking to demonstrate that the absolute truth we look for is the truth already in our possession. To which Rosmini's reply is that man has in his own reason an infinite light which enables him to affirm that his knowledge is not bounded by the limits of sensible experience – a position which the Italian thinker gladly shares with the German idealists – but also one which obviates any claim that the human spirit can compass within itself the infinity of being and truth. The mystery of existence always beckons the philosopher forward, but he can never lay hold of it with both hands.

Among his fellow-countrymen Rosmini's influence was considerable. His gifts as a thinker were widely recognized and the ideas expounded in his voluminous writings gained many sympathizers, especially in his native northern Italy, where it would be no exaggeration to speak of a Rosminian school. But from the start he had his critics as well, one of the earliest being Mamiani, who later became a follower of Gioberti's.[85] But his chief opponent was Gioberti himself, who in Degli errori di Antonio Rosmini attacked what he saw as the basic contradiction in the Rosminian doctrine, that its 'ideal being', being per se, should be described as 'divine' but denied to be God, as also to be at once in the mind yet above it and to be preconditional and indeterminate whilst at the same time the object of reflective thought. Such incoherences, in Gioberti's view, could not but lead to further serious errors, such as that truth has no objective basis and that 'intellectual perception' affords an adequate account of our knowledge of the external world. So far from establishing proof of divine existence the Rosminian metaphysics fails to present any clear concept of God at all. In his judgment the author of the *Nuovo saggio* could avoid scepticism only by embracing a subjective pantheism.

It was this last charge of pantheism which especially stung Rosmini, who was at pains to answer it at some length,[86] again pressing his distinction between the ideal and the real, infinite and finite, necessary existence and contingent existence.[87] He expressly denied that we have any direct intuition of the divine being itself, as Malebranche had held; for what is open to us is no more – if no less – than cognition of that 'indeterminate' being which is the condition of the existence of all particular beings. It presupposes God, but is not itself God, for God is not seen immediately 'in things', and Rosmini vigorously repudiates pantheism in so far as it implies that God cannot be thought of as existing apart from created reality. Nevertheless the allegation was subsequently made by Rosmini's critics that in his posthumous works his position was clearly ontologist, whatever may be said of those published in his lifetime.[88] What perhaps they found difficult to explain was the concept of 'ideal being' as an attribute of God or of his 'Word', and therefore in a true sense *divine*, without its being itself God. For this, we may well concede, is the nub of the matter, since if use of the epithet 'divine' is rightly applicable to ideal being, not simply in a metaphorical way but realistically, as denoting a substantial participation in deity, then in what respect precisely does Rosmini's teaching differ from Malebranche's? His repeated answer, that the difference is between the ideal and the real, may seem to some, in view of the generally idealist stance of his thinking, to amount to no more than a verbalism. Dubious, too, for his orthodox critics was his whole notion of creation as a 'divine synthesis' of ideal, indeterminate being and the innumerable possible determinations of it that are pre-existent, or anticipated, in the mind of God. For basically Rosmini conceives of God first as Being in the sense of absolute Subject whose eternal act is one of 'self-thinking', then as Being in the sense of absolute Object, the Word, who is likewise personal. But the Word has a dual aspect, not only as that of a subsisting divine Person, but as that also of being as pure possibility, the potential reality of all things. It is this latter which Rosmini characterizes as ideal and indeterminate, divine yet not God – God, that is, in his personal self-centredness as eternal subject – nor even as his personal 'outgoing' Word. It is from this pure potentiality, Rosmini tells us, that God conceives determinate existence, so that the ideal 'possible' becomes the concrete 'actual'. The objection to this theology is that by it God's act in creation is not properly creative at all; for if being is itself eternal what takes place in creation is only a form of divine self-limitation. So that ultimately God and the world are one. Rosmini of course denies this conclusion, emphasizing the distinct and substantive reality of particular existents. Again, however, the question arises of his self-consistency. He may in all earnestness wish to avoid the apparent implications of his metaphysical principles, but can he do so except by sacrificing logic? In short, does not Rosmini's idealist ontologism involve him in the same fundamental ambiguities as are latent in Hegelianism?

In spite therefore of the Vatican *dimittantur* of 1854, criticism of Rosmini's religious philosophy was not silenced and found renewed voice after his death. The *Civiltà cattolica* and the *Osservatore Romano* repeatedly carried articles impugning his orthodoxy.[89] Statements by the Congregation of the index in 1880 and again in 1881 indicated that the *dimittantur* simply meant that no prohibition was placed on Rosmini's writings and should not be assumed to imply that they were entirely free from error. But the *Civiltà* was not satisfied and in 1885 again denounced Rosmini, this time not only as philosophically a pantheist but as a Jansenist in theology and a liberal in politics – in fact, as a continuing source of danger to the unsuspecting faithful. The Vatican thereupon reopened the whole issue of Rosmini's soundness as a thinker and in 1887 the Holy Office formally condemned forty propositions culled from his posthumous works and touching not only on his theories of ideal being and creation but on the origin and nature of the soul, the dogmas of the trinity and the incarnation and various other theological matters. It was a comprehensive survey, although none of the opinions cited was singled out for special theological censure. It was also borne in mind that Rosmini had not himself published the writings which contained the alleged errors and that it might properly be supposed that had he lived he might have revised or even retracted them.[90]

Rosmini is a philosophical thinker who, one feels, has still not received the recognition that is his due, even from the standpoint of the historian. Outside Italy he made little or no impact, while in his own country the type of philosophy which he expounded, albeit with fullest conviction that it supplied the most appropriate metaphysical context for orthodox Christian and Catholic doctrine – that it was, in a very precise sense, a 'Christian philosophy' – was not favoured by theologians who saw neo-Thomism as the only philosophy congruous with ultramontane integralism. In many ways his ideas, as did Gioberti's, anticipate those of Maurice Blondel, and today it is possible to appreciate the distinctiveness of his contribution to modern Catholic thought without having to defer to the officially countenanced criticisms which for many years cast a shadow over his work. Himself a

Catholic by unshaken conviction, whose own mind was steeped in the tradition of the *philosophia perennis*, he nevertheless saw the need for the Catholic church to speak with a voice that could command respect in cultural and social conditions that had undergone radical change. His intellectual powers were both original and constructive, his practical interests were many-sided and his dedication to his priestly calling was never at any moment open to doubt. Indeed the term 'Rosminianism' is very nearly a synonym for the entire revival of Catholic spirituality in Italy in the first half of the nineteenth century.

7

Lamennais and *Paroles d'un Croyant*

A PARADOX of early nineteenth-century romanticism, forced upon it no doubt by the political and social turmoil of the period itself, was the seeming contradiction between its uncurbed individualism and its yearning for a reintegrated and reconstituted society, an ideal 'collective' imaginatively projected either behind it into the past or forward into the future. Against the back-cloth of the Revolution, and the socially atomistic rationalism which had so largely contributed to it, it is little wonder that the utopianism of the Romantics should in the main have been conservative. Not that all political conservatism drew inspiration from this source. The reactionary policies of Metternich and the architects of the Holy Alliance were motivated chiefly by fear and jealousy for the privileges of the existing ruling class. But genuinely romanticist political and social theory arose from the urge to maintain or reassert the ties which bound men one to another; ties, however, which had to be compatible also with their liberties. In fact individualism as a socio-political principle was too little adequate to the organic nature and vital needs of human society to be permanently effective, as the Revolution itself had demonstrated. 'Society', declared Henri de Saint-Simon, 'does not live on negative ideas, but on positive', and pointed back to the middle ages for a paradigm instance of an 'organic' social order such as he and his contemporaries desiderated. Moreover, what had given society its cohesion in the past and alone, they held, would restore it in the future was religious belief. As Edmund Burke had said: 'We know, we feel inwardly, that religion is the basis of civil society.' And religion for the Romantics was not a matter of the individual rational judgment, but of tradition, of the established principles and usages of a historic institutional authority. Indeed it is this which explains the wave of converts to Roman Catholicism, particularly in Protestant Germany. For as Goethe observed: 'Protestants feel a void; they want to create a new mysticism', and he himself had long considered that Protestantism had given the individual 'too much to carry'.

But it was in France, a traditionally Catholic country in which the Enlightenment had nevertheless gained many of its most spectacular advances, that hopes for a rejuvenated Catholicism as the foundation of a just and stable Christian social order received clearest articulation. This is what we have in the 'traditionalism' of Bonald and the new ultramontanism of Joseph de Maistre and Lamennais – the last-named the outstanding representative among Frenchmen of his generation of religious romanticism and a man in whom personally the ardour, the passions, the doubts and the distresses associated with the Romantic movement are epitomized.

Hugues-Félicité Robert de Lamennais (1782–1854), like Chateaubriand a Breton from Saint-Malo,[1] entered on a clerical career in March 1816, when he had reached his thirty-fifth year. But his ordination to the priesthood took place only with the deepest misgivings and much hesitation on his part, the result probably of his melancholic indecisiveness of temperament.[2] Not that this step, when at last ventured on, brought him peace of mind. On 25 June of the same year he wrote to his elder brother, Jean-Marie, himself an abbé and a strong personal influence in helping Félicité to his decision: 'I believe that I can and should explain myself to you once and for all. I am, and henceforth cannot but be, extraordinarily unhappy.'[3] Highly strung, introspective and moody, he tended throughout life to oscillate between the extremes of disillusionment and mental torpor and a sanguine impetuosity. In his youth he had swung from the simple Catholicism in which he was nurtured as a child to the deism of the *philosophes*: at one time he was a fervent disciple of Rousseau, and was himself, one might almost say, a product of *Emile*, thanks to the influence of his rather free-thinking uncle, Robert des Saudrais, to whose care he was committed, so far as his education went, after his mother's death. But by 1804 he had returned to the faith, a change of conviction for which we have something of an apologia in the two letters which he wrote years later to an English acquaintance,[4] although it is more than probable that, with such a disposition of mind as his, this recovery of belief was the outcome of pressures other than purely intellectual. Assuredly religion offered no easy consolation to a man who could feel moved to write: 'Human life has but one springtime, and I still do not know what it is; I have learned of it only by hearsay.'[5]

Yet for all his besetting *Weltschmerz* Lamennais's intellect was keen and vigorous. Largely self-instructed – and he was an omnivorous reader in half-a-dozen languages – he taught mathematics in his early years at the *collège ecclésiastique* at Saint-Malo, but for reasons of health he gave up his post and went to live at the family property of La

Chênaie, between Combourg – Chateaubriand's ancestral home – and Dinan. Here he threw himself into study, always his most willingly chosen pastime, but his psychological *malaise* did not improve, and he even expected death. He went back to Saint-Malo to resume his teaching, but with characteristic restlessness again abandoned it and returned to La Chênaie, the one place on earth, it would seem, where he came nearest to finding happiness. Nevertheless he had been able to embark on literary work in collaboration with his brother, and in 1809 published a small volume of *Réflexions sur l'état de l'Eglise en France pendant le XVIIIᵉ siècle, et son situation actuelle*, as well as assisting Jean-Marie with another and much more extended venture, *Tradition de l'Eglise sur l'institution des évêques*, although the printing of this was delayed until the time of the first Restoration in 1814.[6] The former was intended mainly as a tract for the clergy and is of interest to the student of Lamennais as already containing the seeds of the later Mennaisian philosophy. It hails the prospect of a Catholic revival, however strongly the current of anti-Catholic and even anti-religious opinion might still be flowing. The church had endured many evils in the past, and especially during the preceding century, but better times could now be expected – not least, the author is at pains to suggest, through the beneficence of the emperor, whose concordat with the Vatican was a recent memory, and to whom Lamennais pays some rather fulsome compliments. His dislike of Protestantism – and throughout his career he displayed a particular animus against it – is already evinced. Society, for its health and stability, needs to be founded on the right principles, and these the Protestant reformers of the sixteenth century had gravely compromised, thus undermining the bases not only of religious but of social order. They established the rule of anarchy in church and in state by attributing sovereignty to the people and the right of private judgment in belief to each individual.[7] Of this deplorable innovation the doctrines of the *philosophes* had been the progeny, with their disastrous outcome in the Terror, since it had been in the vaunted name of liberty that 'twenty-five million men groaned in the most abject slavery'.[8] The French church had no doubt done its best in extremely difficult circumstances, but its apologists had lacked the requisite literary sophistication – no slight disadvantage when seeking to address a highly literate public.

Lamennais, however, is not concerned only with a general diagnosis; he goes on to propound specific remedies. The church must be strengthened, which means that the clergy must be improved (and at the time he was writing their quality was sadly mediocre), there should be bishops' meetings, synods of the clergy, mission-priests organized in 'teams' (as we nowadays would say), rural deans, new church schools;

but above all more vocations to the priesthood, for the numbers had sunk low. All this reads tritely enough in the light of developments in after years, but such ideas at the time were novel.[9] Unfortunately for its author, at the moment of the book's appearance Napoleon was in open conflict with Pius VII; its tone was not approved and copies were seized by the Paris police.

Tradition de l'Eglise, of much greater bulk than *Réflexions*, was indicative of another of Lamennais's major concerns. It was a frontal attack on Gallicanism, defending the inalienable because divine right of the pope to institute bishops; to negate that right would be to subvert the papal primacy itself and thus destroy the Catholic church's very constitution. It was in fact a manifesto of ultramontanism, granting to the Holy See not only the highest dignity but absolute rights. Indeed, as between the throne of Peter and its successive occupants no distinction was to be drawn, nor was the papal infallibility to be construed as mere indefectibility. Much historical learning – Jean-Marie's most likely – was brought up in support of this thesis, but the thrust of the whole argument, which owes something to the later views of Bonald, who likewise opposed the Gallican position, is doctrinal and polemical. The idea of development – if not of dogma then certainly of the church's institutions – is also present. But the most significant feature of the work, in view of Lamennais's subsequent career, was its total dedication to the idea and institution of the papacy. Lamennais, together with Joseph de Maistre, whose volume *Du Pape* appeared a few years later, in 1819, could be said to be the founder of modern ultramontanism.

Surprisingly or not, *Tradition* aroused little criticism or comment. The publication that made Lamennais's name was, beyond all question, that of the first volume of the *Essai sur l'indifférence en matière de religion* three years later, in 1817. If it was not the most important work of Catholic apologetic to appear during the nineteenth century it certainly was the most sensational, turning out to be a landmark in the history of the French church in modern times. Its success was immense. The first edition was exhausted within two months, and by the end of the year it had sold 13,000 copies.[10] Its author was hailed as a second Bossuet, with the intellectual acumen of a Pascal and the literary style of a Rousseau added. Assuredly nothing at all resembling it had been published in the French language since Chateaubriand's *Le Génie du Christianisme*.[11] Not least surprised by this acclaim was Lamennais himself, now on the way to acquiring a European fame as the *Essai* was translated into several tongues.[12] Today of course it is of no more than historical interest, its argument carrying weight only in face of an intellectual and social situation like that of its own day.[13] But when it made its *début* it was saluted by the younger French intellectuals, not by any means necessarily themselves Catholics, as a masterly defence of the nation's traditional faith. A second volume was published in 1820, and a third and fourth in 1823; a fifth was planned but never completed, although in 1821 the author produced a *Défense de l'Essai sur l'indifférence* in which he re-presented his case against objectors. But these subsequent volumes did not make the same impression on public opinion as the first. It was the trumpet-call of 1817 that resounded throughout France and beyond. Joseph de Maistre called it 'a clap of thunder beneath a leaden sky'.

The 'indifference' which Lamennais denounces is not mere heedlessness, complacent or trifling. He was concerned rather with matters of intellectual principle: *l'indifférentisme* might perhaps have been a better word. Broadly the view he was assailing was one which maintains that moral and social conduct has no necessary connection with formal beliefs, that religious doctrines are at best of only very secondary importance and that a right disposition is all that counts – much the same attitude, in fact, which was opposed in England by John Henry Newman as 'liberalism'. But, says Lamennais, the contrary is the truth.

> Man acts only because he believes, and men in the mass always act in conformity with what they believe, since the passions of the multitude are themselves determined by its beliefs. If belief be pure and true, the general tendency of actions is right and in harmony with order; if belief be false, actions contrariwise become depraved. For error corrupts, and truth perfects.[14]

For the good of society therefore the beliefs generally held within it should be sound; unbridled freedom of opinion is ruinous, since where each follows his own notions order will be undermined. Indifferentism Lamennais sees as of three main kinds. The first is that of sophisticated non-believers who nevertheless profess to hold that religion is good for the common people – or, in plain words, is politically useful as a means of restraint. This had been the view of many among the ruling classes under the *ancien régime*. The second is that of the deists and their successors, the *idéologues*. Religion is desirable and even credible, but not in any 'supernaturalistic' form, an opinion Lamennais considers must eventually lead to atheism. Thirdly, there is Protestantism. Here, too, private judgment is the guide, there being no authority beyond it. But the outcome has been the fragmentation of Christendom, and as with deism total unbelief is likely to be the end result. All three positions rest upon a fatal individualism.

The first volume of the *Essai* was mainly polemical and negative; the positive side of Lamennais's new apologetic emerges more clearly in the second. Here the appeal is to authority, without qualification. This in truth was not quite novel, Bonald having already urged it.[15] But Lamennais does so with greater boldness and point.

> Re-establish authority! [he proclaims in his preface] Order will be entirely reborn, truth will again be set on an unshakeable base, the anarchy of opinion will cease, man will listen to man, minds united by one and the same faith will dispose themselves around their centre, which is God, and will draw life again from the source of light and life.[16]

But where is such authority to be found? The answer is in tradition, the 'general reason', the *sens commun*, of mankind. Lamennais expresses the matter succinctly in his *Défense de l'Essai*. In order, he says, to avoid the scepticism to which the belief of the isolated individual leads one should not look to oneself for the certitude of a primary truth, but start from a fact – namely, that insurmountable faith which is intrinsic to our nature – and admit as true that which all men invincibly believe. Authority, or the general reason, or what all men are agreed upon, is the rule for governing the judgments of the individual man.[17] The ground of this general reason, which *philosophie* in its popular meaning is so apt to pervert, is God's primal revelation to mankind; its first principle, in fact, is that of God's existence, something which all men by their very humanity – when uncorrupted – unite in testifying. But Lamennais hurries his argument forward; deists admit divine existence, yet divine truth is the possession of Christianity alone, and within Christianity, of the Catholic church. 'Since Jesus Christ what authority dare anyone compare to that of the Catholic church, the heir of all the main traditions, of the first revelation and of the Mosaic revelation, of all the truths known to antiquity, whereof its teaching is only the development?'[18] Outside Catholicism Lamennais finds no authority, no religion even, worth speaking of.

Resounding though Lamennais's *succès d'estime* was, there also were many who demurred. The author of the *Essai* was plainly an asset to the Restoration but his anti-Gallicanism at least did not commend him to the government, nor in truth to the majority of the French clergy, especially the bishops. On the question of authority his doctrine of the *sens commun* looked to some – the theologians of St-Sulpice, for example – dangerously equivocal. It assigned too much room to faith and not enough to reason – and the Cartesian inheritance in the seminaries was still a force. So controversy arose and Lamennais was thrown increasingly on the defensive. The Jesuits particularly came out as firm opponents of Mennaisian views. Although Lamennais's sense of mission was if anything intensified under attack, and he had convinced and energetic disciples like Olympe Gerbet and Henri-François Rohrbacher, he decided to refer matters to Rome, in which he

181

had implicit trust and whither he journeyed in the spring of 1824. He was welcomed in the Holy City as a distinguished visitor and received in audience by Leo XII with undisguised warmth of feeling. Lamennais had every reason at this stage to feel confident of Vatican support.

The truth is, however, that he was not in the strict sense of the words either a philosopher or a theologian. His real interests were social and political, and notably the border region between theology and social ethics. These it was which now increasingly determined his purposes and action, fired by his passionate and impulsive nature. His belief in the social role of the church, moreover, grew. He had no wish to see the *ancien régime* restored intact and he felt no commitment to the reactionary monarchism of the 'ultras' of the Right. The throne might serve the altar, or it might not; his own prime loyalties were in no doubt. The direction of his thinking was made very evident in his next book, *De la Religion considérée dans ses rapports avec l'ordre politique et civile*,[19] which was published in two parts, the first in May 1825 and the second in February of the following year. Its theme expressly was the peril of too close an alliance between altar and throne. French public opinion, he declared, was becoming more and more democratic, not to say secularist, the secularism encouraged especially by the state educational system, the Université, established under Napoleon. No good would come to a church thus conjoined with a political order increasingly atheist in outlook, whatever its religious professions. The church's proper task was that of restoring, or creating, a truly Christian society, the spiritual power being 'the supreme defence of justice and of the rights of humanity'.[20] The Gallican theory was thus an impediment to its fulfilment.

> The true dignity, the real strength, of bishops and priests alike depends today on their detachment from public affairs; there is enough for them in the work of the church. The future of religion is assured; it will not perish, its foundations are unshakeable. Separate it, then, from what is collapsing. Why try to combine things that do not belong together?[21]

What Lamennais, ever the visionary, thus seemed to desiderate was in the end a theocracy; but a theocracy in which the pope, society's supreme defender of justice, was to be acknowledged as God's undisputed vicegerent.

Lamennais's principal opponent was Mgr Frayssinous, vicar-general of the archdiocese of Paris, who as grand master of the Université was effectively the government minister for public instruction, and who used his very considerable influence with the episcopate and the government to discountenance both Lamennais's ultramontanism and his questionable 'taditionalist' philosophy.[22] The upshot was

Lamennais's being convicted and fined under the law by a police tribunal, although the terms of the judgment were surprisingly tempered and even respectful. It was the prosecution, rather, which cut a poor figure.[23] The effect, however, was to weaken still further Lamennais's regard for the existing authorities and to drive him towards an avowed liberalism.

His next work, *Des progrès de la Révolution et de la guerre contre l'Eglise*, which came out in 1829, was prompted by the royal ordinances of the previous year relating to church schools and aimed in particular at excluding the Jesuits from their control. It reveals its author's thinking to have reached a transitional stage. In the preface he boldly demanded for the Catholic church the liberties promised under the *Charte* of the Restoration, along with freedom of conscience, freedom of education and freedom of the press – the objectives, in fact of the liberal movement then fermenting in Belgium. A national return to Christianity would come, he declared, only within the conditions created by such freedoms. A merely reactionary royalism like that of the restored monarchy was obsolete. Between the alternatives of despotism and anarchy a new Christian order offered the sole hope, and to establish it Catholic and liberal must unite. The church's part was crucial, for only a spiritual society could safeguard both order and liberty. Catholics should place themselves above party, while if need be the connection between church and state would have to be severed. On its appearance *Des progrès de la Révolution* was immediately denounced by the government press, and Mgr de Quélen, the archbishop of Paris, condemned it in a pastoral letter as the work of a presumptuous and mischievous upstart, however talented. Lamennais's reply, in the form of open letters to the archbishop himself, was no less trenchant and uncompromising.

The famous *Avenir* began publication on 16 October 1830, shortly after the revolution which overthrew Charles X and forced him into exile. The time was ripe, in the eyes of Lamennais's friends and followers, for a new daily newspaper openly identifying itself with views not only Catholic but liberal. It proclaimed its standpoint at once. Since the outbreak of the Revolution of 1789 various *régimes* had come and gone, but two things had stood firm in men's hearts: God and liberty. Combine them and France would recover her stability. Lamennais directed the *Avenir*, but was strongly supported by two close companions and sympathizers, the Dominican friar Henri de Lacordaire and a young nobleman Count Charles de Montalembert. The Breton priest however was its moving spirit and his utterance set the whole tone of it. Its programme was laid down in summary form in the issue of 7 December, and covered the freedoms for which its editor had called in his last book. Freedom in education was a pressing concern; the state monopolized teaching and private schools were forbidden. But the policy of the Université was secular, and as such repugnant to the Catholic conscience. It was this conviction which induced Lacordaire and Montalembert, somewhat melodramatically, to open a private school of their own in defiance of the law, an act which resulted in Montalembert's prosecution. The *Avenir*'s argument was that exclusive state control was a plain violation of parental rights. And of freedom in education that of publication, of the press, was a natural concomitant. The tight government hold on the expression of opinion – warning, fine, suppression was the sequence – was intolerable. The policy was moreover dangerously short-sighted: the only effective remedy for abuses was public protest, and any attempt to forbid that would inevitably lead to disaster.

A third demand was for freedom to form associations, in particular religious communities, the establishment of which was at the time prohibited, mainly for fear of secret societies. Cases of hardship and injustice were readily cited in detail. Fourthly, *Avenir* demanded freedom of worship. Again instances were reported of unwarranted and provocative government interference. In the regulation of worship – the question of burials was a special irritant – the state had no authority. Not that the ecclesiastical authority was behind the *Avenir*'s campaign: it too suffered the lash of the editorial tongue. Total separation of church and state – the withdrawal of the government's stipend would be no cause for grief – was a price well paid for liberty. Gallicanism was no better than a euphemism for the church's actual subservience, and Bossuet had wrought more harm in France than ever Luther had done. Nor was the *Avenir* afraid to venture into purely political areas; it called alike for universal suffrage and administrative decentralization.

In pursuing this agitation Lamennais's newspaper prepared trouble for itself. The attitude of the French episcopate shifted from embarrassment to hostility, particularly when Lamennais set about organizing a 'liberal' association, the Agence Générale pour la Défense de la Liberté Religieuse, announcement of which, with Lamennais himself as president, was made on 16 December.[24] The *Avenir* was denounced in one pastoral letter after another and the reading of it was prohibited in all seminaries and in several dioceses. Obviously it was impossible for a Catholic journal to continue in France in open antagonism to the hierarchy, however little Lamennais himself cared for episcopal views; to him the only true authority was Rome, and to Rome he made up his mind to appeal, regardless of events in his own country. On 15 November 1831 the last issue of the *Avenir* made its appearance. In the end indeed shortage of funds not less than ecclesiastical disapproval silenced it. Immediately Lamennais and his intimates Lacordaire and Montalembert took the path to Rome, arriving there on 30 December with the intention of submitting their aims and hopes, with all candour, to the Holy See.

On 3 February 1832 a *mémoire* – almost entirely the work of Lacordaire – was addressed to the pope, Gregory XVI, setting out Lamennais's version of the facts about the *Avenir* and its purposes but couched in the most studiously deferential terms. The three of them came, it stated, as pilgrims to the Chair of Truth, before which they laid their beliefs unreservedly; the supreme pontiff's word was enough. Towards the end of the month Cardinal Pacca, dean of the Sacred College, replied that while the Holy Father gave all credit for the good intents as well as the talents of the contributors to the *Avenir* he deplored their imprudence in raising so many matters of controversy; nevertheless he promised that a careful inquiry would be made into their principles. This would of course take time and he advised them meanwhile to return to France. However, Lamennais and his friends pressed their request for an audience and were received by Gregory on 13 March, in the presence – presumably as a witness – of the French Cardinal de Rohan. The interview was disappointingly brief – a bare fifteen minutes – and conversation was restricted to affable generalities. Afterwards Lacordaire departed for Paris, although Lamennais chose to stay on in Rome. Montalembert also remained, but spent a good deal of his time in visiting other parts of Italy. In July the pope issued a brief to the bishops of Poland enjoining obedience to the established order. The papal statement was a blow to Lamennais, who in the columns of the *Avenir* not only had urged French Catholics to take the road of liberty but had pleaded on behalf of the same cause elsewhere in Europe – in Ireland, in Poland, in Italy itself. The brief, therefore, inevitably boded ill for his present mission. Yet he lingered on, still hoping for the best. If the Vatican continued to say nothing it had at least not condemned. As the days passed, though, even he felt it pointless to remain in Rome any longer and he left for Munich. Near the end of July a document drawn up by the archbishop of Toulouse and some dozen other French bishops was received at the Vatican. It contained a list of propositions culled from the writings of Lamennais and his follower Gerbet which in the view of the prelates who signed it deserved censure,[25] although what in the main they objected to was the philosophy of the *sensus communis*. Whilst at Munich Lamennais, who now had been joined by Lacordaire as well as Montalembert, was personally handed a copy of the papal encyclical *Mirari vos*, dated 15 August, with an accompanying letter from Pacca, making clear

Gregory XVI's disapprobation of the opinions of the *Avenir* on matters of public concern which it had taken up.[26] The encyclical itself did not refer either to the journal or to Lamennais by name and was less overtly anti-Mennaisian than is sometimes alleged. But on certain issues it was outspoken – for example, to say that the church is in need of regeneration is described as 'absurd' and 'insulting', or to plead for liberty of conscience as 'sheer madness'. Freedom of the press is strongly reprobated as 'abominable and detestable', and the call for the separation of church and state is denounced as impious. The idea of forming associations of Catholics and members of other religions the pope found especially distressing. Obedience to sovereign princes, 'our dear sons in Jesus Christ', was, he reminded them, a Christian duty.

The same evening on which the encyclical reached them Lamennais and Montalembert drew up an instrument of submission, which on 10 September was countersigned by others of their collaborators on the *Avenir*. The journal itself was of course still suspended and the Agence Générale was already in process of dissolution.

2

Lamennais, the extreme papalist, had confidently appealed to the authority he so revered, and yet it had decided against him on matters touching his conscience at the quick. The spiritual power he had employed all his energy and eloquence to promote had condemned the very causes for the endorsement of which he had had recourse to it. Thus his whole standing-ground seemed to have crumbled beneath him. What was he to do? His immediate reaction – that of dutiful submission – alone seemed logical. But how far was such submission really to go? Had it no limits? Was it indeed a case now of burning what he had hitherto adored? Lamennais, for the sake of his own integrity, was bound to reflect gravely on the predicament in which he now found himself. In a letter of 30 November to a friend, Abbé Guéranger, afterwards abbot of the famous abbey of Solesmes, he wrote:

> We have always considered the Encyclical as an act of diplomacy solicited by the sovereigns [i.e. of the Powers] in order to halt the Catholic action that was alarming them. We were only too well acquainted with the facts to be deceived for a moment, and we were none the less bound as Catholics to obey. That is what we have done, and our declaration implies no more than that.[27]

By the beginning of 1833 Lamennais had left Paris and was back at La Chênaie. The indefinite suspension of the *Avenir* and the winding-up of the Agence Générale apparently spelled the end of the liberal Catholic movement. This at least was the earnest hope of its opponents, for not only had Lamennais quitted the public scene but had told his friends that his purpose now was to devote all his time to the revision and completion of his philosophical system – an occupation for the next two years, as he calculated.[28] The only appropriate response to the papal encyclical, other than an act of formal submission, was, he judged, silence, cost him what it might to his feelings to maintain it. But his mind was awake and active, and certainly far from contemplating any retraction of the opinions and aims propounded in the *Avenir*. What, however, might well be altering was his view of the church itself. The latter had shown plainly enough that it was wholly unwilling to lend its support to political and social change, believing that its interests, which it evidently identified as purely temporal and material, lay with the old order. At all events such was the attitude of the hierarchy. But the church was not the hierarchy alone; it was the entire body of the faithful, and for their good it should be kept intact, with nothing done likely to cause dissension and schism. A letter of 12 March to a correspondent in Mexico is a clear disclosure of the drift of Lamennais's thoughts. The world, he wrote, was in a state of crisis, trying to free itself from a lifeless past and to start on a new era.

> Nothing will stop this magnificent movement of the human race, directed from above by Providence. But several causes are holding it back. The welfare of society reposes on two principles which, rightly understood, comprise all its laws: 'No liberty without religion', and 'No religion without liberty'. Now our old Europe is divided into two parties, one of which wants liberty without religion, and the other religion without liberty; that is to say, both alike are striving to realize the impossible. The only remedy, then, is to attach the Catholics to the cause of liberty, in order to win back the friends of liberty to Catholicism. That is what we tried to do in the *Avenir*, and, if I may say so, with success, both by its extent and by its promptness. But the absolute sovereigns, who were alarmed by our progress, have sought to stop it. For that purpose they have allied themselves with Rome and the episcopate, who unfortunately are imbued with the notion that religion would perish without the material support of the powers of the earth, and who, moreover, are on principle (*en théorie*) enemies of liberty. So as not to put ourselves in a false position as regards Catholicism we have had to suspend our efforts, or at least modify their form; for it would be an additional and immense calamity to bring trouble and division upon the Church. The obstacles which prejudice, passion and interest put in the way of the good will disappear. God will intervene by means that are unknown to us. Until then we ought, without abandoning his work, to avoid everything which would tend to loosen, even momentarily, the sacred bonds of unity. Without any doubt there are happening before our eyes strange things which should cause profound groaning and which would shake the very elect if God were not sustaining them. But great scandals always announce a great manifes-

tation of Providence. Let us then await it with faith, and hasten it by our prayers.[29]

In his own deeper mind Lamennais was less convinced that a pro-gramme of liberal social reform could be enacted without a large degree of support from his fellow-Catholics; and were that really the case then the cause of liberty would have to be advanced by a broader humanitarian appeal – humanitarian, but no less certainly Christian for all that, when the freedom of mankind is seen to lie in the purpose of God. Writing to Montalembert he was frank about 'changing our position', by which he meant 'transposing our action ... outside the Church, by ceasing on the one hand to occupy ourselves with matters proper to religion, and on the other by refraining from treating any question from the theological point of view'.[30] He even confessed that he had no real interest now in what went on at Rome, knowing as he did how things were manipulated there.[31] But the fact also was that he no longer viewed the papacy itself in the way he formerly had done. It had for years been clear to him that the actual holders of the papal office had often shown themselves little capable of rising to the full responsibilities of their position.[32] He now felt that Gregory XVI had been sent by Providence, as he put it, 'to close a long period of crimes and ignominy' and 'to show the world just how low the human part of the divine institution can sink'.[33]

How, then, did the doctrine of papal infallibility now stand with him? That there had to be a visible centre of faith he had no doubt; without some external authority able to serve as such unity of belief was not possible; and the pope speaking in the name of the whole church on earth must therefore be held to be infallible. But the supreme pontiff's personal opinions were an altogether different affair, the difficulty being to distinguish between one pronouncement and another. He was confident nonetheless that 'there always comes a time (époque) when this discrimination is made, with certitude, by a sort of sound sense and general instinct'.[34] More importantly, Lamennais was beginning to take a wider view of the relation of the church to society at large. He had long been imbued with a sense of world crisis and was wont, in voicing his fears, to recall the prophetic language of the Bible.[35] Cardinal Wiseman, who met Lamennais on the occasion of the latter's previous visit to Rome in 1824, noted this tendency in his thinking from personal conversations he had with him.[36] But by 1833 the conviction had settled upon him that the church itself would not escape the approaching catastrophe, that it too would be under judgment, and that out of the destruction divine Providence would cause a renewed church to emerge fit to serve the new age that had dawned. Lamennais, in a letter of 25 January 1833 to his friend, Countess de Senfft, delivered his views on these matters explicitly and eloquently:

> Today everything is in a state of flux; nothing has roots; neither thought nor feeling (*coeur*) is able to attach itself to anything at all. This is the character of great epochs when everything is changing, when everything is renewing itself. The old foundation, worm-eaten and rotten, crumbles into dust and one cannot yet see what is going to take its place. Between a past which can no longer be and a future which does not yet exist, one can dwell only in formless ruins, where the rain, wind and snow penetrate from all sides. But in the very midst of these ruins, beneath the half-collapsed vault where Providence has afforded us a little shelter, one can meanwhile taste a certain peace in contemplating these preliminaries of a new creation and, so to speak, this amazing work of God. The world in its old form was used up. Men had abused everything, they had de-natured, corrupted everything. That is why the old Hierarchies, political and ecclesiastical alike, are disappearing; they are no more than two spectres that embrace one another in a tomb. God, by means which to me are unknown, will without doubt regenerate his Church; she will not perish; she is immortal, for she is nothing other than the society of the human race under the law of the Redemption wrought by Jesus Christ. But in what form will she appear when the purifying fire has consumed the dry envelope which conceals her today from nearly all eyes? I know not. One knew no more when the Synagogue expired, or rather, when it underwent the transformation that had been predicted.[37]

Such an achievement was, however, beyond the strength of mere men; it would have to be the direct work of God.

It was in this apocalyptic mood, then, that Lamennais conceived *Paroles d'un Croyant*, which, although not published until a year later, was writen in the early summer of 1833.[38] In no respect did he feel that the cause to which he must henceforth devote himself implied any recantation of his formal submission to Rome. It was simply that he could not admit the pope's authority in the political sphere, apart, that is, from certain 'mixed' questions concerning which agreement should properly be sought between the spiritual and the temporal powers. As a citizen he judged himself to be entirely free to pursue aims that were inherently secular and did not directly involve matters of faith or morals. Further, in advancing his 'Christian' politics he conceived himself to be following up quite logically the principles set out in his earlier writings. The basic principle indeed had been that the 'universal reason' is itself infallible, whereas individual reasoning may well be erroneous. When the former has declared itself then the latter must keep silence. In fact the essence of his doctrine was *vox populi vox Dei*. But granting its truth in philosophy there is no ground, he would have said, for denying it in politics. The judgment and will of the majority must therefore be right, and the introduction of universal suffrage, by which alone that universal will and judgment can be registered, becomes for the state an obligatory commitment. And by the same token the church would put itself in the wrong to oppose it. On this Lamennais's conscience was clear and firm. But he evidently as yet did not perceive whither his argument might eventually lead him.

Paroles d'un Croyant was very likely influenced, although not actually suggested, by a publication which appeared at the end of April 1833 and with which Montalembert was closely associated as a translator, namely a French version of *Le Livre des pèlerins polonais* by the Polish poet and scholar Adam Mickiewicz.[39] Lamennais was greatly taken with it. Describing its author, in a letter to the Marquis de Coriolis, as 'sans contredit le premier poète de notre époque', he said there were in the book 'choses ravissantes', and he even found it – without of course forgetting the distance that separates the word of God from the word of man – 'beau comme L'Evangile'. Resembling Lamennais's own book in its biblical tone and style, it was a kind of apocalypse written to encourage the Polish exiles in their adversity, and thus struck a deeply responsive chord in the French patriot's heart. The truth would appear to be that the minds of both, as Catholic Romantics and apostles of liberty, were really moving along the same lines. For both believed the spirit of the New Testament to be capable of guiding and sustaining the masses of their own time in their aspirations towards freedom and justice. *Le Livre des pèlerins polonais* was denounced however by the Gallican paper *L'Ami de la religion* as 'a continual eulogy of revolt and a Philippic against the sovereigns', and critics of the Mennaisian circle were prompt to see in it evidence of its members' insincerity as well as of their subversive intents. Yet Lamennais himself made a fresh declaration of his submission in a letter to the pope through the bishop of Rennes.[40]

As for *Paroles d'un Croyant*, Lamennais on 23 March 1834 informed Montalembert of his decision to publish it.[41] Montalembert answered urging him not to do so, for that would produce 'an immense scandal'.[42] The archbishop of Paris also wrote to him expressing the hope that rumours of an impending publication which had reached his ears were false, to which Lamennais replied assuring him that his little book dealt only with political concerns and that no word would appear in it regarding any positive and dogmatically determinate form of Christianity and that the church would not once be mentioned.[43] So on 30 April 1834, despite the pleas of Lamennais's brother as well as of intimate friends, *Paroles d'un Croyant* was given to the public, having been seen through the press by Sainte-Beuve.[44] A sort of *poème en prose*, it is a difficult book to describe succinctly, partly because of its style, at once passionate, hortatory and aphoristic, but still more because of the strange prophetic and apocalyptic imagery in which its message is arrayed.[45] Lamennais adopted this manner, he said – though it combined the forthright with the cryptic – in order to communicate that message the more readily to 'the People', to whom the book is dedicated.[46] He was conscious of its faults, but, as he told Sainte-Beuve, were it able nevertheless to give rise to 'generous sentiments in some souls [his] wishes would have been fulfilled', and he asked for no more. Theologically it is scrupulously orthodox, the author identifying himself plainly with the main doctrines of the Catholic faith. Nor was his aim in any wise to destroy or subvert in the political sense. As he wrote to Baron Eckstein on 23 June:

> I do not want to level anything, but I would wish to 'elevate' much. I would wish that all things might progressively rise step by step to a better state. I would wish that instead of arming the rich man against the poor the laws had bowels of mercy for him; I would wish that all the means could be made easier for him to get out of his misery, not by pillage but by labour, and that instruction more widely diffused would prove more fruitful. I would wish that the barriers were broken down which, on all sides, are raised about him as though to imprison him in a state of eternal need. And it is here that I shall say what I mean by the people. I call that unhappy class the people which is deprived in part of common rights; that suffering class which possesses nothing and will possess nothing, as long as hateful laws take from them all real capability of acquiring and of creating property for themselves by the sweat of their brow; that class which is despised and rejected by the others, and which forms nonetheless 86 per cent of the human race – for such everywhere is pretty well the proportion of the poor to the rich. And I mean by the poor him who, living by his toil, has need during part of his life of the help of charity, and dies without leaving sufficient to bury him.[47]

Hardly very revolutionary words, even then, one might have supposed. But what in the forty-two brief chapters of the *Paroles* he assailed was the carapace of insensitivity which the ruling classes displayed towards the importunity of the vast mass of the populace even in the most civilized countries. The truth he proclaims above all is the brotherhood of man:

> Ye are the sons of the same father, and the same mother hath nourished you; wherefore then love ye not one another as brethren? Wherefore call ye one another enemies?

> He who loveth not his brother is cursed seven times, and he who maketh himself the enemy of his brother is cursed seventy times seven.

> It is for this that kings and princes, and all those whom the world calls great, have been cursed; they have not loved their brethren, and they have treated them as enemies.

> Love ye one another, and fear not the great, nor princes, nor kings. They are strong against you only because ye are not united, and because that ye love not one another as brethren.
>
> Say not, 'He is of one nation, and I of another people'; for all nations have had on earth the same father, who is God.
>
> If one member be smitten, the whole body suffereth. Ye are all the same body; nor can one of you be oppressed without all being oppressed.

And he goes on to ask:

> Wherefore is it that animals find their nourishment, each seeking that which is appropriate to his own species?

And answers:

> Because, among them, none stealeth that which belongeth to another, and because each one is content with that which satisfieth his necessities ...
>
> Justice is life, and charity is yet another life, still sweeter and more abundant ...
>
> Men, equal among themselves, are born for God alone; and whosoever speaketh contrary to this, speaketh blasphemy ...
>
> The law of God is the law of love; and love raiseth not itself above others, but sacrificeth itself for others.
>
> He who sayeth in his heart, 'I am not like other men, but other men are given to me, that I may command them and dispose of them and theirs according to my caprice'; such a one is the child of the Devil.
>
> And Satan is the king of this world, for he is the king of all those who think and act thus, and those who think and act thus are by his counsels made the masters of the world ...

Lamennais also relates a parable of sweated labour and worker exploitation – the parable of a man 'wicked' and 'accursed of Heaven', who says to his workmen:

> Ye work during six hours, and for your labour there is given unto you a piece of money; work during twelve hours, and you may gain two pieces of money; and ye may live better, ye, your wives, and your little ones.
> And they believed him.
> Afterwards he said to them: ye work no more than half of the days in the year: work all the days of the year and your gain will be doubled.
> And again they believed him.
> But after that it came to pass that the quantity of work having become greater than a half, without the demand for work becoming greater, the half of those who before lived by their labour, no longer found persons to employ them.
> Then that wicked man, whom they had believed, said unto them, I will give work to you all, upon condition that you will work for the same length

of time, and that I shall not pay you more than the half of that which I now pay you: for I would willingly do you a service, but I am not willing to ruin myself.

And as they were sore pressed with hunger, they and their wives and their little ones, they accepted the terms of this wicked man, and they blessed him; for, said they, he giveth unto us life.

No doubt some of Lamennais's imagery is far-fetched and over-wrought – kings drinking blood out of skulls, and so on – though not of course without biblical precedent in this respect. But in general his vision of a corrupt and oppressive world is telling. Moreover, the corruption and the oppression implicate the church itself: 'the priests of Christ' are won over 'with riches, with honour, and with power', to serve the ends of temporal rulers. In one passage Pope Gregory XVI is introduced – after some highly unflattering allusions to contemporary monarchs, King William IV of England among them – although it did not appear in editions previous to that of 1837, by which time Lamennais had abandoned his priestly functions. The senility of the supreme pontiff is dwelt on mercilessly, no doubt on account of the pact Lamennais believed him to have concluded with the tsar of Russia, Nicholas I – a schismatic as well as the autocrat of a wholly subject people.

Yet one who reads the *Paroles d'un Croyant* today, to whom many of its verses will inevitably now seem rather trite, is likely to have little idea of the amazement, elation or outrage that seized those who first scanned its pages in the early weeks of May 1834. As regards circulation its success was enormous, and such as to make it one of the outstanding literary productions of the entire Romantic era. Copies sold in their tens of thousands. People are said to have queued up to read it in the public reading-rooms. A crowd of young folk in the Jardin du Luxembourg listened to it being declaimed aloud.[48] The *Revue de Paris* cited it at length and commented on it ecstatically. 'M. de la Mennais', it declared, 'is reproached with being a republican; may it please God that all priests were republicans like M. de la Mennais, and all republicans were as religious as he.'[49] The little book was variously described as 'a red bonnet stuck on a cross', ''93 celebrating Easter', 'Robespierre in a surplice', 'Satan's apocalypse'.[50] Its author's fame, or notoriety, spread across all Europe. 'I never open a newspaper', Montalembert wrote to him while travelling in Austria, 'without seeing your name on the front page.'[51] It was reported that the effect caused by the book in Vienna was 'terrible': 'Ce ne sont qu'anathèmes, et, chez les plus doux, gémissement et larmes', an allusion to an Augsburg newspaper article which exclaimed that 'si le Diable venait au monde il tiendrait ce livre à la main'. Edition after edition appeared in France,[52] and translations were brought out in several European languages, the first English version bearing the title *The Words of a Believer: and having thus spoken, was eternally condemned by the Pope of Rome for having uttered them.*[53] On 11 June 1834 *The Times* newspaper published a feature on *Paroles* from its Paris correspondent, who sanctimoniously noted that 'the Abbé de Lamennais flatters the lower classes with as much address as perfidy, and his words are calculated to excite that envy which sleeps, but which never ceases to exist in the breasts of those who suffer when they come in contact with those who enjoy. This work, of which it grieves me to have to speak, will spread over the whole of Europe'.

Lamennais himself seems to have experienced relief once he had got his burning indignation off his chest. He had manifested before the world his claim to speak freely on political matters, regardless of the pope. 'My intention', he wrote to Charles de Coux, 'is to remain submissive to the Church and free outside the Church.' But he admitted he foresaw the church's undergoing a 'necessary transformation', although none might know in what it would consist and thus could not feel called upon to operate it. He felt it his duty to stay loyal to it, or at least to 'all that was good and true in it'.[54] He feared, however, that Rome, at the behest of the reactionary European governments, would not only frown on it but proceed to some form of condemnation, even though the book contained nothing objectionable on the score of faith.[55] He drew some comfort from the thought that the great popular welcome accorded it and the danger of affronting public sentiment might have the effect of mitigating blame were it to be attached to him. The religious journals meanwhile expressed widely diverging views. *France catholique* extolled the book, the *Univers religieux* and the *Ami de la religion* bitterly criticized it, the latter finding in it nothing but a headstrong and menacing opposition to all authority whatsoever. *La Dominicale* adopted a middle-of-the-road position: publication of the book was an error of judgment, but there was no reason to think that Lamennais was deliberately preaching revolution. On the other hand, anticlerical papers like the *Populaire* applauded the author, if only in mockery of the church authorities. 'S'il nous vient', observed its editor, M. Cabet, 'une religion nouvelle et un Dieu nouveau, les prêtres devront rassembler à M. de Lamennais.'

An independent and fairly weighty theological voice against the *Paroles* was that of abbé Louis Bautain, of the faculty of letters in the university of Strasbourg and a philosophical thinker of some standing.[56] He considered the book 'bizarre', written in a style too studied and artificial, and lacking in any really solid thought. Besides which its influence would, he feared, prove noxious – 'le *Contrat Social* présenté sous forme apocalyptique'. Its author's viewpoint was distorted by political bias and everything he said was affected by it.[57]

But powerful forces also were in motion against Lamennais. On 16 May 1834 Metternich wrote to the Austrian ambassador in Rome, Count Lützow, referring to Lamennais in the most opprobrious terms and observing that a priest who abuses the sacred books in order to corrupt the world and who, whilst pretending to be inspired, dispenses what he must know to be poison, is an 'abject being'. Would that he could be burnt as a heretic! But the Austrian chancellor was anxious to learn what the pope's own attitude was and what he was likely to do, since some action plainly was necessary. The ambassador replied informing Metternich that the Holy Father fully shared his opinion and judged *Paroles d'un Croyant* to be 'a work of the most shameful and wild impiety', and that the Vatican would act in the matter was certain.[58]

And act it did. On 15 July Lamennais received news of the publication of a new encyclical, *Singulari nos*, in which his book was condemned outright as, 'if small in size, immense in perversity' (*libellum ... mole quidem exiguum, pravitate tamen ingentem*), as potentially subversive of the political order, and as an audacious reassertion of principles which had already been formally censured in *Mirari vos*.[59] But although the main object of the pope's displeasure was the *Paroles* he also had a thrust at 'a fallacious system of philosophy, recently invented', by which presumably was meant the doctrine of the *sensus communis*. There can be no doubt that the promptitude and vigour of the papal response were attributable to pressure from outside Rome, and Lamennais himself was surprised and rather shocked by it. But he interpreted it as in essence political, not doctrinal, and affected to treat it rather lightly.[60] But the pope had never countenanced Lamennais's distinction between the two so long as it implied the latter's right to discourse on highly controversial political issues as freely as he chose.

Whatever the reasons, or the causes, which moved the pope to make his pronouncement, *Singulari nos* spelled the end of the Mennaisian school. One after another its leading members – Gerbet, Salinis, Rohrbacher, Jean-Marie de la Mennais – made their submission. Montalembert, most loyal of all Lamennais's friends, was the last to do so and the act cost him much grievous heart-searching. His immediate impulse was to write to Lamennais urging him too to submit. 'You will reply, I know, that conscience is invincible, but I myself will say that after much reflection on this point I am persuaded that the Christian ought not to obey *his* conscience exclusively and that there are cases in which he ought above all to *obey*.'[61] Lamennais could not of course agree: 'Je connais ton coeur et tu connais le mien.'[62] Montalembert's heart, however, was in the last resort attached to the church, and towards the end of the year (8 December) he informed Cardinal Pacca of his unqualified submission to both encyclicals.[63] To Lamennais himself he offered such justification of his decision as he could, for since he was a layman the act had not strictly been necessary.

> I had to do great violence to my more deeply rooted convictions in order to bring myself to adhere to an act like that of the Encyclical of 15 August [i.e. *Mirari vos*], which conflicts with these convictions in the most formal manner; but I have preferred this violence to the chance of finding myself one day outside the Church which alone offers me consolations for those intimate sufferings that no political or intellectual activity would relieve ... What matters for me, I repeat, is that I should preserve a refuge from the troubles of the heart, which after all are life's sharpest thorn. This refuge exists for me only in Catholicism.[64]

Lamennais and he kept up their correspondence for a year or two after this, but their relations eventually terminated when it became obvious to both that they had ceased to have a common mind on what once had meant so much to both.

Lamennais was now isolated, and the course of events was such as inevitably to cause him further serious reconsideration of his position. On 15 February 1836 he wrote to an old friend, Benoît d'Azy, stating that his convictions had certainly changed on a number of points, although as to what these were none shared his confidence. 'I do not have to account to anyone for my inner thoughts, and no one has the right to put his conjectures in place of my avowals.'[65] But his links with the church were breaking, though when finally he ceased to regard himself as a member cannot be said with certainty. In any case he was never formally excommunicated. He seems still to have been attending mass in the summer of 1836.[66] In February he wrote to another old acquaintance, Baroness Cottu, that although his ideas had developed and expanded they had in no way essentially altered. 'Le bourgeon est devenu feuille, voilà tout.' It is strange that although he corresponded with his friends regularly and at length he rarely opened his mind to them. Thus in marking out the great changes which his views unquestionably underwent between the end of 1834 and 1840, by which time he had decisively broken with any form of orthodox religion, one has to have recourse to his published works. Of these the most important is *Affaires de Rome*, which came out in May 1836 and in which his rupture with the Vatican is manifest, although the long preface to his *Troisièmes mélanges*, a collection of articles already printed mainly in the *Avenir*, which had appeared over a year before, had already given clear enough indication of whither he was moving.[67]

Affaires de Rome purports to be a straightforward, documented account of its author's dealings with the Holy See, and from the purely literary point of view is probably his most satisfactory work, exhibiting his skill as a writer at its most consummate. But it is by no means free of the polemical spirit, although expressed ironically, *sotto voce* and by innuendo. The papacy, Lamennais argues, is in a dilemma: either it must renounce teachings which it has ever declared to belong to the tradition of the apostles and the early Fathers and thus to form part of divine revelation, in which case its present actions would amount to apostasy; or else it must confess to having been mistaken in its teaching and to have misunderstood that same revelation, in which case it would have forfeited its claim to authority. All it can do therefore is to cling to its present policies and accept the consequences.[68] He himself must wash his hands of 'the pope's Christianity' and follow that 'of the human race'. For the papacy, by allying itself with the absolute powers in their opposition to freedom and democracy, has denied the people's aspirations for a juster society and so has turned its back upon the future, in which it henceforth can have no creative role to enact. The Christianity of Rome – and Lamennais, true at least in this to his former convictions, will not consider any alternative[69] – is moribund, a thing of the past. The new Christianity which will emerge with time will however be such as to voice and to meet mankind's deepest needs. He also states his belief and desire that the book should be looked on as bringing to an end the series of writings published during the preceding years.[70] Rome's reaction was to place the volume on the Index.

One other book belongs to the mid-thirties, although it did not see print until 1841, namely, *Discussions critiques et pensées diverses*, consisting of a miscellany of pieces culled mostly from his private journal for the years 1833 to 1838 and detailing his views on a range of subjects, theological, philosophical and political. From it it is not difficult to gather that Lamennais's attitude to Catholic doctrine itself was now in process of a radical shift towards deism. Catholicism, he thinks, has ossified into a system of formal beliefs and the Catholic church has lost touch with the spiritual life, its concerns being merely secular. The appeal to authority can no longer be upheld; reason has to be the criterion, and by the light of it the supernatural – if by that be meant the miraculous interventions in the natural order to which orthodoxy is committed – altogether fades, and with it, more or less inevitably, the whole idea of an external revelation. The Bible has no greater authority than any other religious writing, and the true knowledge of God is to be sought in nature. The papacy, needless to add, is reproached in the bitterest terms. On 26 February 1841 he stated in a letter to the editor of *Le Semeur*, a Protestant journal, that until Rome had required of him an act which, rightly or wrongly, had wounded his conscience, he had applied himself with the utmost attention and sincerity to keep within the bounds of the strictest orthodoxy, but when he saw the choice before him to be that either of continuing to adhere to the orthodox creed or of following his conscience he had, for the sake of his own peace of mind, to examine the bases of that authority which in all such matters had hitherto been his rule.[71] In no way did he desire to impose his personal views on others, but neither should they try to impose theirs on him. What finally counted was not men but truth.

3

The course of Lamennais's career from the publication of *Réflexions sur l'état de l'Eglise en France* down to that of *Affaires de Rome* would seem on the face of it to be sheer paradox. From royalist to republican, from authoritarian to democrat, from establishmentarian to one calling for the complete severance of the church from the state, from ardent ultramontane to a denunciator of the pope as a perverter of the gospel, from traditionalist churchman to philosophical deist – this romantically volatile cleric and *littérateur* appears consistent only in his inconsistency. And at the level of personal feelings it is the same. A priest honoured by one pontiff and condemned by another, a leader of dedicated disciples who ended by being abandoned by them all – even the beloved Montalembert – a seeker after solitude whose longing was the salvation of society, a poet in imaginative vision who nevertheless committed himself unreservedly to the logic of his rational principles, a man acutely sensitive to the opinion of others but who was little disposed to mitigate the acerbity of his judgments on them – this indeed would seem to be a personality and a character beyond the reach of any readily plausible explanation. Thus failing to 'rationalize' him adequately one may feel tempted simply to label him as another 'typical' Romantic. Range his views and his qualities side by side and what you would appear to have is only a catalogue of disparities suggestive of intellectual anarchy.

However, examine Lamennais's changes of front as they occur over the years and a consistent pattern of thought does emerge. But it cannot be appreciated except in the light – or sometimes, it has to be confessed, against the obscurity – of his nature and temperament. For a Romantic Lamennais most truly was, and perhaps in the entire record of that many-faceted movement there is no personality more typical of it.

According to Sainte-Beuve – writing in 1834 – Lamennais's polemical and doctrinal life was composed of two contrasting parts, during which he pursued the same goal but by very different procedures.[72] What in the first instance struck him was the state of sheer indifference regarding religion, the spiritual tepidity and materialistic corruption, of the society of his day. His whole effort was directed, one might say, to the revivification of a corpse; for what he sought was the moral and spiritual regeneration of that society. Such was his vision, his inspiration and his practical objective alike; and it imparted a basic unity to all he thought and did. But the methods he adopted to attain and realize it were conflicting. In his earlier years democratic ideals did not attract him, for what could be hoped for from the mass of mankind when left to its own resources? What was needed was strong leadership of a kind that only authoritarian governments could exercise. But even governments could not do without unified direction, and this, in Catholic Christendom, the Holy See alone could provide. Governmental authority, that is, was essentially utilitarian; it was the means, the channel, through which the benefits of truth and justice could be made available to the multitude. But when it became apparent that governments were failing in this their authority for him declined and he saw them as a hindrance rather than a help. More and more therefore did the Roman papacy present itself to him as the sole authority capable of controlling the earthly destinies of mankind, and hence to be worthy of receiving total allegiance. But alas, when the papacy's own light ceased to shine in a dark world, when it evidently preferred the very darkness which it was its office to dispel, Lamennais's disillusionment was swift. Rome had to all intents apostatized, so forfeiting its own claim to authority and the right to be obeyed. Salvation would now be found, if found at all, only in the 'people' themselves, illuminated by a pure 'gospel' of which they, rather than a backward-looking and worldly hierarchy, were the providential custodians. *Paroles d'un Croyant* was thus a trumpet-call to the masses to rise to the height of their responsibility and so fashion their own destiny on earth:

> Something which we know not of is stirring in the world: God is at work there.
> Is not each of us on the alert? Is there a heart which does not beat faster?
> Mount the heights, O Son of Man, and proclaim what thou seest![73]

Once the general direction of Lamennais's thinking is understood the literary landmarks that punctuate the route become intelligible. In the early days *Réflexions* was a survey of the church's condition as the intellectual disintegration of the previous century, followed by the social upheaval of the Revolutionary period, had left it – weak in its organization and undecided even upon its mission. The deadly egoism of the *philosophes* had to be repudiated and the institution itself strengthened by a properly trained and disciplined clergy. Of the attainment of these ends the Concordat seemed to give hope, but the actual moment of the book's appearance was not, as we have seen, auspicious. The imperial government did not appreciate it and the reading-public was indifferent. *Tradition de l'Eglise*, published contemporaneously with the restoration of the Bourbon monarchy, could point out that 'in the political as in the religious society the Church teaches us to reverence a power which comes from God, and which commands in the name of God; a power ... which is responsible solely to the all-powerful Being whom it represents and who instituted it'. The two heads, the civil and the spiritual, have equal right to men's obedience in their respective orders, providing that neither offends against the natural and divine law, just as neither is to be confused with the other. 'Let them remain sincerely united, without seeking to invade one another's authority.'[74] But Lamennais's anti-Gallicanism is throughout an unmistakable presence: the church is not the creature of the state, which, on Gallican principles – its spurious 'liberties' – it could easily become. Against this stifling patronage the rights of the papacy are the great safeguard. With the *Essai sur l'indifférence* Lamennais took in the whole field of apologetics. His target was the superficial, divisive and reductive values of the *Eclaircissement*; his plea, that Christianity, so far from being irrational, has ever struggled to secure the paramountcy of reason, and even the deism and atheism of the *philosophes* have left it basically unmoved. But Lamennais's approach is not that of a metaphysician; if he defends the Christian creed it is because he believes that social renewal depends on the supremacy of Catholicism. Opinion has its outcome in action, and when we know what men's faith is we can predict their conduct. Indeed, rereading the *Essai* one constantly feels, I think, that its author's real interest in religion springs from its power to put men in right relation to their environment, creating the order and fixity which he himself so passionately desired.

It was, in short, an 'ideology', as we now would say, by which alone could social cohesion be secured and maintained. But this meant that society had to be monist, not pluralist, even at the cost of the sacrifice of the individual. The principle of unity given in history is Catholicism, its foundation the church of Rome, which itself could not exist apart from the pope. Lamennais thus declares himself an ultramontane, out and out. The volume of 1825, on the relation of religion to the temporal order, shows how, if ultramontanism should prove inconsistent with political and civil society as it actually exists, then church and state must go their separate ways and Gallicanism be exposed as a hollow sham. It is at this point, therefore, that Lamennais reveals his incipient liberalism, with its eventual appeal to the general mass of men. In the meantime, however, his confidence in Rome stood unshaken. *Des Progrès de la révolution et de la guerre contre l'Eglise* takes account of the new revolutionary movement gaining impetus all over Europe and marks out a further advance in its author's thinking, for in it his 'liberal Catholicism' comes to birth. It is an appeal to the church to free itself from the shackles of the past. 'Sortez de la maison de servitude', he exhorts her, 'entrez en possession de la liberté'; and the programme of liberalization he here draws up was to provide the basis for the entire *Avenir* campaign. The theocratic ideal still beckons him onwards, but he has come to believe it realizable only through a church which is itself a free agent within society. Thus he calls on bishops and priests simply to devote themselves to the duties of their office. No dignity, no function in the civil order, he warns them, 'is comparable with the liberty of your ministry'.[75] But whether as yet he had come to recognize the fully pluralist implications of his policy may be doubted. Probably he still did not realize how the appetite for freedom grows by what it feeds on.

The *Avenir* venture was, then, aimed at achieving practical results. Its lack of success with the French clergy as a body was a sad disappointment to Lamennais and his circle. What they themselves demanded seemed so reasonable, so proper, that Rome if not the French hierarchy would be bound to welcome it. But Rome's initial coldness and subsequent hostility proved utterly disillusioning. For Lamennais personally the *Singulari nos* was a blow under which his faith in liberal Catholicism collapsed. It was now manifest that liberalism and Catholicism, as what the latter again showed itself to the world to be, were incapable of reconciliation. Society, he was convinced, must ever look to religion for its salvation, but only through a religion the actual forms of which did not yet exist. It was in this mood that his 'words of a believer' were uttered. His quittance of the priesthood was likewise a natural and probably inevitable outcome of it. But his spiritual utopianism was not shared by his friends and followers. Far from being volatile, his disposition all along revealed a consistency, even an intransigence, which with his guiding principles was bound to lead him on to a solitary road. And having taken it he kept to it to the end.

A student of Lamennais interested only in ecclesiastical history may feel that after 1836 there is no point in pursuing the record of his career further. To the student of ideas, however, this would be an unwarrantable curtailment of the story. Lamennais outside the Catholic church loses nothing of his fascination, since in his case it is the man, rather than the ecclesiastical setting in which he operated, that continues to hold attention. We ought therefore to cast a glance over the final years, even though the literary work he went on producing is such as to deserve a more careful survey: the disenchanted idealist of the 1840s is not to be overlooked. In the late 'thirties' it seemed that Lamennais wished to break with his own past as far as possible. Thus he simplified his name, choosing to be known no longer by the aristocratic style of Félicité de la Mennais but as F. Lamennais merely. No less significant was his abandonment of his Breton retreat of La Chênaie, in former days always so congenial to him, and his settling in Paris (29 May 1836), where the remainder of his life was to be spent. He also sold off his fine library to help meet his financial needs. For a few months in 1837 he edited Le Monde with the assistance of George Sand, to whom he had been introduced by the composer Franz Liszt two years previously. Another friend and loyal helper at this time was Charles Didier, author of Rome souterraine. December saw the publication of Le Livre du peuple, in some respects among the most attractive of his books, although Le Semeur dismissed it as 'vulgar rationalism'. His rejection of Christianity in anything other than a purely ethical sense, even if he retained some sort of theistic belief, was apparently complete.[76] Twelve months later he brought out De l'esclavage moderne, and in October 1840 a pamphlet, Le Pays et le gouvernement, attacking the July monarchy, which he despised, and the 'citizen king' personally for having betrayed France both internally and externally. For this he was tried, convicted and sentenced to a year's imprisonment and the payment of a fine of two thousand francs. The event nevertheless gained him widespread public sympathy, often very openly expressed. A result of his incarceration in Sainte-Pélagie – from 4 January 1841 to 3 January 1842 – was the composition of Une Voix de prison, a little collection of prose poems, and Du Passé et de l'avenir du Peuple. In the latter he enlarges on his idea of human progress, which will, he is confident, come to pass 'through the development of intelligence and love'. That the domain of the intelligence is growing is not in doubt, but the advance must go hand in hand with charity. 'He who loves not is dead to every good.' Whereas faith changes with time in accordance with the progress of knowledge, love is not time's creature but is unchanging and eternal. 'It is liberty joined with love that will save the world.' The book thus can be read as a manifesto of religious socialism, provided that the socialism be understood as that of a moralist not an economist. The inequality of the classes he sees as the result of two great evils, the selfishness of the rich and the ignorance of the masses. But he has practical proposals too. The right of association he upholds with firmness, but he again shows himself far from being a revolution-

ary. He voices indeed the spirit of revolt, along with strident indignation and the withering sarcasm which was always prompt to his
tongue. But basically Lamennais reveals here what he himself always
was, a man of order.

Imprisonment, however, did nothing to soften the asperities of his
temper. Early in 1843 he published *Amschaspands et Darvands* –
names signifying the opposing powers of good and evil in ancient
Persian religion – which turned out to be a frenetic onslaught on the
established authorities; in calling it 'violent et désordonné' the *Revue
des deux mondes* did not exaggerate. It was ill-received generally.
Among the objects of Lamennais's attack was, it may be added, George
Sand's feminism. January 1846 saw a translation from his hand of the
gospels, with notes and comments. Once more the reviews were severe:
'more affectation than originality' was a representative opinion. Rome
put it on the Index. Even the Paris prefect of police remarked upon it as
'dangerous'.

With the outbreak of revolution on 24 February 1848, Lamennais,
pen ever at the ready, lost no moment in founding *Le Peuple constituant*, the first number of which went on sale on the 27th,[77] so as to
lend his support to the new-born republic. On 23 April he was elected
last of the thirty-four deputies for the *département* of the Seine with
104,871 votes. Appointed a member of the Constitution commission,
he himself drew up a far-reaching programme of reform, to include
thorough-going decentralization, election of the president of the
republic by universal suffrage, abolition of the Université's monopoly
of education, separation of church and state, suppression of the *budget
des cultes* – and with it of course government payment of clergy
stipends – progressive taxation and the abolition of the death penalty.
In May 1849 he was re-elected on the candidature of the Comité
Démocratique Socialiste (with 113,331 votes), supported the Moun-
tain and took on the journalistic task of editing *La Réforme*. His
political views at this time I have characterized as broadly socialist, but
Lamennais temperamentally was always an individualist and his social
theory was not likely now to be such as to minimize individual rights.
Indeed a society in which individuals were not free was not a free
society. And the mainstay of individual freedom was, he was convinced, private property. 'All questions of liberty resolve themselves, in
practice, into questions of property', he wrote in the *Peuple constituant*
(30 May 1848). In an article of his in the same paper of 27 April, he had
endeavoured to make his position clear. If by socialism, he explained, is
meant one of the many systems which, since Saint-Simon and Fourier,
had cropped up everywhere and of which the general character is the
negation, explicit or implicit, of property and the family, then he

certainly was not a socialist. But if, on the one hand, socialism stands for the principle of association regarded as one of the basic articles of the social order which ought to be established, and, on the other, the firm belief that under the invariable conditions of life itself, both physical and moral, such order will constitute a new society, to which nothing in the past can be compared, then yes, a socialist he was. But he would say to the people at large: Desire and demand whatever is just and possible, though not more; for to demand more would only be to play into the hands of your enemies. Do not run after chimaeras; it is reason which will save you.[78]

The *coup d'état* of 2 December meant Lamennais's speedy return to private life. He then undertook a new translation of Dante's *Divine Comedy*, preceded by an introduction – in the event unfinished – which was no more than a long diatribe against the papacy. It did not, however, appear in print until 1855, a year after Lamennais's death, which occurred on 27 February 1854 at his sparsely furnished lodging in the rue du Grand-Chantier, near the Temple. In his last illness he refused all religious consolations, and when, early on a damp and foggy morning – it was Ash Wednesday – his body was interred in a common grave at Père-Lachaise, it was without any religious rite and no address was given, although a considerable crowd of people followed the hearse to the cemetery.

This chapter is not concerned either with Lamennais's apologetic or with his philosophical position in general, since I have offered a description of both elsewhere.[79] But it cannot well be concluded without some reference to the major literary undertaking of his post-Catholic phase, namely the *Esquisse d'une philosophie*, the first three volumes of which were published in November 1840. He had been working on them for several years and regarded them as his most serious effort in the purely intellectual field. Virtually all his other works had been occasional and more often than not polemical, whereas this one was intended to be a systematic and dispassionate statement of philosophical truth.[80] A fourth volume came out in 1846, while part of the third volume, the chapters on aesthetics, was published separately in 1864 as *De l'art et du beau*. That Lamennais should have entitled a work planned on so extended a scale as a mere 'sketch' may seem a little wilful, since his aim clearly was to set out a comprehensive metaphysic encircling the entire realm of human know-ledge. Also, romanticist though he was, he did not adopt the psychological or 'subjectivist' approach, but true to the tradition of Catholic philosophy adhered to the ontological method. His starting-point, that is, is not man and the relativities of human knowledge but the absolute being of God, and on this ultimate and immutable basis his whole scheme is made to rest. Moreover, although his philosophy no longer takes account of revelation it retains a trinitarian concept of the divine framed ostensibly in purely rational terms. He even seeks to preserve his doctrine of the *sens commun* in all moral matters as the ground of certitude, while at the same time admitting the principles of the critical reason, individually exercised, as the final criterion of what can or cannot be believed. It thus seems obvious that at the time when Lamennais was composing this work his thought was suspended between his earlier views as a Catholic and the free-ranging rationalism to which his general abandonment of an external authority in all areas of philosophical and moral belief was in fact conducting him. The 1846 volume on 'science' betrays a similar duality of perspective. There are two realms of science, he maintains, that of God and ultraphenomenal reality, and that of the physical and sense-experience. The overall purpose of a scientific philosophy is to secure their coordination.

Lamennais's ambitious attempt to synthesize all knowledge on a broadly theistic foundation is remarkable for its boldness, considering the date of its publication – Comte's *Cours de philosophie positive* was its exact contemporary – rather than for the rigour of its analysis. The *Esquisse* was hailed by some of Lamennais's admirers as a masterpiece – Béranger and Hauréau, for instance, spoke of it in glowing language; but the socialist *doctrinaire* Proudhon attacked it mercilessly, as did Lamennais's old enemy, the *Ami de la religion*, which wrote it off as 'une publication sans orthodoxie ni talent'. A former disciple, abbé Rohrbacher, took the opportunity in the same journal to denounce its author as an 'apostate' and even to suggest his mental derangement. *Le Semeur*, as usual when referring to Lamennais, was unsympathetic, as likewise was the academic 'establishment': the *Revue des deux mondes* pronounced it 'the effort of a great mind to reunite in a complete and ordered system doctrines of which no prestige of style can disguise the basic inadequacy'.[81]

Lamennais remains even yet something of an enigma. It is not really possible to separate his religious thinking from his social and political, so closely are the two intertwined. In the earlier phases of his public career he was an ardent Catholic, but the force of his conviction, at least as registered in the *Essai sur l'indifférence*, was impelled more by what he opposed than by what he affirmed. In youth he was something of a sceptic, even when quite prepared to put up a defence of Catholicism,[82] and he had reached manhood before he made his first communion. The hesitation and even horror with which he approached ordination is well known. Between the inner and the outer man, in fact, there somehow was a curious disjunction. As Henri Bremond perceptively commented: 'One always feels oneself to be in the presence of two people, or rather of a man and a system.'[83] Was the man, as distinct from the author of the system, less than a genuinely convinced Christian? At any rate he seems never to have felt the truth of religion in his heart. Thus Catholicism in its social and political aspect appealed to him more than in its personal, which probably accounts for his consistent antipathy towards Protestantism: he detested it because he could not understand it as he understood, whether rightly or wrongly, the historic institutions of Roman Catholicism. With the errors and inadequacies of unbelief he also could engage, since its attractions he knew within himself, a knowledge which contributed largely to his skill as an apologist. But the reasons for rejecting unbelief were usually presented by him in terms of its social consequences. For unbelief, or even mere *indifférentisme*, might everywhere be seen to lead to doubt of all positive and collective values, and so to social disintegration and anarchy. The thought of beholding outwardly what he so often had to endure inwardly – spiritual chaos and conflict – appalled him. His memories of the Revolution fuelled these fears. If religion could only prevent this it must be supported to the uttermost, and Catholicism extolled as the indispensable foundation for social reconstruction. His welcome of the Bourbon restoration was, accordingly, at the time unfeigned; the alliance of altar and throne promised well. But the shortcomings of the accompanying Gallicanism soon became apparent and an alliance in which the church, the spiritual realm, was a wholly subordinate partner to the temporal was objectionable and not to be tolerated. Only the papacy seemed to possess the authority necessary to uphold the freedom of the spiritual as the determining ethical force in society. But this hope also was to be shattered. Even so Lamennais did not jettison his cherished principle; a 'secular' Christianity of his own devising was to be the goal. Indeed Lamennais may be looked on as probably the first to envisage such a secularization of the religious ideal as has gained widespread adherence in the latter years of our own century. For it is a type of 'religionless' Christianity, identified with the cause of liberty, democracy and social amelioration (if not revolution), which found expression in *Paroles d'un Croyant* and *Le Livre du peuple*. But as soon as the essentially secular 'pull' of the gospel – or what Lamennais took to be such – was recognized by him the supernatural and dogmatic structure collapsed, as the *Discussions critiques* make evident. His personal tragedy was that in the end he lost belief not only in the possibilities of social renewal through religion but even in the objectives of politics itself, and was left only with a vague and visionary utopianism. In him the romanticist tension between faith and reason, tradition and progress, past and future finally snapped. His last years, in which disillusionment joined hands with ill-health and advancing age, thus brought a turbulent life to a sombre close.

8

Auguste Comte and the Religion of Humanity

THE NAME of Auguste Comte, unlike that of Lamennais, does not immediately invoke the spirit of romanticism. The founder of positivism and the creator, for such he may be said to have been, of the scientific discipline of sociology – its hybrid name was certainly his invention – would appear to have drawn no inspiration whatever from the soaring flights, poetic or philosophic, of the Romantic imagination. Rather would he have conceived himself to be, on that very account, a deliberate anti-Romantic. Nevertheless the romanticist elements in his thought are by no means difficult to trace, whether in his consistent drive towards 'wholeness' of view, in his overweening sense of personal mission, in his dedication to 'Humanity' to the point of its becoming for him the divinity of a new religious cult, in his quasi-mystical obsession with the 'eternal feminine' – symbolized by the adored Clotilde de Vaux – in his sentimental idealism, which grew upon him as the years passed, even in his tendency to mental instability, all of which are more reminiscent of romanticist ardours than of the hard-headed *scientisme* of a later generation of positivists, however much indebted these were to one whose declared purpose was both 'to organize our scientific conceptions and to systematize the art of social life'. The truth is that the theories of this most gifted of the disciples of Saint-Simon were compounded of ideas and sentiments which did not consort well together and in retrospect suggest a confusion of standards and objectives, coupled with an evidently megalomaniac disposition, that has long since caused the most eminent of mid-nineteenth-century French thinkers to be set aside, then as now, as little more than an object of derision.[1] Assuredly the Romantic movement, in its time, gave birth to nothing more bizarre than Comte's pseudo-Catholic 'Religion of Humanity'.

Positivism's ultimate goal, as Comte himself repeatedly stated, was 'the spiritual reorganization of the West', a process to be effected first in the realm of ideas, then in that of morals, and finally in social institutions. In this Comte's thinking was, I believe, consistent throughout. Some interpreters indeed have held that the development of Comtism falls into two differing phases, with a recognizable point of cleavage between them. The first represents the work of a logician and theorist, the second, contrastingly, of a prophet and reformer, a man whose supreme concern is with society. It is a view not without plausibility for a number of reasons, the most obvious being that there are passages in Comte's writings which indicate as much: thus he can speak of two separate if connected 'careers' in his public life, the one philosophical, the other religious, his conversion from the former to the latter being brought about by his meeting with Madame de Vaux, which made him realize the superiority of the heart to the intellect. Again, the first three volumes of the *Cours de philosophie positive* would seem to show their author as an epistemologist pure and simple. His purpose there is to define the aims of the various sciences, to determine their relations, to distinguish their respective methods, to observe their development and to assess the value of their achievements. Beyond this he does not venture. Moreover, the attitude of many of the Comtists themselves would appear to confirm this opinion: the theoretical part of his work they readily accepted; where they could not follow him was on his excursions into morals, politics and religion.

All the same, the notion that Comte in middle life, and as the direct result of an amorous crisis, was suddenly converted to social messianism is not to be sustained, as the facts of the matter contradict it. His social concern was made abundantly clear in an essay written in 1822, when he was twenty-four years old: the *Plan des travaux scientifiques nécessaires pour réorganiser la société*.[2] In this he contemplates the unhappy condition of French society since the Revolution – one of 'a profound anarchy, of ever-growing extent' – and its continuance could prove mortal. This revolutionary period must therefore be brought to a close, as the best minds of the age all recognize. Social equilibrium will be regained only when *order* is established in such a form as not to impede *progress*. But to attain to this a consensus of belief is necessary, the recovery of a faith *pour régler le présent au nom de l'avenir déduit du passé*. Such too was, as we have seen, the inspiration of Lamennais, as also of the fiercely anti-Revolutionary doctrines of Maistre and Bonald, to whose influence, particularly of Maistre in his *Du pape* (1819), Comte himself was to some extent indebted.[3] But in his view this reactionary 'traditionalist' approach to the problem was fundamentally mistaken. The ideas and institutions of the pre-Revolutionary era could not be restored. They had proved of value in the past, but their day was over and they could no longer meet the needs of the present with its vastly changed outlook. In fact the advocates of a return to the old order themselves knew that compromise was unavoidable. Could the expansion of knowledge or new ideals in literature and the arts be discounted? Was it possible any more to envisage as the foundation of a reconstituted society ancient theological dogmas now neither agreed upon nor even properly understood? Unanimity of conviction could not be reached on the basis of the unintelligible or the incredible. Yet if the traditionalist case will not stand, neither, in Comte's estimation, will that of outright commitment to 'the principles of the Revolution'. Revolutionary principles may well serve to destroy – as recent history had proved – but they are insufficient for reconstruction. In a sound socio-political order authority will be respected, not held in suspicion or contempt. Unlimited freedom to criticize in any sphere – intellectual, moral, legal – does not make for the stability of institutions. The 'Western sickness', says Comte – in words that are a striking echo of Lamennais's – lies in the failure to recognize any other authority in things of the mind than that of individual reasoning, especially on the really vital issues. 'Une insurrection mentale de l'individu contre l'espèce', he calls it. Nor does the young Comte accord any more approval to the other revolutionary shibboleths. Egalitarianism he dismisses as plainly contrary to all evidence and denies that men in association can possess equal rights. The doctrine of popular sovereignty he repudiates as an elevation of the mediocre and no more acceptable than that of the divine right of kings. Nor does he see any good in emphasizing personal 'rights', for what men need to be instructed in is their duties. Such half-measures and self-contradictions as are found in English constitutionalism he rejects, with a fine Gallic insolence, as totally inadmissible to a people like the French, capable of consistent thinking.

All 'bastard' solutions must, then, be cast aside and the problem confronted in a spirit entirely new. Anarchy in the political and social spheres springs from a like anarchy in belief. The remedy depends on discovering a principle on which the minds of the most intelligent can unite. But where is it to be found? To Comte the answer seemed obvious: what is needed is a body of propositions which no reflecting man can, or will wish to, contest. Intellectual unity will produce emotional harmony, which in turn will induce a convergence of action. Thus the young Comte's optimism led him to his *philosophie positive*, to which, he was confident, the unbiased thoughtful would inevitably rally. Its foundation would be the scientific knowledge of nature with its proper divisions and procedures. After this it would be possible to face and resolve the problem of constructing a positive science of society, a science whose practical outcome would be secured by the very methods the success of which in all other scientific fields was already manifest. In other words, this new science of man would give rise to a 'rational social art', an art as well established in its techniques as that of medicine. By its application alone would the Western sickness be healed. As soon as men realize that societies evolve in accordance with ascertainable laws they will see that the art of politics requires a degree of competence analogous to that of medical science and that mere 'arbitrary fancies' in the one will need to be as rigorously excluded as they are in the other. For the truth is that most men are ignorant of the nature and the complexity of human societies, and when brought to recognition of their ignorance will concede the necessity of leaving such matters 'to a small number of select intelligences, which the most careful (*la plus forte*) preliminary education, appropriately followed by studies of a more direct nature', will gradually have prepared them to meet successfully. The task ahead, then, can be identified by most persons of intelligence, but only those who adopt the right standpoint will be in a position to take due measure of it.

Born at Montpellier in 1798 of an ardently Catholic and royalist family, Comte whilst still a schoolboy let it be known that he had 'naturally ceased to believe in God' and had also embraced republicanism. Admitted at the age of fifteen to the Paris Ecole Polytechnique, he devoted himself to scientific studies, in which his precocity was obvious, but his stay there was short – he was somewhat refractory to its discipline – and on leaving became personal secretary to Saint-Simon, from whose ideas and opinions he imbibed much, but with whom he broke some six years later.[4] In 1826 he began a course of private lectures covering the entire range of science as known to him. Unhappily this enterprise was cut short by a mental breakdown which after a suicide attempt necessitated his confinement in an asylum for a time. Two years later he had recovered sufficiently to be able to resume his teaching and in 1829 he set to work on the composition of his *opus magnum*, the *Cours de philosophie positive*, publication of which, in six volumes, was spread over the twelve years 1830 to 1842. Two or three minor educational appointments secured him a modest income, but in 1842 the loss of his post as examiner for admissions to the Ecole Polytechnique reduced him to a condition verging on poverty. Fortunately for him some of his English admirers, led by John Stuart Mill, raised enough money to tide him over for a while, and subsequently Emile Littré and others of his compatriots exerted themselves to do likewise. On completing the *Philosophie positive* he turned to the application of its principles to his grand design for the reconstruction of society, the outcome of which was the *Système de politique positive* that appeared in four volumes from 1851 to 1854. But his views received a more immediate and practical expression with his founding in 1848 of the 'Société Positive' and in the free public lectures which he gave until silenced by government order in 1851. Indeed this side of his work alienated not a few of his followers, who were prompt to dismiss it as unscientific and fanciful; as a betrayal, in fact, of the true positivist spirit. Their disapproval was evoked especially by the *Catéchisme positiviste* (1852), the *Appel aux conservateurs* (1855) and the *Synthèse subjective* (1856),[5] by which time of course he had become the 'high priest' of his Religion of Humanity. Comte died in 1857, worn out by toil and embittered by the isolation to which public misunderstanding – as he thought – and increasing neglect had reduced him. The great personal event of his life, the one to which, as I have said, he looked back as its turning-point, was his passionate attachment to Clotilde de Vaux, short though it was, for she died only two years after her first meeting with him and at the moment when her husband's decease rendered her free to marry him.[6]

It was natural enough that one whose interests and training were scientific, not metaphysical, should, when he nevertheless undertook the role of philosopher, have followed his native bent. To Comte as to Saint-Simon all things were relative, nothing absolute. Facts, he held, can be known by us only in their relation to other facts, or more precisely, to their antecedent constants. Generalized, these relations can be stated as 'laws', but 'ultimate causes' and 'substances' are beyond our understanding, since both imply the absolute and unconditioned. Herein lies the fundamental principle of the whole positivist system;[7] a principle, however, which is everywhere assumed by Comte though never actually demonstrated, the assumption itself being an indicator of the positivist spirit and outlook. The system, he would have said, rests on the principle: concede the one and the other ensues. But of the necessity of the principle Comte had no doubt whatever if the practical end of the *philosophie positive* was to be attained, namely the 'salvation' of humanity. The procedure therefore which positivism required was threefold: the establishment, first, of a generally recognized body of scientific beliefs, then of a more particular set of truths relating to social science, and finally a moral and political creed derived from social science itself. Its successful achievement depended on two essential conditions: the attitude and standpoint proper to the solution of scientific and philosophical problems and the method or methods proper to the pursuit of knowledge in the various sciences. The term 'positive' fits them both. What, then, did Comte take it to mean?

The answer is to be sought in his famous 'law of the three stages' (*la loi des trois états*), stated at the very outset of the *Cours de philosophie positive*. According to this:

> The entire development of the human intelligence ... is subject to an unvarying necessity ... Every one of our main conceptions, every branch of our knowledge, passes through three different stages: the Theological, or fictitious; the Metaphysical, or abstract; and the Positive, or scientific.[8]

Comte does not tell us what precisely he understands by the human intelligence in this context, or indeed by law,[9] but it is clear from his commentary that he thinks that in every epoch some kind of explanation has been felt to be necessary to account for the relations of things.[10] Thus his *états théoriques* represent the differing ways of explaining, or 'methods of philosophizing'.[11] The first stage, the theological, is that in which man looks for the ultimate or primal cause or causes of events and discovers them, as he believes, in personal agencies regarded as superhuman beings, or in the case of monotheism, in one such only. So we have the age of the gods or of a single God. The most primitive form of this type of thinking is fetishism – or, as we today would say, animism – where inanimate objects are personalized. To this succeeds polytheism, where the gods are no longer identified with things but are thought of rather as acting upon things externally. The final development at this level is the monotheistic, where instead of the gods forming a community they coalesce into or give place to one, conceived as supreme or unique and as perfect. The second stage, the metaphysical, substitutes abstract causes or essences, usually regarded as entities in themselves, for supernatural agents. But the attitude of mind it signifies differs little basically from that represented by the theological stage.[12] Natural phenomena disclose a pattern too regular to have proceeded from mere personal volition, liable as that is to caprice. Anthropomorphism, therefore, will no longer provide an explanation. Nevertheless the metaphysical causes and essences are but analogues of the deities of the theological stage. The great example of this is the seventeenth- and eighteenth-century idea of 'Nature' – as in Hobbes or Buffon, for instance – which, unless simply a camouflaged divinity, is no more than a tautology for natural phenomena and hence explains nothing. The fault with both these earlier stages, in which emotion and imagination play a major role, is that they cannot dispense with the notion of an absolute.

The third stage, the positive, introduces an altogether new frame of mind, the scientific. Here the futile search for ultimate explanations is abandoned and the quest of the absolute recognized to be illusory. Knowledge, it is now understood, depends on observation and exact reasoning in a way which correlates phenomena in terms of 'law'.[13]

Such laws are no more than descriptive, but their use is in making prediction possible. Positive knowledge thus combines certainty with utility, without aspiring to what in the nature of the case cannot be known. At the same time we should appreciate that the need for explaining things – and in the end *all* things – is an irrepressible one; the intelligence seeks always to push on a bit further. Indeed the pursuit of unity is reason's vocation. This is why the theological understanding itself exhibits a succession of phases. The theological stage reaches the highest perfection of which, intellectually, it is capable when it substitutes the providential action of a single deity for a fraternity of independent divinities. And we find the same route followed by the metaphysical understanding in reducing its various entities to one, namely '*nature* envisaged as the sole source of all phenomena'. Thus it is not unreasonable to conceive the positive understanding itself as aiming at a single comprehensive law from which all others are theoretically deducible. However, it would be unreasonable to expect this in practice; the urge to unify is, we might say, instinctive, but the positive spirit is aware both of the limitations of the human intelligence and of the immense complexity of phenomena.[14] At the very moment, therefore, at which Comte promulgates his palmary law of the mind's historical development he bids us recognize that the grasp of reason is not boundless – we are, after all, human – and a certain intellectual humility is a proper and permanent element in the positivist outlook.

In fact, when we consider the law of the three stages in relation to the mind's inherent desire to unify we are in a position to comprehend the true character of man's intelligence. A law which 'explains' history is itself a natural law, since history is not a reversal but a prolongation of nature. History, that is, *realizes* nature, in the most active meaning of the word. So in the fifty-first lecture of the *Philosophie positive* Comte declares that his law is not simply a hypothesis subject like any other to continuous verification, an abstract principle requiring to be sustained empirically, but rather a fundamental truth grounded in 'the exact knowledge of human nature'.[15] In Comte's view the mental development of the human race generally is to be observed microcosmically in that of the individual from childhood through adolescence to mature manhood. 'When contemplating his own history', he asks, 'does not each of us recollect that he has been successively *theologian* in his infancy, *metaphysician* in his youth, and *physicist* in his maturity?'[16] This developmental pattern may thus be seen to be typical of humanity as such, something written into human nature itself, and therefore inevitable. Yet there can be no doubt that Comte's theory rests upon his reading of history, although the cast of his thought is sufficiently aprioristic for him to wish to found it on what he sees as psychological necessity rather than a more or less tentative empirical inference.

Individual psychology, however, is a precarious foundation for a principle valid for overall historical interpretation. The historical evidence, on the other hand, is not without plausibility when taken very broadly. The intellectual frame of reference for the modern world, as contrasted with the middle ages, or even with the era of the Enlightenment, is that of science. Modern man, at least when dealing with phenomena, no longer treats either 'God' or 'Nature' as an explanatory concept, but resorts to scientific hypothesis. At the same time, to suppose that Comte's law can be applied in any hard-and-fast way to historical epochs would clearly be a mistake, and to be fair to Comte himself he does admit this. The stages overlap. Thus he says that:

> We shall have to regard the theological epoch, for example, as still existing in so far as moral and political ideas have retained their essentially theological character, despite the transition of other intellectual categories to the purely metaphysical stage, even when the genuinely positive stage has already been reached in respect of the more simple of such categories. Likewise it will be necessary to prolong the metaphysical epoch, properly speaking, into the beginnings of positivism.

In this way, he thinks, 'the essential character of each epoch will remain as pronounced as possible, while the spontaneous preparation of the epoch which follows is clearly brought out'.[17] Of course we may expect to find a hangover from one epoch persisting into another – German idealist metaphysics in Comte's own day furnished him with a good example; but in human affairs such complications are always to be encountered and do not affect the basic plan.

Comte's interpretation of history obviously rests upon an *a priori* progressivist assumption. The positive stage is not only necessary, it is desirable. Not that the two antecedent stages are simply to be written off as ages of mere intellectual darkness; Comte concedes that in their time they were not only unavoidable but appropriate, as fables are educative in childhood and abstract speculations in youth. It is simply that in mature thinking they have no place. The positive stage is marked by the scientific attitude, based on tested knowledge. Further-more, the stages are to be seen as not simply a matter of theoretical understanding; each is associated with a distinctive form of social organization. Thus with the theological stage we connect, historically, a social order founded on authority and militarism, while the meta-physical is correlated with doctrines of 'natural right' and popular sovereignty – types of social theory which Comte regards as no more than transitional. For positivism the proper social expression is industrialism, man's interest at this stage being focused on his economic life. In other words, scientific knowledge is geared to technology, on which industrial production depends. But here Comte is nothing if not an optimist, since he believes that the consistent pursuit of economic ends can only produce peace. Of revolutionary class-war he offers no hint. However, as between advances in the natural sciences and the reconstruction of society which he desiderates, a further body of knowledge is requisite, namely a 'positive' science of man in his social relations – *sociology*. How man should best organize his life will relate, that is, to the way in which he can grasp and utilize the principles on which society is constituted, and in particular those which govern change within it.

But before approaching Comte's social theory we must pause briefly to consider his view of the sciences and the procedure he adopts in classifying them. For he holds such classification to be possible inasmuch as, for all their apparent diversity, they are bound one to another in close solidarity.[18] Not of course that one could actually have been deduced from another, as with consequent and antecedent. Progress in the sciences is attainable only because each can rely upon certain others for both its methods and its results, as biology relies upon chemistry and so ultimately upon physics. But in classifying the sciences Comte adopts two distinct points of view which he nevertheless regards as complementary. In the former case one moves from the simple to the complex, or from the abstract to the concrete; in the latter one takes the historical perspective. From the standpoint of logic the sciences can be arranged according to the mode of their interdependence, the pattern of advance being one of growing complexity. But the validity of this procedure can also be demonstrated from the historical or social standpoint, for if the more complex sciences need to borrow from the simpler ones, as to both methods and results, those that were the first to establish themselves historically must also have been the simplest and most abstract. The more complex emerged later, and in the order of their complexity. Logically the science of physics, as that of nature in its greatest generality, is primary. But physics is both inorganic and organic. The inorganic subdivides into celestial and terrestrial – astronomy, physics proper and chemistry – chemistry depending on physics as physics in its turn depends on astronomy. Similarly organic physics subdivides into biology, the science of life as such, and 'social physics' or sociology, the latter depending on biology as biology depends on chemistry. Thus there develops a chain of interconnecting disciplines, the whole sequence of which can be shown ultimately to rest on mathematics as its 'true rational basis', without which astronomy would not be possible. So the scheme of human knowledge is complete.[19]

When, next, we look at it from the historical angle we find that history bears out the conclusions of logic. Men have indeed been occupied with the various sciences in all ages, but in earlier times progress was achieved only in those that are logically the prior ones. A science has not established itself until it has acquired an exact idea of its own domain, of the methods appropriate to it and of the unchanging principles which it must assume. Mathematics had its beginnings in antiquity, although it needed the work of Descartes, Leibniz and Newton in modern times to complete it. Astronomy was the second science to take shape, the ancients again making the first observations of the heavens, but immense advances occurred in the sixteenth and seventeenth centuries with the work of Copernicus, Kepler and Galileo, leading on to that again of Newton. Physics made no effective appearance until the seventeenth and eighteenth centuries, while chemistry had to emerge from mediaeval alchemy before being set on the right road by Lavoisier and others toward the end of the eighteenth century. Biology made good headway in the seventeenth century, but its greatest achievements – although Comte wrote before Darwin – had to await the nineteenth. Sociology, however, remained still to be constituted. But the way forward was clear enough.

When we turn to the *Système de politique positive* we find this scheme of classification continued, but with certain interesting differences. In the wake of the six sciences just listed Comte introduces a seventh, ethics, understood as the method by which conduct, both individual and social, is to be regulated. Its basic principle is altruism, but it is to be ranked as a science inasmuch as it consists of knowledge both of the human faculties themselves and of the laws by which the life of societies is governed. Yet it also is an art, since it aims at instructing us in the right *praxis* alike of individuals and of groups. Its own laws, however, through its being more complex and concrete, are more immediately apparent than are those of sociology, from which it has therefore to be distinguished as a separate form of knowledge. But there is a further point to be noted. Comte, while in no way qualifying his idea of the solidarity of the sciences, is concerned nevertheless to discriminate among them on the score of value. Some are more important than others – those, namely, that are of more direct use to humanity; and of none of them is this more obviously so than ethics, the science and art of human living, although it is sociology that furnishes ethics with its needed information on the nature of society as such. Thereafter, although this time in reverse order, come biology, chemistry, physics, astronomy and mathematics. In fact the more complex a science is the more *evident* is the operation of its laws, and *vice versa*. This in no way affects the logical order of the sciences, and mathematics, probably to the ordinary man the most remote of all, remains fundamental. But a hierarchy of relevance, of utility, has to be recognized, Comte thinks, in which the humane sciences are and must be pre-eminent. Of course any given science has primarily to be studied on its own account, but if its relation to the whole body of the sciences is overlooked it degenerates into a mere mental exercise.

Thus Comte will not have knowledge purely for its own sake; life itself is of more value than 'scientific puerilities', and the wise man will not waste time on a futile erudition. Every science should be reduced to the minimum content necessary for the constitution of that which is immediately subsequent to it in complexity and human significance. And in the end the science which all others subserve as the most important is ethics.

Comte is well aware that the study of human society is no new thing; novelty lies in approaching it along scientific or 'positive' lines. Hitherto as a rule social theorizing had been no more than an enterprise in utopia-building, an imaginative projection bearing little relation to the circumstances of existing societies and directed in the main by the particular author's moral concerns. But 'ideal' societies cannot be constructed *in abstracto*. Social phenomena, like any other, are subject to specific conditions or laws, and these must be clearly understood if deliberate social action is to be effective. For human societies, as Lamennais was wont to insist, are more like organisms than mechanisms, and to that extent their life could only suffer from over-drastic modification. Revolutions carried through on *a priori* principles spell disaster, not benefit. Not that Comte had no mentors in this field: Montesquieu was one, certainly,[20] Turgot another, while Condorcet he often referred to as his 'spiritual father'. But for all their high intelligence and insight these men lacked an adequate scientific basis for their social thinking, as well as sufficiency of historical knowledge or indeed any clear idea of the nature of human progress. Comte believed that he himself possessed this equipment. To meet the need of the hour, therefore, was his responsibility.

He too, be it said, began with a large presupposition, the concept of Humanity, 'le Grand Etre'. This 'Great Being', however, is 'always subject to the totality of the natural order, of which it constitutes the noblest element'.[21] It comprises, first, mankind as it actually is, the sum of all living human beings; but also, secondly, mankind of the past, though still in a real sense alive, whether through the sustained effects of its actions in the present or in the historical memory; while thirdly there is mankind yet to be, our posterity, of which we nevertheless can form some anticipatory notion. The Great Being may thus be conceived as a vast organism continuously developing, and it is this which is the object of genuinely scientific social inquiry. But are we, then, to understand that sociology is really no more than an extension of biology? Some Comtists have maintained this, but Comte himself is guarded on the point. There is, he holds, a close parallelism between living organisms and human societies, but it should not be carried too far, since the differences between them are significant, chiefly so in the fact that an organism constitutes a unity in a way that no grouping of human individuals can ever do. Sociology therefore cannot be looked on as a 'simple appendix to biology'. On the contrary, it is a quite distinct science, directly founded on bases proper to itself. Its material is the general and unchanging laws by which human societies subsist and develop, and it comprises two areas: social statics and social dynamics.

Observation of human societies reveals to us certain elements common to virtually all, out of which, at any given period, organizations of various kinds are seen to develop. In every society there is division of labour, giving rise to distinctive group interests and loyalties. Institutions – political, economic, religious, judicial, military – also come into being, thus establishing a certain *order* or equilibrium more or less permanent. The 'science of order', in this particular sense, is social statics. Further, the various organizations which grow up in society stand to one another in a reciprocal relationship, so creating a *consensus*, a community of mind and outlook, which operates as a stabilizing and conservative force in society. This too is the concern of social statics. But the actual life of man in society is not determined by order alone; there must also be progress, and progress that is continuous.[22] Comte certainly does not go so far as to claim that the human race is steadily moving towards a condition of manifest wellbeing and happiness. Whether in this world human felicity does or does not increase with the passage of time he judges to be not only unanswerable but pointless: happiness depends on a correlation of desires with circumstances. What Comte means is simply that the human race is continuously changing and so learns to adjust itself with increasing adaptability to the differing *milieux* in which it evolves. But the conditions of social change similarly have their own laws or principles, and these it is which are the interest of social dynamics. As the former investigation, we may say, provides the theory of order, so the latter provides the theory of progress. The laws which it sets out are basic and governing; knowledge of them enables us to appreciate humanity's past and to assess the factors which have contributed to form the present. It also will help us to anticipate the future and even to calculate how best to promote coming developments. Such is the task before us. It is not sociology's responsibility either to justify existing political arrangements or to condemn them, but to regard them simply as subjects of study.

The means which Comte believes sociologists must adopt for success-ful pursuance of their aim are categorized by him as follows: observa-tion, which should be as far-reaching as possible; experiment, limited though it obviously is in its applicability to society; comparison, since different types of society, primitive and civilized alike, need to be appraised in relation to each other; and finally, use of the historical method, which has as its goal determination of the conditions for the advancement of human freedom and assessment of these conditions in their relation to one another, an undertaking which not only deepens our appreciation of the extent to which the present is rooted in the past, but also stimulates the social feeling which for Comte is necessary for the ultimate regeneration of mankind. In introducing the historical method sociology completes the channels of positive research. Science will now have the resources with which to push its inquiries to the limit.

2

In none of his discussions of the *loi des trois états* does Comte employ the word 'religion'; instead he speaks of 'theology' and the 'theological stage' in human thought. Religion, it is evident, is associated by him with feeling or sentiment, and as such – in contrast with theology – its day is by no means over. Rather can the history of humanity be represented as in a sense – to quote Levy-Bruhl – 'an evolution which proceeds from primitive religion (fetishism) to definite religion (posi-tivism)'.[23] Comte even envisages a kind of fourth stage in which the mind frees itself from science in much the same way as it has come to free itself from theology and metaphysics, the scientific stage being repre-sented as in the end little more than a transition to the purely positive, although in no respect does Comte go back on his claim that his 'great law' is 'the fundamental law of our intellectual development'.[24]

Comte's theory of religion is thus an aspect of positive philosophy in its explanatory function, as in the law of the three stages. Now we have seen that Comte believes this law to be rooted in the very nature of the mind and its development, and at this point it will be well to look more closely at what he says. Comte speaks of a 'natural and irresistible inclination' in man to adopt the theological view.

> Man's personal action on other beings is the only one the manner of which he understands, through the feeling he has of it. He is led therefore to represent the action which external bodies exercise on him in an analogous

way, as well as the action they exercise among themselves, of which he directly sees only the results.

In other words,

> Man necessarily begins by seeing all bodies which hold our attention as if they were other living beings, with a life like our own, but in general superior to ours because of the more powerful action which most of them exert.[25]

In the fifty-first lecture of the *Cours de philosophie positive* Comte takes up this argument again, and he states his position very clearly:

> The inevitable necessity of such an intellectual development has as its first and basic principle man's primitive tendency involuntarily to transfer the inward sense (*le sentiment intime*) of his own nature to phenomena generally.[26]

Consequently,

> If man, on the one hand, necessarily regards himself as in origin the centre of all things, he is likewise, on the other, to be no less inevitably disposed to set himself up as the universal pattern.

A spontaneous anthropocentrism, that is, implies an equally spontaneous anthropomorphism. Thus

> Man can conceive no other ultimate explanation of phenomena in general than to assimilate them as far as possible to his own actions – the only ones by which he can ever believe himself able to understand the essential mode of production, through the natural sensation which directly accompanies them.[27]

This means that every cause is to be understood as a psychological fact, whereas to explain natural phenomena as 'caused' is really to confuse the psychological with the physical. For, as we have already observed, he rejects the notion of 'psychological facts', holding that the primary task of positivist criticism is to banish the idea of causation as expressive of mind, will and purpose. To confuse the *how* with the *why* of things is to turn explanation into justification.

The error at the centre of this confusion is clearly exposed by the law of the three stages. Man has a natural tendency to conceive the external world anthropomorphically; in this sense it may fairly be said that he 'knows nothing essentially but himself'.[28] The feeling both for his own being and for those differing modes of being which his actions effect constitutes a kind of spontaneous knowledge that precedes and directs the mind's first efforts to comprehend his environment. Historically, that is, man's attempt to understand the world he lives in has no other starting-point than himself. He sees a natural event not as a mere happening but as something done or suffered or achieved; there is intentionality behind it. But for this very reason positivism is concerned to avoid the psychological approach. Comte himself, as I say, is so far from ignoring the anthropomorphism inherent in human thinking that he considers it the dominating feature of the primitive intelligence. What he denies, however, and what he believes the positive spirit is bound to eliminate, is the idea that any account of nature which assumes the operation upon or within it of 'supernatural' personal agencies can possibly be regarded as scientific. Even when the positivist speaks of what he has himself experienced he really is doing no more than state what in certain situations he has *felt*. An experience, *per se*, cannot tell us what objectively has been cognized.

Comte's law thus shows that progress in knowledge must come to exclude all such subjectivism. 'Causes' will be replaced by natural laws that make no reference to psychological conditions or to ideas that can never be wholly detached from their subjective matrix. And if in particular the study of man himself is to rank as a science in the proper sense of the word then recourse to the 'psychologism' which would turn interior sensations into objectively observable facts will have to be set aside. This anti-psychological bias in Comte is highlighted further by his method of classifying the sciences. It is a classification which, as we have observed, follows an order of increasing complexity. But this 'logical' order has an anthropological significance in that its culmination is the science of man himself, since human phenomena are the most complex and individualized of all. And it also is historical, as the order in which the various sciences have actually acquired their positivity in the course of time. Sociology, as the last of the sciences to be established, demonstrates how history reflects logic. And the reason for its being the last is that the study of human phenomena is the most difficult of all to free from 'psychologism'. Comte makes the point succinctly when he rephrases his law thus: In the history of the relations between mind and the external world an original anthropocentrism and anthropomorphism direct the rational understanding from man to the world, but with the advance of knowledge the process is reversed, the rational understanding now proceeding from the world to man.[29]

In Auguste Comte's thinking religion in all its historic forms belongs to the theological stage of man's mental development. But what preconception of religion on his part does this suggest? It is to be noted that the word consistently used by him is 'theology', i.e. the *logos* of *theos*, and is referred to belief in divine beings, or, as in theology's most sophisticated form, monotheism, a single divine being. But in Comte's view the purpose of this belief is explanatory; whatever shape theology assumes it is always, he thinks, essentially cosmology. From the most primitive fetishism to the most metaphysically refined theism the divinity is represented as fulfilling a cosmic function. This, it could be said, is positivism's philosophy of religion. 'God' always denotes *cause*, whether immediate or ultimate. But when science compels us to drop the very idea of causality the theological interpretation of the world is bound to disappear with it. Positivism, in pursuing the methods of science, is content to take the universe as it is; the task of 'explaining' it, even if comprehensible, is outside its competence.

Comte sees in religion, therefore, a perfectly natural development as an expression of man's need to account for the world about him. And his most spontaneous way of doing this is to invest it with human characteristics. Thus he speaks of the 'spontaneous origin' of theological thinking and of 'our primordial tendency' to regard even inanimate objects as having a life analogous to our own.[30] He has to conclude therefore that religion marked a necessary stage in the evolution of the human intelligence by teaching it to frame hypotheses. The difficulty facing the scientist is that a hypothesis has to be constructed if useful and orderly observations are to be made, while at the same time no hypothesis is possible unless and until such observations have been made.[31] What the theological imagination did was to break this vicious circle by devising 'hypotheses' not based on observation; or, as Comte phrases it: 'This fatal logical antagonism was evidently incapable of any other solution than that naturally procured by the inevitably primitive flight of theological philosophy in assimilating, as far as possible, all phenomena to human actions.'[32] If his intelligence had failed to make this venture man would never have embarked on the long quest which has led him at last to understand the universe scientifically. The original hypothesis we now recognize to have been non-rational, but the important thing is that the urge to *explain* was given effect.

Here we may note, in passing, Comte's generally rather low estimate of the vitality of human reason, believing as he did that man's psycho-physiological constitution is such as to render keen intellectual effort more or less uncongenial to him. That man is aware of the need to find an explanation for things is not in doubt, but he tends to shirk the trouble of doing so.[33] For confirmation of his opinion that human pride should not on this score be flattered he appeals to man's historical record. To accomplish anything beyond the mere satisfaction of his basic necessities man has to be emotionally stimulated, and such stimulus has as a rule been provided by remote or even impossible ideals. Nothing shows this more plainly than the 'infantile curiosity' which hankers after the knowledge of 'absolutes', of that ultimate *why* which in the nature of things cannot be answered. Paradoxically, however, it is this very longing which in the modern world has brought mankind to seek not intellectual chimaeras but 'true facts'.[34]

For the founder of positivism, then, dreams will often be the gateway to reality:

> However vain these puerile speculations must appear to us now, it should not be forgotten that, on any matter, always and everywhere, they alone have been able to lift the genius of man out of its primitive torpor in supplying his permanent activity with the one spontaneous nourishment capable of existing at the beginning.[35]

Thus it is by the non-rational that reason is first awakened. So when we say, as Comte thinks we must, that religion originated in an attempt to explain the world, we cannot blink the fact that the explanation is not a rational one. Yet irrationality is not essential to it – the individual mind in infancy is not rational. What matters, on a long view, is not the content of the explanation but its intent.

The evolution of the theological mode of thought throws light on the intrinsic nature of religion itself. The transition from fetishism by way of polytheism to monotheism is assuredly an advance, but at the same time it represents, as Comte sees it, a certain weakening of the theological standpoint and at least a move towards the positive.[36] Theology, that is to say, becomes more sophisticated with the gradual reduction of its overtly non-rational elements. In seeking to unify experience by eliminating multiple causation it takes a long step nearer that total abandonment of the whole notion of 'causality' which distinguishes the scientific attitude.[37] Development *within* the theological stage is thus itself part of an intellectual process of both generalization and concentration. In this respect the emergence of monotheism is of particular interest to Comte, for he sees it – evidently in complete disregard of the religious history of ancient Israel – as a consequence of the deliberate exercise of philosophical reason among the Greeks. It is a product, we are to believe, of exclusively intellectual reflection:

> The rational understanding reached the point where the direct and general contradiction which the disorderly crowd of capricious deities presented to it revolted it, as compared with the spectacle, daily ever more fixed and regular, that man came by degrees to perceive in the external world as a whole.[38]

Hence in the *Politique positive* Comte assures us that 'as monotheism was never just polytheism reduced and concentrated, its appearance was not the result of any spontaneous and popular tendency. It has always rested upon a long series of philosophical meditations which could occur only within a body of abstract thinkers whose opinions gained a hold through teaching.'[39]

But, although the monotheistic development reached its climax in Christianity, the popular hold of Catholicism was maintained for centuries by drawing upon polytheism for whatever could be adapted to faith in a unique deity, especially through the cult of the Blessed Virgin, the intercession of the saints and the ministry of angels. Yet in its origin and substantive character Christianity's fundamental doctrine is the product only of critical reflection, and as such marks, he thinks, a derogation from what the ordinary worshipper has usually understood in religion.[40]

The growth of monotheism, then, so far from being a true expression of the religious consciousness, simply represents the demand of the critical intelligence that causality be limited to a single source, provided that that source is located beyond the natural order and so in the literal sense of the word is 'supernatural'. But this implies that the divine is wholly exteriorized and far removed from the world of humanity. As a result the religious spirit is debilitated. For if religion is essentially a way of explaining phenomena every act of worship and devotion must be directed by that belief, whereas the idea of an entirely transcendent deity deprives men in their ordinary daily experience of virtually all awareness of the divine as immediately operative in their lives. So the supreme Author of nature becomes ever more remote, and if the concept of transcendence does not destroy the religious spirit altogether – although Comte, as we shall observe, does not believe that it has – it certainly devalues theology as a category of explanation. Not until God is understood as *le Grand Etre*, Humanity itself, that is, will the true interiority of religion be rediscovered. For man will then become God.

Compared with the biblical view Comte's opinions must strike the reader as perverse. Not only is the Old Testament experience ignored, so too is the Christian doctrine of the incarnation. For all Comte's professed admiration of Catholicism he is entirely deficient in his comprehension of the religion of the New Testament – the figure of Jesus he does not admire and in the gospels he sees only a 'mental and moral void' – while for Protestant biblicism and the individualism which he thinks it encourages he has nothing but contempt. A God *historically* revealed, and a view of religion which is not simply a mode of explaining natural phenomena, were completely beyond his ken.[41]

However, Comte commends monotheistic theology at least for the form of social organization produced by it or at any rate adapted to it. This basically is why the mediaeval Catholic church – 'immense et admirable organisme' – wins his praise.[42] The ecclesiastical structure is constituted by the hierarchy centred on the papacy. Graeco-Roman antiquity united the spiritual power of the priesthood with the temporal power of the magistrate. Catholicism, on the other hand, has separated them, to the undubitable good of humanity generally. To place government in the hands of philosophers, Comte thinks, would be absurd because they are not fitted for it; their interest is focused on the past rather than on the present, and anyhow they consider themselves above matters of mere detail. A nation's leaders ought rather to be men of average intelligence but with a gift for the practical. At the same time there must be a fund of sound ideas available to them if they are not to court disaster. Side by side therefore with the men of action must be the *savants*, the experts, to advise them. This happy arrangement, Comte supposes, had been achieved in the middle ages, when the papacy reached the summit of its moral authority and exercised a power quite distinct from the temporal, acting directly and publicly through its official pronouncements, and covertly but no less effectively through the confessional. It also had at its disposal another potent arm, excommunication, with which to influence public opinion, since the object of the church's ban was excluded not only from its spiritual ministrations but very largely from the society of his fellow-men. Moreover, in the mediaeval system the clergy as a learned class exerted a civilizing influence. It was they who possessed such knowledge and understanding as then existed, combined with the dignity and prestige accorded to a recognized social estate having its particular and by universal consent superior responsibilities, its special ethos and even its own language; a class which, nevertheless, was preserved by the rule of celibacy from becoming a caste and which saw recruitment and preferment, whatever the abuses that might be tolerated, as dependent in principle on personal vocation and merit. It was this class which, to an eminent degree, maintained the cultural standards of Christendom.

For education itself rested with the church. Admittedly it was traditionalist, formal and quite unscientific, but it inculcated the idea of fundamental obligations incumbent on all. This teaching authority, which the penitential system could impose on the conscience of each individual, was based on dogmas which, although in substance false, served as a means of social cohesion. Especially favoured by Comte were the doctrines of *extra ecclesiam nulla salus*, purgatory, with its offer of eventual salvation to sinners, and the real presence of divinity in the mass, which confers upon the officiant a mysterious and sacral character; while the sacraments which punctuated the course of the believer's life from the cradle to the grave also bound him to the ecclesial community. As the self-proclaimed prophet and hierarch of a regenerated society Comte could not but expatiate on the wisdom and beneficence of such an order, illusory though its theoretical foundations were.

The ecclesiastical structure is matched on the temporal side by feudalism, with its system of hereditary fiefs. Together they formed a dual power which, in the idealizing eye of the nineteenth-century philosopher, was a model still for the kind of society he envisaged. To be admired above all, though, was the church's universal ethic, to which the whole of mediaeval life was subject. The city-states of antiquity had had, along with their tutelary deities, their own codes or traditions of morality. But under Christianity this moral relativism disappeared and all nations and classes acknowledged the same ethical principles, disseminated by education, explained by the church's preaching and upheld by its penitential discipline. From it men's lives derived their whole meaning. As with creed and dogma, however, it was not the specific content of this moral teaching which attracted Comte; some of its provisions no doubt were salutary, but in the main it was narrowly individualistic and took little account of the needs of society as such, throwing as it did the entire weight of emphasis on the attainment of individual salvation hereafter. Yet in imposing individual self-discipline, and through that a general consistency of action, it was able to sustain the social organization, whilst its method of rewarding moral and spiritual excellence by formal beatification set an example which other societies resting on a different ideological foundation might well emulate. Further, the Christian ethic had borne fruit in social amelioration. It had largely removed slavery, even if, at first, only to replace it with serfdom, although the free association of skilled artisans in the mediaeval guilds was to follow. Important too – and Comte readily concedes the fact – was the scholastic development of philosophical reason; scientific knowledge indeed was absent, but the intrepid rationalism of the schoolmen had the effect of diminishing religious credulity and preparing the way, in due course, for the scientific observation of man's environment. Again, the mediaeval synthesis of faith and culture had achieved a marvellous efflorescence in the visual arts and music, for on the beauties of Catholicism Comte waxes almost as lyrical as Chateaubriand. Like any Romantic enchanted by the wonders of the middle ages he denounces the merely 'frivolous philosophy' which could describe as 'barbarous and dark' the epoch which produced a Thomas Aquinas, an Albert the Great, a Roger Bacon or a Dante.

Yet, great though the attainments of the theological stage were, in many respects, it was a phase of thought that was bound to pass away; first, as a consequence of the break-up of the unity of the spiritual and temporal powers through their mutual rivalry and conflict, but also because of the increasingly manifest incompatibility of Catholic dogma with intellectual progress. Dogma claimed to be absolute, but as knowledge advanced faith saw itself to be more and more under threat from reason. Religious belief, looking always to the past, could not move with the times, so admitting to all intents that it was to the past alone that it belonged. The age of theology had therefore to give place to another, more open to the future. Nor could an ethic which linked virtue only with the fear of hell or the hope of heaven continue to preserve its authority.[43] Thus in the words of Comte's modern biographer, 'Dieu est parti sans laisser de question.'[44]

As the law of the three stages informs us, however, the theological outlook did not yield to the positivist immediately; a transition stage, the metaphysical, intervened. This in part was destructive, in part constructive. The former carried out, initially unconsciously but subsequently consciously and deliberately, the necessary task of demolition; the latter made a path for the advent of positivism itself. Social forces were ubiquitously operative: the decadence of the papacy, the growth of the spirit of nationalism, the appearance of a bourgeois and mercantile class, and so forth. But a powerful negative element, doctrinal as well as social, irrupted in the shape of the Protestant Reformation. Protestantism opposed traditional beliefs and accorded the individual the right to criticize them, subject only to the 'truth' conveyed in the biblical revelation – a proviso more characteristic, be it said, of the earlier phases of the Protestant movement than of its subsequent developments, since in the end it conceded the right of free inquiry without restraint, 'le dogme absolu et indéfini du libre examen individuel'. Thus 'classical' Protestantism collapsed into deism and finally atheism. For to the age of Enlightenment every rational man was his own authority in belief and morals. Dogma and the church were despised even when not overtly opposed, the hostility being encouraged by the idea that an abstract and critical philosophy could unite men's hearts and that radical changes in their institutions would suffice to renew the world. The prophets of this confident rationalism were Hobbes, Spinoza and Bayle, its apostles Fontenelle, Voltaire and Diderot. The gospel of Reason was, however, necessary if error was to be exposed and banished. But the constructive efforts of the metaphysical stage were less successful because its presuppositions were basically those of its predecessor, reified abstractions taking the place of anthropomorphic divinities.

The positivist therefore stands on the threshold of a new era. The old world, with its theological interpretation of life, has passed away, or at any rate is passing. Yet much remains to be done. It is not enough only to amass detailed information; a sense of the whole needs to be

fostered. The social order of the future demands a planned reorganization of humanity's resources. Industry, for example, requires systematic action to rationalize it, art should have a social objective, while
science, already over-departmentalized, too frequently dissipates its
energies in futile research; it likewise needs to reorientate its efforts. All
these necessary ends it is for positivism to clarify and coordinate. In the
light of the new sciences of social statics and social dynamics man now
is in a position, Comte claims, to reconstitute society in a manner befit-
ting his knowledge. So will it combine order with progress.

3

The constructive programme of positivism is set out in the *Système de
politique positive* and the *Catéchisme positiviste*. How is it to be
realized? Not apparently by the abolition of social classes. Comte is no
egalitarian and thinks any attempt to enforce social equality undesirable. It is knowledge which will bring social amelioration. But what
knowledge especially? The answer of course is sociology; and one thing
of vital import it does tell us is that what in the past has controlled and
guided the conduct of individuals and brought them into harmony with
each other has been *religion*. (The word itself indicates this, for religion
is 'that which binds', *quod religat*.) For here history affords abundant
witness; the evolution of humanity has been dominated by that of its
religious ideas. I said earlier that Comte's rejection of theological thinking, in accordance with the requirements of his law, did not mean that
religion itself was otiose. As explanation no doubt it was; but not as
sentiment. And at this point we cannot but turn to Comte's own life for
illumination of his attitude. Between 1842, when the *Philosophie positive* was completed, and 1852, when the first volume of the *Politique
positive* made its appearance, Comte had passed through a phase of
mental development which in one respect at least was revolutionary.[45]
His hitherto prevailing intellectualism had been shaken by the
emotional experience of his relationship with Clotilde de Vaux. Not
that he became in any sense a 'new man' as a result of it, and the attempt
of some who found the later expressions of his thought repugnant to
attribute the Religion of Humanity to the baneful effects of a sentimental infatuation is, as I have said, unwarranted. But that Mme de
Vaux greatly stimulated his emotional sensibility – never far below the
surface of his nature – causing him to assign to the 'heart' a role in
thought as in life itself which he hitherto had not contemplated, seems
to me not open to denial. He spoke of her in language of effusive admiration, the sincerity of which is not to be questioned. Above all, she
taught him, on his own warm asseverations, the meaning of love.[46]

For now feeling must be given its due place in a vision of life resting on knowledge. The revolt of reason against feeling had been disastrous, not because reason was misguided in its aims but because it was exclusive in its purview. Morality grounded in love is indispensable, since humanity is not a metaphysical abstraction but something that demands to live in the hearts of men. Hence if a social order is to be established which properly reflects man's humanity it must embody an appropriate *religion*, such as will unite knowledge, aspiration and love, and furnish the individual with a goal for his activity and an object for his affections. But how? The theological way of thinking is effectively no more; the metaphysical, with its 'absolute' causes and substances, persists only as an intellectual illusion. If men are to have a new religion it must be, in the modern sense of the word, a rational one, and the elements of it are supplied, Comte believes, by sociology. A religion of Humanity is thus both needed and possible.

We live, he says, in the 'Grand Milieu' of space, our evolution having occurred on the 'Grand Fétiche' of earth, and we are all of us members of the 'Grand Etre' of the human race.[47] This last consists of the living, of the dead who yet survive in the memories of the living, and of those still to be born but who are proleptically present in the imagination. To this great human reality each one of us owes everything – his material subsistence and welfare, the result of the cumulative thought and toil of past generations; his dearest and most intimate sentiments, be they aesthetic, moral or religious; his understanding, his information, his techniques, his very language. Humanity therefore is for each of us a true Providence, replacing the mythological 'Providences' and 'Destinies' of the old religions with their divine legends and miracles. As such it should be the abiding object of men's thoughts, for on it they wholly depend. It offers us a religion the truth of which is self-evident but which also has the power to inspire the heart and direct action.

Comte, however, is not content with general praise of his humanistic faith; he is nothing if not specific, and in this the influence of his Catholic upbringing is all-pervasive. Every religion, he submits, has had its dogmas, its cultus and its polity, and the religion of humanity must be similarly equipped. In regard to positivist doctrine Comte has already made himself clear: it is the substance of the *philosophie positive* itself, the sum of positive knowledge furnished by the sciences. There can be no other 'truth' than this. No form of theism, therefore, is to be admitted. 'To the extent that I worked out the positivist dogmatic the more incapable I became of returning to supernaturalist beliefs.'[48] He spoke contemptuously of 'sophismes monothéistes', dismissing the whole idea of 'the one God' as vague and incoherent.[49]

He could even say that 'our intelligence would be better guided by a wisely condensed polytheism than by any sort of monotheism'.[50]

The question of worship, however, occasioned him more difficulty. A cultus certainly was wanted, but how could *sociolatry* – the term is his – be established? Individuals, he thought, would need above all to be imbued with reverence for humanity and a deep sense of their total dependence upon it. Here Catholicism might point the way, for, although instead of God-as-Providence faith in Man-as-Providence would be substituted,[51] the institutions of the Catholic church had nevertheless been well tested down the centuries and could readily be adapted to the requirements of the new religion. Positivist worship, like its Catholic exemplar, would assume two forms, a private and a public. A major feature would be its hagiology, a due commemoration, on a carefully elaborated basis, first, of the honoured dead, then of the living, who are our actual collaborators, and finally of our posterity, who will continue their predecessors' good works. The attitude of mind to be fostered is one of gratitude and love; though also, where necessary, of condemnation. Private worship would be either purely personal or domestic. The former would consist in 'the intimate adoration of the *feeling* sex', for if the guardian angels of Catholic piety are only fictitious authentic ones do exist in the shape of *women*. Woman is the 'soul' of the family – as mother, or wife, or daughter primarily, but also as sister and even maidservant. Whatever her role be, woman stands for one thing in particular: sympathy, love, devotion. She is humanity's true type and example. Let man, then, see in her his guardian angel, as she will see hers in her own mother, her spouse and her son.[52] Both man and woman should offer prayer three times a day – morning, noontide and evening – prayer too that is spoken, since verbal utterance enhances its psychological effect. And let prayer always be poetic, for poetry goes to the heart.

Domestic worship has a different object, that of uniting family and fatherland. To this end Comte finds the Catholic sacramental principle useful, and he devises sacraments – social sacraments – of his own; nine of them, in fact – two up on the Catholic seven.[53] Baptism becomes the ceremony of 'Presentation', with godparents assisting. 'Initiation' follows at the age of fourteen, the equivalent of confirmation, when the youth will come under the tutelage of positivist 'priests' to strengthen his heart against his intellect. At twenty-one comes 'Admission'; studies now are over and adult life, directed to the service of humanity, has to be faced. 'Dedication' at twenty-eight marks the choice of a career and a solemn resolve to give oneself to it. 'Marriage', for men, is not below the age of twenty-eight, or, for women, of twenty-one. (Comte thinks that as a rule a man should not marry after thirty-five, or a woman after twenty-eight.) 'Maturity' is reached at forty-two and lasts for twenty-one years, sixty-three being the age of 'Retirement', at which time a man must have decided on his heir. Death, finally, brings to a close a well-regulated and useful life, accompanied by 'Transformation', Comte's counterpart of the church's extreme unction, in which the priest of humanity encourages the dying with the hope of a blessed immortality in the memory of men. Seven years after death 'Incorporation' ensues, a solemn judgment at which the deceased, if deemed worthy, will be incorporated into the Great Being of virtuous humanity.[54] Should he, however, be unworthy, his reprobated remains will be consigned to the burial-place of executed criminals, suicides and duellists! The dead man's widow, as in the early church, will not remarry.

Public worship will be taken up with the celebration of civic festivals. All who have contributed significantly to the organization of order and progress will receive solemn commemoration of a kind to provide occasions for the production of new works of art and music. Such ceremonies will fortify the individual's sense of social solidarity. This public cultus will also of course have its temple, situated in the burial-ground of the honoured dead and oriented towards Paris, 'the normal centre of positivism'. The temple sanctuary will contain a symbolic figure – that of a young woman of about thirty years with her infant son in her arms – while side-chapels will likewise have their token images. A presbytery will house the priests and their families, with another edifice nearby to serve as a school for instruction in the positivist creed. Banners, 'Sacred' emblems of various sorts and edifying inscriptions – 'Order and Progress' (the motto of the new republic), 'Live for Others', 'Live for the Great Day' – will have their appropriate places. Nor does Comte forget a suitable 'positivist gesture' to supersede the sign of the cross.

Comte's obsessive concern with the accessories of his new religion is nowhere shown more clearly than in his plan for the calendar. The order and character of the successive festivals are scrupulously detailed. The year is to consist of thirteen months, each of four weeks – the feminine month – of seven days, with one day added every year, plus another each leap year. The months are to be dedicated either to the various social relationships on which 'order and progress' depend – humanity itself, marriage, paternity, filiation, fraternity and domesticity – or to the great epochs in the history of human religious development – fetishism, polytheism, monotheism – or, lastly, to the four social classes or groups – women, the priesthood, the patriciate and the proletariat. The days of the week retain their familiar designations, but each will have special associations – the name of some hero of thought along with that of one of the positive sciences: Homer and mathematics, Aristotle and astronomy, Julius Caesar and physics, St Paul and chemistry, Charlemagne and biology, Dante and sociology, and Descartes and ethics. (Jesus, we may note, does not figure in the list.)[55] A sequence of festivals will be connected with each month in turn; thus womanhood will be celebrated with the festivals of mother, wife, daughter and sister. The extra day in each year is to serve as a commemoration of the dead, that in a leap year, a holy woman. Attendance at these recurrent ceremonies will be obligatory.

So we reach the positivist polity, or system of organization. As already remarked, the middle ages separated the spiritual and the temporal powers: the papacy instructed, secular rulers paid heed to its monitions. This happy arrangement should be restored. Positivism must have its own 'spritualty', propounding wisdom, as well as a 'temporalty' giving its counsels practical embodiment. Experience gained in the past may in this way profit the future.

Education will be the prime responsibility of the spiritual power. To the schools adjoining the temples seven priests will be attached, together with their assistants ('vicaires'), all of whom will be married. To relieve them of any material concern they will receive an adequate stipend, but, like Plato's Guardians, they will have no personal property. To become a cleric in the Religion of Humanity a man must prove himself to be of superior character and abilities. At twenty-eight he would be admitted to the grade or order of 'aspirant'; at thirty-two, to that of 'vicaire'; not until the age of forty-two would he be eligible for that of 'priest'. A supreme pontiff, 'le Grand Prêtre de l'Humanité', will have absolute authority to nominate to office, and suspend or remove from it unsatisfactory ministers. His province is to be all France and his place of residence Paris; but he will have the assistance abroad of seven superiors, one each for Italy, Spain, Germany and England, with three others for overseas missionary work. Priests would on no account be admitted to the seats of government, nor allowed to draw on any source of income other than their official stipends. In any case a large part of their time will be taken up with cultic duties, on which assiduous care must be bestowed to maintain the beauty and dignity of the religion. The high priest, however, will have the special authority and responsibility for advising and warning those who exercise temporal power, in the latter case by appeal, first, to the feelings, though failing this to reason; should that also not succeed then public opinion must be invoked, particular weight being attached to the views initially of the female sex and then of the common people generally. If this too proves of no avail recourse must be had to 'social excommunication', involving the banishment of the offender from the community of his fellow-men. Should he die unrepentant the posthumous honour of 'Incorporation' will be denied him. The high priest of positivism – a role for which Comte cast himself – will thus be the 'Pope of Humanity'.

Strong emphasis is laid by Comte on the integrity of family life as the foundation of society and humanity. Husband and wife stand for the present, their children for the future, the husband's parents for the past. All will live together, the dwelling-place being the property of the family that occupies it, and it must afford sufficient room for the separation of children from parents and of the children themselves according to sex. An oratory also will be required. The family will be the woman's particular charge and concern, although only as subject to her husband – Comte is no feminist – since he is her superior in knowledge and understanding as well as physical strength.[56] She, on the other hand, is his superior in natural altruism and tenderness of disposition, and the children's education will at first be in her hands. Her instinctive sympathy and goodness, moreover, qualify her to advise her spouse in all matters; but it is his duty to sustain her in her proper sphere of hearth and home. Legal divorce is not envisaged and the ideal of matrimony demands lifelong chastity. Indeed a perfect marriage, in Comte's own exalted view, would be a mystical union of souls, with physical union replaced by artificial insemination, although in his day science had not yet opened up this utopian possibility.

Comte's blue-print for the organization of 'secular' society need not detain us – though as between 'secular' and 'sacred' the prophet of the Religion of Humanity would of course allow no substantive difference. Suffice it to say that it is characteristically grandiose, schematic and idealistic, assuming a perfectibility in human nature which history does little to countenance as probable. The philosopher is not unaware, however, that any immediate transformation of society as it is into society as the positivist doctrine would have it to be is in no way feasible. So he indicates certain intermediate policies the implementation of which would take up much of the rest of the century. Two main operations would be necessary: first, Western society would have to be won over to acceptance of the positivist philosophy, religion and polity both as a matter of principle and as a goal actually to be sought; and secondly, a start would have to be made to convert the more backward and tradition-bound peoples of the globe, notably in Asia and Africa, an undertaking obviously of vast complexity and difficulty the measure of which Comte was quite unable to grasp and on which his opinions are naive and simplistic to a degree. In Comte's estimation the trouble with the Western world of his time was its individualistic rationalism and disaffection towards external authority of any kind.

This regrettable disposition, he thinks, could be overcome by the gradual dissemination of the positivist faith. The work would be uphill, but Comte is ready with a time-table for its accomplishment, covering three periods of seven, five and twenty-one years respectively.[57] He himself had great hopes for the régime of Louis Napoléon, which he welcomed as putting an end to democratic aberrations and the imposition of firm political rule and social discipline. The way would thus be prepared for the philosopher himself to assume the role of Humanity's pope and Napoléon's inspired personal counsellor. By means of this collaboration much could be achieved in a short while, including the abolition of the existing system of education, the *budget des cultes* and the reactionary Institut Français, together with – need it be said? – the national legislative assembly, since to make laws is in the competence of sociologists, not the elected representatives of an ignorant populace. The old Revolutionary device, 'Liberty, Equality, Fraternity', will give way to Comte's own shibboleth of 'Order and Progress'.

The immense constitutional changes in society which Comte plans to occur over these decades – suppression of the armed forces and their replacement by a national *gendarmerie*, the radical decentralization of the country, the return of Algeria to the Arabs, and so forth – we again may disregard. Revolutionary violence might indeed have effected them, as it did in Russia in 1917 and after, but this Comte certainly did not envisage or desire. All is to be achieved by the quietly persuasive voice of reason, whose powers, it would seem, are limitless. Optimism about human nature could not, in fact, have been less inhibited than with the author of the *Politique positive*. When the new order at last comes into being humanity, without God and without kings, will live in perpetual peace and harmony. Even so, progress will continue, though the phantoms of theological and metaphysical thinking will have nothing to contribute to it, the way forward into the blissful future having been laid by knowledge, by science. No longer will man ask himself questions that cannot be answered or seek goals impossible to reach. Where reason is the touchstone all obstacles will vanish, for in Comte's sight there is nothing whatsoever in the character of man himself to impede either the advance of his rational understanding or the realization of his natural altruism.

It is easy to ridicule Comte's cosmic visions, which even his followers and admirers were apt to find disconcerting and an embarrassment.[58] The Religion of Humanity – 'Catholicism *minus* Christianity', as it has been dubbed, though presumably Comte himself would not have seen the remark as a gibe – is as far-fetched a piece of speculative Romantic theorizing as can be cited. Even Schelling's flights of metaphysical fancy are not less credible, because less of a challenge to one's feeling for what is or is not feasible in a world where men's passions or inertia are by no means always subject to their reason. That Comte was devoid of a sense of humour goes without saying. My main comment here is to call attention, rather, to the authoritarianism of Comte's doctrine as an amalgam of dogmatic positivism and Catholic institutionalism, an aspect of it which drew John Stuart Mill's regretful criticism, especially as in the Englishman's opinion it had no organic connection with the authentic substance of the positivist philosophy, of which it was no more than a superfluous and repugnant adjunct.[59] Yet it was the authoritarianism of the Catholic system, as well as its institutional formalism, which so strongly appealed to him.[60] In his judgment there could be no loss of liberty in submitting to the truth. The submission demanded by the Catholic church was not in itself objectionable, but only the false theological doctrines – 'croyances chimériques' – on which its claim to obedience rested. Positive religion rightly demands such submission because its truth is proven – 'démontrable et démontré'. It now is the 'normal régime', the 'final régime' and a 'real faith', which will have no decline. Not all indeed can *know* that it is true, but all can and must believe it on the authority of those who have such knowledge. The common people need a religion which gives them a feeling of security, for only so will the cohesion of society be sustained. Thus in Comte's system – and it is more 'positive', he insists, than any science[61] – there is no room for either heresy or doubt. Nothing is to be feared from the subordination of reason to faith, any more than that of the mind to the heart. Man cannot be oppressed by his own humanity.

Unfortunately Comte's later thinking has had the effect of devaluing the *philosophie positive*. His originality, however, must be conceded. Unlike all other thinkers of his age he owed nothing, or nothing directly, to Kant, while to Kant's idealist successors he presents an abrupt contrast; or at least appears to do, for beneath the overt divergences between them – above all his emphatic rejection of metaphysics – similarities are detectable. As I have suggested, Comte is an expression of the ethos of his time scarcely less characteristic than were they. His positive philosophy was not, in his view, simply the sum of the particular sciences but also a way of looking at the world, a *Weltanschauung*. What really separates Comtism from idealism is a radical difference of aim. The post-Kantians wished to preserve, even if they found it necessary to reshape, not only the ethical values but – as in the case especially of Hegel – the basic dogmatic principles of the Christian theological tradition; and it was in this spirit that they opposed Enlightenment rationalism. Comte, on the other hand, had no room for anything approaching a metaphysical doctrine of faith, breaking completely with both Christian theology and the types of spiritual philosophy to which it had been adapted. His own objective was the operation of a purely humanistic culture on the firm foundation of modern science and free of the metaphysical ambiguities and obfuscations by which European thought was in his opinion still encumbered; a humanistic culture, nonetheless, which could simulate the forms and institutions of Europe's immemorial religion, the social value of which he regarded as unquestionable. In this purpose there was nothing inherently to invite ridicule. Absurdity arose only from the unremitting literalism with which Comte strove to articulate it. His belief that the only real knowledge is that provided by science has been widely accepted in the present century, although, for all his conviction of the essential unity of science, he was not dogmatic about its methods. And he had sense enough to realize that of itself science is unable to answer all the problems of human existence and that man cannot dispense with ideological goals. His influence has been far greater than is usually admitted, and the detraction he has suffered at the hands of the historians does not negate the fact that his was one of the seminal intelligences of the nineteenth century. As Emile Faguet observed: 'We meet him at every step in modern thought.'

9

Ernest Renan and the Religion of Science

IT IS NOT UNUSUAL to regard Ernest Renan as the most eminent of Comte's followers, a status, however, assured to him less perhaps for his attainments as a systematic thinker than for his gifts as a writer, since as a *prosateur* he is among the best of his century. But if he is to be counted as a positivist it must be so with qualification. 'I felt quite irritated', he observes in *Souvenirs d'enfance et de jeunesse*, 'at the idea of Auguste Comte being dignified with the title of a great man for having expressed in bad French what all scientific minds had done for the past two hundred years as clearly as he had done.' I am not now concerned to assess the justice of this judgment on Comte himself, but it is surely not open to doubt that in its substance at least Renan's own philosophy is a positivism not far removed from Comte's. Where he diverges from Comte is in the tone of its presentation and in his coloration of scientific rationalism with a large infusion of Romantic idealism, though not without a significant residue of Catholic sentiment inherited from his childhood and youth. 'I was formed', he tells us, 'by the Church, I owe to it what I am, and I shall never forget it.'[1] No wonder he could say 'Je suis double' – 'I was predestined to what I am, a romantic in protest against romanticism ... '[2] It is evident, then, that behind the *penseur* there is the complex, many-faceted personality of the man. He who, whilst still under training for the Catholic priesthood, decided to reject both Catholicism and Christianity, since he found himself unable to admit the Protestant compromise – something always difficult for a Frenchman – could yet envy German Protestant scholarship its ability to reconcile a spirit deeply religious with that of modern criticism.[3] Catholic supernaturalism, he was convinced, could not be adjusted to the scientific outlook of the nineteenth century, but modern man is still in need of a faith, a need, he believed, that would have to be met with an adequate response. Science, he was confident, could give this – were but science rightly understood. It is easy to remark, therefore, that 'no one knew better than Renan how to gild positivism with religiosity and throw around the operations of the scientific intellect a vague aroma of the infinite'.[4] And indeed in his later years he seemed deliberately to cultivate the *persona* of the sceptical dilettante, elegant, learned and trifling. But his sincerity is not to be questioned when he declared that Catholicism sufficed for all his faculties except the critical reason – if of course critical reason were to have the final word.

Renan's was the dilemma, typically nineteenth-century, of the Romantic traditionalist driven to choose faith *or* knowledge. That his thinking was profoundly influenced by German idealist philosophy, and in particular by Herder and Hegel, is hardly open to question. But the influence was powerfully tempered by scientific rationalism. In that sense too Renan could be said to characterize his age, with romanticism and science as the great mutually confronting forces, always in tension and not seldom in open conflict. He himself was a Romantic at least to the extent that he clearly saw the insufficiency of the Enlightenment concept of human reason. For the eighteenth-century thinkers were preoccupied with what is definable because static – with clear and distinct principles and entities. What was in process, and thus more or less inchoate, they disregarded, a restriction of view fatal to any realistic appraisal of life as we know it. 'The infinite, the developing, escaped them. The mystery of origins, the prodigies of instinct, the spirit that moves the crowds, the spontaneous in all its forms, passed them by.'[5] It was this feeling for the infinite, for the spontaneity of the primitive and the collective, for the continuous flux of historical development, that Renan himself drew from the Romantic idealists. The eighteenth century had on the whole little sense of history, which it failed to understand. Nor could it really appreciate the spirit of religion. On the other hand the speculative bent of the romanticists needed to be curbed. The basic themes and sentiments of romanticism were a reflection of and a response to the needs and aspirations of life as it is lived and not merely analysed, but scientific knowledge had to be assigned its place, with its rightful demands and seemingly unlimited fields of applicability. It could not be thrust aside therefore by the impatience of a soaring imagination only too eager to leave the solid earth. Philosophical idealism required the sobering and even chastening contact of the scientific reason, as indeed Hegel himself had very fully realized. Romanticism had by no means abandoned the rational, but what was wanted was a fusion of the diverse and supple romanticist view of reason – the speculative *Vernunft* – with the factual and positive view, covering the aims and methods of the sciences, both natural and human. A religion purged of its antiquated supernaturalism and conjoined with a science guided and stimulated by philosophy could supply modern man with the spiritual nutriment for which he now looked. Such at any rate was Renan's hope and assurance.

Ernest Renan was born at Tréguier in Brittany on 28 February 1823, the youngest child of a not very prosperous seafaring man who disappeared in mysterious circumstances in 1828. His mother maintained herself and her family of three by running a small grocery business. Ernest, whose health was delicate, attended the local *collège ecclésiastique*, with ordination to the priesthood ahead of him. His intellectual abilities were already apparent, and in 1838 Mgr Dupanloup, afterwards well-known as bishop of Orléans, selected him for entry to his *petit séminaire* of Saint-Nicolas-du-Chardonnet in Paris. Like his fellow-Bretons Chateaubriand and Lamennais, he was deeply attached to his native province and its associations and felt himself to be an exile in the French capital; but he applied himself eagerly to his studies – exclusively literary: science was not taught – in a way to leave no doubt in his teachers' minds of his brilliant promise as a scholar. His life – at this time somewhat forlorn, it has to be said – was one of hard work, though also, as far as his religion was concerned, of unfeigned piety, in accordance with his upbringing and his own disposition: to the end of his days he carried about him something of the aura of the sacristy, although a priest he was never to become. His recollections of these early years are set down, with all the literary grace for which he was by then famous, in *Souvenirs d'enfance et de jeunesse*, published in 1883.[6] While at Saint-Nicolas he attended philosophy classes at the Issy annexe of the *grand séminaire* of Saint-Sulpice, although his private reading took in the German idealists, especially Kant, making him increasingly dissatisfied with the drab Cartesianism, along with the no less uninspiring 'common sense' philosophy of Reid and the Scottish school, which were largely the fare offered him in the ordinary curriculum. In 1843 he transferred to Saint-Sulpice itself, where theology, dogmatic and apologetic, dominated the scene. But his critical faculties were now much sharpened. In apologetics, for example, the stock answers given to objections seemed to him weak and tortuous, tending, for a keen intellect, to undermine faith rather than support it. Moreover his interest was turning towards philology, by way of the Semitic languages. Thus he seized the opportunity to follow the Hebrew course at the Collège de France, and he also began Arabic. But the doubts already lodged in his mind were becoming more and more pressing. He sought the advice of his elder sister Henriette, to whom he was devoted, but she – herself by now a free-thinker – so far from helping to allay his misgivings, suggested that he should travel before finally committing himself to an ecclesiastical career. In 1848 he received the tonsure, although not without strong scruples. Yet he still adhered at least formally to Christian belief, fortified by his reading of Pascal, who at the time was his great admiration.

The fact, however, was that theologically his faith was disintegrating. He no longer accepted the doctrine of a life after death, nor that, probably, of the divinity of Christ, or even of a personal deity. He still prayed, seemingly in the vain hope that some 'miracle' might deliver him from the straits in which, as an ordinand, he now found himself. His difficulties, it would appear, were not primarily metaphysical. Indeed he stresses that they were not; much less was it any metaphysical criticism of Catholic dogma that shook him than the problems raised by biblical exegesis. 'My reasons', he states, 'were all of the philological and critical order; they were not metaphysical, political, or moral.'[7] The Bible, as the document of divine revelation, was on examination discovered to be full of 'fables, legends and traces of its quite human composition', and 'a single error proves that the Church is not infallible; a single error proves that a book is not revealed'.[8] Despite, then, the anguish which his decision would cause his ageing mother he resolved to quit the seminary, separate himself from the church and contrive to live as best he could on such modest financial resources as he possessed or might secure to pursue his vocation not of a priest but of a scholar. Yet he had to equip himself with the requisite qualifications, and after two years of concentrated study – and necessarily austere living – he passed his *agrégation de philosophie* with the highest distinction. In the meantime he attended the course given by the famous orientalist Eugène Burnouf at the Collège de France on the languages and ancient culture of India. To maintain himself in food and clothing he took up a teaching post at the *pension* Creuzet, where he first met his lifelong friend Marcellin Berthelot – seven years his junior – destined for eminence as a scientist and as a figure in public life.

The revolution of 1848 made Renan politically conscious. His sympathies were with the masses as against the *bourgeoisie*, of whose interests the despised July monarchy had for long been a prop. But his politics did not deflect him from his true concerns; the previous year had seen the publication of his first book, an *Essai historique et théorique sur les langues sémitiques en général et sur la langue hébraïque en particulier*, which won him the Prix Volnay, and he now began to contribute to periodicals, notably the *Revue philosophique*, which carried an article of his on the origin of language, and *La Liberté de penser*, in which he wrote in its July 1849 issue on current intellectual activity in France. However, the most important literary task at that time was the drafting of *L'Avenir de la science*, although it was not published until some forty years later. At the end of 1849 he was appointed one of the two members of a government commission to inspect public and monastic libraries in Italy and to report on any Syriac manuscripts that he might come across, though also to be on the look-out for any *trouvaille* of interest bearing on French literary history. Shortly afterwards he visited England on a similar errand. It was most probably on the strength of his report on his investigations that he was given a post in the department of oriental manuscripts at the Bibliothèque Nationale.

In 1852 Renan gained his doctorate with a thesis on *Averroès et l'averroïsme*. He was now twenty-nine, and his sister – twelve years his elder – was keeping house for him 'at the bottom of a little garden near the Val-de-Grâce'. In all respects they suited each other, with like tastes and opinions, while a more conscientious secretary he could not have found. Nevertheless, in 1856, he married, his bride being Cornélie Scheffer, niece of the then well-known painter Ary Scheffer. At first difficulties were encountered with Henriette, who felt slighted and was jealous, but they seem to have been resolved and the two women shared his house and company more or less harmoniously. Two daughters were the fruit of the union, although the first-born died in infancy. It was in 1856 too that Renan was elected to membership of the Académie des Inscriptions et Belles-Lettres, and thus could now feel that his status as a writer and scholar was acknowledged. He had published numerous essays and reviews on historical, ethical and literary topics which had won him the praise of the leading critics of the day, among them Augustin Thierry and Sainte-Beuve, who were soon to be followed by Hippolyte Taine. But as a philologist and student of the religions of antiquity it was his growing ambition to produce above all a magisterial 'History of Christian Origins', and as the necessary preparation therefore he made up his mind to tour the Near East. An opportunity for this arrived when in 1860 he was invited to lead an official archaeological mission to the lands of ancient Phoenicia, with his sister for companion and *aide* and every assistance afforded him by the officer in command of the French troops at that time stationed in the Lebanon. Unhappily, in September 1861, both he and Henriette caught malaria. It was a serious attack and when he himself regained consciousness it was to learn that his sister was already dead. He felt it as a grievous blow, but the first draft of the *Vie de Jésus* was in his baggage when he made his way back to France.

His friends in Paris now urged him to apply for the vacant chair of Hebrew at the Collège de France as his suitability for the job was obvious, and in January 1862 he was duly elected. His inaugural lecture, delivered on 21 February before a large audience, dealt broadly with the subject of the history of religions, dwelling especially on the moral elevation of Judaism and suggesting the possibility that the world might actually have been won over to it but for the emergence, from within its own bosom, of Christianity. But it was when he alluded to Jesus as 'an incomparable man' and went on to speak of him as 'so great that, although in this place [i.e. the Collège de France] everything ought to be judged from the point of view of positive science, I should not wish to contradict those who, struck by the exceptional character of his work, call him "God"' that murmurs of dissent arose. His words, although delighting younger members of the audience, gave offence when repeated in influential clerical circles. The upshot was that his lecture-courses were summarily suspended. Renan defended his attitude in an address to fellow-academics, but without rancour, and he refrained entirely from controversy. He continued, however, his instruction in the Hebrew language and literature as part of the professional duties for which he drew his salary. He himself had no doubt of his ability and right as a non-believer to treat the history of Christianity from a strictly historical–critical angle. Indeed he held that only one who had formerly been a believer could possess the 'inside' knowledge necessary for an empathetic understanding.

1863 saw the publication of the *Vie de Jésus*, the success of which in terms of the book's sales has probably not been rivalled by any other work of its kind. Within a few months of its appearance it had run through eleven editions and sold in its tens of thousands, with translations into foreign languages either already in print or in preparation. Before the century was over it is likely that more than half a million copies were in circulation. The charm of its style is to be conceded, but a haze of sentiment hangs over it which was by no means to all tastes even among its first readers, and German scholars were quick to deprecate it as both superficial and over-speculative, the author's own imagination having too often supplied what the historical evidence lacked. That Catholic opinion was affronted by it goes without saying, and Renan was bitterly attacked by hostile pamphleteers and frequently suffered personal insult. Opposition from the French hierarchy, moreover, was so far effective with the imperial government that he was eventually deprived of his chair at the Collège, although by way of compensation – if such it were – he was offered a new appointment at the Bibliothèque Nationale. That he became for a time the idol of the anti-clericals and café atheists afforded him no satisfaction.

Authorship engrossed his time and energy during the ensuing years, in which he produced the successive volumes of the great work on Christian origins that had for so long been his dream and of which the *Vie de Jésus* was now the first instalment.[9] In November 1864 he and his wife embarked on an extended tour of the Near East, his purpose being to feed his imagination on the scenes of early Christianity. They first visited Egypt, then the Lebanon and Syria, paying respect to Henriette's grave near Beirut, and finally traversing Asia Minor in the footsteps of St Paul, to reach Athens on 13 February 1865. From there they went on to Corinth and Philippi, bringing their tour-pilgrimage to an end at Istanbul. The following June saw them back in France.

But Renan's scholarly pursuits and travels did not quench his interest in political affairs and in 1869 he even stood as a candidate for election to the Legislative Assembly in the Seine-et-Marne constituency of Meaux, but without success. Perhaps, like John Stuart Mill in similar circumstances, he was too much of a philosopher for the average elector.

The outbreak of the Franco-Prussian war was the cause of much mental suffering to him, not only as a French patriot but as a consistent admirer of Germany and what he believed to be the essentially liberal and forward-looking spirit of the German people. Events in Paris following the French defeat particularly saddened him, and he felt obliged to turn aside from his historical studies to write *La Réforme intellectuelle et morale de la France*, published in November 1871, in which in messianic mood he expounds the somewhat authoritarian measures that he deemed necessary if his country were to be delivered from its plight, and which conveys the substance of his mature political thinking.[10] Renan's pen was indeed especially active in these years. With the fall of the empire he had been reinstated in his chair at the Collège de France, which meant of course the resumption of his lecturing, while weighty articles by him appeared in the *Journal des Débats* and the *Journal des savants*. A work of particular importance from the point of view of the present chapter was his *Dialogues et fragments philosophiques*, not published until 1876 but containing matter dating back to the early sixties,[11] as in the case of the very revealing letter to his friend Berthelot, written in 1863. Frank in its utterance, with its account of his youth, of his loss of religious faith and of the ideas and beliefs by which this had come to be replaced, it gained him a wider readership than did any product of his historical erudition apart from the *Vie de Jésus*, aided above all by the felicity of his literary style, clear, graceful, nuanced. The Third Republic he had brought himself resignedly to accept, since his own preference would have been an Orleanist restoration as a constitutional monarchy. But his personal standing as a great *savant* and public personage was by now firmly established, a fact testified by his election in 1879 to the Académie Française in succession to Claude Bernard. Five years later he became administrator of the Collège de France, having thus achieved all that a

French scholar could hope for in the way of public recognition. His delightful reminiscences of his early life, *Souvenirs d'enfance et de jeunesse*, came out in 1881. But by now he was entering upon his last period, a period of a more relaxed, sceptical and, as some would say, irresponsible outlook on life, to be summed up in the word *dilettantisme*. His four *Drames philosophiques* of 1878 to 1886 – published together in 1888[12] – were criticized on this score, and not least, it may have been, for a rather curious vein of eroticism that appears in them, although Renan had always tended to harp on the allurements of chastity, with his 'dreams of a *veiled* and amorous flesh'. But the dilettantism showed itself mainly in an increasing proneness to treat moral issues from the standpoint simply of an observer, aesthetically attracted but not personally involved. For example, in one of his *Dialogues philosophiques* he puts into the mouth of a speaker words which, it may be thought, reflect not altogether unfaithfully his own gift of 'negative capability':

> I myself enjoy the universe in much the same way that one feels gloomy in a gloomy town and cheerful in a cheerful one. In this way I enjoy the pleasure of the voluptuary, the debauches of the debauchee, the worldliness of the worldly and the austerity of the ascetic. By a kind of subtle sympathy I enter imaginatively into their minds. I applaud the scholar's discoveries and rejoice in the ambitious man's successes. Were anything missing from the world I should be sorry, for I am conscious of all that it holds. My only regret is that this age has sunk so low that it no longer knows what pleasure is.[13]

But Renan's variegated nature enabled him to continue to hold his basic moral and philosophical convictions, as his *Examen de conscience philosophique*, also dating from 1888, would seem to indicate. In any case the great scholarly achievement of these final years was the five-volume *Histoire du peuple d'Israël* (1887–92), a pendant to his earlier survey of the rise and development of Christianity.[14] Moreover he had by now many disciples, including some – an Anatole France, a Jules Lemaître – who affected to outdistance even their master in pursuit of a cynically tolerant worldliness. His last days were passed, as frequently as possible, in his beloved Brittany, although when the end came, on 2 October 1892, it occurred appropriately enough in Paris. His seventy years were not a great age, but his physical powers were exhausted. Mentally, however, he was still much alive and made it plain – to forestall any possible claim by the church – that he retracted nothing of what he had professed and taught during the near half-century since he abandoned Catholicism at the portals of Saint-Sulpice.

The elderly Renan – intellectual coquette, as he could easily be taken to have been – presents one aspect of the man, but it is far from being the whole. Neither the dilettante nor the ironist can hide the devoted scholar in lifelong quest of the historical truth, who back in his seminary days learned a lesson he never afterwards forgot: 'l'amour de la vérité, le respect de la raison, le sérieux de la vie'.[15] At no time was he satisfied with the merely easy solution, the conventional view, even though to press the inquiry might lead only to uncertainty and doubt. That is why he favoured the dialogue as a literary form; using it, he could look at a question from several different angles and finally turn away from any definite answer.[16] Dogmatism was repugnant to him, and he distrusted the *esprit de système*. That he was an emotional man is evident, and like Montaigne he was 'ondoyant et divers'. Widely informed as he was, he absorbed more than he could readily come to terms with and properly order. He was plainly a Romantic, if categorize him we must, but one whose romanticism was strongly countered by his positivism: he was, as he said of himself, 'a Romantic protesting against romanticism'. The result philosophically was eclecticism, but an eclecticism that tended to drift into self-contradiction. In later life he won such popular esteem that after his death a reaction was inevitable. A man of his public status and acclaim should, it was felt, have committed himself to a more determinate message. The minor key, the pessimistic shading, the irony and moral ambiguity – his 'dandified despair', in William James's phrase – ceased to attract, and for some decades his fame was clouded, although his talents as a writer could never be impugned. Today, I fancy, we are in a better position, while recognizing his weaknesses, to appreciate his strength.

2

It would be idle to seek in Renan any compact scheme of doctrine. What we have is a series of orientations, a variety of perspectives, a sequence of intellectual explorations. He was always subjective, even in his historical work. But he took learning seriously and had the profoundest respect for the critical spirit. Both characteristics have to be set over against his temperamental aestheticism, not to mention his occasionally intrusive sentimentalism. An individualist who ever chose his own way, he nevertheless made it his principle as a historian and student of the achievements of man in society that, as he stated in *L'Avenir de la science*, the individual is nothing, humanity everything. The paradox here offers a clue to the overall direction of his thinking. Renan always preferred the long and comprehensive view, and he realized that the nature of man is the product of his history, to the knowledge of which 'philology' – a favourite term of his – gives the entry. Through history he had himself found intellectual freedom, glimpsing in it, from the outset of his career, the source from which the constitutive elements of his philosophy would have to be drawn. For the content of philosophy, as he saw it, is basically humanity, not nature.[17] In fact 'philosophy' and *philologie*, according to the *Avenir*, are essentially one, its author meaning by this, so evidently we are to assume, that philosophical method is properly experimental and descriptive.[18] And as he himself is concerned with the human mind in its historical development it was appropriate from his standpoint – given also his personal aptitude for linguistic studies – that philology should present itself as the true science of man; not man in some abstract, eighteenth-century sense as a fixed and definable quantity, but in his perpetual 'becoming', his *devenir*, of which history supplies the record. Philology, as Renan uses the word, a usage akin to that more usually found among German scholars, affords insight into the very nature of the human mind, since it is the science of its most characteristic products;[19] the science, that is, whose function it is to study past civilizations from their languages and documents. As such it is one that calls for imagination, sympathy and intuition, beyond mere classification and analysis, in that it has to penetrate the rational to reach the unconscious. The *esprit de géométrie* will be of no help here: 'enthusiasm' and criticism, Renan says, are far from being mutually exclusive; and he considers philology to be especially profitable the farther back into the past it delves, because it is in the primitive stage of a civilization that the human mind is discovered at its most spontaneous and creative. Hence the importance of *myths* in the process of man's mental development, in that the myth is a form of thought which later reflection will by no means dismiss as childish credulity. Myths rather are 'great divine poems wherein primitive peoples have deposited their dreams of the supersensible world'.[20] In this matter Renan could look to German Romantics like Friedrich Creuzer for informed guidance.

We observe here the significance which Renan, at least in the *Avenir de la science*, attaches to history. He does not see it simply as a record of past events reconstituted by means of such disciplines as archaeology, epigraphy and philology. Its deeper purpose is to recover as far as possible the living mind, the actual ways of thinking, of peoples now long distant from us in time and correspondingly alien in outlook. Nor is this itself only an antiquarian exercise; it is an attempt to understand the human consciousness as such, to comprehend the very nature of man's self-awareness and self-identification. To that extent the future itself may be anticipated. But this of course is to envisage a *philosophy* of history, or at least to suggest the feasibility of some general law of interpretation such as Comte believed he had established. No doubt it would be 'subjective', in being framed from our own point of view in time; but this is inevitable, total objectivity being unattainable by minds that are themselves part of history's ceaseless movement. The simple fact that 'definitive' history is never actually written proves it; the past has constantly to be reassessed, not only because of the possible discovery of new facts but because our angle of vision itself shifts with the years. Were this not the case, were we able to suppose that we ourselves could somehow stand 'outside' the historical in order to appraise it objectively, history would simply fail to yield up its secret. Engagement is necessary for understanding. For when rightly understood history is itself philosophy. On this Renan is quite explicit: 'The history of the human mind', he says, 'is the true philosophy for our time. Each of us is what he is only because of his situation in history.'[21] He goes even further and claims to be able to build a new ethic on man's developing 'consciousness'. Obviously his assumption is that in such development the 'good' is realized. He can even convince himself that true religion is 'intellectual culture'.[22]

The idea underlying Renan's interpretation of history is therefore one of a continuous progress discernible over the ages. Each generation contributes its quota to it, though without as a rule perceiving what actually it has accomplished, much as a weaver at work on a big tapestry is scarcely aware of the complex design he is helping to create. In the *Avenir* Renan ventures to offer his own 'law of the three stages': those, namely, of 'syncretism', which characterizes early times, of 'analysis', or the critical awareness which follows later and which conspicuously distinguishes the modern outlook, destructive as this is of religion and 'poetry', and finally of 'synthesis', a state yet to be reached when the rational and affective aspects of life are once again reconciled in an enlightened harmony. This consummation Renan thinks it not inappropriate to deify, so that God becomes the realization by man of his moral and spiritual ideals. All of which invites comparison with the doctrines of Auguste Comte, whose *Système de politique positive* appeared not long after Renan had drafted his *Avenir de la science*. The younger man's interest in race – a subject on which he dwells at some length – was, it is true, of little concern to Comte, who also sees morality in a less personal light than Renan, his own ethical views, as we noted in the previous chapter, depending on his conception of sociology as a science standing in close relation to biology. And Comte quite certainly does not share Renan's sympathy with the life and practice of religion in its existing forms. But there is in the ex-seminarian's philosophical musings an element of positivism more firmly based than its author probably realized.

Of positivism as a system, however, Renan was distinctly critical. It clearly was not congenial to him temperamentally. Comte's mind was utterly prosaic, his prose itself being stiff and laborious, whereas Renan, awake to every nuance of sentiment, was a master of rhetoric. Comte, again, seemed to move only in a world of rigid categories and classificatory schemes such as the other, with all a Romantic's sense of the infinite variety of things, instinctively sheered away from. Renan's love of the vague, the ambivalent, the elusive – admittedly his major weakness as a philosopher – was repelled by the wooden symmetry of Comtist thinking. And of course he had no sympathy with positivist materialism. To him it lacked all spiritual sensitivity, besides being devoid of that romanticist feeling for the infinite which he himself, unbeliever though he was in the 'credal' sense, never forswore. On the contrary, while Comte detested Christianity – as distinct from Catholicism, or at least those aspects of it of which he approved – Renan's nostalgic affection for the religion of his youth was genuine and lasting. His naturally 'clerical' disposition and manner were frequently remarked upon by those who met him personally.[23]

But Renan's attitude to the past generally, and not only the Christian, was emotional. He deeply respected it and believed that really great achievements were possible only to those who themselves felt this respect and looked back to the past for their inspiration. He himself viewed it, with truly Romantic enthusiasm, as a vast epic of humanity which through the imagination of the poet-historian could again be brought to life. Indeed it was because of this continuous possibility of resuscitation that it revealed itself as progressive. So far from being dead, it was living and ongoing, the experience thus accumulated by humanity producing a 'consciousness' ever fuller, more varied and more perceptive, in which the *divine* becomes increasingly manifest. Such at any rate was the vision of the *Avenir*. With the passing of the years and first-hand encounter with history in its current phase Renan's progressivist faith underwent modification, although it was never lost. His one-time political hopes were not realized, compromises having always to be made. European power-politics – as the Franco-Prussian war so brutally demonstrated – were far from idealistic. Even that new and intellectually revolutionary expression of modern scientific insight, the Darwinian theory, could hardly be said, on a more reflective assessment of it, to encourage the notion that evolution and progress are identical. Nonetheless, whether or not the course of history is also an advance to a brighter future, it is to history and to history alone that man can go if he is to contemplate his true visage. That truth Renan never doubted. Moreover, one lesson history quite certainly teaches is the relativism of the time-process. Every succeeding period is what it is, and is to be appreciated accordingly. It is a mark of the critical historian's tact that he should be able to see the past in the right perspective, as only so can the life and culture of former times be understood, relived and enjoyed afresh. But impartiality implies tolerance. Differences are to be treated with sympathy and not merely condemned, since the yardstick of one age is not necessarily applicable to another. And if the rationale of human existence, as the philosopher discerns it, is to be sought in the overall advance of human consciousness then error, intellectual and moral, also has its place in the educative process. As Renan grew older this sympathetic tolerance of all experience became so settled an attitude as to look like moral indifferentism.

In the *Avenir* the developing nineteenth-century conflict between religion and science is already present as a personal issue for the author himself. The scientific view of life had to be accepted – Renan had relinquished his Catholic allegiance because of his conviction that science and Catholic supernaturalism were incompatible – but he was scarcely less convinced that acceptance of science does not imply the abandonment of religion, provided the word 'religion' be taken in a very broad sense and with a firm apprehension of its poetic connotation. For both science and religion he held to be necessary to our humanity. With the former unquestionably modern man cannot dispense: science he has to recognize to be autonomous, uncircumscribed by anything else. But so comprehensive also is it that it is potentially a religion in itself. Henceforth science alone will create symbols; as science alone can resolve for man the eternal problems whose solution his nature imperiously demands.[24] For it is science which will instruct mankind in the true meaning of life and point forward to its real destiny. Renan's book is in fact a prophetic view of the future of science as fulfilling a religious role, teaching not only the truth about the universe but inculcating that spirit of cosmic awe and *pietas* which ought to accompany such knowledge. 'The true way of worshipping God is to know and to love that which is.'[25] It was a vision and an enthusiasm which was never afterwards really dimmed or weakened. Knowledge, he was always to believe, would 'resolve the enigma of life', explain man to himself and provide him with 'the symbolism which religions used to offer ready made and which he can now no longer accept'.[26] In short, Renan embodied all the nineteenth century's hope for science and confidence in its ultimate capacity for good, even when not only philosophers but scientists themselves were beginning to have their doubts.

But it is science with considerable overtones of religious feeling. Positivism was too abstract, too constricted in outlook, too much wanting in *la poésie* for Renan's willing endorsement. He looked on

Comte himself as 'un esprit borné', a perhaps not altogether fair judgment in view of the control which sentiment came to exercise over his later thinking. But Comte, for all his emotionalism, especially where the opposite sex was involved, was no poet, and aesthetic sensibility is little in evidence in positivist doctrine. His Religion of Humanity may display all the outward appurtenances of Catholicism, but it has nothing of its inner spirit. Such could not be said of Renan, who was peculiarly sensitive to visual beauty and with whom an undercurrent of feeling is present even in his purely scholarly work. He was never the dry intellectualist. For him thought was compounded of reason, imagination and emotion; rational demands, in all matters of factual knowledge, were paramount, but could not be divorced from the affective side of life. Aesthetic values especially were as real as any others and their place in man's total apprehension of the truth of the world about him had to be acknowledged. The analytical stage in human thought would properly stress the determining role of the critical intellect, but the previous century had so exaggerated its function as seriously to misrepresent the nature of reason itself and the extent to which it is linked with the emotions – a fatal mistake which romanticism had to repair. For feeling is no mere adjunct of thought, it is of its substance, a truth which in the coming age of 'synthesis' would be fully recognized. And of that synthesis Renan saw his own work, in both history and philosophy, to be the herald. The 'complete' man would be one who is simultaneously poet, philosopher and scholar, as well as a man of virtue; and that not intermittently but continuously, through an intimate penetration of each by the other – the poet in being a philosopher, the philosopher in being a scholar.[27]

But an additional respect in which Renan's attitude to religion differs radically from Comte's, as indeed from that of some Catholic apologists, is that he sees it not as a prop for the social order, or still less a mere sop to the feelings of the common man, but as something inherent in human nature. It is to be cultivated and valued for its own sake, not exploited for purposes which have nothing to do with it. So long as humanity survives, Renan believes, religion will also, as expressing a basic psychological need.[28] No doubt when it aims to be 'objective' and scientific, when it attempts metaphysical demonstrations of the ontic truth of its object, it can only mislead. Both 'natural' theology, professing to lay the intellectual foundations of faith, and 'revealed', which pretends to formal knowledge of the facts of the supernatural order, are unacceptable because they misrepresent what religion essentially is. But this is not to say that intuition and spiritual sensibility, the 'heart', are not means to truth. Consider knowledge as bare 'reasoning' and it is at once deprived of its real significance. The teachings of deism were only a debilitated, sapless theology, without poetry or emotional resonance, while declared atheism is brash and superficial.[29] Mankind needs some sort of religious ideal if life is to have true moral worth and dignity. Thus Renan's conception of religion – albeit a 'religion of science' – is very much more inward than Comte's. For what Comte had in mind was no more than contrived forms of organization and ritual which he imagined would serve the new positivist society in much the same way as Catholic institutions had functioned in the past, whereas Renan is trying to combine his rational belief in the standpoint and methods of modern science with the ethos of a faith he continues to respect.[30]

This emerges plainly enough in the attitudes the two thinkers adopt towards religious liberty. Comte insists on uniformity: dissent would be banned. Renan, because he sees religion in a strongly personal light, holds freedom to be a right which the state must not infringe.[31] This too is why he, unlike both Comte and Lamennais, is sympathetic to Protestantism, which preserved the spirit of religion while less committed than Catholicism to authority and dogma. Hence his regret that, given the historic religious traditions of France, Protestantism in that country afforded no real option for a Catholic who had relinquished the faith of his upbringing. He could only be a *libre-penseur*. Incidentally, of the 'liberal' Catholicism of his day he entertained a poor opinion, dismissing it as an 'insipid compromise'.[32] But Renan was convinced that life could not be lived in its wholeness unless the needs both of reason and of the heart were satisfied, and each by the other: knowledge and aspiration should go hand in hand. His hopes and expectations for the future were therefore in the creation of a 'scientific philosophy', which would be neither profitless speculation, without any real object, nor an arid and exclusive scientism, but one which, in achieving completeness, would be both 'religious and poetical', since poetry is itself the soul of religion.[33] Any 'scientific' religion that is only a thinly disguised logical system is scarcely to be thought of as religious at all. 'God is the product of the conscience, not of science and metaphysics.'[34]

The great difficulty with Renan is of course his habit of shifting the meaning of his key-terms, the same word being used to denote one thing in one context but something rather different in another. *Philologie*, defined as 'the science of humanity', is a prime example, but so too is *science* itself, which can carry as wide a connotation as simply 'the exercise of the mind in an ordered (*régulier*) way',[35] while as the 'sainte poésie des choses' it can even refer to the 'truth' and 'sincerity' of life.[36] But *philosophie* is equally malleable, as too is *existence*. The persuasiveness of Renan's argument often depends on this semantic sleight-of-hand. At times his use of language reminds one of Newman's, whose own reasoning likewise draws on carefully evoked sentiment when its logic begins to falter; and both writers knew well enough the rhetorical effect of irony.[37] The result is that instead of presenting a clearly stated position with which a critical reader can actively engage we tend to have only insinuations and suggestions, a standpoint adopted for the nonce and then quietly abandoned when discussion takes a new turn. In this respect Renan's elusiveness recalls Montaigne's 'diversity'.

In the strict sense of the word Renan is not a philosopher, any more than Newman was. For like Newman he had no real mental aptitude for metaphysics or at any rate for the particular kind of rigorous thinking that philosophy properly demands. Newman distrusted metaphysical arguments, and his Gallic counterpart, in this at least a Kantian, wrote them off altogether. Renan indeed is ready enough, when he chooses, to equate philosophy with science, but not if by the former is meant *a priori* speculation about the ultraphenomenal, although the distinction between philosophy and metaphysics is not always clearly made by him. Science, he holds, must follow *a posteriori* methods, whereas metaphysics as 'une science première' never gets beyond abstractions. Yet he also believes that science must eventually become philosophy, by so broadening its scope as to include within it a great deal more than the term is designed to convey in positivist usage.[38] For 'what indeed is left', he asks, 'if you deprive science of its philosophical goal?'.[39]

However, as Renan insisted, his own intellectual problems as a seminarist were not of a metaphysical kind but rather 'philological'. He could not avoid pondering the implications of German biblical criticism regarding such matters as the unity, authorship and historicity not only of books of the Old Testament like Genesis, Isaiah and Daniel, but of the gospels themselves. And to the intelligent and thoughtful youth brought up in the straightest Catholic piety the result was profoundly unsettling.

> My initiation into German studies [he afterwards wrote] put me in a completely false situation; for, on the one hand, it showed me the impossibility of an exegesis which made no concessions; and on the other, I saw perfectly well that these gentlemen at Saint-Sulpice were right not to make concessions, since a single admission of error ruins the edifice of absolute truth and brings it down to the level of mere human authorities, where each makes his own choice according to his personal taste. In a divine book, indeed, everything is true, no contradiction must be found there.[40]

Yet the Bible, the very source of divine revelation, with an authority not to be questioned at any point, was discovered to contain too many evidences of its essentially human composition. Renan saw no means of compromise, given his own position. An infallible authority must never be seen to be in error.[41] For if the basis of the church's dogma is detected to be thus insecure what can be said for the security of the superstructure itself? Metaphysical speculations were something that could be argued about, perhaps indefinitely, but philological objections were matters of fact capable of being critically investigated and finally determined.

Renan's views on metaphysics are well set out in a short essay addressed to Adolphe Guéroult, a philosopher of some standing in his day, entitled 'La Métaphysique et son avenir', first published in the *Revue des deux mondes*, 15 January 1860.[42] The great speculative systems, culminating in that of Hegel, are, he maintains, things of the past. The sciences, both the natural and the historical, have now replaced all such schemes, and there is no sort of 'preliminary' science which can be accepted as containing in itself all the rest, and which affords a basic knowledge not only of the universe and of man, but even of God. The human spirit will always be prone to speculate on what it cannot actually know; such curiosity is as natural to man as his imaginative and emotional creativity. But for any serious attempt to understand the nature of reality it is to the positive sciences that one must go. 'The glory of philosophy', Renan concludes, 'is not to resolve problems but to pose them.'[43] And he ends his essay in characteristically ironic vein with a prayer of blessing to the 'Heavenly Father' for having in the end remained hidden and a mystery. 'For thus our minds and hearts are free.' Three years later, in the letter to his friend Marcellin Berthelot also published in the *Revue des deux mondes*, he restates his position.[44] 'I formerly denied the existence of metaphysics as a distinct and progressive system; I do not deny it as a body of unchanging concepts in the way that logic is. These sciences teach us nothing, but they serve well to analyse what we do know. In each case they are wholly outside the realm of fact.'[45] Obviously, then, speculation about the infinite, the absolute, freewill and so on has no status alongside knowledge empirically grounded.

It can hardly be denied that Renan's statements are tantalizingly ambiguous and confusing. Sometimes he approximates philosophy and metaphysics, at others he distinguishes them radically. At one moment he can describe the former as 'the general result of all the sciences',[46] a phrase which has a definitely Comtean ring, while at another he declares that 'to philosophize is to know the universe'[47] and that philosophy's role is to be 'the science of the whole',[48] which seems to bring us close to the traditional view of metaphysics. I suspect that it is impossible to fix Renan's meaning precisely. The nearest we can get to doing so is perhaps to say that although for him the only real knowledge is factual, 'how things actually are', for which of course we have to go to the empirical sciences, he nevertheless wants such knowledge, when *conceived as a whole* – assuming, that is, the possibility of so conceiving it – to be regarded not merely as the sum of its parts but as a 'world-view', a *Weltanschauung*, to the final shaping of which subjective factors, moral and aesthetic, make a vital contribution. But what the logical status of such a 'higher' knowledge would be we are not told.[49]

3

But may it not be that 'philosophy' for Renan is no more than another name for what he calls 'the religion of science'? Man's religious consciousness he sees to be real and permanent. 'That which is inherent in humanity, and which in consequence will be as eternal as humanity, is the religious need, the religious faculty.'[50] An affirmation like this evidently takes him far beyond science as positivism understands it. The question is whether Renan conceives religion to be anything other than moral idealism, an aspiration of the heart, or whether the word 'God' can be used with some recognizably transsubjective content. The answer, however, is a long way from clear. Renan is not afraid to speak of God, but he does so after a fashion which leaves no doubt of the influence upon him of the immanentist and subjectivist tendencies so characteristic of Romantic philosophizing. His theology – if the term be appropriate – is a singular amalgam of positivism, idealist metaphysics and Christian sentiment that falls short, in the end, of anything amounting to a coherent doctrine. What exactly its components are we must now attempt to identify.

Renan has a notion of deity, but his God is not 'outside' the universe, in an eternal transcendence; on the contrary, it is wholly within it, not indeed as its state at any given point of its development, but in the development itself, 'in the category of *fieri*, of slow evolution'.

> Like a mighty heart overflowing with a vague and impotent yearning, the universe is continually in the pangs of change ... There can be felt an immense universal striving towards the realization of a plan, the filling of a living mould, the creation of a harmonious unity or a consciousness. The consciousness of the whole has remained until now extremely vague and does not seem much more clearly defined than that of the oyster or the polyp, but it exists.[51]

Strictly speaking, nothing ever *is*, in the sense of subsisting without change. All things change and evolve, although not without aim or direction. 'Notre planète travaille à quelque oeuvre profonde', he tells us. But the aim and direction are intrinsic. Plainly the shade of Hegel is present here: God is the objective of the universal evolutionary process, which attains an ever-enlarging self-awareness in what Renan calls 'consciousness' (*la conscience*), something not very different, it would appear, from Hegel's *Geist*. Through the clouds, he says, of a still embryonic universe we perceive the laws of the progress of life, the consciousness of Being as ceaselessly growing, and the possibility of a condition in which all things will have reached a definitive state, in the way that the countless buds of a tree are in the tree, or the myriads of cells of a living organism are in the living organism – a state wherein the life of all things will be complete. The realization of that end will be deity, God.

That the universe exists is not a matter of doubt; we see it in process, in its endless *becoming*. That God as the ideal exists cannot, however, be stated, Renan thinks, with an equal certainty, although we should not hesitate to affirm it. Or as Theophraste, one of the speakers in the dialogue entitled *Certitudes*, puts it in answer to Euthyphron's question, 'You think, then, like Hegel, that God is not, but that he will be?': 'Not precisely. The ideal exists; it is eternal, but it is not yet materially realized; it will be one day.' Renan seems to be saying that God as the ideal has yet to be, but his being is already latent in the process of the universe and is inwardly directing that process: 'The idea appears ... as the principle of deifying evolution, as the creator *par excellence*, the end and the first mover of the universe.'[52] God therefore is to be thought of as both the goal and in some sense the cause of things, inasmuch as the end is in the beginning. In his letter to Berthelot Renan is a little more explicit: 'One must admit within the universe what one discerns in the plant or animal, an inner force which causes the seed to follow a pattern already traced out.'[53] But surely language of this sort is beguiling him into the forbidden realm of metaphysics? If such a thought does occur to him Renan is evidently undeterred. He continues:

> The idea [i.e. God] is of a potentiality which seeks being; matter gives it concretion, makes it actual, real. The two poles of the universe are thus the ideal and matter. Nothing is without matter, but matter is the condition of being, not the cause. Cause, efficiency, belongs entirely to the idea. *Mens agitat molem.* It is the idea which really is, which alone is and aspires unceasingly to full existence in giving rise to the material combinations suitable for its production... We thus reach the position where we attribute perfect existence to the idea alone, or rather to the idea conscious of itself, to the soul.[54]

In short, 'God will be and God is. As reality he will be, as ideal he is.'[55]

The universal process, then, is to be conceived as a cosmic 'enfantement du divin', a deification of the world itself. God is the immanent cause of what, in the consummation of things, will manifest him as the ideal fulfilment towards which reality has all along been moving. But this, as I say, carries us well away from positivism – back indeed to those metaphysical notions of a self-evolving Absolute which in the positivist stage of thought are completely abandoned. Renan's philosophy is, in fact, only another instance of the evolutionary immanentism which the nineteenth century found so attractive, especially when adorned with progressivist ideas; *immanentism*, that is, as distinct from pantheism, at least in so far as Renan, like others of his contemporaries wedded to some form or other of Hegelianism, seems also to claim that God's being is not simply equivalent to the totality of the universe. He even seems ready to affirm that God exists as, in some manner, the *prius* of the universal process, the conceptual 'absolute' in which the actual substance and course of things are ideally, immutably and eternally anticipated or prereflected. So again it is the shade of Hegel that appears; moreover of Hegel as interpreted by his disciples of the 'Right', who for the most part believed their master to be upholding the essential doctrines of Christianity. Must we not ask, then, whether Renan's own vestigial Christianity had not been getting the better of him as the years went by? In the *Avenir de la science* he was propounding an altogether different view, more or less in conformity with orthodox positivism. According to this, 'God' is really no more than a projection of man's moral idealism, a symbol of his spiritual aspiration, and to that extent Renan's use of the word is a perfectly intelligible part of the humanist vocabulary. But in his later thinking God is not just a symbol, he is the causal principle of the universe and so for human consciousness objective, something the reality of which man's moral idealism can only presuppose.[56] In this case, however, the reader is left to conclude either that since 1848 Renan had changed his mind – as he was fully entitled to do – having returned to Christian theism by way of idealist immanentism, or else his imagination and sentiment have betrayed him into the simultaneous entertainment of intellectual positions that are essentially incompatible. For what he says in his letter to Guéroult, for example,[57] that nature is only an appearance and man a mere phenomenon, with an eternal and infinite 'absolute' beyond them – 'according to the Jewish expression ... *He who is*' – is neither naturalism nor positivism nor agnosticism but a throw-back to Romantic metaphysics or even Christian Platonism.

Yet Renan's 'religion of the spirit'[58] is not simply a metaphysical dream, it also implies an ethic. And in fact it is by the ethic that the religion is proved. The whole evolutionary process has culminated in man, in whom it attains consciousness, especially in the more advanced stages of his civilization. Renan is prepared to allow to the lower organisms a measure of consciousness, but it is in the human species alone that it has achieved self-reflection. Not indeed that the plenitude of consciousness is shared by all its members; among the masses of mankind it still is only of comparatively low degree. But in the most thoughtful and cultivated representatives at least of Western civilization Renan finds a clear pointer to that future consummation of humanity's innate spiritual powers by which God will stand revealed. Renan's view is unquestionably intellectualist; it is in the development of the things of the mind, in an ever-growing cultural awareness – the 'progress of reason', as he calls it – that mankind's advance depends. But his intellectualism must be given a broad meaning, to include moral and aesthetic sensibility as well as science and scholarship.[59] What he offers is thus a humanism, in the sense that supreme value is to be attached to those features of man's existence in which his humanity is most amply demonstrated.[60] But it is an elitist not an egalitarian humanism. The spearhead of evolutionary progress is the relatively small band of the intellectually and morally proficient. This *aristocratisme* was in truth characteristic of Renan's attitude all his life. Personally fastidious and exacting in his tastes and judgments, he genuinely felt that the aristocrats of intellect – not mere technocrats but men of both knowledge and wide spiritual discernment – possess in regard to man's future what can best be described, in the language of the biblical tradition, as a messianic vocation. It is for them, that is, to guide the unthinking majority into paths that will lead the race forward, and to show whither the world ideally tends. For if a man learns anything from life it is that he must take it seriously and realize that he has a responsibility in the shaping of it. As Renan declared in *Souvenirs d'enfance et de jeunesse*, life is vain unless it is lived from a sense of duty, even if on other occasions – as, for example, in his play *L'Eau de jouvence* – he so far came to modify this austere doctrine as to believe that the way of virtue was for the spiritual aristocrat alone, leaving the diversions of pleasure for the many.[61]

Man's sense of a spiritual destiny, Renan maintains, is not an illusion. 'La nature n'a mis dans l'humanité rien de trompeur.' We are called to assist in the process of 'deification', confident that its achievement is a possibility. 'For us to obey nature is to collaborate in the divine work.'[62] Renan is thus a romantic optimist: process means progress, difficult, intermittent and fluctuating no doubt, but eventually certain. We have to follow nature; to refuse to do so is a sin.[63] Yet Renan can at the same time look on nature in an altogether different light. The operation of general law, he reminds us, is entirely insensitive to human desire or need; and he can even speak of nature's 'transcendent immorality'.[64] Not only is it indifferent, it is maleficent.

So again we are offered a paradox, being at one moment told that nature is working towards a moral end, the promotion of good, and that our vocation is to cooperate with it, and yet at another that the 'natural' man, like the animals, is moved only by self-concern, and indeed that he has 'an actual interest in not being virtuous'.[65] It has, I think, to be said frankly that there is no way of reconciling these opposing views. But it is evident that Renan, being the man he is, is once more speaking with two voices, both of which are authentically his own. The one is that of the positivist, for whom nature is not responsive to human values and purposes, and man unable to escape his inborn selfishness. The other is that of the moral idealist who recognizes that humanity must be guided by an ethic if the higher spiritual consciousness is to be reached. The question therefore is whether Renan believes that man creates the values by which he is to live, in spite of the indifference and even the hostility of nature – an existentialist, Sartrean interpretation perhaps – or whether he holds these values to be implicit in the process of nature itself, such that man's clear duty is to give them explicit status in his personal life. To this query our author's reply is characteristically ambiguous:

> The universe, in man's eyes, appears as a deceitful tyrant who subjects us to his designs by Machiavellian tricks and contrives that few detect these deceits, since if all were to see them the world would be impossible. It is evidently to the interest of nature that the individual be virtuous. From the viewpoint of personal interest this is a deception, inasmuch as the individual will derive no profit from his virtue. She has provided for this by the categorical imperative – the greatest, the true, the unique revelation. The surest virtue is that which is grounded in speculative scepticism ... We are knowingly duped by nature with a view to a transcendent end which the universe intends and which surpasses us completely.[66]

This rather cryptic utterance is less the philosophy of a positivist than the faith of a believer, even if a faith which sits very uncomfortably with reason. For how can virtue be obedience to nature if man, as himself part of nature, is unable to do otherwise than submit to it? When Renan actually states that 'morality reduces itself to submission' is he not destroying the very thing in which, as he elsewhere claims, man's worth and dignity essentially lie? And why should he strive to cooperate with that which he cannot resist? Yet if the 'religion of the future' is to become a reality the contradiction – Renan seems to imply – must be suffered. Life, we must recognize, has to be lived in polarity.

But if Renan looks to the future for the creation of a new religion capable of preserving those human values which mere *scientisme* overlooks, does he also think that the historical religions have anything of importance to contribute to it? As a critical scholar he cannot but dismiss them on purely intellectual grounds, made up as they are, he would point out, either of myths and legends that are often puerile and unedifying or else of abstruse metaphysical speculations without practical significance. Indeed that the positive content of these faiths renders their acceptance impossible for the instructed modern mind was a conclusion he arrived at in early manhood and never afterwards retracted. But eighteenth-century 'rational' religion does not satisfy him either. He sees it as having nothing whatever to offer since it had no spontaneous origin in feeling but arose only from a desire to prove the truth of abstract propositions. The failure of natural religion need not therefore be regretted, especially as its supposed proofs have all been shown to be fallacious. Men are not elevated spiritually and morally by mere argumentation, even when logically firm. However, Renan believes, as we have seen, that the religious impulse is natural to our humanity and as such calls for expression in worship which is 'in spirit and in truth' and in the cultivation of the 'absolute' values of truth, goodness and beauty. Let a man but hearken to his conscience and sensibility, heeding what they tell him. At any rate to suppose that religion will have no part in the perfect humanity of the future is an absurdity. For this reason man can learn much from the historic religious consciousness, if he approaches it from the critical standpoint of *la philologie*. For the positive religions are a reliable index to the feelings and needs of ordinary men for whom a mediator between 'God', the ultimate reality, and themselves is a necessity. The form of this association may in the past have been crudely conceived, but its essential purpose is not to be doubted. Even the least admirable of existing cults has, in the final analysis, something in it of that sense of the infinite which a sound faith will enable us, if not to comprehend rationally, at least to affirm emotionally.

The religion to which Renan naturally turns for inspiration is Christianity. Its doctrines will require reinterpretation, but their spiritual substance is perdurable. Its idea of eternal life, for example, is basically right. Catholic teaching on immortality is, as it stands, quite inadmissible, but dedication to promoting the good and the true is to impart to one's life an 'eternal' quality that gives final meaning to all human existence. 'It is in the memory of God', says Renan, 'that men are immortal.'[67] The remark is of course ambiguous, but it can at any rate be construed as a belief in the conservation of man's highest values. Final blessedness will be genuinely attained when all men share in the light of the human spirit itself and the beauty and perfection of which it is capable, thus coming to know the happiness which these will bring.[68] It is even possible to think of life as having a transcendent dimension, an aspect of mystery the reality of which may never be grasped philosophically – 'For now we see as through a glass darkly' – but which man will ever feel the urge within him to seek.[69] Yet this is as it should be if faith is to have moral worth, far above a rational calculation of probabilities.[70] Renan also has a theory of evil. It may be ignorance and the failure to cultivate the things of the mind – such at least is the viewpoint of *L'Avenir de la science* – or, as he later came to think, it may be wilful disobedience to 'nature' and its ends; for here too there is a conscience to be followed. In the overcoming of evil lies the way of spiritual advance, or 'sanctification' in the traditional language of Catholicism. Worship also has its place, in that to know and love that which is is 'to adore God',[71] just as the love of God consists in the knowledge of the absolute virtue of truth, goodness and beauty. Such love and adoration are the expression of a natural humility and piety.[72] Moreover, all who participate in this experience constitute a fraternity imbued with the same fundamental purposes and moving towards the same goal – an 'invisible church' of enlightened humanity.[73] Nor is it inappropriate, Renan evidently thinks, even to speak of a 'resurrection of all consciousnesses', since 'all souls live in God that ever have lived'.[74] The hierarchy of the new religion will be the men of spiritual and intellectual insight and ability: scientists, philosophers, artists, scholars. These indeed are the apostles of progress and their achievements will be preserved in institutions responsible for maintaining the cultural heritage.

It is thus that Renan conceived how the supreme need perhaps of his age, the reconciliation of religion and science, might be met. For he is never tired of insisting that science and religion both are necessary to the life of modern man. Science must provide the criteria of knowledge, but religion, together with the arts, offers a great part of the substance of what human sensibility and moral aspiration have to feed on. A 'true theology', he thinks, will be 'the science of the world and of human-ity'.[75] It is a belief resting on both sympathy and scepticism. Sympathy there must be; what man has built for himself throughout the long history of his civilization is to be treated with respect and understand-ing – iconoclasm was totally foreign to Renan's nature. Tolerance therefore is vital. Religion has become irrevocably an affair of personal aptitude and men have the inalienable right to believe or not, as they may choose. The mind has to be persuaded, it cannot be coerced. But scepticism is a condition of knowledge, or at any rate of perceptive understanding, and scepticism was certainly native to Renan's own disposition. A merely negative attitude, Voltairean mockery, or the mood of indifference or indolence, he of course deplores; it is a form of barbarism and its effect can only be destructive. A fruitful scepticism, however, is of a different kind, 'le grand scepticisme', as he terms it.

This is philosophic and methodical, requiring that the sources of our knowledge be always subject to rigorous examination. But such scepticism is also awake to the distortions of human prejudice, of which irony is the corrective. But irony was something which for Renan himself was an all too handy tool. In his famous 'Prière sur l'Acropôle' he actually invokes the goddess Athène to deliver him from a 'perverse philosophy' for which the opposites of good and evil, of beauty and ugliness, of wisdom and folly merge imperceptibly into one another like 'the colours on the neck of a dove'.[76] 'Wisdom then consists in neither loving nor hating anything absolutely.' He was conscious of this propensity in himself as a weakness, a lurking distrust even of the truth which he recognizes. But one has, he insists, to believe in the truth, though one knows that the truth one possesses is not absolute. In this sense a man's dogmatism must always be critical, tempered with doubt.

But although Renan made his prayer to Athène in all good faith, the query which confronts the reader of his last works is whether he ever did free himself from the 'perverse philosophy' of scepticism for scepticism's sake. For the ironical element seems over the years to have become more corrosive, the inquisitive spirit more flippant, less and less responsible even in the service of truth. Increasingly he appears to smile at his own philosophy which, like other such constructions, is best viewed, he suggests, with a sense of humour.[77] Not that he wishes to question the verities of science; to that extent his positivism is unshaken. But the important thing now seems to be self-realization through pleasure.[78] Of course one continues in quest of truth, but assuredly not to the point of self-martyrdom. Life is to be enjoyed. Why give yourself a headache for the sake merely of exchanging one error for another? 'At twenty years of age' – he is addressing the young – 'amuse yourself; only work as well.' Renan himself was now elderly, supremely articulate as ever, and celebrated as one of the outstanding *esprits* of the age. In a word, he had 'arrived', and he knew it. The comforts of a successful career were not to be despised at the bidding of the austere ethic he had imposed on himself in his youth. This mellow hedonism was also better suited to his growing agnosticism about matters lying beyond the finite and immediate. All, he muses, who once considered themselves to be right are now seen to have been mistaken; would it not be foolish presumption on our part to suppose that the future will not judge us as we ourselves judge the past? 'The Gods pass away as do men, and it would not be good that they should be eternal. The faith that one has had ought never to become a chain. One has finished with it when one has wrapped it in the purple shroud in which the dead Gods sleep.' The religion of science may well prove to be no less mortal. Why should not a man just comfort himself with dreams, however illusory?

Whenever one thinks that one has seized Renan one finds that the old charmer can still shake off one's grasp. Nevertheless is it not possible finally to summarize his position? On the ultimate things he is, I say, agnostic, and quite frankly so. There are matters that one does not and cannot know; absolute beginnings and absolute ends are conceptually beyond our ken. One can entertain speculations and conjure up views, but certainty is impossible. With the historical we can fare better, admittedly. It is through history that man learns to understand himself, discovers, if painfully, who actually he is. But history has its limitations; the necessary data may be lacking and we have to make do with a perhaps very imperfect picture, since even at its best history is but 'a poor, conjectural little science', incapable of showing us the past as it really was in all its detail, or of telling us what truly was in the minds of men of generations long dead. For what we can firmly know of the past, in comparison with what we evidently do not know, brings home to us the immensity of our ignorance. Renan cannot forgo reminding us of all this, and clearly takes some ironical pleasure in doing so.

But before I close this chapter it is necessary to say something further of Renan's achievements in the fields in which he would rightly have claimed to be a professional and which he designates collectively as *la philologie*, 'the science of the products of the human mind'. The great bulk of his published work is the outcome of his historical interest and expertise, and it is by this that he should mainly be judged. For as a philosopher he was no more than an amateur, and his place in the history of technical philosophical thought is but incidental, that of a footnote. As a historian and biblical exegete, however, he has every justification for being considered seriously and compared closely with other workers, chiefly of course German, in the same area. And of this the *Origines du christianisme* imposes the principal demand on our attention.[79] The work was planned in six volumes, but Renan found he required a seventh to complete it.[80] At the time of its publication it proved highly controversial, appearing as it did in a land steeped in the traditions of Catholicism and where Catholic opinion still carried political weight. Following the *Vie de Jésus*, *Les Apôtres* treats of the early community at Jerusalem, the founding of the church at Antioch and the first Christian missions. The volume on *Saint Paul* outlines the apostle's career as presented in Acts and provides an analysis of the epistles. *L'Antéchrist* carries on the narrative from Paul's arrival in Rome to the end of the Jewish revolt which culminated in the fall of Jerusalem. The author thinks it appropriate to include here a review of the remaining books of the New Testament – apart, that is, from the gospels themselves – since he assigns the composition of Revelation to the period of Nero. The literary history of the synoptic gospels is recounted in *Les Evangiles*, but Jewish Christianity is also assessed, along with certain writings of the post-apostolic group known as the Apostolic Fathers, notably the First Epistle of Clement and the Ignatian letters. *L'Eglise chrétienne*, covering the years 117–60, comprises others of the same group as well as the Johannine writings, gnosticism, Justin Martyr and the formation of the New Testament canon. The volume on Marcus Aurelius, besides providing an obviously sympathetic study of the philosopher-emperor himself, introduces the reader to the Montanist movement, Irenaeus and the church in Gaul, and the work of the later Greek apologists. The whole constitutes a scholarly undertaking of magisterial scope, placing the New Testament writings in the general context of the contemporary history and without muddying the historical waters, as Protestant scholars invariably did, by drawing a theologically motivated distinction between the canonical and the extra-canonical writings. Renan also strikes a fair balance between the narrative of events in so far as this can be constructed on the available evidence, and the internal development of early Christianity. He is right, too, as scholars nowadays would agree, in seeing Christianity as the product of Judaism, with Jesus himself, unequivocally a Jew, as its true founder – an opinion running counter to the idea encouraged by so much nineteenth-century German biblical scholarship, which preferred to ascribe that distinction, in its own eyes altogether dubious, to St Paul. As Renan observes, the historical Jesus would have made no mark in Greece had his mission been carried on there.[81] It is also the fact that men have been won to Christianity by the 'legend' of Jesus much more readily than by the theology of his great apostle.[82] Indeed Renan thought Paul far less representative of the real spirit of Jesus than was St Francis or the author of the *De imitatione Christi*.

The *Marc-Aurèle* makes explicit certain assumptions underlying Renan's account of the early church. He believes Christianity to be, of all religions, the most enlightened ethically, but judged that its existing forms, Protestant as well as Catholic, had become ossified. The only hope for the future lay in an alliance of liberal Protestantism, a forward-looking Judaism and idealist philosophy. The personal example of Jesus would ever remain its inspiration, but his gospel of the Kingdom, the moral idealism of the Sermon on the Mount, the witness of the Christian martyrs, the 'difficult and dangerous art of spiritual direction', the need of a spiritual society in support of family and fatherland – these and much more the Catholic church, he thinks, has still to offer the world. 'It will become unnecessary only at the price of reducing life to a despairing aridity.' The important thing is that the ecclesiastical society should not weaken the civil, that it should have no power in the temporal sphere, and that the state, in turn, should not concern itself with the affairs of the church, whether to control it or to patronize it.[83]

The *Origines* remains an impressive demonstration of its author's learning and the general soundness of his historical insight, even though scientific New Testament study since his time would revise many of his particular conclusions in matters of dating, historicity and so forth. In the French-speaking world of his day the state of biblical scholarship was abysmally low, and his own work, disturbing though its impact on Catholic opinion was, beyond all doubt met a need; while from the standpoint of pure historical criticism it had the effect of modifying the extreme views associated with Baur and the Tübingen school by ascribing roles of equal importance to both Petrine and Pauline Christianity, thus discountenancing the idea that any fundamental rift had existed between them.

Renan reviews the history of the origins and early development of Christianity strictly from the angle of the scientific historian, with no supernaturalist assumptions and no concern whatever to make his work serve a doctrinal or apologetic interest. His purpose is simply to explain the rise of the Christian religion in terms of the cultural, social and political conditions prevailing in the Graeco-Roman world during the first two centuries. He implies throughout, however, that the growth of Christianity is a classic illustration of his thesis that cultural evolution begins at the purely instinctive or 'syncretistic' level, where the human mind is at its most spontaneous and creative, and proceeds by a continuous enlargement of self-awareness, becoming ever more fully cognizant of ends and means which at the outset were taken for granted. It is a process, that is, of increasing rational reflection or 'analysis'. Christianity's first stage, as an expression of Jewish religious consciousness, was, as the gospels reveal, instinctive, immediate. Jesus himself was typical of it; his teaching is the direct utterance of his feeling. He simply states his message, he does not argue it. In no sense is he a theologian or philosopher. The task of intellectual articulation was assumed later, by St Paul first and most originally, then by the author of the first gospel, and eventually by gentile thinkers inevitably subject, through their education, to the influence of Greek philosophical categories. And along with theological formulation went an institutionalizing movement. What the growth of Christianity, as the historian sees it, thus discloses is a perfectly intelligible process of natural development that requires no doctrine of providence, no allegation of miracles, to account for it. Philology, the method of critical historiography, is sufficient to bring the entire sequence of events, and the diverse forces – Judaic, Hellenic, Latin – which operated upon them, into a coherent pattern of scientific knowledge. But it is only as and when this objective assessment becomes possible, when theological notions of providential ordering, special revelation and extra-natural evidences are seen for what they are and relegated to the realm of mythical thinking generally, that the sophisticated intelligence, having now reached the synthetic stage of thought, is able to distil from the traditional beliefs what is of permanent value in them, so contributing to that advance of the human consciousness which in the Renanian philosophy is history's goal.

Renan prided himself on being a historian *tout court* and not merely a 'church historian' in the usual sense – something which he despised.[84] His overall achievement, in and for its time, was impressive. He brought to his work a humanist sympathy, sagacity and tact, along with a degree of literary talent, which the equivalent German scholarship in his chosen field rarely if ever displayed.[85]

To the modern New Testament scholar the defects of the *Origines du christianisme* are obvious. It is not simply that the movement of New Testament study during the present century now leaves Renan with an old-fashioned look; the subjective element in his work is altogether too much in view. He indulges speculation to excess – for example, as to the mind of a Nero or a Marcus Aurelius – coupled with a persistent tendency to read not only himself but his contemporary circumstances into the persons and events he is describing. His own temperament colours all he writes, not only in the notorious *Vie de Jésus* but in the succeeding volumes as well, whilst the prevailing aestheticism, including even the grace and suppleness of the prose itself, has an enervating effect on both subject-matter and reader alike. All the more remarkable is it therefore that Renan should have referred to himself as 'the least literary of men': the *Origines* is too literary. Its author dilates too much on the 'beauty' and 'charm' of primitive Christianity – 'la belle morale de Paul ravissait les bons Lycaoniens', he tells us – even its 'mollesse féminine'. A more serious fault, however, is his apparent lack of interest in its doctrinal content; in particular his treatment of Christology is so summary as to be useless; and although he does recount the teachings of Paul and others they clearly do not engage his attention at any depth and his discussion is never more than perfunctory. It is only the moral idealism of the early church that wins his praise, thus conveying the impression that the burden of the Christian community's preaching was the gospel ethic rather than its faith in the risen and exalted Christ.

In Renan the tension between reason and romanticism attains its height. Sentiment and imagination drew him in one direction, science and scholarship in another. Both sides of his nature called out for satisfaction, but any really constructive compromise between them proved difficult, if not impossible. Hence the ambiguities and recurrent inconsistencies of his position. He extols morality, but a morality devoid of any profound sense of obligation and thus of normative strength. He is optimistic about human nature, but mainly because he shrinks from contemplating its darker side. The world he prefers to look out upon is the relatively narrow one of the aesthetic sensibility and cultivated erudition of the *savant*. Of such, he all but says, is the kingdom of heaven (always, of course, on earth). Man's divinity is to be realized in all that a person of his own disposition, hopes and ideals may, not without reason, expect to be achieved with time. He was tolerant, imaginative, learned, at a certain level wise, but egocentric in all he attempted and desired. More contemplative than truly introspective – why Amiel should have written his journal he could not understand – he never, one suspects, established authentic self-identity. He admitted, rather, that he saw himself as 'a tissue of contradictions'. Although even then he has to add: 'I do not complain, since this moral constitution has brought me the liveliest intellectual enjoyment that one can experience.' We may admire his frankness and be ready always to concede the insinuating appeal of his personal and literary style. But if he fails to convince it is because, in the end, he himself lacked convictions.

Notes

1   Romanticism, idealism and religious belief

1   A. O. Lovejoy, *Essays in the History of Ideas* (Baltimore, 1948), p. 232.

2   As, for example, by René Wellek in 'The Concept of Romanticism in Literary History' (*Concepts of Criticism*, New Haven, Conn., and London, 1963, pp. 128–221). Cf. Jacques Barzun, *Romanticism and the Modern Ego* (London, 1943).

3   Though Lovejoy himself goes so far as to assert that the contrast between the eighteenth-century view of the cosmos as 'an infinite static diversity' and the romantic emphasis upon its 'dynamic diversity' is the most significant and distinctive single feature of the Romantic revolution. See *The Great Chain of Being* (Cambridge, Mass., 1936), chap. 10.

4   Cf. H. J. C. Grierson, *The Background of English Literature* (London, 1925), p. 235.

5   As Wellek rightly says: 'Goethe, while under the impression of his trip to Italy, for a time expounded a classical creed, especially in his writings on the plastic arts, and he wrote some works which must be considered in any history of neo-classicism ... Still, however successfully their classical spirit could be defended, Goethe's greatest works are the subjective lyrics, *Faust*, the very influential *Meister*, and, of course, *Werther* ... All the artistic power of Goethe is in these, where there is scarcely any trace of classicism' ('Concept of Romanticism', p. 162).

6   See Friedrich Meinecke, 'Die Idee der Staatsräson', *Werke*, I (Stuttgart, 1959).

7   Cf. Meinecke, 'Die Entstehung des Historismus', *Werke*, III (Stuttgart, 1963).

8   *Lectures on Modern History* (London, 1906), 1960 ed., p. 38. Cf. Acton's correspondence with Mandell Creighton in 1887 (*Essays on Freedom and Power*, ed. G. Himmelfarb, London, 1956, pp. 328–45).

9   For a statement of the case against a romanticist interpretation of the Oxford Movement see H. N. Fairchild, 'Romanticism and the Religious Revival in England', *Journal of the History of Ideas*, II (1941), pp. 330–8. The writer justly stresses the elements of authority and self-abnegating discipline in Tractarian thought.

10   First published in English under this title in 1933, the original Italian – *La carne, la morte e il diavolo nella letteratura romantica* (Milan and Rome, 1930) – gives clearer indication of its contents.

11   'All theory, dear Friend, is grey; life's golden tree is green.'

12   See L. Brunschvicg, *Spinoza et ses contemporains* (3rd ed., Paris, 1923), p. 333.

13   T. F. O'Meara, *Romantic Idealism and Roman Catholicism: Schelling and the Theologians* (Notre Dame, Ind., 1982).

2   **Schleiermacher on the religious consciousness**

1   For a detailed account of Schleiermacher's early life see W. Dilthey, *Das Leben Schleiermachers*, part I (Berlin, 1870; 3rd ed. by M. Redeker, 1970. Part II was edited by Redeker in two volumes and published in 1966). While at Landsberg Schleiermacher had translated the sermons of Hugh Blair of Edinburgh and of the English preacher Hugh Fawcett.

2   Its full title is: *Ueber die Religion: Reden an die Gebildeten unter ihren Verächten*. A second edition, considerably revised, appeared in 1806. Two more editions, in 1821 (again revised) and 1831 respectively, came out in Schleiermacher's lifetime. Rudolf Otto's critical edition was published at Göttingen in 1926. The first English translation was that of J. Oman, *On Religion: Speeches to its Cultured Despisers* (London, 1893; repr. with an introduction by Otto, New York, 1958). Throughout the present chapter I quote from this version, referred to as *OR*.

3   *OR* (ed. 1958), p. xi.

4   Cf. *OR*. p. xii: 'The taste of the time and the stylistic influence of the Schlegelian ambience are illustrated clearly in the rhythmical and measured cadences, which occasionally degenerate into affectation, in the use of archaic turns of phrase, mythological images and references, and the elevated pathos and classical stiltedness of tone that marks the whole.'

5   A second edition appeared in 1831. An English translation edited by H. R. Mackintosh and J. S. Stewart was published at Edinburgh in 1928 under the title *The Christian Faith* (referred to below as *CF*). The full German title is: *Der christliche Glaube nach dem Grundsätzen der evangelischen Kirche im Zusammenhange dargestellt* (referred to in the text as *Glaubenslehre*). There is a modern critical edition by Redeker in two volumes (Berlin, 1960).

6   *Protestant Theology in the Nineteenth Century* (English translation by B. Cozens and J. Bowden, London, 1972), p. 427.

7   *Grundlegung zur Metaphysik der Sitten*, part II, *Werke* (ed. G. Hartenstein, Leipzig, 1867–9), V, p. 34.

8   *OR*, p. 17.

9   *OR*, p. 18.

10   *OR*, p. 20.

11   *Die Mystik und das Wort* (Tübingen, 1924), p. 34.

12   *OR*, p. 16.

13   *OR*, p. 36.

14   *OR*, p. 41.

15   *OR*, p. 43.

16   *OR*, p. 44.

17   *OR*, p. 46.

18   *OR*, p. 39.

19   *OR*, p. 37.

20   *OR*, p. 36.

21   *OR*, p. 44.

22   *Reden* (ed. Otto), p. 49.

23   *CF*, p. 6.

24 Cf. *OR*, p. 59: 'Uninterruptedly, like a sacred music, religious feelings should accompany the active life.'

25 *Dial.*, p. 429. The *Dialektik* comprises Schleiermacher's notes on epistemology and logic covering the period 1811–31. He had begun to prepare them for publication only a short while before his death in 1834. They are printed in the *Sämmtliche Werke* (Berlin, 1834), part III, vol. 4 (ii). The passages in this work dealing with the common basis of thinking and willing in feeling, although difficult, merit careful study.

26 *CF*, p. 13.

27 *CF*, p. 15.

28 *CF*, p. 16.

29 *CF*, pp. 16f.

30 *CF*, p. 18.

31 *OR*, p. 16.

32 *CF*, pp. 22f. Schleiermacher uses the term 'sensible consciousness' in *Der christliche Glaube* (section 5:1), where he distinguishes three levels of consciousness; the 'animal-like' (*tierartig*), the 'sensible' (*sinnlich*) and the 'religious', i.e. the feeling of absolute or utter dependence. At the first and lowest level there is no realized distinction between the self and its environment; it is, says Schleiermacher, a dream-like state, to be compared perhaps with the consciousness of a very young infant. At the second level, however, the antithesis of self and not-self is already occurring. It covers 'on the one hand, the gradual accumulation of the perceptions which constitute the whole field of experience in the widest sense of the word, and, on the other hand, all determinations of self-consciousness which develop from our relations to nature and to man', thus including the social and moral feelings no less than the self-regarding. While obviously at this level the mere 'animal' consciousness has been transcended and left behind, the third level, with its feeling of absolute dependence, does not annul the second, which, on the contrary, persists in it as a necessary condition. For the feeling of absolute dependence is awakened only when the sensible self-consciousness embraces as it were the totality of being and is brought to the question of the *whence* of this totality. See *Der christliche Glaube* (ed. Redeker), I, pp. 30ff (*CF*, pp. 18ff).

33 Rudolf Otto is similarly at fault in claiming for Schleiermacher that the reality of God is something intellectually inferred from the experience and not an inherent part of it. Thus he writes: 'According to Schleiermacher I can only come upon the very fact of God as the result of an inference, that is, by reasoning to a cause beyond myself to account for my "feeling of dependence"' (*The Idea of the Holy*, English trans. by J. W. Harvey (6th ed., London, 1931), p. 10).

34 *CF*, p. 26.

35 *OR*, p. 39.

36 This is why a factitious 'natural theology' cannot provide the basis of a religious community. Cf. *CF*, p. 48.

37 *OR*, p. 50.

38 Cf. *OR*, p. 217: 'You will then find that the positive religions are just the definite forms in which religion must exhibit itself.'

39   Cf. *OR*, p. 234: 'If a definite religion may not begin with an original fact, it cannot begin at all.'
40   Cf. *OR*, pp. 222f.
41   *OR*, p. 238.
42   Cf. R. B. Brandt, *The Philosophy of Schleiermacher: the Development of his Theory of Scientific and Religious Knowledge* (New York, 1941), pp. 175–84. Brandt advances the opinion that in the 1806 edition of the *Reden* Schleiermacher intended to discontinue using *Anschauung*, but made the change systematically only in the second and third speeches, thereafter – perhaps because he was in a hurry – substituting 'feeling' or 'idea' or 'view' indiscriminately. The difficulty however is in determining whether or to what extent the exclusive use of 'feeling' is meant to cover 'intuition' as well, and to regard religious feeling as having a cognitive aspect.
43   *OR*, p. 101.
44   *Dial.*, p. 77. Cf. p. 319.
45   Cf. *CF*, pp. 131ff.
46   *Dial.*, p. 322.
47   *Dial.*, p. 162.
48   *Dial.*, p. 433.
49   *Dial.*, p. 162.
50   *Dial.*, p. 167.
51   *Dial.*, p. 168.
52   *Dial.*, p. 119.
53   *CF*, p. 207.
54   *CF*, p. 174.
55   *CF*, p. 194.
56   *CF*, pp. 125ff.
57   *Dial.*, p. 256.
58   *CF*, p. 170.
59   Namely that 'the absolutely timeless causality of God, which conditions not only all that is temporal, but time itself as well' (*CF*, p. 203) and that 'the absolutely spaceless causality of God, which conditions not only all that is spatial, but space itself as well' (*CF*, p. 206).
60   *CF*, p. 211.
61   *CF*, pp. 213ff.
62   *CF*, p. 222.
63   *CF*, p. 171.
64   *CF*, p. 725.
65   *OR*, p. 88. Cf. *CF*, pp. 178ff.
66   *CF*, p. 52.
67   *CF*, pp. 31f.
68   *CF*, pp. 34f.
69   *CF*, pp. 39ff.
70   On Schleiermacher's classification of religions see *OR*, pp. 218ff and *Kurze Darstellung des theologischen Studiums* (1811) in the English trans. by T. N. Tice, *Brief Outline of the Study of Theology* (Richmond, Virginia, 1970), pp. 29f.
71   *OR*, pp. 239, 241.

72   *CF*, p. 140.
73   *CF*, pp. 76ff.
74   *CF*, p. 303.
75   *CF*, p. 535.
76   *CF*, p. 377.
77   *Protestant Theology in the Nineteenth Century*, p. 425.
78   *Ibid.*, p. 454.
79   On Schleiermacher's debt to Spinoza see T. Camerer, *Spinoza und Schleiermacher* (Stuttgart and Berlin, 1903).

3   **Hegel and Christianity**

1   H. S. Harris, *Hegel's Development: Towards the Sunlight 1770–1801* (Oxford, 1972), p. 88.
2   Cf. Harris, *Hegel's Development*, pp. xx, 59.
3   H. Nohl, *Hegels theologische Jugendschrift* (Tübingen, 1907), p. 3. The greater part of this book appeared in an English translation by T. M. Knox with an introduction by R. Kroner (Chicago, 1946) as *G. W. F. Hegel: Early Theological Writings* (repr. Pennsylvania, 1971).
4   Harris, *Hegel's Development*, p. 482.
5   Hegel gave no title to the manuscript, which was printed for the first time by Nohl, *Hegels theologische Jugendschrift*, pp. 75–136. It is, though, less a 'Life' of Jesus than a kind of harmony of the gospels in Hegel's own very paraphrastic translation. It proved to be the forerunner of many other such 'Lives' that appeared in the course of the following century.
6   See Nohl, *Hegels theologische Jugendschrift*, pp. 3–76.
7   Cf. W. Kaufmann, *From Shakespeare to Existentialism* (Boston, 1959), p. 131.
8   Hegel's own title is unknown, as the first page of the manuscript is missing. The essay is reproduced in Nohl, pp. 152–211, and in translation in *Hegel's Early Theological Writings*, pp. 67–143. It is quite probable that Hegel conceived the work before beginning the 'Life of Jesus'. Cf. Harris, *Hegel's Development*, pp. 207f.
9   Knox, *Hegel*, p. 134.
10   *Ibid.*, p. 68.
11   *Ibid.*, p. 78.
12   *Ibid.*, p. 21. In an earlier fragment (Nohl, pp. 48ff; cf. Harris, pp. 508ff: 'Unter objektiven Religion') Hegel had written: 'To make objective religion subjective must be the great concern of the State, the institutions of which must be consistent with the freedom of the individual dispositions so as not to do violence to conscience and to freedom, but to work indirectly on the determining grounds of the will – how much can the State do? How much must be left to each individual man?'
13   For a translation see Knox, *Hegel*, pp. 182–301. The first piece dates from the early part of 1797, when Hegel had moved to Frankfurt, the rest being put together after revision, and with additions, by the author himself in 1799, or perhaps early in 1800.
14   Knox, *Hegel*, p. 187.
15   *Ibid.*, p. 244.

16 By Richard Kroner (Knox, *Hegel*, p. 11).

17 *Ibid.*, p. 289.

18 *Vorlesungen über die Philosophie der Religion.* But difficulties arise because there is no definitive form of the text. Hegel delivered four successive courses on the philosophy of religion at the university of Berlin, viz. in 1821, 1824, 1827 and 1831, the last being just before his sudden and untimely death in the November of that year. To them should be appended the 1829 course on the proofs of God's existence. None of these, however, was published by the author himself. In 1832 a two-volume edition of the *Vorlesungen* was brought out by his disciple Philipp Marheineke, using Hegel's own corrected lecture-notes where available, those of two of his students (one of whom had attended the 1824 course, the other that of 1827), and a notebook belonging to Hegel's son Karl. He also had access to certain of the philosopher's other papers. In 1840 a new edition appeared, considerably enlarged and altered, which, although bearing Marheineke's name on the title-page, was in fact the work of Bruno Bauer, who had been able to draw on further material. It is this 1840 text which was reproduced for Hermann Glockner's *Jubiläumsausgabe* (Stuttgart, 1927; repr. 1959), and which was used for the English version of E. B. Speirs and J. B. Sanderson (London, 1895; repr. 1962). A critical edition involving a considerable rearrangement of the text and the incorporation of more new material was prepared by Georg Lasson in four volumes, first published at Leipzig 1925–9, while a revision of this by J. Hoffmeister began publication at Hamburg in 1955. Hoffmeister's death prevented its completion.

19 *Philosophy of Religion* (trans. Speirs and Sanderson), I, p. 79. For the convenience of the reader I shall as a rule quote from this version (hereafter referred to as *PR*). Where desirable, however, I shall cite the Lasson (or Lasson–Hoffmeister) text in an English rendering of my own, referring to the original as *Phil. d. Rel.*

20 *Enzyklopädie der philosophischen Wissenschaften in Grundrisse* (1817), 564: 'God is God only in so far as he knows himself, his self-consciousness in man; it is the knowledge man has of God which advances to man's self-knowledge in God' (W. Wallace, *Hegel's Philosophy of Mind*, Oxford, 1894, p. 176).

21 *PR*, I, pp. 217f.

22 *PR*, I, p. 33.

23 From *aufheben*, signifying to abrogate, annul or cancel. As Hegel uses it the verb combines this common meaning with the less common one of both 'setting aside' and 'preserving'. Thus in the dialectic a lower stage is cancelled and yet maintained – 'sublated' – as an element in a higher synthesis.

24 *Vorlesungen über die Philosophie der Weltgeschichte.* The English translation by J. Sibree, *Hegel's Philosophy of History*, was first published in 1858 (repr. New York, 1956). There is a modern critical edition of the *Vorlesungen* by Hoffmeister (Hamburg, repr. 1968–70).

25 Cf. *Enzyklopädie*, 163f: 'Universality, particularity, and individuality are taken in the abstract, the same as identity, difference, and ground.

But the universal is the self-identical, with the express qualification that it simultaneously contains the particular and the universal' (Wallace, *Hegel's Philosophy*, p. 294).

26   *PR*, I, p. 25.

27   *PR*, III, p. 3.

28   Cf. *de Trinitate*, IX.

29   Cf. *Die kirchliche Dogmatik*, I (i): *Die Lehre vom Wort Gottes* (Zurich, 1947), II, section 8.1 ('Die Stellung der Trinitätslehre in der Dogmatik').

30   Cf. *Phil. d. Rel.*, III (i), p. 38, where the words are certainly Hegel's own, taken from a rough MS of his: 'That which is implicit must for that very reason be brought forth ... will thus be brought forth through the Idea itself; and nothing which is not implicit will be brought forth.'

31   *Phil. Hist.* (trans. Sibree), pp. 333f.

32   *PR*, III, p. 48.

33   *PR*, III, pp. 52f.

34   Hegel discusses the doctrine in a number of places in his writings, e.g. *Enzyklopädie, Zusatz* to section 24; *Phil. Hist.*, pp. 321f.; *The History of Philosophy*, trans. E. S. Haldane and F. H. Simpson (London, 1892–5), III, pp. 8–10. Hegel's ideas are adumbrated also in *The Phenomenology of Mind*, trans. J. Baillie (2nd ed., London, 1931), pp. 770–2.

35   *Phil. Hist.*, p. 334.

36   *Ibid.*

37   Cf. *Phil. d. Rel.*, III (i), p. 131.

38   *Phil. Hist.*, pp. 336f.

39   *Hist. Phil.*, III, p. 4.

40   *Phil. d. Rel.*, III (i), p. 132.

41   *Phil. Hist.*, p. 326.

42   Cf. *Phil. d. Rel.*, III (i), p. 185.

43   *Phil. Hist.*, p. 325.

44   Cf. *Phil. d. Rel.*, III (i), p. 156.

45   Cf. *Hist. Phil.*, III, pp. 15–21, where Hegel castigates the ancient Gnostics and others who interpreted the gospel history in a way to deprive it of its historical value.

46   Cf. *Phil. d. Rel.*, III (i), pp. 156f.

47   *PR*, III, p. 89.

48   *Ibid.*

49   *PR*, III, p. 91.

50   Cf. *Phil. d. Rel.*, III (i), pp. 157f. Hegel quotes the words 'Gott selbst ist tot' from the Passion-tide hymn 'O Traurigkeit, O Herzeleid'.

51   Cf. *Phil. d. Rel.*, III (i), pp. 155–74.

52   *PR*, III, p. 90.

53   *Phenomenology of Mind*, p. 794.

54   *PR*, III, p. 91.

55   *PR*, III, p. 99.

56   *Ibid.*

57   *Phil. Hist.*, p. 337.

58   *Phil. Hist.*, p. 340.

59   *PR*, III, p. 121.

60   *Phil. d. Rel.*, III (i), pp. 172.

61   *PR*, III, p. 124.
62   *PR*, III, p. 10.
63   *PR*, III, p. 125.
64   *PR*, III, p. 128.
65   *PR*, III, p. 129.
66   *PR*, III, pp. 127f.
67   *PR*, III, p. 133.
68   *PR*, III, p. 134.
69   Cf. *PR*, III, p. 132: 'What we have here is the consciously felt presence of God, unity with God, the *unio mystica*, the feeling of God in the heart.'
70   *Phil. Hist.*, p. 345.
71   *Phil. Hist.*, p. 433.
72   *Phil. Hist.*, p. 460.
73   Cf. *PR*, I, p. 127: 'I am, as feeling, something entirely special or particular. I am thoroughly immersed in determinateness, and am in the strict sense of the word subjective only, without objectivity and without universality.'
74   Cf. Wallace, *Hegel's Philosophy*, pp. 36f.
75   Hegel uses the word *Begriff*, 'concept' – Latin: *concipere* – to describe the 'gripping together' (*begreifen*) into a unity of the different components of a concrete idea. The frequent English rendering of *Begriff* as 'notion' is not very satisfactory and should be avoided.
76   *Phil. d. Rel.*, I, pp. 28f. Cf. *PR*, I, pp. 19f.
77   *PR*, III, p. 151.
78   *PR*, III, pp. 146f.
79   O. Pfleiderer, *The Development of Theology in Germany since Kant* (London, 1890), p. 131.
80   Cf. K. Löwith, *From Hegel to Nietzsche*, trans. by D. E. Green (London, 1965), p. 333.

4   **The idea of God in the philosophy of Schelling**

1   Thus in his *Biographia Literaria*, chap. 9, Coleridge states: 'In Schelling's "Natur-Philosophie", and the "System des transcendentalen Idealismus", I first found a general coincidence with much that I toiled out for myself, and a powerful assistance in what I had yet to do.' But he wishes to tell his future readers that: 'It would be a mere act of justice to myself, were I to warn [them], that an identity of thought, or even similarity of phrase, will not be at all times a certain proof that the passage has been borrowed from Schelling, or that the conceptions were originally learnt from him.' He avers indeed that 'all the main and fundamental ideas [i.e. of his own doctrine] were born and matured in my mind before I had ever seen a single page of the German Philosopher'. (Ed. by J. Engell and W. Jackson Bate (2 vols., Princeton, 1983), pp. 160ff. Cf. pp. lxxviii, cxx–cxxii.

2   The original edition of Schelling's *Sämtliche Werke* was that of his son, K. F. A. Schelling, in fourteen volumes (Stuttgart and Augsburg, 1856–61). This was reprinted unchanged by M. Schröter in twelve volumes (Munich, 1927–54). But work still remains to be done on Schelling's manuscripts despite the loss of some material during the bombing of Munich in 1944. The Schelling-Kommission is however preparing a new critical edition

which will include unpublished writings. Schelling's correspondence was edited by G. L. Plitt, *Aus Schellings Leben: in Briefen* (3 vols., Leipzig, 1869–70), but a new collection of the letters, with detailed commentaries, is being prepared by F. Fuhrmans, the first volume of which appeared in 1962. W. Schultz has edited separately Schelling's correspondence with Fichte (*Fichte–Schelling: Briefwechsel*, Stuttgart, 1968).

3   Among twentieth-century studies of Schelling those especially to be mentioned are: W. Schulz, *Die Vollendung des deutschen Idealismus in der Spätphilosophie Schellings* (Stuttgart, 1955), Karl Jaspers, *Schelling: Grösse und Verhängnis* (Munich, 1955), X. Tilliette, *Schelling: une philosophie en devenir* (2 vols., Paris, 1970), and J.-F. Marquet, *Liberté et existence: étude sur la formation de la pensée de Schelling* (Paris, 1973). For comprehensive bibliographical information see H. J. Sandkühler, *Friedrich Wilhelm Joseph Schelling* (Stuttgart, 1970).

4   Modern critical edition by R. E. Schulz (Hamburg, 1957; repr. 1962).

5   The edition by C. Herrmann (with introduction) (Leipzig, 1928) was repr. at Hamburg in 1954.

6   Plitt, *Aus Schellings Leben*, I, p. 77. J. Hoffmeister (ed.), *Briefe von und an Hegel* (Hamburg, 1969), I, p. 22.

7   Plitt, *Aus Schellings Leben*, I, pp. 39f.

8   *SW*, I, p. 88. This and all subsequent references are to the original edition.

9   *SW*, I, p. 92.

10   *SW*, I, pp. 100, 180, 200, 324.

11   Plitt, *Aus Schellings Leben*, I, p. 75; Hoffmeister, *Briefe*, I, p. 21.

12   *SW*, I, pp. 228f.

13   *SW*, I, p. 165.

14   *SW*, I, p. 202.

15   *SW*, I, p. 287.

16   *SW*, I, p. 337.

17   *SW*, I, pp. 284f.

18   *SW*, I, p. 316.

19   *SW*, I, p. 192. Cf. Plitt, *Aus Schellings Leben*, I, p. 76; Hoffmeister, *Brief*, I, p. 22.

20   *SW*, I, p. 240.

21   These two complementary aspects of the absolute Ego furnish the main subjects of discussion in *Vom Ich als Prinzip der Philosophie* and *Philosophische Briefe über Dogmatismus und Kritizismus* respectively.

22   *SW*, I, p. 318.

23   *SW*, I, p. 208.

24   *SW*, I, p. 319.

25   *SW*, I, pp. 325f.

26   *SW*, I, pp. 195, 208.

27   *SW*, I, p. 209.

28   *SW*, I, pp. 149f.

29   *SW*, I, pp. 184, 177, 163.

30   *SW*, I, pp. 162, 178.

31   *SW*, I, p. 193.

32   *SW*, I, p. 313.

33   *SW*, I, p. 315.

34 Schelling had obviously read Spinoza on his own account, but his interpretation would appear to have been influenced by Jacobi's *Ueber die Lehre des Spinozas in Briefen an den Herrn Moses Mendelssohn* (1798).
35 *SW*, I, pp. 240f.
36 Plitt, *Aus Schellings Leben*, I, p. 77; Hoffmeister, *Briefe*, I, p. 22.
37 *SW*, I, p. 201.
38 *SW*, II, p. 459.
39 *SW*, II, p. 237.
40 *SW*, II, p. 186.
41 *SW*, I, p. 349.
42 *SW*, II, p. 395.
43 *SW*, III, p. 285.
44 *SW*, III, pp. 279, 299.
45 *SW*, III, p. 277.
46 *SW*, III, pp. 288, 14.
47 *SW*, III, p. 285.
48 *SW*, III, p. 307.
49 *SW*, III, pp. 327ff.
50 *SW*, III, p. 380.
51 *SW*, III, p. 587.
52 *SW*, III, p. 594.
53 *SW*, III, p. 597.
54 *SW*, III, p. 603.
55 *SW*, III, p. 627.
56 *SW*, III, p. 619.
57 *Ibid.*
58 Schelling's aesthetic doctrine is elaborated in his lectures *Ueber das Verhältniss der bildenen Künste zu der Natur*, published in Munich in 1807, in which Friedrich Schlegel's influence is very evident, even down to details. In it he treats of the metaphysical significance of art as the finite manifestation of the Absolute, for art, he maintains, is the eternal Idea pictorialized by the imagination. Its affinity with mythology therefore is obvious, the myths of the ancient Greek gods being symbols of the Absolute. What is needed, Schelling thinks, is the revivification of religion by a new mythology.
59 Modern critical edition by O. Weiss and W. E. Ehrhardt (Hamburg, 1974).
60 *SW*, IV, p. 77.
61 *SW*, IV, pp. 114f.
62 *SW*, IV, pp. 119f.
63 *SW*, IV, p. 128.
64 *SW*, VI, p. 13.
65 *SW*, VI, p. 19.
66 *SW*, VI, pp. 26f.
67 *Ibid.*
68 *SW*, VI, p. 38.
69 *SW*, VI, p. 40.
70 *SW*, VI, p. 39.
71 *SW*, VI, p. 42.
72 *Ibid.*

73   *SW*, VI, p. 57.

74   *SW*, VI, p. 61.

75   *SW*, VI, p. 70.

76   In 1816 Schelling was invited to take charge of the faculty of philosophy at Jena. The offer attracted him as providing an opportunity 'to make a gradual and historical transition to theology, and thus, under divine blessing, to do something distinctive for all Germany' (Plitt, *Aus Schellings Leben*, II, p. 366). Nevertheless he turned the offer down.

77   Plitt, *Aus Schellings Leben*, II, p. 187.

78   English translation by J. Gutmann, *Of Human Freedom* (Chicago, 1936).

79   Plitt, *Aus Schellings Leben*, II, p. 78.

80   *SW*, VII, p. 347.

81   *SW*, VII, p. 350.

82   *SW*, VII, p. 374.

83   *SW*, VII, p. 412.

84   *SW*, VII, p. 408.

85   *SW*, VII, p. 357.

86   *SW*, VII, p. 418.

87   *SW*, VII, p. 395.

88   N. Hartmann, *Die Philosophie des deutschen Idealismus: Fichte, Schelling und die Romantiker* (Berlin, 1923), p. 167.

89   *SW*, VII, p. 364.

90   *SW*, VII, p. 380.

91   *SW*, VII, p. 382.

92   *SW*, VII, p. 46.

93   *Die Weltalter*, planned in three volumes, was to have come out early in 1811. The edition of 1946 (Munich) was reissued in 1979; English translation by F. de Wolfe Bolman, *The Ages of the World* (New York, 1942).

94   *SW*, VII, pp. 432f.

95   *SW*, VII, p. 210.

96   *SW*, VII, p. 435.

97   Modern critical edition of the latter by M. Frank (1977).

98   W. Schulz, *Die Vollendung der deutschen Idealismus in der Spätphilosophie Schellings*, for example, sees in the 'positive' the culmination and due outcome of the 'negative', whereas H. Fuhrmans, *Schellings lezte Philosophie* (Berlin, 1940), regards Schelling's attempt to correlate them as misrepresenting the true nature of the latter, which he considers to be in an altogether new mode, and as arising from a natural if mistaken wish not to render his previous work otiose.

99   Plitt, *Aus Schellings Leben*, II, p. 124.

100   *SW*, XIII, pp. 57f.

101   *SW*, X, p. 211.

102   *SW*, XIII, p. 58.

103   *SW*, X, p. 213.

104   Among those who heard Schelling lecture in the winter of 1841–2 was Søren Kierkegaard, who was not much impressed by the celebrated German thinker. As he wrote to his brother: 'Schelling drivels on quite intolerably ... I am too old to attend lectures, and Schelling is too old to

give them. His whole doctrine of Potence displays the utmost impotence...
I should have become utterly daft if I had had to go on listening to
Schelling' (*Journals*, ed. and trans. by A. Dru, London, 1938, p. 104). The
letter is dated 27 February 1842.

105 *SW*, XI, pp. 566ff.
106 *SW*, XI, p. 556.
107 *SW*, XIII, p. 76.
108 *SW*, XI, p. 587.
109 *SW*, V, p. 440.
110 *SW*, XIV, p. 324.
111 *SW*, XIV, p. 66.
112 T. F. O'Meara (*Romantic Idealism and Roman Catholicism: Schelling and
the Theologians*, p. 4) no doubt has right on his side in stating that
'Schelling was the mentor of German Catholic intellectuals. In its perduring influence upon German Catholicism, his long career gives us a framework, the outline of a chart for early nineteenth-century Roman Catholic
thought'; but the important word here is 'early' and I question whether his
influence should be described as 'perduring'. The circles in which it was
effective were small – if distinguished – and authority frowned on it. See
chap. 5 of this book.

5   German Catholic theology in the Romantic era

1   Cf. the present writer's *Liberalism and Tradition: Aspects of Catholic
Thought in Nineteenth-Century France* (Cambridge, 1976).
2   Cf. J. Schmidlin, *Papstgeschichte der neuesten Zeit* (3rd ed., 3 vols.,
Munich, 1933–6), I, pp. 405–13.
3   *Der Primat des Papstes in allen christlichen Jahrhunderten* (Mainz,
1836–8).
4   Sulzbach, 1822. His *Rationalismus* was published in 1835, also at Sulzbach. He was a by no means imperceptive critic of D. F. Strauss' *Leben Jesu*
(*Dr Strauss Leben Jesu aus dem Standpunkte des Katholizismus betrach-
tet*, 1834).
5   *Versuch einer Pastorallehre* (Munich, 1805).
6   *Eine allgemeine Grundlage der christlichen Religion und Theologie*
(Cologne, 1823).
7   *Kirchengeschichte* (Münster, 1823–34).
8   The second did not appear until ten years later, in 1829, also at Münster.
9   3 vols., Münster, 1834.
10   Page x.
11   *Phil. Einleitung*, p. 9.
12   Cf. H. Schörs, *Geschichte der katholisch-theologischen Facultät zu Bonn
1818–1831* (Cologne, 1922), pp. 88f.
13   *Phil. Einleitung*, section 15.
14   *Ibid.*, p. 258.
15   *Ibid.*, p. 264.
16   *Ibid.*, p. 265.
17   *Ibid.*, p. xvi.
18   See *An Essay in Aid of a Grammar of Assent* (London, 1870), chap. 4.

19 *Christkatholische Dogmatik*, III, p. 471.
20 *Phil. Einleitung*, sections 4 and 6.
21 *Ibid.*, sections 18, 25–8, 33.
22 On K. J. H. Windischmann, an admirer and personal friend of Hegel's, who was strongly influenced by contemporary idealist thought, see A. Dryoff, *Karl Josef Windischmann und sein Kreis* (Cologne, 1916).
23 C. M. Hofbauer (1751–1820), a Redemptorist working mainly in Vienna, was an influence on a number of Romantics, such as Friedrich Schlegel and J. A. Möhler. In 1909 he was canonized by Pius X, who described him as 'the apostle of Vienna' and named him a patron saint of the city. See J. Hofer, *St Clement Maria Hofbauer*, Eng. trans. by J. B. Haas (New York, 1926).
24 A full account of Günther's career and writings was published by P. Knoodt in *Anton Günther, eine Biographie* (2 vols., Vienna, 1881). This should be supplemented by P. Wenzel, *Das wissenschaftliche Anliegen des Güntherianismus* (Essen, 1961) and the same author's *Der Freundeskreis am Anton Günther und die Gründung Beurons* (Essen, 1965). See also J. Pritz, *Wiener Beiträge zur Theologie*, IV (1963), and K. Beck, *Wiener Beiträge zur Theologie*, XVII (1967).
25 Baader's *Sämtliche Werke*, ed. F. Hoffmann *et al.*, were published at Leipzig, 1851–60. They have since been reprinted (Aalen, 1963ff.). His letters have been published by E. Susini (Paris, 1943). On Baader generally see D. Baumgardt, *Franz von Baader und die philosophische Romantik* (Halle, 1927), and E. Susini, *Franz von Baader et le romantisme mystique* (2 vols., Paris, 1943). On Baader as a Catholic Romantic see T. Steinbüchel, 'Romantisches Denker in Katholizismus mit besonderer Berücksichtigung der romantischer Philosophie Franz Baaders', in *Romantik: ein Zyklus Tübinger Vorlesungen*, ed. Steinbüchel (Tübingen, 1948).
26 Parts I–IV, Berlin, 1822–4; part VI, Leipzig, 1825.
27 Part I, Stuttgart, 1828; parts II–V, Münster, 1830–8.
28 G. Goyau, *Histoire religieuse de la nation française* (Paris, 1903), p. 82.
29 2 vols., Heidelberg.
30 Coblenz, 1820; Eng. trans. *Germany and the Revolution*, London, 1820.
31 See H. Brück, *Geschichte der katholischen Kirche in Deutschland im neunzehnten Jahrhundert* (4 vols., Mainz, 1887–1901), II, pp. 268ff, and H. Hocedez, *Histoire de la théologie au XIXe siècle* (Paris, 1947–52), I, pp. 195–201.
32 *Gesammelte Schriften*, ed. M. Görres, 9 vols., Munich, 1854–74. Critical ed. by W. Schellberg (Cologne, 1926ff). Görres' *Briefe*, eds. M. Görres and F. Binder, came out in 3 vols., 1858–74. A selection from both is to be found in Schellberg, *Josef von Görres ausgewählte Werke und Briefe* (2 vols., Munich, 1911). More recent biographies than that of J. N. Sepp, *Görres und seine Zeitgenossen* (Nordlingen, 1877), are those of Schellberg (Cologne, 1926) and R. Saitschick (Olten and Freiburg-im-Breisgau, 1953).
33 *Concilium Tridentinum, diariorum, epistolarum, tractuum nova collectio* (1901–65).
34 E. Vermeil, *Jean-Adam Möhler et l'école catholique de Tubingue 1815–1840* (Paris, 1913), although very discursive, is still a most valuable

source of information on its subject. But it is faulty in its assessment of the originality of J. S. Drey in relation to Möhler himself.

35 See S. Lösch, *Die Anfänge der Tübinger Theologischen Quartalschrift* (Rottenburg, 1938).

36 The article appeared in *Archiv für die Pastoralkonferenzen in den Handkapiteln des Bisthums Constanz*. See J. R. Geiselmann, *Geist des Christentums und das Katholizismus* (Mainz, 1940), p. 83.

37 The scholastic theology he described as being 'Abdruch ihres Gemüthes' and its dialectic as 'das Bestreben, die innere religiöse Welt auch nach aussen zu entfaltn' (*Archiv f. d. Pastoralkonferenzen* . . ., I (i), pp. 9f).

38 On Drey's relation to Schleiermacher see K. Eschweiler, *Johann Adam Möhlers Kirchenbegriff* (Braunsberg, 1930), pp. 11ff.

39 *Kurze Einleitung*, preface, vf.

40 *Ibid*., pp. 166ff, especially pp. 207–13.

41 *Ibid*., pp. 214f.

42 *Quartalschrift*, I (1819), pp. 10–18, in particular p. 14.

43 *Ibid*., p. 22.

44 *Ibid*., pp. 369–91.

45 *Ibid*., pp. 566f.

46 Cf. *Quartalschrift*, I, pp. 563f, 569f.

47 His *Untersuchungen über die Constitutionen und Kanones des Apostel* was published at Tübingen in 1832 and was widely praised for its careful investigation of the problem, although its conclusions have not been endorsed by more recent scholarship.

48 *Die Apologetik als wissenschaftliche Nachweisung der Göttlichkeit des Christenthums* (Mainz, 1838–47).

49 See Owen Chadwick, *From Bossuet to Newman* (Cambridge, 1957), chap. 5.

50 Cf. G. Goyau, *Moehler* (Paris, 1905), p. 15.

51 Cf. Goyau, *Moehler*, p. 16. Eschweiler, *Johann Adam Möhlers Kirchenbegriff*, stresses the influence of both Schleiermacher and Hegel. The impression they made on Möhler is not to be belittled, but J. H. Geiselmann, 'Der Geist des Christentums und Katholizismus: Johann Adam Möhler und die Entwicklung seines Kirchenbegriffs', *Tübinger Quartalschrift*, CXII (1931), pp. 1–91, rightly assesses Möhler's debt to Drey.

52 *Athanasius der Grosse und die Kirche seines Zeit* (Mainz, 1827) and 'Anselm, Erzbischof von Canterbury', *Quartalschrift*, IX (1827), pp. 435–97, 585–664, and *Quartalschrift*, X (1828), pp. 62–130 (repr. in J. A. Möhler's *Gesammelte Schriften*, ed. J. J. I. Döllinger, Regensburg, 1839, I, pp. 32–176).

53 Its full title was: *Die Einheit in der Kirche, oder das Prinzip des Katholizismus dargestellt im Geist der Kirchenväter der drei ersten Jahrhunderte* (Tübingen, 1825). There is a modern critical edition by J. R. Geiselmann, Cologne, 1957. On Möhler's ecclesiology see G. Ronzet, 'L'unité organique du Catholicisme d'après Möhler', in *Irénikon*, XII (1935), pp. 328–50, 427–85; P. Chaillet, 'L'esprit du christianisme et du catholicisme', in *Revue des sciences philosophiques et théologiques*, XXVI (1937), pp. 483–98, 713–26; and S. Bolshakov, *The Doctrine of the Unity of the Church in the Works of Khomyakov and Möhler* (London, 1946).

54   *Die Einheit in der Kirche*, p. 165.

55   Vermeil, *Jean-Adam Möhler*, claims that the Tübingen school were the direct ancestors of the Catholic Modernist movement of the last years of the nineteenth century and the opening decade of the twentieth; as too does A. Fonck, *Dictionnaire de théologie catholique*, x, coll. 2048–63 (though cf. art. 'Tradition', x, coll. 1332f). L. de Grandmaison in *Recherches des sciences religieuses*, IX (1919), pp. 387–401, criticized this opinion, as also did S. Lösch, *Quartalschrift*, XCIX (1917–18), pp. 129–52. Loisy himself denied that the Tübingen theologians had any direct influence on Modernism (*Mémoires*, III (1931), pp. 267f). Yet there plainly was an affinity between the religious philosophy of the former and that of the Modernists. The latter, however, were much more powerfully influenced by nineteenth-century biblical and historical criticism than the Tübingen men could have been.

56   *Die Enheit in der Kirche*, pp. 221f and 224.

57   Its full title is: *Symbolik, oder Darstellung der dogmatischen Gegensätze der Katholiken und Protestanten nach ihren öffentlichen Bekenntnis-schriften*. An English translation appeared in 1843. Subsequent editions were modified by the author in a more traditionalist direction. There is, again, a modern critical edition by Geiselmann (Cologne, 1960–1).

58   Möhler was alluding to the work of G. J. Plank and K. Marheineke, 1810–13.

59   *Symbolik*, chap. 5, section 38.

60   *Ibid.*

61   *Neue Untersuchungen der Lehrgegensätze zwischen den Katholiken und Protestanten*. See further: H. Geisser, *Glaubenseinheit und Lehrentwicklung bei Johann Adam Möhler* (Paderborn, 1971); H. Wagner, *Die eine Kirche und die vielen Kirchen. Ekklesiologie und Symbolik beim jungen Möhler* (Paderborn, 1977); and *The Heythrop Journal*, XIX (1978), pp. 46–70.

6   Italian ontologism: Gioberti and Rosmini

1   Concerning ontologism in France and Belgium see B. M. G. Reardon, *Liberalism and Tradition: Aspects of Catholic Thought in France in the Nineteenth Century* (Cambridge, 1976), chap. 8.

2   Gioberti's complete works (*Opere edite e inedite di Vincenzo Gioberti*), published under the auspices of the Istituto di Studi Filosofici (Rome and Milan) with Enrico Castelli as general editor, began to appear in 1938. *Il primato morale* comprises vols. II and III of this *Edizione nazionale* (referred to here as *EN*).

3   *Lettre sur les erreurs religieuses de M. de Lamennais* (Brussels, 1840) and *Lettre sur les doctrines philosophiques et politiques de M. de Lamennais* (Brussels, 1841). On *Paroles d'un Croyant* see chap. 7 of this book.

4   2 vols., Paris and Turin, 1851.

5   Lausanne, 1846–7; repr. in *EN*, vols. XIII-XVIII (ed. M. F. Sciacca, 1940–2).

6   See *Della riforma cattolica della Chiesa: frammenti pubblicati per cura di G. Massari* (Paris and Turin, 1856), of which there is a complete and

revised edition (ed. G. Balsamo-Crivelli) under the title *I frammenti 'Della riforma cattolica' e 'Della libertà cattolica'* (Florence, 1924).

7   Cf. F. Palhoriès, *Gioberti* (Paris, 1919), pp. 329–85 ('Le Réformateur moderniste').

8   On Gioberti's career see L. Stefanini, *Gioberti* (Milan, 1947), and G. de Crescenza, *Gioberti* (Brescia, 1964). A selection from his writings is given in E. Travi (ed.), *Gioberti: scritti letterari* (Milan, 1971). There was a considerable revival of interest in Gioberti in Italy during the fascist period.

9   Of the posthumous works *Della protologia* (2 vols., Paris and Turin, 1857) is the most important.

10   See also B. Croce's chapter on Gioberti as philosopher in *Discorsi di varia filosofia* (Bari, 1945), I, pp. 73–96.

11   The former view is the conclusion not only of the neo-idealist Giovanni Gentile (*Rosmini e Gioberti*, Pisa, 1899) but of the Catholic U.A. Padovani (*Vincenzo Gioberti ed il Cattolicismo*, Milan, 1927).

12   *Introduzione allo studio della filosofia* (Brussels, 1840) (repr. in EN, ed. G. Calò, vols. IV and V, 1939–41). References in the text are to the French version by V. Tourneur and L. Defourny (3 vols., Paris, 1847).

13   Tourneur and Defourny, I, p. 253.

14   *Ibid.*, I, p. 363.

15   *Ibid.*, II, p. 254.

16   Gioberti is convinced of the link between Scottish philosophy of the Reid school and ontologism. 'From Reid's theory of perception to the "vision" of Malebranche and Augustine there is', he says, 'only a step' (I, p. 357).

17   *Ibid.*, II, pp. 26ff.

18   *Ibid.*, I, pp. 382f.

19   *Ibid.*, II, p. 29.

20   *Ibid.*, II, p. 1.

21   *Ibid.*, II, pp. 47f.

22   *Ibid.*, II, p. 46.

23   *Ibid.*, II, pp. 70f.

24   A second edition of the *Teorica* appeared in 1850. Blondel's *Lettre sur les exigences de la pensée contemporaine en matière d'apologétique et sur la méthode de la philosophie dans l'étude du problème religieux* was published three years after *L'Action*, in 1896. It has since been reprinted in *Les premiers écrits de Maurice Blondel* (Paris, 1956).

25   Traditionalism as taught by Louis de Bonald (1754–1840) and others was the doctrine that all metaphysical, moral and religious knowledge rests on a primal divine revelation transmitted over the centuries by a continuous tradition. As likely to lead to scepticism it was censured in a number of official decrees culminating in the constitution 'De fide catholica' of the first Vatican Council (1870). See *Liberalism and Tradition*, chaps. 3 and 4.

26   On Matteo Liberatore (1810–92) see *Dictionnaire de théologie catholique*, IX (Paris, 1926), coll. 629f.

27   On the views of Mamiani see G. Gentile, *Le origini della filosofia contemporanea in Italia*, I (Messina, 1917), pp. 87–137, and G. Alliney, *I pensatori della seconda metà del sec. XIX* (Milan, 1942), pp. 217–23.

28 Quoted by C. Leetham, *Rosmini: Priest, Philosopher and Patriot* (London, 1957), p. xiv.

29 Leetham, *Rosmini*, p. xx.

30 On Rosmini's life and career see mainly G. B. Pagani, *Vita di Antonio Rosmini* (2 vols., Turin, 1880–4; rev. ed. by G. Rossi, Rovereto, 1959), and G. Pusinieri, *Rosmini* (Milan, 1967); but also W. Lockhart (and G. S. Macwalter), *Life of Rosmini* (London, 1883–6), as well as Leetham, *Rosmini*. The complete edition of Rosmini's letters (*Epistolario completo*) comprises 13 vols. (Casale Monferrato, 1887–94). His total literary output, much of it published posthumously, was immense. The *Edizione nazionale* (ed. E. Castelli *et al.*), which began publication at Rome in 1934, although running to over 30 volumes, is still incomplete. For full bibliographical information see C. Bergamaschi, *Bibliografia rosminiana* (Milan, 1967).

31 In his time the family name was Rosmini-Serbati, his grandfather having assumed the patronymic Serbati in order to benefit from a legacy coming to him from his mother's family.

32 *Panegirico alla santa e gloriosa memoria di Pio VII* (Modena, 1831).

33 *Epist.*, I, 453.

34 *Epist.*, I, 322.

35 *Epist.*, I, 294.

36 *Educazione cristiana* (Venice, 1823).

37 *Epist.*, II, 55.

38 *Epist.*, II, 725.

39 Maddalena Gabriela di Canossa (1774–1855), the daughter of a wealthy nobleman, devoted her life to works of charity. She also founded a religious congregation dedicated to educational and medical work. She was beatified in 1941. See I. Giordani, *Maddalena di Canossa* (4th ed., Brescia, 1957).

40 *Massime di perfezione cristiana adotte ad ogni condizione di persone* (Rome, 1830). There is an English trans. by W. A. Johnson, London, 1889 (repr. 1962).

41 Cf. C. J. Emery, *The Rosminians* (London, 1960).

42 2 vols., Milan, 1827–8.

43 4 vols., Rome, 1830; reprinted in *EN* in 3 vols. (ed. Castelli), Milan, 1934. An English trans. was published under the title *Essay on the Origin of Ideas* (3 vols., London, 1883–4).

44 *Epist.*, X, 6113.

45 See *Progetti di costituzione* (ed. C. Gray, in *EN*, Milan, 1951).

46 See *Della missione a Roma ... negli anni 1848–1849* (Turin, 1881).

47 Repr. Milan, 1954.

48 Probabilism, the reader will recall, is the theory in moral theology based on the principle that in case of doubt as to whether an action is or is not morally lawful it is permissible to follow an opinion, favouring liberty, that has substantial probability, even though the opposing opinion, favouring law, should appear the more probable. See R. C. Mortimer, *The Elements of Moral Theology* (London, 1947); or, more fully, T. Richard, *Le Probabilisme morale et philosophique* (Paris, 1922).

49 See *Progetti de costituzione*.

50 Lugano, 1848. An English trans. was made by H.P. Liddon (*The Five Wounds of the Church*, London, 1883).

51 In 20 vols., it was published in Paris between 1690 and 1720, and covered the whole history of the church from the first century down to 1414.

52 *Epist.*, X, 6212.

53 Cf. *Della missione a Roma*, p. 159.

54 *Il comunismo e il socialismo* (Naples, 1849).

55 *Epist.*, X, 6396.

56 Repr. in 4 vols. (ed. G. Rossi) in *EN*, 1941–51.

57 At Turin. The *EN* reprint (2 vols., ed. E. Troilo) is dated 1942–3.

58 For Rosmini's personal reaction see *Epist.*, XII, 7729.

59 *Epist.*, XII, 7739.

60 Cf. Leetham, *Rosmini*, p. 435.

61 In 5 vols. The entire work was reprinted in *EN* in 8 vols. (ed. C. Gray), 1938–41.

62 Repr. in *EN*, ed. G. Pusinieri, 2 vols., Milan, 1955.

63 On Galluppi, see G. Gentile, *La filosofia italiana dal Genovesi al Galluppi*, II (Milan, 1931).

64 Cf. Gentile, *Rosmini e Gioberti*, p. 62; Spaventa (ed. Gentile), *La filosofia italiana nelle sue relazioni con la filosofia europea* (Bari, 1908), p. 14.

65 The *Nuovo saggio* (ed. F. Orestano) comprises vols. III-V of the *EN* (1941).

66 I (ed. 1850), pp. 42f, n. 62. Cf. p. 36, n. 5. Also *Antropologia* (ed. 1884), IV, chap. 4.

67 *Psicologia*, I, p. 56, n. 81.

68 To this account of the soul's immediate self-apprehension – one of the points of divergence between himself and Gioberti – Rosmini gave the name 'ideological psychology' (*psicologia ideologica*).

69 *Nuovo saggio*, II, n. 99.

70 *Ibid.*, p. 171.

71 'E intelletto quegli che s'accorge della sensazione.' Cf. *Teosofia*, V, p. 506.

72 *Psicologia*, I, p. 22.

73 *Ibid.*, p. 148, n. 267; p. 138, n. 251.

74 *Ibid.*, p. 139, n. 254.

75 For a discussion of Rosmini's epistemology see M. F. Sciacca, 'Les éléments fondamentaux de la gnoséologie rosminienne' (*Revue philosophique de Louvain*, 53 (1955), pp. 225–38).

76 Cf. *Il rinnovamento della filosofia in Italia* (Milan, 1836), II, p. 167. The *Rinnovamento* was reprinted in *EN* in 2 vols., Milan, 1941.

77 *Sistema filosofico* (Montepulciano, 1846), nn. 167, 169f.

78 *Principi della scienza morale* (Milan, 1831), chap. 4, art. 5.

79 *Ibid.*, art. 8.

80 *Ibid.*, chap. 3, art. 4.

81 *Introduzione alla filosofia* (Casale, 1850), p. 215. The *Introduzione* (ed. U. Redano) is reprinted as vol. II of *EN* (Milan, 1934).

82 *Sistema filosofico*, nn. 176ff.

83 *Ibid.*, n. 182.

84 Cf. *Antropologia*, II, pp. 48f.

85 Mamiani's criticisms of Rosmini were stated in *Il rinnovamento della filosofia antica in Italia* (Milan, 1834), to which Rosmini's *Il rinnovamento*

was a reply. Mamiani countered this with *Six lettres à l'Abbé Antoine Rosmini* (Paris, 1838).

86 *Vincento Gioberti e il panteismo* (Milan, 1846).

87 Cf. L. Ferri, *Essai sur l'histoire de la philosophie en Italie au XIXe siècle* (Paris, 1869). One of Rosmini's sharpest critics was G. M. Bertini (1818–76), whose *Idea di una filosofia della vita* (2 vols., Turin, 1850) discounted any differences between Gioberti and Rosmini as minimal, since both thinkers had in the author's opinion embraced ontologism with its pantheistic overtones. Rosmini answered Bertini in much the same strain as he did Gioberti, but his *Logica* (1854) and the posthumous *Teosofia* reveal modifications in his terminology which show that he felt Bertini's case needed to be met.

88 Cf. Ferri, *Essai sur l'histoire de la philosophie*.

89 Cf. also G. M. Cornoldi, *Il Rosminianismo, sintesi dell'ontologismo e panteismo* (Rome, 1881).

90 The decree *Post obitum* was published 14 December 1877. The text is to be found in *Rosminiarum propositionum quas S.R.U. Inquisitio ... reprobavit, proscripsit damnavit trutina theologica* (Rome, 1892).

7   Lamennais and *Paroles d'un Croyant*

1 The family name was Robert de la Mennais. Félicité's father had been ennobled on the eve of the Revolution.

2 On Lamennais's early life C. Maréchal's *La Jeunesse de Lamennais* (Paris, 1913) is still indispensable.

3 *Correspondance générale*, edited by L. le Guillou (9 vols., Paris, 1971–81), I, p. 309. Referred to hereafter as *CG*.

4 *CG*, I, pp. 244–52.

5 Lamennais's distress of mind at this time is only too evident in his letters to his brother. Thus on 1 November 1810 (?) he writes: 'Mon seul désir en ce moment est de passer le reste de [ma vie] dans la solitude, *oblitus omnium, obliviscendus et illis*. Il n'est personne au monde dans le souvenir de qui je désire subsister ... Depuis quelques mois je tombe dans un état d'affaissem[en]t incompréhensible. Rien ne me remue, rien ne m'intéresse; tout me dégoûte. Si je suis assis, il me faut faire un effort presque inouï pour me lever. La pensée me fatigue. Je ne sais sur quoi porter un reste de sensibilité qui s'éteint. Des désirs, je n'en ai plus. J'ai usé la vie, c'est de tous les états le plus pénible, et de toutes les maladies la plus douloureuse comme le plus irrémédiable' (*CG*, I, p. 76).

6 The material for *Tradition* had almost certainly been researched by Jean-Marie, and the book was not included in Lamennais's *Oeuvres complètes*, referred to below as *OC* (12 vols. in 6) of 1836. Cf. Maréchal, *La Jeunesse de Lamennais*, chaps. 5, 6 and 8 of part II.

7 *OC*, VI, p. 6.

8 *OC*, VI, p. 68.

9 Cf. C. Boutard, *Lamennais: sa vie et ses doctrines* (3 vols., Paris, 1905–13), I, p. 55.

10 *CG*, I, pp. 397f, 458.

11 See A. Feugère, *Lamennais avant l'Essai sur l'indifférence en matière de*

religion 1782–1817 (Paris, 1906), p. 187: 'Après Chateaubriand, il [Lamennais] croyait qu'il restait à montrer que le christianisme est capable, non seulement à exciter des émotions esthétiques, mais de satisfaire les besoins de la pensée.' On Lamennais's personal relations with Chateaubriand see V. Giraud, *La Vie tragique de Lamennais* (Paris, 1933), pp. 175–85.

12   No English translation appeared until the rather unsatisfactory one by Lord Stanley of Alderley in 1895.

13   Nevertheless such authorities on Lamennais as Maréchal (*La Mennais: La dispute de l'Essai sur l'indifférence*, Paris, 1925, and Boutard, *Lamennais*, p. 146) still considered it of value. But F. Duine, *Lamennais: sa vie, ses idées, ses ouvrages* (Paris, 1922), p. 66, is right in saying: 'Comme d'autres ouvrages, qui ont mérité des contemporains l'épithète d'immortels, il n'est plus qu'un document du passé, un illustre témoin de la Restauration.'

14   *Essai* (ed. Garnier), I, p. 30.

15   Lamennais had read Bonald and he admired him, alluding to him in *Réflexions* as 'un homme de génie' who had penetrated 'avec succès dans cette nouvelle route ouverte aux défenseurs du christianisme' (OC, VI, p. 78).

16   *Essai*, I, p. 49.

17   'Nous sommes donc convenus d'admettre comme vrai ce que tous les hommes croient invinciblement. Cette foi invincible, universelle, est pour nous la base de la certitude; et nous avons montré qu'en effet, si on rejette cette base, si on suppose que ce que tous les hommes croient vrai puisse être faux, il n'y a plus de certitude possible, plus de verité, plus de raison humaine' (*Essai*, IV, p. 313).

18   *Essai*, II, p. 283.

19   OC, VII.

20   OC, VII, p. 255.

21   OC, VII, p. 280.

22   Denis Frayssinous (1765–1841), a Sulpician, who was consecrated bishop in 1822 with a titular see, was also a peer of France. From 1824 to 1828 he was minister for ecclesiastical affairs, but retired from public life after the July Revolution of 1830. His *Vrais principes de l'Eglise gallicane* (1818) propounds a moderate Gallicanism. As a notable apology along traditional lines his *Défense du christianisme*, first published in 1825, besides being repeatedly reprinted was translated into English, Italian, Spanish and German. See A. Garnier, *Frayssinous, son rôle dans l'Université sous la Restauration 1822–1828* (Paris, 1925).

23   Cf. Garnier, *Frayssinous*, p. 424: 'Cette condamnation solennelle et ridicule ne diminua pas l'écrivain devant l'opinion, pas plus qu'elle ne grandit le parti qui l'avait cité en justice.'

24   The Agence's prospectus and its articles of association were published in the *Avenir* on 18 December 1830. See *Articles de l'Avenir* (7 vols., Paris, 1830–1), I, pp. 455–8.

25   The *Censure of Toulouse*, with other documents and a preface, was published in 1835. See in particular P. Dudon, *Lamennais et le Saint-Siège 1820–1834 d'après des documents inédits et des Archives du Vatican* (Paris, 1911), pp. 167–71, 243–63.

26   Lamennais received his copy of the encyclical on 30 August while attending

a dinner given in honour of the French guests by a group of distinguished German writers, among them Schelling and Görres. The incident is described by Montalembert. See P. de Lallemand, *Montalembert et ses amis dans le romantisme 1830–1840* (Paris, 1927), pp. 156f.

27 *CG*, v, p. 227. Cf. his letter to Countess de Senfft, 1 November 1832 (*CG*, v, pp. 208f) in which he is scathing on Rome: 'J'y suis allé, et j'ai vu là le plus infâme cloaque qui ait jamais souillé des regards humains. L'égout gigantesque de Tarquin serait trop étroit pour donner passage à tant d'immondices. Là, nul autre Dieu que l'interêt; on y vendrait les peuples, on y vendrait le genre humain, on y vendrait les trois personnes de la sainte Trinité, l'une après l'autre, ou tout ensemble, pour un coin de terre, ou pour quelques piastres. J'ai vu cela, et je me suis dit: Ce mal est au-dessus de la puissance de l'homme, et j'ai détourné les yeux.'

28 Cf. *CG*, v, pp. 270, 377f.

29 *CG*, v, p. 333.

30 *CG*, v, p. 310.

31 *CG*, v, pp. 377f: 'Or, premièrement, je suis convaincu que toute action catholique, c'est-à-dire, toute action qui suppose le concours du clergé ou au moins sa neutralité, est absolument impossible aujourd'hui et continuera de l'être, jusqu'à ce que Dieu, par des moyens qui nous sont inconnus, ait opéré une immense réponse dans l'Eglise' (letter of 2 May 1833 to Mlle de Lucinière).

32 Cf. *CG*, iii, p. 482.

33 *CG*, v, pp. 389f (letter of 8 May 1833 to Abbé Vuarin).

34 *CG*, v, p. 302 (letter of 5 February 1833 to Count Rzewski).

35 Cf. Y. Le Hir, *Les 'Paroles d'un Croyant' de Lamennais: texte publié sur le manuscrit autographe* (Paris, 1949), Introduction, chap. 2: 'Eschatologie et Messianisme'.

36 Cardinal Wiseman, *Recollections of the Four Last Popes* (London, 1858), pp. 338f.

37 *CG*, v, p. 295.

38 See Le Hir, *Les 'Paroles d'un Croyant'*, pp. 1–4.

39 Montalembert was responsible for the translation only in a very general sense, since he knew very little Polish. Lamennais in a letter to him dated 16 May 1833 states categorically: 'Avant d'avoir lu Mickiewitz, j'avais commencé un petit ouvrage d'un genre fort analogue. Comme ce ne sont pas de ces choses qui commandent à être faites de suite, peut-être le continuerai-je si je m'y sens quelque attrait. Toutefois n'en parle à personne. Je te montrerai ce que j'en ai fait, et ton avis m'encouragera à poursuivre ou m'en détournera' (*CG*, v, p. 395). See Y. Le Hir, 'Mickiewicz et Lamennais en 1833', in *Annales de Bretagne*, 1948, pp. 47–58. On Montalembert's part in the translation see Lallemand, *Montalembert et ses amis*, p. 321.

40 *CG*, v, pp. 44f: 'Je déclare ... que personne, grâce à Dieu, n'est plus soumis que moi, dans le fond du coeur et sans aucune réserve, à toutes les décisions émanées ou à émaner du Saint-Siège Apostolique sur la doctrine de la foi et des moeurs, ainsi qu'aux lois de discipline portées par son autorité souveraine.'

41 *CG*, vi, pp. 49f.

42   CG, VI, p. 580.

43   CG, VI, pp. 80f.

44   It was not, as has sometimes been said, published anonymously. The mistake arose through Lamennais's name not appearing on the title-page but on the back of the volume instead. Cf. A. R. Vidler, *Prophecy and Papacy: a Study of Lamennais, the Church and the Revolution* (London, 1954), p. 244.

45   H. J. Laski describes it as 'a lyrical version of the "Communist Manifesto"' and as 'written in a style that has a splendour and elevation not merely unique in Lamennais's own work, but in the whole range of French literature' (*Authority in the Modern State*, New Haven, Conn., and London, 1919), p. 255.

46   See his letter of 4 May 1834 to Sainte-Beuve: 'J'ai cherché, pour parler au peuple, les expressions les plus communes et le langage le plus simple. Il me semble que je devais tâcher, sous ce rapport au moins, de me rapprocher de l'Evangile' (*CG, VI*, p. 82).

47   CG, VI, pp. 159f.

48   CG, VI, p. 96.

49   *Ibid.*

50   See Boutard, *Lamennais*, III, pp. 38f.

51   CG, VI, p. 647.

52   See Le Hir, *Les 'Paroles d'un Croyant'*, pp. 16–27.

53   London, 1834. A more recent translation is that of C. Reavely, *'The People's Prophecy' by F. de Lamennais* (London, 1949).

54   CG, VI, p. 102.

55   See a letter of 25 May 1834 to Baron de Vitrolles (*CG, VI*, p. 113).

56   On Bautain see *Liberalism and Tradition*, chap. 6.

57   In *Réponse d'un Chrétien aux 'Paroles d'un Croyant'*, a brochure of 96 pages printed at Strasbourg in June 1834. It was answered by an 'ancien professeur de théologie' in *France catholique*, 12 July 1834. See P. Vulliaud, *Les Paroles d'un Croyant de Lamennais* (Amiens, 1928), pp. 123ff. Lamennais observed sarcastically to Montalembert: 'Ce Bautain veut être évêque, mais il y a de grands obstacles du côté de Rome.' In 1838 Bautain had to go to Rome to explain the charge of 'fideism' brought against him by his own bishop.

58   Boutard, *Lamennais*, III, pp. 76f.

59   *Singulari nos* was dated 24 June 1834. See Dudon, *Lamennais et le Saint-Siège*, pp. 427–30. Cf. Lamennais's *Affaires de Rome* (ed. Garnier), pp. 418–33. See also M.-J. and L. Le Gillou, *La condamnation de Lamennais* (Paris, 1982).

60   See a letter of 12 July 1834 to Montalembert (*CG, VI*, pp. 200f).

61   CG, VI, p. 706 (letter of 19 July 1834, sent from Mainz).

62   CG, VI, p. 229.

63   See Dudon, *Lamennais et le Saint-Siège*, pp. 337f.

64   CG, VI, pp. 808f (letter of 13 December 1834, sent from Pisa).

65   CG, VII, p. 35.

66   See A. Roussel, *Lamennais d'après des documents inédits* (2 vols., Paris, 1893), II, p. 254.

67   OC, VII. The preface is entitled 'Du catholicisme dans ses rapports avec la

société politique'. Duine says that it 'peut être considérée comme l'acte public et définitif de la séparation de Lamennais du catholicisme' (*La Mennais, l'homme et l'écrivain: Pages choisis*, Paris, 1912, p. 13).

68 *Affaires de Rome*, pp. 328f.

69 Protestantism he describes as a 'systeme bâtard, inconséquent, étroit, qui, sous une apparence trompeuse de liberté, se résout pour les nations dans le despotisme brutal de la force et pour les individus dans l'égoïsme' (*Affaires de Rome*, p. 338).

70 *Affaires de Rome*, p. 201.

71 *CG*, VIII, p. 39.

72 *Portraits contemporains*, I (ed. 1868), pp. 231–47.

73 Cf. a letter to the Marquis de Coriolis dated 5 April 1836: 'On se récriera tant qu'on voudra; je soutiens, moi, que le peuple, le pauvre peuple, travaillant chaque jour, est partout ce qu'il y a de meilleur, et qu'en lui seul sont les éléments avec lesquels on peut refaire la société' (*CG*, VII, p. 60).

74 *Tradition*, I, p. cxv.

75 *OC*, IX, p. 188.

76 He wrote to Mazzini in 1841: 'Tout l'avenir de l'humanité dépend de sa conception future de Dieu et jusqu'à ce qu'elle se soit formée, le monde, privé de direction, continuera de flotter au hasard, incapable de se fixer, incapable de sortir de la confusion présente' (*CG*, VIII, p. 99).

77 It ran until 7 July 1848.

78 Duine, *Lamennais: sa vie, ses idées, ses ouvrages*, pp. 275f.

79 See *Liberalism and Tradition*, chaps. 4 and 5.

80 Lamennais's lecture-course in philosophy, given first at La Chênaie and later at Juilly, was printed in 1834 with the title *Essai d'un système de philosophie catholique*. A critical edition by Y. Le Hir was published at Rennes in 1954. On Lamennais's philosophy see L. Le Guillou, *L'Evolution de la pensée religieuse de Félicité Lamennais* (Paris, 1966), chap. 5. But P. Janet, *La Philosophie de Lamennais* (Paris, 1890), is still of value.

81 Cf. Duine, *Lamennais*, p. 222.

82 Cf. Maréchal, *La Jeunesse de Lamennais*, p. 13.

83 *L'Inquiétude religieuse*, 2nd series (Paris, 1909), pp. 79f. A notable recent attempt at assessment is by G. Hourdin, *Lamennais, prophète et combattant de la liberté* (Paris, 1982).

8   **Auguste Comte and the Religion of Humanity**

1 A contemporary of Comte's, P.-J. Proudhon, could speak of him as 'cet animal de Comte, le plus pédant des savants, le plus maigre des philosophes, le plus plat des sociologues, le plus insupportable des écrivains' (quoted by A. Desjardins, *La Vie de P.-J. Proudhon*, Paris, 1896, I, p. 217).

2 This 'Plan of the Scientific Researches Necessary for Reorganizing Society' was first printed in *Opuscules de philosophie sociale 1819–1828*, published in 1883.

3 'De Maistre a pour moi la propriété particulière de me servir à apprécier la capacité philosophique des gens par le cas qu'ils en font. Ce système ne m'a jamais horrifié ... Guizot, malgré tout son protestantisme transcendant, le sent assez bien' (Letter dated 24 November 1824. See *Corres-*

pondance générale et confessions, ed. P. E. de B. Carneiro and P. Arnaud, I (1814–40), Paris, 1973, p. 138).

4   Although Comte chose to regard his connection with Saint-Simon as 'disastrous' he was indebted to him for certain key-ideas in his own system. Even if Comte was guilty of some plagiarism, he built on what he borrowed, showing more method and wider knowledge than Saint-Simon. But it is ironical, in view of the subsequent development of his own thought, that he should have deplored what he saw as Saint-Simon's sentimental religiosity. In some respects Comte's attitude to Saint-Simon is akin to that of Schelling to Hegel. Cf. G. Dumas, *La Psychologie de deux Messies positivistes* (Paris, 1905).

5   Its full title is: *Synthèse subjective, ou système universel des conceptions propres à l'état normal de l'humanité*. Only the first volume saw print, the work remaining uncompleted.

6   The standard works on Comte's life are those of H. Gouhier: *La Vie d'Auguste Comte* (Paris, 1931) and *La Jeunesse d'Auguste Comte et la formation du positivisme* (3 vols., Paris, 1933–41). Harriet Martineau's translation and condensation of the *Cours de philosophie positive* was published in two volumes in 1853, and won Comte's personal approval. Cf. 'Discours sur l'esprit positif', prefixed to the *Traité philosophique d'astronomie populaire* (1848). The *Système de politique positive* came out in an English version by J. H. Bridges, F. Harrison and others (*The System of Positive Philosophy*, 4 vols., London, 1875–7), while the *Catéchisme positiviste* was translated by R. Congreve under the title *The Catechism of Positive Religion* (London, 1858).

7   As R. Flint succinctly puts it: 'The aim of Comte was to construct a system in which nothing would be arbitrary but everything determined by a few closely connected laws, proved by the concurrent application of deduction and induction' (*Philosophy of History*, Edinburgh and London, 1874, p. 589).

8   *Phil. pos.*, I, pp. 2f.

9   Comte does not examine the meaning of 'law' in this context, and his use of the term contains the ambiguity of 'descriptive' and 'prescriptive'.

10   *Phil. pos.*, I, p. 6.

11   *Ibid.*, p. 3.

12   *Phil. pos.*, V, p. 17; IV, p. 351.

13   *Phil. pos.*, I, pp. 3f. Cf. IV, pp. 233f.

14   *Phil. pos.*, I, p. 4.

15   *Phil. pos.*, IV, p. 526.

16   *Phil. pos.*, I, p. 11.

17   *Ibid.*, p. 24.

18   It may be added, however, that although Comte believes the unification of the several sciences to be perfectly feasible, and indeed his own positive philosophy claims to have proved it, he did not share Saint-Simon's expectation of discovering a single overall method in science, preferring to regard each one as developing its own. As he states: 'According to my deep personal conviction I consider that attempts to achieve the universal explanation of all phenomena by one unique law as eminently chimerical, even when they are made by the most competent minds. I believe that the

means at the disposal of the human intelligence are too feeble and the universe too complex for such a scientific perfection ever to be open to us' (*ibid.*, p. 44).

19   It will be observed that Comte does not include psychology in his list of the sciences, somewhat surprisingly to the modern reader. But reasons for this apparent omission are not difficult to assign. Mere personal introspection he passed over as incapable of scientific treatment, and clinical psychology had not in his time been established. Thus the study of the human mind had to be divided between biology and sociology.

20   'It is to Montesquieu that we must attribute the first great direct effort to treat politics as a science of facts and not of dogmas' (*Pol. pos.*, IV, p. 106).

21   *Pol. pos.*, II, p. 65.

22   *Pol. pos.*, III, p. 72.

23   *La Philosophie d'Auguste Comte* (Paris, 1900), p. 43.

24   *Pol. pos.*, III, p. 28. Comte seems to restrict 'religion' and 'religious' to the practical aspect of 'theological' thinking. Religion for him, it could be said, is philosophy in so far as it imposes itself as a unifying principle of life, whether individual or collective. Cf. *Pol. pos.*, II, chap. 2: 'Théorie générale de la religion, ou Théorie positive de l'unité humaine'.

25   'Considérations sur les sciences', in *Opuscules*, pp. 182f.

26   *Pol. pos.*, IV, p. 529.

27   *Ibid.*, pp. 527f. Cf. *Phil. pos.*, III, p. 210, and *Pol. pos.*, II, pp. 80f.

28   *Phil. pos.*, V, pp. 34f.

29   *Phil. pos.*, IV, p. 528; cf. III, pp. 209ff, V, pp. 251f.

30   *Phil. pos.*, IV, p. 529. Cf. V, pp. 24, 53; IV, pp. 533, 550.

31   *Phil. pos.*, IV, p. 533.

32   *Ibid.*

33   Cf. *Phil. pos.*, III, pp. 618f, IV, pp. 534f and V, p. 119.

34   *Phil. pos.*, V, p. 511: 'Dans cette enfance intellectuelle, que nous pouvons maintenant si peu comprendre, les faits chimériques l'emportent infiniment sur les faits réels.'

35   *Phil. pos.*, V, p. 534.

36   Of all the religious phases in the course of man's mental development Comte's own sympathies lie with fetishism, which he considers to have been immune from the 'divagations peculiar to theology' and to have anticipated man's later intellectual development. Indeed 'a system which directly places all beings, even the most inert, on the same footing as ourselves is admirably in keeping with man's creative urge in poetry, music and even the plastic arts'. 'Our maturity is led to perpetuate and develop the fundamental dispositions of our childhood, while overcoming the obstacles attributable to the absolute character of primitive conceptions.' See *Pol. pos.*, III, pp. 92–123, 154–61; IV, p. 213.

37   *Phil. pos.*, V, p. 222.

38   *Ibid.*

39   *Pol. pos.*, III, p. 241.

40   'Le régime monothéique, comparé au précédent, constitue une diminution intellectuelle mais prononcée de l'esprit religieuse' (*Phil. pos.*, V,

p. 370).

41 Comte's own knowledge of the Bible was superficial and his appreciation of it slight. He deplored the constant tendency of Protestantism 'à proposer surtout pour guide aux peuples modernes, la partie la plus arriérée et la plus dangereuse des Saintes Ecritures, c'est-à-dire celle qui concerne l'antiquité judaïque' (*Phil. pos.*, IV, p. 121n.).

42 *Catéchisme*, p. 361.

43 'Le catholicisme ne se trouvait compétent qu'envers l'existence personnelle, d'où son ascendant s'étendait à peine aux relations domestiques, sans pouvoir aucunement embrasser la vie sociale' (*Pol. pos.*, II, p. 111).

44 In Gouhier's words, 'Dieu est parti sans laisser de question' (*La Jeunesse d'Auguste Comte*, I, p. 23). Comte's positivism is not so much atheistic as anti-theistic. Theoretical atheism he despised as mere metaphysical speculation. 'Confirmed atheists can be regarded as the most inconsistent of theologians, since they occupy themselves with the same questions but reject the only suitable approach to them' (*Pol. pos.*, I, p. 73).

45 For Comte's letter of dedication of the *Système de politique positive* to Mme de Vaux (4 October 1846) see *Correspondance générale*, III (1846–8), (Paris, 1977), pp. 275–86.

46 'Le positivisme religieux', Comte wrote, 'commença réellement dans notre précieuse entrevue initiale du Vendredi 16 mai 1845, quand mon cœur proclama inopinément, devant ta famille émerveillée, la sentence caractéristique: *on ne peut pas toujours penser, mais on peut toujours aimer*, qui, completée, devint la devise speciale de notre grande composition' (*Testament d'Auguste Comte avec les documents qui s'y rapportent*, Paris, 1884; 2nd ed., 1968). On Comte's relations with Clotilde de Vaux see Gouhier, *La Vie d'Auguste Comte*, chap. 12.

47 Space, Earth and Humanity were for Comte the true, 'unalterable' trinity (*Synthèse subjective*, p. 24).

48 *Testament*, p. 9.

49 *Pol. pos.*, III, pp. 247, 331f, 492.

50 *Ibid.*, p. 101.

51 Cf. *Pol. pos.*, III, p. 621.

52 Cf. *Pol. pos.*, II, p. 64; IV, pp. 118f.

53 *Catéchisme*, pp. 115–21.

54 *Ibid.*, p. 122.

55 Comte's disapproving attitude towards Jesus as a merely 'religious adventurer' is off-set by his warm admiration of the apostle to the gentiles, 'the incomparable St Paul', with his 'intimate acquaintance' – as Comte supposes – 'with the true thinkers of Greece'. Paul was 'the true founder of Catholicism' (*Pol. pos.*, II, p. 115).

56 For Comte's 'Lettre philosophique sur le mariage' (11 January 1846), addressed to Mme de Vaux, see *Correspondance générale*, IV (1846–8) (Paris, 1981), pp. 47–61.

57 'I am convinced', he told a correspondent on 22 April, 1851, 'that before the year 1860 I shall be preaching positivism at Notre Dame as the only real and complete religion' (*Correspondance inédite d'Auguste Comte*, 4 vols., Paris, 1903–4, III, p. 101).

58 Emile Littré (1801–81), Comte's most committed disciple among his

fellow-countrymen, fully accepted the teachings of the *philosophie positive* – 'elle suffit à tout, ne me trompe jamais, et m'éclaire toujours' (*Auguste Comte et la philosophie positive*, 2nd ed. (Paris, 1864), pp. 662f) – but rejected the Religion of Humanity. On Littré see S. Aquarone, *The Life and Works of Emile Littré* (Leyden, 1958).

59 J. S. Mill (*Auguste Comte and Positivism*, London, 1865) deplored Comte's *Système de politique positive* as 'the most complete system of spiritual and temporal despotism that ever issued from the brain of any human being, except perhaps Ignatius Loyola'. But Mill, it has to be remembered, was unacquainted with Marxism.

60 *Pol. pos.*, III, p. xxxix.

61 *Pol. pos.*, IV, p. 533.

9 Ernest Renan and the Religion of Science

1 *L'Avenir de la science, Oeuvres complètes* (ed. H. Psichari, 10 vols., Paris, 1947–61, referred to below as OC), III, p. 1121.

2 OC, II, p. 795.

3 OC, II, pp. 865f.

4 I. Babitt, *The Makers of Modern French Criticism* (Boston and New York, 1912), p. 271.

5 OC, II, p. 1102.

6 Repr. OC, II, pp. 711–931.

7 OC, II, p. 869.

8 OC, II, p. 866.

9 The *Origines du christianisme* comprises vols. IV and V of the *Oeuvres complètes*.

10 *La Réforme intellectuelle* was reviewed by Matthew Arnold in the *Academy*, 15 February 1872 (see *The Complete Prose Works of Matthew Arnold*, VII, ed. R. H. Super, Ann Arbor, Mich., 1971, pp. 40–50; cf. pp. 407–12).

11 Repr. OC, I, pp. 545–714.

12 Repr. OC, III, pp. 369–710.

13 OC, I, p. 625.

14 Volume VI of the *Oeuvres complètes*.

15 OC, II, p. 789.

16 On Renan's liking for the dialogue form cf. the preface to *Dialogues et fragments philosophiques* (OC, I, pp. v f).

17 OC, I, p. 696.

18 OC, III, p. 939.

19 OC, I, p. 700.

20 OC, III, p. 940.

21 OC, II, p. 74.

22 OC, III, pp. 988f.

23 As he himself said: 'J'étais né prêtre a priori ... je ne fus pas prêtre de profession, je le fus d'esprit' (OC, II, pp. 798, 796).

24 OC, III, p. 746.

25 See *L'Avenir de la science*, chap. 7.

26 OC, III, p. 746.

27   *OC*, I, p. 703.

28   *OC*, III, pp. 1113f, 790.

29   *OC*, III, pp. 1105f.

30   'Mon Catholicisme est celui de l'Ecriture, des conciles et des théologiens. Ce Catholicisme, je l'ai aimé, je le respecte encore; l'ayant trouvé inadmissible, je me suis séparé de lui' (*OC*, II, p. 871).

31   Cf. *Nouvelles Etudes d'histoire religieuse*, preface.

32   'Ce fade compromis, bon pour les laïques, qui a produit de nos jours tant de malentendus' (*OC*, II, pp. 871f).

33   *OC*, III, p. 968.

34   *OC*, I, p. 710.

35   *OC*, III, p. 801.

36   *OC*, III, p. 827.

37   For an instructive comparison between Renan and Newman see J. Guitton, *La Pensée moderne et le Catholicisme. Parallèles: Renan et Newman* (Aix-en-Provence, 1938).

38   *OC*, III, p. 731.

39   *OC*, III, p. 759.

40   *OC*, II, p. 866.

41   *Ibid.*

42   *OC*, I, pp. 674–714.

43   *OC*, I, p. 714.

44   *OC*, I, pp. 633–50.

45   *OC*, I, p. 643.

46   *OC*, I, p. 695.

47   *Ibid.*

48   *OC*, I, p. 701.

49   For an existentialist interpretation of Renan see J. Chaix-Ruy, *Ernest Renan* (Paris, 1956).

50   *OC*, III, p. 1114. On Renan's religious ideas generally see J. Pommier, *La Pensée religieuse de Renan* (Paris, 1923); also M. Weiler, *La Pensée de Renan* (Grenoble, 1945).

51   *OC*, I, p. 571.

52   *OC*, I, p. 586.

53   *OC*, I, p. 644.

54   *OC*, I, pp. 586f.

55   *OC*, I, p. 631.

56   *OC*, I, p. 573.

57   *OC*, I, p. 578.

58   *OC*, III, p. 1106.

59   *OC*, I, pp. 703f.

60   *OC*, III, p. 809.

61   *OC*, II, pp. 1140f.

62   *OC*, I, p. 577.

63   'Le mal, c'est de se révolter contre la nature ... Son but est bon; veuillons ce qu'elle veut' (*OC*, I, p. 581).

64   *OC*, I, p. 565.

65   *OC*, I, p. 573.

66   *Ibid.*

67   *OC*, I, p. 628.
68   *OC*, III, p. 906.
69   *OC*, III, p. 804.
70   *OC*, I, p. 714.
71   *OC*, I, p. 829.
72   *OC*, I, p. 711.
73   *OC*, I, p. 580.
74   *OC*, I, pp. 649f.
75   *OC*, I, p. 705.
76   *OC*, II, pp. 759ff. Cf. H. Psichari, *La Prière sur l'Acropôle et ses mystères* (Paris, 1956).
77   *OC*, I, pp. 556f.
78   'Le moyen de salut n'est pas le même pour tous. Pour l'un, c'est la vertu; pour l'autre, l'ardeur du vrai; pour un autre, l'amour de l'art; pour d'autres, la curiosité, l'ambition, les voyages, le lux, les femmes, la richesse; au plus bas degré, la morphine et l'alcool. Les hommes vertueux trouvent leur récompense dans la vertu même; ceux qui ne le sont pas ont le plaisir … La plus dangereuse erreur, en fait de morale sociale, est la suppression systématique du plaisir' (*OC*, II, p. 1153).
79   Other works by Renan on the history of religions include *Etudes d'histoire religieuse* (1857), *Nouvelles études d'histoire religieuse* (1884) and *Mélanges religieuses et historiques* (1904).
80   The titles of the successive volumes are: *La Vie de Jésus* (1863), *Les Apôtres* (1866), *Saint Paul* (1869), *L'Antéchrist* (1873), *Les Evangiles et la seconde génération chrétienne* (1878), *L'Eglise chrétienne* (1879) and *Marc-Aurèle et la fin du monde antique* (1881). In 1860 Renan told Sainte-Beuve that 'une histoire critique des origines du christianisme, faite avec toutes les ressources de l'érudition moderne, en dehors et bien au-dessus de toute intention de polémique comme d'apologétique, a toujours été le rêve que j'ai caressé' (quoted A. Albalat, *La Vie de Jésus d'Ernest Renan* (Paris, 1933), p. 26.
81   *OC*, IV, p. 871.
82   *OC*, IV, p. 1089.
83   *OC*, V, p. 1148.
84   *OC*, V, p. 299.
85   For Renan's comments on the Tübingen school see *OC*, IV, p. 1097; cf. *OC*, II, p. 893: 'Quand la réaction viendra contre cette école, on trouvera peut-être que ma critique, d'origine catholique et successivement émancipée de la tradition, m'a fait bien voir certaines choses et m'a préservé de plus d'une erreur.'

Index

Index

Index

Index

Jena, university of, 88, 90, 91, 101, 111, 140, 277
Jesuits, 150, 160, 161, 181, 183
Jesus Christ, 17, 50, 53–4, 62, 63, 64, 72–7, 102, 170, 242, 292, 263–4
Judaism, 62, 64
justification by faith alone, 143

Kant, Immanuel, 15, 17, 20–1, 26, 27, 29, 31, 32, 35, 53, 59, 62, 64, 67, 71, 92, 108, 112–13, 120, 121, 126, 150, 164, 168, 169, 235, 239
Katterkamp, J. T., 119
Kierkegaard, Søren, 1, 2, 10, 28, 116, 277
Kingdom of God, the, 76–7, 79, 109
knowledge, Rosmini's theory of, 164–5, 166–8
Kritisches journal der Philosophie, 91
Kuhn, J., 139
Kurtze Darstellung des theologischen Studiums (Schleiermacher), 270
Kurtze Einleitung in das Studium des Theologie (Drey), 136, 137–8

Lacordaire, H. de, 183, 185
Lamennais, Félicité Robert de Lamennais (1782–1854), 12, 13, 28, 117, 118, 154, 158, chap. 7 (*passim*), 208, 209, 217, 239, 251, 285–9. See also *Avenir, L'*; Catholic liberalism; Gallicanism; *Mirari vos* (papal encyclical; *sensus communis (le sens commun); Singulari nos* (papal encyclical); socialism, religious; traditionalism; ultramontanism
Lamennais, J.-M., 177, 178, 190, 195, 285
Laski, H. J., 288
Law of the Three Stages (la loi des trois etats), Comte's, 211–14, 219–21
Lasson, G., 272
Lenau, N., 2, 8
Leo XII, Pope, 182
Leopardi, G., 2, 7, 15
Lessing, G. E., 11
Lévy-Bruhl, L., 219
Liberatore, M., 154, 282
'Life of Jesus' (Hegel), 62
Littré, E., 292–3
Livre des pélérins polonais, Le (Mickiewicz), 198

Livre du peuple, Le (Lamennais), 202, 206
Logica (Rosmini), 163
Logos, doctrine of, 103, 104
Loisy, A., 142, 281
Lotze, H., 27
Lovejoy, A. O., 267
Louis Napoléon, 234
Louvain, university of, 147

Maistre, J. de, 12–13, 16, 117, 131, 177, 179, 180, 208
Malebranche, 147, 173
Mamiani della Rovere, Count T., 156, 172, 282, 284–3
Manzoni, A., 156, 157, 158–9, 163, 289
Marheineke, P., 60, 86, 272
Marx, Karl, 60
Maxims of Christian Perfection (Rosmini), 159
Mazzini, G., 147, 148
mediaevalism, 11–12, 79, 136
metaphysics, 252–4
Metternich, Prince, 132, 195
Michelet, J., 23
Mickiewicz, A., 190, 287
Mill, J. S., 210, 235, 243, 293
miracles, 26, 50, 122
Mirari vos (papal encyclical), 185, 186, 187, 195, 196
modernism, Catholic, 130, 142, 155, 281
Möhler, Johann Adam (1796–1838), 133, 139, 140–5, 279
monotheism, 51, 52, 212, 213, 223, 224, 229–30, 231, 291
Montaigne, 245, 252
Montalembert, Count C. de, 183, 186, 188, 190, 193, 195, 196, 198, 287, 288
Montesquieu, 271, 291
morality and God (in Rosmini), 169–70
Munich, Academy of Fine Arts, 105, 110
Munich, university of, 130, 131, 132, 133, 140
music, Romantic valuation of, 10
Mythengeschichte des asiatischen Welt (Görres), 133
mythology, myths, 114–15, 241

300

Index

Index

Index